The New Paradigm in Architecture

multiple coding

GUGGENHEIM LAS VEGAS.
Design Rem Koolhaas.
Installation Frank Gehry.

Fractal Architecture

FEDERATION SQUARE, MELBOURNE, 2002.
LAB, Bates Smart and Karres en Brands.

THE NEW PARADIGM IN ARCHITECTURE

The Language of Post-Modernism

Charles Jencks

Yale University Press New Haven and London

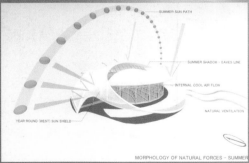

biomorphic

KASAHARA AMENITY HALL, Gifu,
Prefecture. Kathryn and Ushida Findlay
Laboratory (with Tomoko Taguchi and
Takakuni Yukawa). (Katsuhisa, Kida).

Copyright © by Charles Jencks 2002

Designed by Beatrix McIntyre
Set in Walbaum
Printed in Italy

Cover illustrations: *Front*: Daniel Libeskind, Jewish Museum, Berlin 1989–2001; *back*: LAB with
Bates Smart, Federation Square, Melbourne, 1997–2002.

ISBN   0 300 095120 cloth
        0 300 095139 paper

Library of Congress Control Number: 2002106785

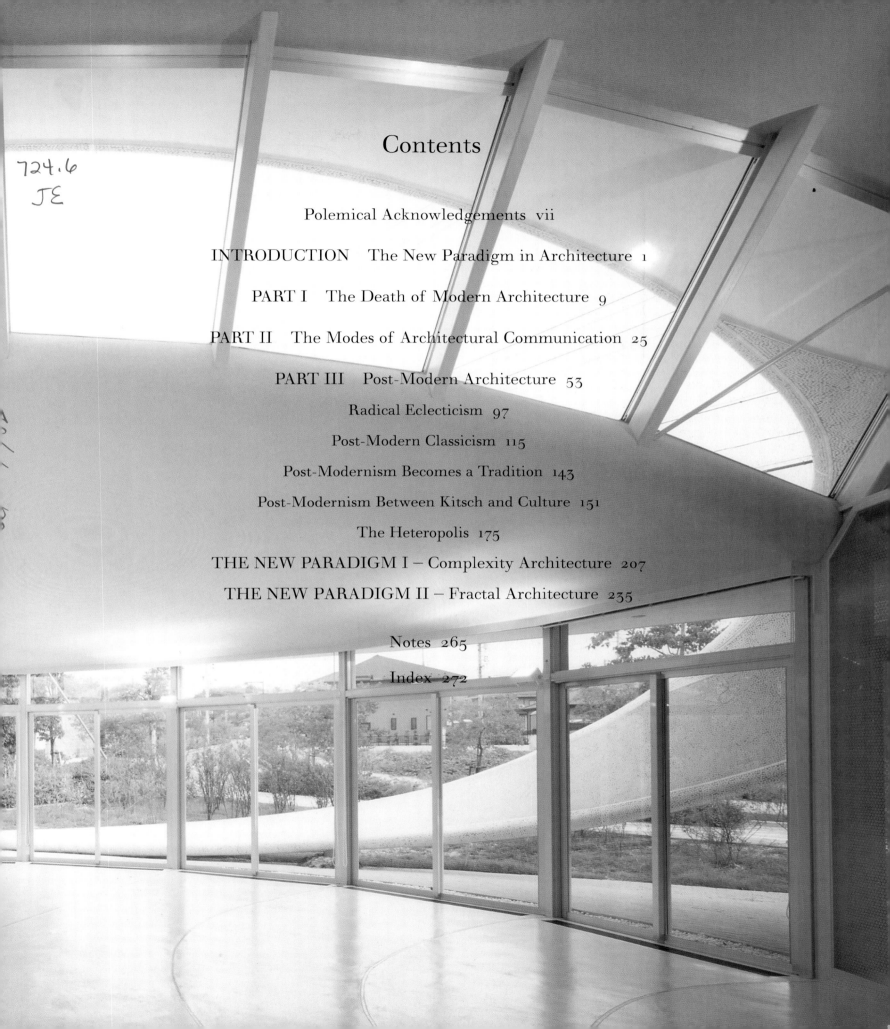

Contents

Polemical Acknowledgements vii

INTRODUCTION   The New Paradigm in Architecture 1

PART I   The Death of Modern Architecture 9

PART II   The Modes of Architectural Communication 25

PART III   Post-Modern Architecture 53

Radical Eclecticism 97

Post-Modern Classicism 115

Post-Modernism Becomes a Tradition 143

Post-Modernism Between Kitsch and Culture 151

The Heteropolis 175

THE NEW PARADIGM I – Complexity Architecture 207

THE NEW PARADIGM II – Fractal Architecture 235

Notes 265

Index 272

fractal landform

DIAMOND RANCH SCHOOL, Pomona,
California, 2001. Thom Mayne and Morphosis.

Polemical Acknowledgements

How does one give credit and thanks for twenty-five years of influence, debate and friendship? I started writing on Post-Modernism in 1975, the first edition of this book was published in 1977, and have thus incurred much too many debts to acknowledge in the proper way.

The easiest to credit are the photographers. When known they are listed at the end of each caption and, where not acknowledged, they have been often denoted by the architects gratis. Thus the lack of a photo credit means that either I took the slide (the usual case) or that the architects supplied me with them. I am grateful for the architects' help in this crucial matter not only because it allows a very wide spectrum of buildings to be illustrated, but also to be shown with fresh images; these I prefer to the over-publicized and often sanitized views.

The hardest obligations to admit are those ideas that I have absorbed so completely as to believe they are my own. The concepts I know to have influenced this book come from the most general sources, such as the Modern and Post-Modern Movements, from Le Corbusier and Umberto Eco among others. The former I have written on extensively, and the latter I was lucky enough to meet in the early 1970s, invite to London to lecture and get to know. A more particular obligation is to contemporary architects with whom I have had long-term friendships and debates. Among these I am particularly grateful to Frank Gehry, Rem Koolhaas, Peter Eisenman, Daniel Libeskind, Terry Farrell, Hans Hollein, Leon Krier and the late James Stirling. These, of course, were sometimes the leading protagonists of architecture, if not always of Post-Modernism (with which they all had *some* important relationship). It is fortunate that my path has continually criss-crossed with theirs for thirty years, and in circumstances most propitious for thought – over meals, drinks and at international meetings, or in their ateliers. I feel honored to count them among my close friends, even though we do not always agree (as the reader will find). A critic must, like a baseball umpire, call the balls and strikes as he sees them – and they do not exist until he does. Unlike this game, and very happily so, the status of a critic's judgement does not determine the ontology of the result: a building goes on being what it is, oblivious to mere praise or censure. I am grateful that the architects have been generous enough to remain good company in spite of my critiques *and* effusions.

Among particular intellectual debts there are also some obvious ones to the theories of Robert Venturi, Christian Norberg-Schulz, Colin Rowe and Greg Lynn. My views on complexity, or multivalence as a theory of value, have come from S. T. Coleridge by way of I. A. Richards, the literary critic I was lucky to meet when I was at Harvard in the late 1950s. Concepts of nonlinearity and complexity theory stem from Stuart Kaufmann, and the Santa Fe Institute which I visited a couple of times. Other conceptual debts are acknowledged in the text or cited in the footnotes.

This polemic is part of a never-ending dialogue with Modernism and, as such, puts a slightly different case for the role of creativity and what Howard Gardner calls the Exemplary Creator than did the Modernists. Under that term, and the book *Creating Minds*, Gardner describes the lives and achievements not of God but the chief Faustian characters of the twentieth century: Freud, Einstein, Picasso, Eliot, Graham, Stravinsky and Gandhi. The typical Exemplary Creator had to overthrow a discipline, field or institution and, as they did so, they characteristically cast off their friends, their lovers or wives and even their identity – as they forged new selves. Post-Modern creators, with less revolutionary ends to achieve, often stay with their wives and companions and are happy to acknowledge their help. Hence, in some of the brief 'portraits' sketched below, I have followed suit and mentioned the aid and shown the presence of 'the other half' – something not done in portraits of the Modern Exemplary Creators. My photos, like much else, are gently polemical.

There are a few who have particularly helped me in this the seventh edition of *The Language of Post-Modern Architecture*. They include my PA, Bunny Firth, who has patiently re-set, and edited the text and composed several layouts. Louisa Lane Fox who has given me helpful comments and pruned my effusions. Beatrix McIntyre, at Yale University Press, has both edited and laid out the final copy, the first time I have ever benefited from this arrangement where two interrelated jobs are sensibly combined into one. Usually the layout competes with the sense, or does not, as it should, underscore the argument. Madelon Vriesendorp has, very kindly and under duress, created the incisive and amusing visual analyses of Frank Gehry's New Guggenheim in Bilbao, and John Nicoll has not only commissioned and overseen the whole project, but skillfully helped me throw off some excess baggage along the way.

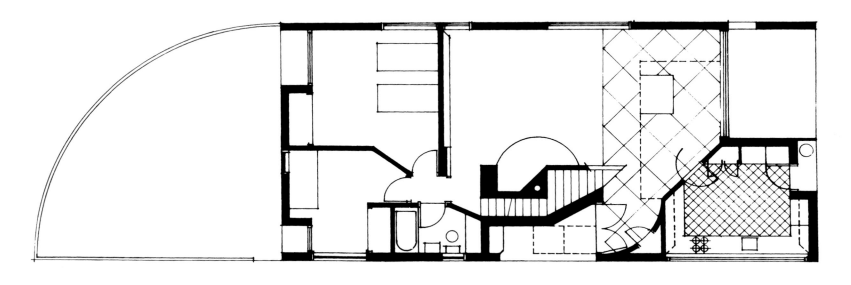

The New Paradigm in Architecture

A change of heart, a new paradigm in architecture? It appears to be so, but one should be wary of all such pronouncements and predictions, especially since, for the last two centuries, they have been made so often, and with some unfortunate effects. Does anyone really *want* another new architecture? Again perhaps, yes, it depends on which one and where it may be going.

My argument is that we are at the *beginning* of a new way of constructing architecture and conceiving cities, that it has grown out of the Post-Modern movement in the sciences and elsewhere, but that it has not yet grown up. The new paradigm exists but somewhat ambiguously. It is past the birth pangs, but still in infancy, and there is much to be decided on how it is going to develop and mature. Will it produce a more convivial, sensuous and articulate environment than before? I think so. One that is more sustainable and urbane? At the moment it is hard to say. These are some of the questions to be asked. No doubt, given the stereotyping of most building, a shift in architecture is to be welcomed, and beyond this a new movement is always exciting and full of hope and promise. Yet a dose of scepticism is in order also, as we examine the case, and not a little bit of irony will be found sprinkled throughout my text, signalling a nuanced appreciation. New paradigm or not, good intentions or bad, its growth will most be helped by an appreciative *and* critical attitude.

If there is a new paradigm, or way of thinking in any field such as architecture, then it obviously stems from a larger cultural shift, a change in worldview, in religion, perhaps politics and certainly science. The Gothic, Renaissance and Modern periods all showed these larger transformations in perspective. By these standards there is today more of a slide than jump.

On the one hand, there is a deterioration of previous cultural formations. Christianity and Modernism, the two reigning worldviews that were supposedly celebrated at the Millennium are both, if architecture is any measure, just hanging on. The millennial celebrations revealed the disquiet and confusion over religious, spiritual and public values. So in these areas we are still very much at the end of the old paradigm and, as I argue in a section of this book on univalent content, the implications of this for architecture are damaging. Architecture without a public content and spiritual direction loses its way.

On the other hand, in the sciences and in architecture itself a new way of thinking has indeed started. It stresses self-organising systems rather than mechanistic ones. It favors fractal forms, self-similar ones, over those that are endlessly repeated. It looks to the notions of emergence, complexity and chaos science more than to the linear, predictable and mechanistic sciences. In more technical terms it is based on non-linear dynamics, and a new worldview coming from contemporary cosmology. From this perspective it sees our place in a universe that is continuously emerging, as a single creative unfolding event. This event is very much an activity, something that has been going on for about thirteen billion years, an affair that contains us in its narrative. We do not live in a cosmos, as was represented in Greek, Christian or Modern architecture, but in a cosmogenesis, a *process* of unfolding and sudden emergence, a surprisingly creative universe. This is one of the great insights of our time to be celebrated in architecture as in all the arts.

This book is not about science and the new worldview, however, but recent architectural history. This starts about the middle of the 1970s, when Post-Modernism came on the scene. As we will see, the new paradigm of thinking pervades the practice of building in all sorts of ways. In the early 1960s it shaped the way Jane Jacobs conceived a new urbanism based on the life sciences and their notion of organized complexity. It also formed Robert Venturi's notion of complexity and contradiction in architecture in 1966 (1); by the late 1980s it allowed us to understand the growth of complex, fractal cities. Complexity theory, the sciences of complexity as they came to be known after the 1980s, is very much a common thread. But above all the new paradigm was aided by computer design and production. This resulted in what I called for in the first editions of *The Language of Post-Modern Architecture* 1977: "computer modelling, auto-

1 ROBERT VENTURI, *Vanna Venturi House*, Chestnut Hill, Penn., 1963–65. Venturi's complexity theory, derived largely from literary theory, focussed on formal problems and varied references. This house for his mother amplified some elements, such as the pediment, displaced others to increase the scale, such as the windows and string course, and combined many forms, such as doorway, arch, and (not visible) stairway and chimney. "Complexity One" here leads to ambiguity and the multiple-functioning element, ideas expressed in Venturi's *Complexity and Contradiction in Architecture*, 1966, that were to affect PM architecture for the next thirty years.

2 FRANK GEHRY, *Fish Sculpture*, Vila Olympica, Barcelona, 1989–92. The first structure by Gehry using the CATIA computer programme to produce a curved construction, something that became normal in his office by the mid-1990s. The computer is the microscope and telescope of Post-Modernism that reveals how complexity can emerge from simple systems that grow: cells, cities, galaxies and buildings. By 1984 the Santa Fe Institute was set up to unearth "the complexity sciences of the twenty-first century," and they did so with the computer. For Gehry and architects the new paradigm came ten years later, although it had been long predicted (for instance in this book in 1977). The Fish Sculpture is a perfect illustration: part computer-fabricated structure, part handcrafted skin of copper strips. A new personalized architecture has emerged with natural overtones, "Complexity Two."

mated-production, and the sophisticated techniques of market research and prediction that allow us to mass-produce a variety of styles and almost personalized products. The results [would be] closer to nineteenth-century handicraft than the regimented superblocks of 1965." It has happened. Computer production now allows curved, folded and sensuous buildings to be produced, such as those by Frank Gehry (2). These are now almost as cheap and easy to build as the ubiquitous dumb box of Modernism.

Yes, the era of stupid and inarticulate slabs is over, the age of repetitive cliché is finished — at least in so far as the excuse of mass-production has been its chief justification. And, in the words of Le Corbusier, Mies van der Rohe and Walter Gropius this *was* the rationale for endless repetition.

The new form of individualized production is a welcome part of the changes seen over the last thirty years, but it goes much deeper than this. Fundamentally it concerns a new way of viewing the world, one less disenchanted than the Modern perspective that holds the universe to be some kind of giant machine, or super computer. The new paradigm, as argued in *The Architecture of the Jumping Universe*, 1995, shows the cosmos to be continuously jumping to new levels of organization, to be unpredictable and more creative than previously thought. Why is this new framework of thought important for architecture? Aside from complexity theory

itself, because all architecture, in the end, presents and represents a cosmology and worldview. When they change, then everything else will change, sooner or later. This is why I believe with confidence that we are at the beginning of a new era.

DEFINING THE NEW PARADIGM

What are the characteristics of the new architecture? It is committed to pluralism, the heterogeneity of our cities and global culture, and it acknowledges the variety of taste cultures and visual codes of the users. From participatory architecture to close consultation with the client is the route travelled, it insists on the wider ecological and urban tissue in which buildings are placed even if it cannot do much about these large issues on a global scale. It is fractal in form and closer to nature and the nature of perception than highly repetitive architecture. It may employ non-Euclidean geometries — curves, blobs, folds, crinkles, twists or scattered patterns. It sends complex messages, ones that often carry ironic, dissenting or critical meanings, those that challenge the status quo. It may be explicitly based on complexity theory, and emerge as a surprise to the designer from the belly of a computer.

Need it be said that no single building fits this compound definition? There has never been an architect who was totally Gothic, Baroque or Modern. A virtue of the new thinking is that it critiques totalizations, it allows statistical and fuzzy categories, and it is obvious that the architects I will be following are sometimes Post-Modern, and other times not.

Let us therefore clarify some terms. Post-Modernism is a broad category that includes a diverse set of architects shown in the evolutionary charts on pages 50–51. It is a historical formation that grows out of the 1960s counter-culture; not only Jane Jacobs, Robert Venturi and their complexity theories, but Rachel Carsons, the student movement, post-industrial society, the electronic revolution, contextualism, adhocism, metabolism and more "isms" than one cares to remember. It is thus a rainbow coalition that resists the excesses of Modernism — a *critical*, not anti-Modernism. Let us make no mistake. As I will point out many times, some of the best PM's (Post-Modernists) are former Modernists critical of their own tradition. To clarify this idea let me give as an example an architect whom everyone perceives as *the* Modernist, Norman Foster.

His 1999 conversion of the Reichstag building in Berlin has many of the Post-Modern definers previously mentioned (3, 4, 5). Its outer form is both reminiscent of past domes and critical of them — a non-dome dome, the paradox of a parabolic circle whose top is opened up to the heavens (and the rain). It combines several functions and shapes to produce multiple readings. Not only is it a see-through fish bowl that is an explosive beacon at night (a powerful mixed metaphor suitable to a new democracy), but with its helical ramps, teeming with people, and an asymmetrical sunshade cranking around following the sun, it is a glowing head sparkling with movement. Yes, a glowing "face" (the anthropomorphic metaphor underlies so much PM).

It relates to the urban context. Indeed the rooftop terraces celebrate a democratic taking possession of the city, with views over the previously divided metropolis given a spectacular framing. In effect, citizens of the new German democracy are encouraged to walk all over their representatives' heads, and look out over their countryside. The politicians meet below in the auditorium and look up to see the weight and importance of the people as a collectivity. More than this, it makes a positive drama of traversing recent German history. Scorch-marks from Hitler's 1930s coup remain. Shrapnel wounds from 1945 are preserved, graffiti from the Russian occupiers are accentuated. Rather than being whitewashed over, as it has been in Russia and Japan, history since the late nineteenth century is confronted and turned into a form of Realist ornament (3). Signs vary from Russian slogans and swearwords to *Mokba*, Moscow, the equivalent of "Kilroy was here." Foster and the German government accept that architecture must symbolize events – even when tragic – making this one of the few significant public monuments of our time.

The building also celebrates the ecological potential of new technology. Not only is it energy efficient, but there is a heating and cooling system that runs on vegetable oil. Such technology is dramatized as an essential part of the architectural experience, so when you climb up the thin, hovering ramps and seem to fly over the city, you pass within touching distance of an extraordinary invention, a gigantic blind that rotates with the sun and cuts down glare and heat. This ascent culminates in an open-air oculus, like the Pantheon in Rome, a round disc that transforms the sky visually into a dome. Thus the whole building can be experienced as a climb through German history to present politics and then to the cosmos, an appropriate and moving narrative.

Well, is Norman Foster a Post-Modernist? Certainly not, but he has in this case adopted typical PM concerns: contextualism, symbolic form, a cosmic metaphor, an equal emphasis on past, present and future as if all these times were valid, and so on. The example of the Reichstag conversion illustrates the basic point, that traditions run through many channels and that no single architect is likely to be loyal, always, to a single tradition. We could say that Post-Modernism directs the architect as much as the architect adopts PM. But there are further distinctions to be made. Troubling ones.

Since the mid-1980s, since Post-Modernism caught on and became a global movement, like its parent Modernism; since Michael Graves started building for the Disney Corporation and Margaret Thatcher gave her blessing to the decorated shed, it has suffered the usual problems of success.

It has become mass-produced, clichéd and too big. In a word, the first period of PM turned into PoMo, and expired. The homophobic overtones of this last label are to be regretted, as is the turn to Thatcherite architecture, but the term has stuck and it does refer to the kitsch and slackening which is covered in a later chapter. It also suggests why scepticism and irony are to be recommended when approaching anything like a movement in architecture. They all carry aspects that have to be contested and continuously re-appraised.

What about the death of Modern architecture and the failure of Mies van der Rohe's work to communicate with its users? I believe, along with the historian John Summerson who made the point, that the death of Modernism is a very liberating idea. It frees one from the pernicious notions that there is a zeitgeist, or a single orthodoxy, or something deterministic about history and, furthermore, cues one to the deleterious views of Modernism that dominated the architectural profession. So I remain unrepentant, and leave my parable as a cautionary tale and reminder: beware of orthodoxies.

This warning takes on new meaning after the mid-eighties. As the architect Terry Farrell said, "now everyone is a Post-Modernist," even many of the people who attack it. No

3 NORMAN FOSTER, *Reichstag Renovation*, Berlin, 1995–99. Graffiti on the walls.

4, 5 NORMAN FOSTER, *Reichstag Renovation*, Berlin, 1995 –99. A Modernist responding to the Post-Modern agenda. At night the parabolic dome lights up like an Expressionist beacon of hope, the radiant crown of crystal that so many 1920s architects put at the center of their utopian schemes. By day one sees tiny figures walking up and down the helical ramps and traversing terraces of the old building, taking possession of the city and a democratic forum. Historical fragments and graffiti are accentuated, the ecological imperative is addressed, the ascent to the sun and sky becomes the narrative for architectural expression. (Nigel Young).

6 STANLEY TIGERMAN, *The Sinking of the Titanic*, collage of Mies van der Rohe's Crown Hall, IIT, 1978. Or is it rising? In the 1920s, the diagonal was preferred by the Modernists to the horizontal and vertical.

7 PETER EISENMAN, *Staten Island Project*, 1996, 1999 +. A ferry terminal is the point where car, bus, pedestrian and other forms of traffic meet to turn into both a place of movement and a museum. Functions and forms are merged together in a fluid continuum that mirrors the movement, land and water, but still keeps a heterogeneity of parts and spaces. For Eisenman "the shift from the mechanical paradigm to the electronic one" (his words) is the change, and it deforms all habitual categories of perception.

matter how they classify themselves, they have assumed several of the definers mentioned at the outset of this section. This changes the situation, the background against which I criticize Mies van der Rohe. Two major exhibitions in New York City recently re-appraised his meaning for architecture and it is time to look at his contribution again. In 1975 I lampooned his architecture for being the ultimate mechanistic metaphor of blankness and for not communicating with its users, either literally or metaphorically. It is the basic Malaprop of Modernism, a misfired metaphor. But today, when everybody is a Post-Modernist in some respects, if not in name, his perfected blankness is a minority position. Not every downtown is papered over with dumb boxes, as it threatened to be when I wrote those words. So Mies' work, as a minority position, is more acceptable. To appreciate the present ambivalence look at the PM collage made by Stanley Tigerman in the late 1970s, it shows a prize icon of Modernism, Mies' Crown Hall, sinking like the Titanic beneath the waves (6). This building was heavily criticized because it mis-communicated and suppressed non-architects, for visual reasons, in the basement. Today, when Mies is no longer a threat, there is another reading of this image. Perhaps the *SS. van der Rohe* is really rising up from the depths, resurrected on the sacred diagonal of Modernism. We can now enjoy Modernist Minimalism, as long as it remains a relative rarity. Nonetheless, the critique below must be left to clarify the way architecture is a language, and one for which the architect is explicitly responsible.

On the whole the Post-Modern shift has been partly effective. If most architects now (alright not *everyone*) acknowledge urban context, the linguistic metaphor, history, the role of the client, and so on, much has been accomplished. With these real changes in attitude and practice, *and* the debacle of PoMo, the movement of Post-Modernism has reached its second main stage. This stage is termed the New Paradigm, or Complexity Two. It signals the way that the complexity theories of Jacobs, Venturi, Ungers, *et al.*, have been transformed by the new complexity sciences. Let me reiterate: this is *not* a book on what were called "the sciences of the twenty-first century," by the Santa Fe Institute that named them, but it assumes the philosophy and worldview coming from these sciences. There are now many good books on complexity theory and they reveal the key role played by the computer in developing it.[1] Complexity Two stems directly from the earlier work in the 1960s on systems theory, the new paradigm grows out of the Post-Modern movement in science, so there is both a continuity *and* change. In architecture this is very clear. The complexity architecture of Robert Venturi and James Stirling confronts different styles, contrasts taste cultures, makes an architecture of opposing codes; but in the second stage the heterogeneous architecture of Peter Eisenman, Daniel Libeskind and Frank Gehry folds in difference, laminates oppositions into a smoother continuity. Complexity One and Two are committed to pluralism – that is why they are both Post-Modern – but in very different ways (7). The new paradigm in architecture develops the notion of heterogeneity in a viscous and layered way, as will be argued in the last chapters.

A MOVEMENT IN SIX PARTS

This book has a strange history and form, since it was rewritten over twenty-five years as Post-Modernism waxed and waned in all the arts and sciences, and changed shape. It was not, as is often said, the first word on Post-Modernism – a phrase that goes back to the nineteenth century – but rather the first book that defined the movement.[2] This led to many translations and editions and a great debate as to whether Post-Modernism really is a new cultural formation. First written at the start of the movement in the middle 1970s, it has gone through six incarnations, six editions, each one that staked out the territory of battle. The virtue of the war report is its immediacy; the vice is its lack of hindsight. These slices of history do have one advantage over the rear-view mirror; they give a feeling of what the issues looked like at a particular moment, and this helps explain why one stage of Post-Modernism led to another.

They also result in a new genre I have called an "evolvotome," an evolving treatise that tries to keep up with the change in perspective that new evidence entails. Now, thanks to a computer and the ability to scan in the whole text, it has been possible to rewrite it from scratch. But the constant shifts in time mean the book can be read in different ways. As a straight historical narrative the story can be picked up at Part III where it begins, but, if one is to understand the social, moral and linguistic roots of Post-Modernism then the first two parts should be looked at. The "Death of Modern Architecture" and its failure to adequately communicate with its inhabitants – its urban failures – have to be appreciated, or else the social and semantic goals of Post-Modernism do not make much sense.

The covers of the previous editions reveal the changing pattern (8). The supergraphics of a building in Tokyo, containing fourteen bars, show the hybrid language of PM at its outset, its compound of different codes – basically Modern and commercial – that communicates a complex mixture of urban functions and meanings. The third edition, featuring the colorful Piazza d'Italia, shows how diverse in reference this language could become when used to give social identity to a minority community in New Orleans. The fourth and fifth editions show the shift to Post-Modern Classicism, the double-coded hybridization of Modernism with Classicism that characterized a more public and civic architecture. The sixth shows the shift away from explicit reference towards a subtle urban abstraction, and one based on the local landforms of Arizona; and the seventh, and present cover, shows the latest synthesis of a continuous, layered heterogeneity. Each one of these buildings, and editions of the book, is a modification of a previous position and in this sense a ceaseless critical dialogue with the immediate past.

Interestingly one of the buildings, Minoru Takeyama's set of bars, reacts against its own first incarnation with a more abstract second version. In this dialectic, of a new position modifying the previous one and reacting to pressures outside architecture, is a pattern I have called Critical Modernism.[3] Critical Modernism is not a single philosophy or approach, but a distributed process that is picked up throughout the many Modern movements that typify the last two hundred years, a hidden tradition that reveals itself more in hindsight than foresight.

Post-Modernism is just one part of this larger debate, and it will continue to exist so long as the problems of modernization – economic, ecological, social and cultural – are so pressing. One must remember it was spontaneously created again and again over the last fifty years in perhaps one hundred separate disciplines (there is even a Post-Modern dance). It is always reinvented in reaction to such things as the Holocaust, Hiroshima, overpopulation, the Vietnam War, Chernobyl, the industrialization of education, the Communist state, and the art market – that is, perceived failures implicated with modern instrumentalism. Instrumentalism? Modernism, in the end, is based on the Newtonian mechanistic paradigm and Adam Smith's economics that grew directly *and* explicitly from it. These lead people to treat each other as machines and as means to their end, to sacrifice values for profit, to root up whole cultures for their gain. Modernism has many things to recommend it (and that is why Post-Modernism keeps a hyphen in the title and marks the paternity case) but it has this great fault-line running through its worldview. This leads to its many failures. So it is appropriate that with architecture, and the following text written in 1975, we start with two of them: the breakdown of mass housing, and the rather dim-witted educational factory.

8 Six editions of *The Language of Post-Modern Architecture*, from 1977 to 1991, various points in a continual critical debate.

9 MINORU YAMASAKI, *Pruitt-Igoe Housing*. St. Louis, 1952–55.
Several slab blocks of this scheme were blown up in 1972 after they were
continuously vandalized. The crime rate was higher than in other developments, and Oscar Newman attributed this, in his book *Defensible Space*,
to the long corridors, anonymity and lack of controlled semi-private space.
Another factor: it was designed in a purist language at variance with the
architectural codes of the inhabitants.

Part I
The Death of Modern Architecture

Happily, it is possible to date the death of Modern Architecture to a precise moment in time. Unlike the legal death of a person, which is becoming a complex affair of brain waves versus heartbeats, Modern Architecture went out with a bang. That many people didn't notice, and no one was seen to mourn, does not make the sudden extinction any less of a fact, and that many designers are still trying to administer the kiss of life does not mean that it has been miraculously resurrected. No, it expired finally and completely in 1972, after having been flogged to death remorselessly for ten years by critics such as Jane Jacobs; and the fact that many so-called Modern architects still go around practising a trade as if it were alive can be taken as one of the great curiosities of our age (like the British monarchy giving life-prolonging drugs to The Royal Company of Archers or The Extra Women of the Bedchamber).

Modern Architecture died in St. Louis, Missouri on July 15, 1972 at 3.32 pm (or thereabouts) when the infamous Pruitt-Igoe scheme, or rather several of its slab blocks, were given the final *coup de grâce* by dynamite. Previously it had been vandalized, mutilated and defaced by its inhabitants, and although millions of dollars were pumped back, trying to keep it alive (fixing the broken elevators, repairing smashed windows, repainting), it was finally put out of its misery. Boom, boom, boom (9).

Without doubt, the ruins should be kept, the remains should have a preservation order slapped on them, so that we keep a live memory of this failure in planning and architecture. Like the folly or artificial ruin — constructed on the estate of an eighteenth-century English eccentric to provide him with instructive reminders of former vanities and glories — we should learn to value and protect our former disasters. As Oscar Wilde said, "experience is the name we give to our mistakes," and there is a certain health in leaving them judiciously scattered around the landscape as continual lessons.

Pruitt-Igoe was constructed according to the most progressive ideals of CIAM (the Congress of International Modern Architects) and it won an award from the American Institute of Architects when it was designed in 1951. Why? Because it carried out the major doctrines of modern city planning. It consisted of elegant slab blocks fourteen storeys high with rational "streets in the air" (which were safe from cars, but as it turned out, not safe from crime); "sun, space and greenery," which Le Corbusier called the "three essential joys of urbanism" (instead of conventional streets, gardens and semi-private space, which he banished). It had a separation of pedestrian and vehicular traffic, the provision of play space, and local amenities such as laundries, crèches and gossip centres — all rational substitutes for traditional patterns. Moreover, its Purist style, its clean, salubrious hospital metaphor, was meant to instill, by good example, corresponding virtues in the inhabitants. Good form was to lead to good content, or at least good conduct; the intelligent planning of abstract space was to promote healthy behavior.

Alas, such simplistic ideas, taken over from the philosophies of Rationalism, Behaviorism and Pragmatism proved as irrational as the philosophies themselves. Modern Architecture, as the son of the Enlightenment, was an heir to its congenital naivetes, too great and awe-inspiring to warrant refutation in a book on mere building. This first part will concentrate on the demise of a very small branch of a big bad tree; but to be fair it should be pointed out that Modern Architecture is the offshoot of Modern Painting and the Modern Movements in the arts. Like rational schooling, rational health and rational design of women's bloomers, it has the faults of an age tying to re-invent itself totally on rational grounds.

These shortcomings are now well known, thanks to the writings of Ivan Illich, Jacques Ellul, E.F. Schumacher, Michael Oakshott and Hannah Arendt, and the overall misconceptions of Rationalism will not be dwelt upon. They are assumed for these purposes. Rather than a deep extended attack on Modern Architecture showing how its ills relate very closely to the prevailing philosophies of the modern age, this will be a caricature, a polemic. The virtue of this genre (as well as vice) is its license to cut through the large generalities with a certain enjoyment, overlooking all the exceptions and subtleties of the argument. Caricature is of course not the whole truth. Daumier's drawings did not really show what nineteenth-century poverty was about, but rather gave a highly selective view of some truths. Let us then romp through the desolation of Modern Architecture and the destruction of our cities, like some Martian tourist out on an earthbound excursion, visiting the archaeological sites with a superior disinterest, bemused by the sad but instructive mistakes of a former architectural civilization. After all, since it is fairly dead, we might as well pick over the corpse.

CRISIS IN ARCHITECTURE

In 1974 Malcolm MacEwen wrote a book of the above title which summarized the English view of what was wrong with the Modern Movement (capitalized, like world religions), and what we should do about it. His summary was masterful, but his prescriptions were wildly off the mark: the remedy was to overhaul a tiny institutional body, the Royal Institute of British Architects, by changing a style here and a heart there, as if these sorts of things would make the *multiple* causes of the crisis go away. These act together as a syndrome and, if we are to make any effective changes in architecture, it is well to find out which parts of the system are closely connected and might be changed most easily.

Let us make use of MacEwen's analysis, not his solution, taking as a typical grotesque of Modern Architecture one building type: modern hotels. The new Penta Hotel in London has 914 bedrooms, which is almost nine times the average large hotel of fifty years ago, and it is "themed" (a word of decorators) in the International Style and a mode which could be called Vasarely-Airport-Lounge-Moderne (10). There are about twenty of these leviathans near each other, on the way to airport (it is known in the trade as Hotellandia), and they create a disruption in scale and city life which amounts to the occupation of an invading army – a role tourists tend to fulfil. These newly formed battalions with their noble-phoney names include The Churchill (500 bedrooms, named after Sir Winston and themed in the Pompeian Palladian style by way of Robert Adam); the Imperial Hotel (720 bedrooms, International outside, fiberglass Julius Caesar inside); and the Park Tower (300 bedrooms, themed in Corn-on-the-Cob and various sunburst motifs inside).

A recurring aspect of these hotels, built between 1969 and 1973, is that they provide very modern services, such as air-conditioning, themed in old-world styles which vary from Rococo, Gothic, Second Empire, to a combination of all three styles together. The formula of ancient style and modern plumbing has proved inexorably successful in our consumer society, and this Ersatz has been the major commercial challenge to classical Modern Architecture. But in one important way, in terms of architectural *production*, Ersatz and Modern Architecture contribute equally to alienation and what MacEwen calls the crisis.

I have tried to untangle the different causes of this situation (11), at least eleven in number, and show how they operate in the two modern modes of architectural production (listed in the two right-hand columns of the diagram). For contrast, the first column on the left refers to the old system of private architectural production (operating largely before World War I) where an architect knew his client personally,

10 RICHARD SEIFERT, *Penta Hotel*, London, 1972. The English government subsidized these kinds of hotels in the late sixties to cope with the tourist boom. Twenty or so, with about 500 bedrooms, sprang up on the main route in from the airport. On the outside they are uptight International Style; on the inside Lapidus Ersatz. (R. Seifert & Partners).

and probably shared his values and aesthetic code. An extreme example of this is Lord Burlington's Chiswick Villa, an unusual situation where the architect was the builder (or contractor), client and user all at once. Hence there was no disparity between his rather elite and esoteric code (a spare, intellectual version of the Palladian language) and his way of life. The same identity exists today, although on a more modest scale and as a relative rarity, for instance, the "Handmade Houses" which are built outside urban centers in America, or the boat house community of Sausalito, in San Francisco Bay, where each boat house is built by the inhabitant in a different, personalized style (12). These self-built houses testify to the close correspondence there can be between meaning and form when architectural production is at a small scale and controlled by the inhabitant. Post-Modern architects such as Ralph Erskine, Lucien Kroll, Charles Moore and Frank Gehry began to recover such an accord between the architect's and user's codes in the 1970s through various interactive processes (see p. 71, *Adhocism and participatory design*).

Other factors that influenced this type of production in the past include the *mini-capitalist economy* where money was restricted. The architect or speculative builder designed relatively *small* parts of the city at one go; he worked *slowly*, responding to well-established needs, and he was *accountable* to the client, who was invariably the user of the building as well. All these factors, and more that are shown in the diagram, combined to produce architecture understood by the

	SYSTEM 1 - PRIVATE private client is architect user	SYSTEM 2 - PUBLIC public client and architect users differ	SYSTEM 3 - DEVELOPER developer client and architect users differ
1 ECONOMIC SPHERE	Mini-Capitalist (restricted money)	Welfare-State Capitalist (lacks money)	Monopoly-Capitalist (has money)
2 MOTIVATION	aesthetic inhabit ideological use	solve user's problem housing	make make money money to use
3 RECENT IDEOLOGY	Too various to list	progress, efficiency, large scale, anti-history Brutalism, etc.	Same as System 2 plus pragmatic
4 RELATION TO PLACE	local client user architect in place	remote users move architects to place	remote and absent changing clients draughtsmanship
5 CLIENTS RELATION TO ARCHITECT	Expert friend same partners small screen	Anonymous Doctor changing designers large team	Hired Servant doesn't know designers or users
6 SIZE OF PROJECT	"small"	"some large"	"too big"
7 SIZE/TYPE OF ARCHITECTS OFFICE	small partnership	large centralised	large centralised
8 METHOD OF DESIGN	slow, responsive innovative expensive	impersonal, anonymous, conservative, low cost	quick, cheap and proven formulae
9 ACCOUNTABILITY	to client-user	to local council and bureaucracy	to stockholders developers and board
10 TYPES OF BUILDING	houses, museums, universities etc.	housing and infrastructure	shopping centres hotels, offices, factories, etc.
11 STYLE	multiple	impersonal safe, contemporary vandal-proofed	pragmatic cliche and bombastic

11 *CRISIS IN ARCHITECTURE* a diagram of three systems of architectural production. The left column shows the implications of the old, private system of production, while the right columns show the two modern systems. Critics of Modern Architecture have emphasized several of these eleven causes of the crisis, but clearly the causes are multiple and work as a system tied to the economic sphere. The question is: how many variables must be changed for the system to change?

client and in a language shared by others. A prime motive of Post-Modern architecture is to find new languages that, while being widely shared, do not suffer the stereotyping of either Ersatz or Modernism.

The second and third columns refer to the way most architecture is produced today and show why it is both out of scale with historic cities and alienating to both architects and society. First, in the economic sphere, it is either produced for a public welfare agency which lacks the money necessary to carry out the Socialist intentions of the architects; or it is funded by a Capitalist agency whose monopoly creates huge investments and correspondingly gigantic buildings. For instance, the Penta Hotel is owned by the European Hotel Corporation, a consortium of five airlines and five international banks. These ten corporations together create a monolith that by financial definition must appeal to mass taste, at a middle-class level. There is nothing inherently inferior about this taste culture; it is rather the economic imperatives determining the size and predictability of the result which have coerced the architecture into becoming so relentlessly pretentious and uptight (13).

Secondly, in this type of production, the architect's motivation is either to *solve a problem*, or in the case of the developer's architect, to make money. Why the latter motivation does not produce effective architecture as it did in the past remains a mystery, (unless it is connected with the com-

12 *SAUSALITO BAY BOAT HOUSES*, 1960. Like the Handmade Houses of California, these boat houses depend on the oldest form of architectural production — self-build. Each one is tailor-made by the inhabitant in a different style, and you find cheek-by-jowl, a Swiss chalet boat house and a converted caravan, or here, the Venturi style next to the A-frame Fuller style.

pelling pressures of predictable taste). But it is quite clear why "problems" do not produce architecture. They produce instead "rational" solutions to over-simplified questions in a chaste style.

Yet the greatest cause of alienation is the *size* of today's projects: the hotels, garages, shopping centers and housing estates which are "too big," like the architectural offices which produce them. How big is too big? Obviously there is no easy answer to this, and we await the detailed study of different building types. But the equation can be formulated in general, and it might be called "the Ivan Illich Law of Diminishing Architecture" (parallel to his discoveries of counter-productive growth in other fields). It could be stated as follows: "For any building type there is an upper limit to the number of people who can be served before the quality of the environment falls." The service of the large London hotels has fallen because of staff shortages and absenteeism, and the quality of tourism has declined because the tourists are treated as so many cattle to be herded from one ambience

13 *PENTA RESTAURANT* interior with its royal, fiberglass cartouche *Dieu-et-mon-droit*. Actually Holiday Inns, the biggest multinational in hotels, prefabricates these fibreglass symbols and then sends them out to some of their 1,700 concessions. The multinationals have been instrumental in standardizing world taste and creating a world consumption community. The National Biscuit Company foresees the goal of two billion biscuit munchers eating their standard average cookie.

14 *DISNEYLAND*, opened in 1955 as a dream of Walt Disney, started the new form of ride-through parks where people are put on a continuously moving assembly line and then shunted past "experiences." Sometimes the ride is effortless and you aren't aware of the mechanisms. At other times long queues form and you are ushered into people pens. Multinationals such as Pepsi, Ford, General Electric and Gulf have heavily invested in Disney Enterprises.

to the next in a smooth and continuous flow. Programmed, continuously rolling pleasure, the shunting of people into queues, pens and moving lines, a process which was perfected by Walt Disney, has now been applied to all areas of mass tourism, resulting in the controlled bland experience (14). What started as a search for adventure has ended in total predictability. Excessive growth and rationalism have contradicted the very goals that the institution of tourism was set up to deliver.

The same is true of large architectural offices. Here design suffers because no one has control over the whole job from beginning to end, and because the building has to be produced quickly and efficiently according to proven formulae (the rationalization of taste into clichés based on statistical averages of style and theme). Furthermore, with large buildings such as the Penta, the architecture has to be produced for a client whom no one in the office knows (that is, the ten corporations), and who is, in any case, not the user of the building.

In short, buildings today are nasty, brutal and too big because they are produced for profit by absentee developers, for absentee landlords, for absent users whose taste is assumed to be clichéd.

There is, then, not one cause of the crisis in architecture, but a *system of causes*; and clearly to change just the style or ideology of the architects, as is proposed by many critics, is not going to change the whole situation. No amount of disaffection for the International Style or Brutalism, for high-rise, bureaucracy, Capitalism, gigantism, or whatever else is the latest scapegoat is going to change things suddenly and produce a humane environment. It would seem we have to

change the whole system of architectural production at once, all eleven causes together. And yet perhaps such a radical move is not necessary. Perhaps some causes are redundant, some are more important than others, and we only have to change a few. For instance, if large architectural offices were divided into small teams that were given a certain amount of financial and design control, and put in close relation to the ultimate users of the building, this might be enough. Who knows? Experiments must be tried with different variables. All that can be said at this point is that the situation has systemic causes that have to be varied as a structure if deep changes are to be made. The next three sections will examine only two causes of the crisis: the way the Modern Movement has impoverished architectural language on the level of form; and has itself suffered an impoverishment on the level of content, the social goals for which it is actually built.

UNIVALENT FORM LEADS TO CONFUSED MEANING

For the general aspect of an architecture created around one (or a few) simplified values, the term univalence will be used. This contrasts with a multivalent architecture where many meanings are linked together to create a coherent, or manifold ensemble. No doubt in terms of expression the architecture of Mies van der Rohe and his followers is one of the most univalent formal systems, because it makes use of few materials and a single, right-angled geometry.

Minimalism was the style he preferred, after 1925, and the slogans of an architecture where "less is more" and the building is "almost nothing." Although it can be relevant in some contexts this reduced style was justified as generally rational (when it was often uneconomic), and universal (when it fitted only a few functions). As a result of his persuasive arguments, and example, the glass-and-steel box has become the single most-used type in Modern Architecture, and it signifies throughout the world "office building."

Yet in the hands of Mies and his disciples this system has also become fetishized to the point where it dominates all other concerns, just as the leather boot dominates the shoe fetishist and distracts him from more relevant parts of the body. The architectural fetishist is typically obsessed by materials, or a consistent geometry, and sublimates further issues to this central concern. Are beams and plate glass appropriate to the home? That is a question Mies would dismiss as irrelevant, or at least secondary to visual consistency. Surprisingly, his first, classic use of the curtain wall was on housing, not for an office, and it was used because he was interested in perfecting certain formal problems. In this case, on Lake Shore Drive in Chicago, he concentrated on the proportion of the I-beam to the infill panels, the setbacks, glass area, supporting column and articulating lines. He kept full-scale details of these members close to his draughting board so he would never lose sight of the elements he loved (15).

A larger question thus did not arise: what if housing looked like offices, or what if the two functions were indistinguishable? Clearly the result would diminish and compromise both functions by equating them: working and living would become interchangeable on the most banal level,

and the particular virtue of each would be obscured. The psychic overtones to these two very different activities would remain unexplored or accidental.

Another masterpiece of the Modern Movement, the Chicago Civic Center designed by a follower of Mies, shows similar confusions in communicating the diversity of its content (16). The long horizontal spans and dark corten steel express "office building," "power," "purity," while the variations in surface express "mechanical equipment." All this is as intended, as far as it goes, but the primitive (and occasionally mistaken) meanings do not express anything deep or complex about working in the city. On a literal level the building does not communicate its important civic functions, nor the social and psychological meanings of this significant building task (a meeting place for the citizens of Chicago).

How could an architect justify such inarticulate building? The answer lies in an ideology that celebrates process, which symbolizes only the changes in technology and building material. The Modern Movement revered the means of production, the Machine Aesthetic, and metaphors such as Le Corbusier's: "the house is a machine for living." In one of those cryptic aphorisms, too delirious to overlook, Mies gave expression to this fetish: "I see in industrialization the central problem of building in our time. If we succeed in carrying out this industrialization, the social economic, technical and also artistic problems will be readily solved." (1924)[4]

What about the theological and gastronomic "problems"? Problems; again the Modernist propensity to see architecture as a problem to be solved. The bizarre confusion to which this reductivist approach can lead is shown by Mies himself in the Illinois Institute of Technology campus in

15 MIES VAN DER ROHE, *Seagram Building*, New York, 1958. Corner detail and plan. The plane of I-beams is extended out a few inches from the column line so that the corner a clearly articulated with angles of steel. The interior curtains now can only be raised to pre-selected, harmonious positions. Mies kept full-scale I-beam details by his desk to get the proportions just so. He thought this member was the modern equivalent of the Doric column, but as Herbert Read once said: "In the back of every dying civilization sticks a bloody Doric column."

16 C. F. MURPHY, *Chicago Civic Center*, 1964. In terms of Mies' curtain wall this solution shows the horizontal emphasis — long spans and under-played verticals in brown, specially rusted steel. Except for the Picasso sculpture and flags out front, you would not recognize the civic importance of this building, nor the various political functions that occur within. (Hedrich-Blessing).

17 MIES VAN DER ROHE, *Siegel Building*, IIT, Chicago, 1947. Is this an astrophysical research lab? The whole campus is in the universal aesthetic of steel, glass and beige brick, except for the most important building. (See 21)

Chicago, a large enough collection of varied functions for us to regard it as a microcosm of his surrealist world. IIT is a place of higher learning and as such it carries the burden of inculcating values, teaching students what is important, and how to see the world. In this idealized setting, Mies has applied his universal grammar of I-beams, brick and glass, to speak about the varied functions of what amounts to a small town: how to live and assemble into collective spaces; how to work in classrooms, or meet in the student union, chapel, and so forth. If we look at a series of these buildings in turn we can see how confusing his language is, both literally and metaphorically.

A characteristic rectangular shape might be deciphered as a teaching block where students churn out one idea after another on an assembly line: the factory metaphor suggests this interpretation rather strongly (17). The only recognizable sign in one of these blocks, a lattice-work disc at the top, further suggests that the students are budding astrophysicists, but the architect did not intend this single bit of literalism. Someone else added it, destroying the purity of his statement. What he can claim credit for, and what has exercised great architectural debate (a disputation between two English deans, Sir Leslie Martin of Cambridge University and Lord Llewelyn-Davies of London University), is his solving of the *problem* of the corner (18). These two British scholars disputed, with medieval precision and inconsequentiality, whether the corner symbolized the "endlessness" of the modern world, or the "closedness" of the past. Was it perhaps the open road of Jack Kerouac, or just the Modern equivalent of a Renaissance pilaster? The fact that it could symbolize both or neither, depending on the code of the viewer, or the fact that larger issues of factory symbolism and semantic confusion were at stake – such questions were never raised.

Not far away from this disputatious corner is another architectural conundrum, designed in Mies' universal lan-

18 THE INFAMOUS IIT CORNER of the previous building. The corner looked like a full visual stop to Leslie Martin, yet Llewelyn-Davies argued it looked "endless" because it was stepped back with two I-beams and an L-beam. The fact that the whole building signified "factory," when it was for teaching, was typically overlooked i n this fetish for details and esoteric meaning.

19 MIES VAN DER ROHE, IIT *Cathedral/Boiler House*, Chicago, 1947. The traditional form of a basilica with central nave and two side aisles. There are even clerestory lights, a regular bay system and campanile to show that this is the cathedral.

guage. Here we can find all sorts of conventional cues that suggest a reading: most apparent is a rectangular structure in the general shape of a cathedral with a central nave. Two side aisles are expressed on the eastern front. The religious nature of this building is heightened by the regular bay system of piers. It is true there are no pointed arches, but there are clerestory windows on both aisles and the nave elevation. Finally, to confirm our reading, we find a brick campanile, the bell tower that dominates the basilica (19).

Alas, this minimalist cathedral turns out on the inside to be a boiler house. But wait, the hard bracing wit of this solecism may have a deeper meaning and one that cannot be fully divined until we have hauled in the real chapel (20). This looks — brilliant move — like a boiler house! Oh university turned on its head, oh tough Chicago built on the stockyards and Al Capone, oh brave new industrial world of IIT students, dig deep to decode the hidden message. Perhaps, on this pragmatic American campus, Mies is teaching an honest lesson in European realism and confronting the major dilemma of western civilization, the schisms between culture and industry, religion and science, those divides which rip up the two cultures. For it looks as if he is making a comment on Henry Adam's famous lament in *The Education of Henry Adams*, that the lovely Virgin of Chartres has been upended by industrial energy, the Dynamo. Why this interpretation? Because the chapel is so underplayed, so minimal, so almost not there as to be "almost nothing." Indeed it is the most unassuming box sandwiched by hard materials, placed balefully between dormitory slabs and, to drive in the point, it has a search-

light attached — all signs which confirm a reading of tough-minded utility, industry supplanting sentiment. But even this reading is open to question.

Because, as we arrive at the most important position on campus, the central area, there is a temple constructed in the most expensive of materials, and these signs distinguish it from all the prosaic structures (21). The temple is raised on a plinth, it has a magnificent colonnade of major and minor orders (large and small I-beams) and a grandiose stairway of white marble planes that miraculously hover in space, as if the local god has worked ultimate magic. It must be the president's house, or at very least, the Administration Center.

Actually it is where the architects work — what else could it be? So, to summarize the narrative, we find the factory is a classroom, the cathedral is a boiler house, the boiler house is a chapel, and the president's temple is the School of Architecture. Mies is saying that the boiler house is more important than the chapel, and that architects rule, as pagan gods, over the lot. Of course he did not intend these propositions, but his commitment to reductive formal values inadvertently betrays them. The problem with univalent form is that it can lead to aberrant readings, or the kind of mistakes that have made Mrs Malaprop into such an enjoyable household figure. This is the one of the most lovable qualities of Modern architecture.

21 MIES VAN DER ROHE. IIT *President's Temple/School of Architecture*, Chicago, 1962. The black temple hovers miraculously from a giant order of steel trusses and a minor order of I-beams. The building occupies a major point on the campus, as the President's house should. (John Winter).

20 MIES VAN DER ROHE, *IIT Boiler House/ Church*. A dumb box placed to either side of high-rise buildings, which are in the same vernacular. Blank on three sides and lit by a searchlight — clearly this is the boiler house.

UNIVALENT FORMALISTS AND
INADVERTENT SYMBOLISTS

Lest we think Mies is special, let us look at similar cases that stem from a reaction against his particular language. Two responses occurred to this type of minimalism in the 1960s, the formalist reaction in America and the Team Ten group that broke away from orthodox Modernism in Europe. Frank Lloyd Wright's last work, the Marin County Civic Center (22), is characteristic of the first, American response, the use of historicist imagery, in this case a Roman aqueduct. The building is based on the endless repetition of strongly emphasized patterns that are wildly uncertain in their overtones: baby-blue and gold baubles on the rooftop oscillate in the imagination somewhere between a flying saucer and a boudoir. No danger of Modern honesty here. Arches, the ultimate form of compression, actually hang in tension and to underline this contradiction they are made to look like cardboard and given further hanging struts. A golden minaret-totem-pole, which like these struts has Indian and Mayan associations, crowns the site of this city center (which is missing only its city). One can applaud the conviction, consistency and kitsch with which the dishonesty is carried through, no one could accuse it of hiding its dissimulations. It has a madcap excess enjoyable as a giant Pop statement, but as a serious building communicating a complex idea it is another malaprop. Like the Chicago Civic Center, already mentioned, it does not tell us anything profound about the role of government today or the citizen's relation to it, beyond the fact that it is surrounded by automobiles and divorced from the city. The unintended humor stems, probably, from Wright's advanced age (he was in his nineties) and the fact that he died before it was carried out, so it is not representative of his best work; but it is revealing of the formalist trend.

The work of I. M. Pei (23), Ulrich Franzen, Philip Johnson,

22 FRANK LLOYD WRIGHT, *Marin County Civic Center*, San Rafael, California, 1959–61. The great Pont du Gard made out of cardboard, gilt and golden bauble, surmounted by an Aztec minaret, with interior bowling alleys of space and a baby-blue, opaline roof with cookie-cutter hemicircles. An excellent piece of Kitsch modern, unfortunately unintended.

23 I. M. PEI, *Christian Science Church Center*, Boston, 1973. Very hard-edge Le Corbusier – in fact, Chandigarh done with precision concrete. From the air you can appreciate the fact that this center is laid out like a giant phallus which culminates, appropriately, in a fountain. Ledoux designed a phallus-planned building as a brothel, but there is no further indication here that some elaborate message is intended.

Skidmore, Owings and Merrill, and other American architects of this period, has a similar erratic signification: there is usually a striking formal statement, a reduced but potent image, and inadvertent meanings. For instance, Gordon Bunshaft's Hirshhorn Museum, the only collection of modern art on the Mall in Washington, is in the very powerful form of a white masonry cylinder (24). This simplified shape, ultimately stemming from the eighteenth-century Modernists, Boullée and Ledoux, was meant to communicate power, awe, harmony and the sublime. And so it does. But, as *Time* and other journals pointed out, with its battered walls, impenetrable heaviness and 360-degree machine-gun slit, it symbolizes more accurately a Normandy pillbox. Bunshaft is accidentally saying "keep modern art from the people and open fire if they approach." So many cues, in such a popular code, reinforce this meaning and make it obvious to everyone not retrained in the architects' code. Had the designer intended the idea of an elitist bunker, it might have been an ironic and multivalent statement of this notion, but, as with the unintended witticisms of Mrs Malaprop, all credit for humor must go to the subconscious.

The disparity between elitist and popular codes can be found everywhere in the Modern Movement and often the better the architect the more he attends to formal analogies and the less to obvious meanings. Herman Hertzberger's Old

Age Home is a case in point (25). On a sophisticated level it is the delightful casbah he intended, with many small-scale places and a closely grained urban fabric where the individual is psychologically hidden and protected by the nooks and crannies of articulated space. As an abstract piece of form it communicates humanism, care, intricacy and delicacy. That is, as a Chinese puzzle the various interlocking elements and spaces convey these meanings by implication. Yet such a subtle analogy is hardly enough when more potent, metaphorical meanings are accidentally overemphasized. For what are the obvious associations of this Old Age Home? Each room looks like a black coffin placed between white crosses (in fact a veritable war cemetery of white crosses). Despite his humanism, the architect is inadvertently saying that old age, in our society, is rather fatal.

Ah well, these "slips-of-the-metaphor" happen to the top Modernists and they can even be made by architects who understand that architecture is a social language — by Peter and Alison Smithson. It is interesting that, like other apologists for the Modern Movement since 1850, they justify their work in terms of the linguistic analogy, and they look to previous languages of architecture for their lesson. They say of the city of Bath: "it's unique … for its remarkable cohesion, for a *form language understood by all, contributed by all.*"[5] Their analysis of this Georgian city of light and dark stonework shows it to have a widely appreciated repertoire, a consistent language, from humble details such as street grilles, to grand gestures such as porticoes (26). These porticoes

24 GORDON BUNSHAFT and SOM, *Hirschhorn Museum,*Washington DC, 1973. Symbolism at its most inadvertent – a concrete pillbox meant to protect art from the people? A marble doughnut? (Hirschhorn Museum).

25 HERMAN HERTZBERGER, *Old Age Home,* Amsterdam, 1975. An intricate puzzle of small-scaled elements, a human scale in the details. But this is multiplied to vast proportions. The incessant symbolism of white crosses containing black coffins is equally unpremeditated and unfortunate.

the Smithsons characterize as metaphors for large doors, and pediments as metaphors for cheaper doors. In short, they are acutely aware of the way architectural language depends on traditional symbolism.

This makes their own anti-traditionalism all the more poignant. The Smithsons, as veritable descendants of the Romantic age, follow the Wordsworthian injunction "to make it new" each time they design a building, and this is to avoid the stigma of conventionality. Thereby, of course, they also avoid communicating the distinctions they find in Bath, for all developed languages must contain a degree of conventional usage, if only to make innovations and deviations from the norm more correctly understood. One reason for the misunderstanding is that their linguistic analogy is based on machine production rather than human usage. For instance, when speaking about a possible Modern language, Peter Smithson comes down firmly, like a 1920s Modernist, in support of a machine aesthetic: "for the machine-supported present-day cities only a live, cool, highly controlled, rather impersonal architectural language can deepen that base-connection, and resonate with culture as a whole."[6] Culture as a whole, integrated culture, or culture treated in the abstract and as a totality has been a dream of Modernists since the Enlightenment and, although it is a worthy ideal in many respects, it overlooks the variety of competing groups and subcultures that make up society.

The dangers of this position became well known at the beginning of the Post-Modern period, during the early 1960s. Yet many architects remained committed to universal solutions because of their training in processes of mass production, and an ideology of progress. They still believed in a *zeitgeist* and one determined by machinery and technology,

26 JOHN WOOD II, *Royal Crescent*, Bath, 1767–80. One of the first examples of housing treated as a palace – the Colosseum was another model. Although making a grand urban gesture, the individual houses still have an identity, marked by vertical separation and several variations in articulation (chimneys, fire walls, fences). The Smithsons are acutely aware of this symbolism, which makes their failure to provide its equivalent all the more poignant. (Bath City Council).

27 ALISON and PETER SMITHSON, *Robin Hood Gardens*, London, 1968–72. Unrelieved concrete (except for curtains), popularly identified now with the image of an industrial process. The variations of vertical fins are not strong enough to identify each apartment The packed-in scale gives the feeling of a dense human wall.

so the buildings they produced managed to symbolize these old-fashioned demons rather clearly.

The great irony is, however, that these same architects also believed in providing essentially humanist values of "place, identity, personality, homecoming" (the quote comes from several Team Ten sources, and the Smithsons were leaders of this breakaway group). How can such meanings be communicated if the language to be used is both completely new and based on the machine metaphor? Post-Modernists, as we will see, are looking for other metaphors such as those derived from nature and the body, and it is in social housing such as Pruitt-Igoe – at the deprived end of the economic scale – where these metaphors become most important. If one is building mass housing for the public, then it would be hard, practically impossible, to be both "cool, impersonal and machine-like" and also give a sense of "place, identity, personality and homecoming." The Smithsons, in their Robin Hood Gardens, in the East End of London, have not pulled off the miracle (27).

In spite of the large urban gesture and U-shaped plan, Robin Hood Gardens is not a modern version of the Bath Crescent. Although Peter Smithson admires Bath for being "unmistakably a collection of separate houses," his design does not accentuate the identity of each house. It suppresses separate identity in favor of visual syncopation, a partially randomized set of vertical fins and a horizontal continuity – the notion of a communal street deck (28, 29). These "streets in the air" have, surprisingly, all the faults that the Smithsons had previously criticized in other similar schemes. The street decks are under-used; the collective

entries are paltry, and a few have been vandalized. Indeed, they are dark, smelly, dank passageways, places where, as Oscar Newman argued in *Defensible Space*, crime may occur more frequently than elsewhere. There is little "sense of place," few collective facilities and fewer "identifying elements," which the architects had reasonably said were needed in Modern buildings.

The Smithsons claim they have provided a sense of place: "On the garden side the building is unified. It is an urban place, a part of the definition of a city, provided it does not become a repetitive pattern which organizes a homogeneous space."[7] Indeed, the space is not homogeneous, it has kinks and an artificial mound near the center. But these deviations from the norm, and the subtle cues of visual separation, are hardly strong enough to override the repetitive pattern and homogeneous material. These signify more strongly "council housing," "anonymity," "the authorities did not have enough money to use wood, stucco, etc" – in brief, they signify "social deprivation." The Smithsons' laudable intentions of providing a community building on the scale of the Bath Crescent and offering the same degree of individual expression and identity in an architectural language understood by all – these positive aims – are denied by the built form.

Such contradictions between statement and result have reached impressive proportions in Modern Architecture, and one can speak of a credibility gap that parallels the loss of trust in politicians. One cause of this stems from the kind of language architecture is. As something rooted in peoples' childhood experience of crawling around on flat floors and perceiving such normal elements as vertical doors, it is by necessity partly tradition and slow changing. But also it is partly rooted in a fast-changing society, with its new functional tasks, new materials, new technologies and ideologies. On the one hand, architecture is as conservative as spoken language (we can still understand Renaissance English); and, on the other, as revolutionary and esoteric as modern art and science. The result is that architecture is *radically schizophrenic*, and this fact leads directly to the Post-Modern strategy of double-coding. As we will see, Post-Modernists design buildings with mixed languages that recognize the basic duality.

Put another way, there are two forms of getting to know architecture. Children, as indeed tourists, learn the cultural signs that make any urban place particular to a social group, an economic class and real, historical people. But professionals and modern architects spend their time unlearning these particular signs while they master the science of building and the arcana of an advanced industrial civilization. Furthermore, following modern novelists, sociologists and idealistic planners, they have constructed the ideal type of the universal man, the abstract client, the average user. This Mythic Modern Man may not exist, except as a historical fiction, but he became a logical necessity for architects and others who wanted to generalize a statistical average and design for the unknown client, the absent user. Tom Wolfe has criticized novelists for writing about such non-existant creatures, and the same points could be made about architects.[8] They try to provide Modern Man with a mythic consciousness, with consistent patterns reminiscent of tribal societies, refined in their purity, full of tasteful "unity in variety," and other such geometric harmonies (30). But, in fact, Modern Man is nothing so much as the architect and professional talking about their own tastes, projecting forward their mid-dle-class values as if they were universal. Signs of status, history, commerce, comfort, and ethnic domain are sacrificed for abstract space, light, and pure geometry. Modern architects are not trained in the popular and slow-changing codes, they do not care to get close to this reality.

Too bad: society can go on without architects, or personalize housing estates, as is being done, or blow them up (as was happening once a month by the middle seventies in Britain). It can hire interior decorators or design every building twice. It does not matter, except for the poor, or state-run housing. Post-Modernism became a radical movement, in the late 1970s, in Communist and authoritarian countries for this reason. The present book went into several editions, including underground ones in the Soviet sphere, because of the way Modernist housing, social coercion and an abstract bureaucracy formed a powerful syndrome. For the middle class, in a relatively free market place, the situation of anonymous mass housing was never as acute because there were several architectural options, as well as other, more realistic professionals ready to move in where Modernists feared to tread.

In any case, before we finish with the case against Modernism, we should look at an aspect of the dilemma that is not caused by architects, but one that has a very important effect on the language they use: the problem of content.

28, 29 SMITHSONS, *Robin Hood Gardens*, street in the air, and collective entry. The long, empty streets in the air don't have the life or facilities of the traditional street. The entry ways, one of which has been burned, are dark and anonymous, serving too many families. The scheme has many of the problems which Oscar Newman traced to a lack of defensible space. Here architectural critic Paul Goldberger mimes a mugger's threatening gesture – commonplace in these corridors.

30 LAS VEGAS *Social Realism, capitalist style*. Modern architects have disregarded this level of symbolic detail and particularity. Most cities contain ethnic diversity, but what large development incorporates the Chinese restaurant, the front of the local butcher? Architects have been removed from this level of detail, and will be, until they are retrained as anthropologists, or journalists, to understand social reality.

UNIVALENT CONTENT

What are the prevalent building types that have engaged the skill of architects in this century? Uplifting types such as churches and public squares, or mundane ones, such as boutiques and offices? A certain disinterest is needed to engage this question, because the truths are hard to swallow and the solutions not forthcoming. Many will gloss over the social realities behind architecture because they are so trivial and of no one's desire, no one's fault. On this score the major mistake architects made in this century is to have been born at all.

Let us look at the major monuments of Modern Architecture and the social tasks for which they were built. Here we will find a strange but unnoticed deflection of the Modern architect's self-image, his assumed role as one who brings social amelioration and progressive liberation. What has become of the avant-garde prophet and utopian healer?

31 Top right: PETER BEHRENS, *AEG Factory*, Berlin, 1909. Often regarded as one of the first great modern buildings, the fountainhead too of industrial design, this work set the factory as the major metaphor for subsequent building. Here the marriage was made between big business, "good design," and the functional style. This union was eagerly sought for at the time by the German Werkbund, and it bore multinational fruit sixty years later. (Bauhaus Archive).

32 Right: FRANK LLOYD WRIGHT, *Johnson Wax Building*, Racine, Wisconsin, 1938. Columns taper downwards and are supported on brass shoes. Everything takes up the curve theme in this "total work of art." The idea of a unified corporate image became standard by the fifties for such multinationals as the CBS, IBM, Olivetti, etc. (US Information Service).

One finds he has actually built for the reigning powers of a commercial society, and this surreptitious liaison has taken its toll, as illicit love affairs will do. The Modern Movement of architecture, conceived in the 1850s as a call to morality, and in the 1920s (in its Heroic Period) as a call to social transformation, found itself unwittingly compromised, first by practice and then by acceptance.[9] Think of the ironies. In the nineteenth century these Pioneers of the Modern Movement (as they were called) wished to give up their subservient role as "tailors to society" and what they regarded as "a corrupt ruling taste"; instead they would become "doctors," "prophets of the new," or at least midwives, to a new social order. But for what order did they build?

Monopolies and Big Business: Some of the accepted classics of Modern Architecture were constructed for clients who today are multinational corporations. Peter Behrens' Berlin Turbine Factory was for the General Electric of its day, AEG (31). This building of 1909 is often considered the

first great work of European Modern Architecture because of its pure volumetric expression, its clear clean use of glass and steel, almost the curtain wall, and its refinement of utilitarian products – the beginning of industrial design. Further landmarks of this tradition were Frank Lloyd Wright's curvilinear poetry of Pyrex tubing and streamlined brick, built for a large wax company, the privately owned near-monopoly Johnson's Wax (32). Another milestone was Gordon Bunshaft's classic solution for the office tower, two pure slabs set at right angles, one on top of the other, erected for the multinational Lever company, based on soap. Then this line culminated in Mies van der Rohe's dark, Rolls-Royce solution to the curtain wall built for the Seagram's Whiskey giant on Park Avenue and, a bit later, Eero Saarinen's sleek black parallelepiped for the giant media company CBS.

Near CBS, on Sixth Avenue in New York, one finds a veritable necropolis of blank boxes dedicated to refinements of the curtain wall and the fortunes of soft drink companies, tobacco chains, international banks, oil companies and *Time-Life*. How should one express the power and concentration of capital, the mercantile function, the exploitation of markets? These building tasks would be the monuments of our time, because they bring in the extra money for architecture; and so their streetwise Darwinism mocks the social idealism of the Pioneers all the more. Was the Revolution of Modernism really fought to make Fifth Avenue safe for Armani? (He hired the Guggenheim as a giant catwalk for a Post-Millennial hard sell). Were the barricades of the 1871 Commune put up so that Walter Gropius could discharge 10,000 businessmen from his Pan Am Building (33) right on top of the most congested site in New York? Were Cubists, Dadaist and Surrealists invented to give MOMA the monopoly on Modernism? Inadvertently, for Modernists, "yes, yes and, yes." Boom boom boom. Modernism chokes on such contradictions many times.

International Exhibitions, World Fairs: Another genealogy of Modern Architecture is traced from the Crystal Palace of 1851 to the Theme Pavilion at Osaka 1970 (34). This line of descent has a series of technical triumphs to its credit, resulting in the new language of lattice structures, the open girders of Eiffel, the pin-jointed parabolas of industrial sheds, the translucent and geometric domes of Buckminster Fuller, and the soaring tents of Frei Otto (these tents always soar in architectural criticism). Indeed these triumphs also did a great deal to aestheticize the experience of architecture, make us so dazzled by the structural gymnastics that we took our eyes off the obvious motivations. Thus modern historians and critics skip lightly over the content of the structures, their propagandist role, and focus on their spatial and optical qualities. The mass media follows suit. Overlooked was the nationalism and ersatz ambience that constituted ninety per cent of the World Fairs. Why? Because this

33 WALTER GROPIUS, with TAC, *Pan Am Building*, New York, 1958. While Gropius was preaching social responsibility he was, at the same time, producing a compromised version of Le Corbusier's Algiers skyscraper, and congesting the busiest hub of New York. Modernists in such blatant contradiction produced the Post-Modern critique.

34 KENZO TANGE, *Theme Pavilion*, *EXPO 70*, Osaka, 1970. A megastructure carrying various services was finally built after being contemplated by the avant-garde for ten years. World Fairs often allow such grandiose and creative ideas to be realized, and have therefore played an important role in the evolution of Modern Architecture. (Masao Arai).

subject matter was so obviously hedonistic and lacking in subtlety and, perhaps, because there was no appreciation of how blatant content might work in a mass culture to become more humorous, creative and provocative.

Factories and Engineering Feats: From Walter Gropius Fagus Factory, 1911, to Le Corbusier's "house as a machine for living," 1922, we have the birth and establishment of the major metaphor for Modern Architecture: the factory (35). Housing was conceived in this image, and however reactionary and evil they were, the Nazis were not altogether wrong in attacking the first international manifesto of this metaphor, the *Weissenhof Siedlungen*, 1927, for its inappropriateness. Why should houses adopt the imagery of the mass production line, and the white purity of the hospital?

More recent mass housing in England, for instance that in London, or Milton Keynes, has followed this pervasive twentieth-century metaphor. That no one asked to live in a factory did not occur to the doctor-Modern-architect, because he was out to cure the disease of modern cities, no matter how distasteful the medicine. Indeed, better if it tasted like castor oil and caused convulsions, because then the transformation of bourgeois society was more likely to be complete. The patient would reform his petty acquisitive drives and become a good collectivized citizen. (In Russia such housing blocks were called "social condensers" and like some mad electrical instrument they were meant to "condense" private property out of the individual).

Such mechanistic metaphors have been rejected on almost all housing where they have been tried — exceptions are in Germany and Switzerland. But they have quite rightly taken hold in areas where the machine, power and production are more appropriate: stadia, sports grounds, aircraft hangars, and grand engineering projects (36). Here the poetry of process is exhilarating without being wildly surreal, and, on the level of content, we can claim the unmitigated triumph of Modern Architecture.

Consumer Temples and Churches of Distraction: Someone from an alien culture would be amazed to see, if he took a quick helicopter trip over our sprawling cities, that urban man worshipped at institutions devoted to commercial gods. Modern architects have not altogether mastered this territory of Disneyworld and ride-through parks, of King's Road and Sunset Strip, but they are beginning to try, and we can already count some bittersweet triumphs. First, in the middle 1960s, were the technological jewels of Hans Hollein, (a later Post-Modernist). In the center of Vienna he perfected the emergent genre of the 12-foot-square boutique and candle shop, the high-gloss mausoleum given over to selling religious relics for the dining table or wedding finger (37). So much design talent, and mystery, expended on such small shops would convince an outsider that he had at last stumbled on the true faith of this civilization. And when he came to see the same medals worshipped in the large hotels, constructed in the theological material of mirrorplate, his interpretation would be confirmed. The culture idolizes tinsel, personal adornment, private jewellery (38). The more adept the archi-

36 KENZO TANGE, *National Gymnasium for the Olympic Games*, Tokyo, 1964. Two buildings in subtle counterpoint are placed on a podium. The concrete masts, which hold the hyperbolic curves, end in the conventional Japanese slant that has become something of a cliché. The gentle curves and structural expression are also traditional signs.

37 HANS HOLLEIN, *Jewelry Shop*, Vienna, 1975. Hollein uses voluptuous, shiny marble to set off the polished mechanical equipment. The contrast of circle and fissure, of skin-like marble and glistening gold lips folding over each other, is explicitly ironic and sexual. Tight space is cut up to loosen the customer's libido even further. Perhaps only a Viennese could have brought off this mixture of commerce and sensuality.

38 JOHN PORTMAN, *Bonaventure Hotel*, model, Los Angeles, 1976. Portman has revived the nineteenth-century tradition of the grand hotel – at least the cost part of this tradition – with lavish Regency Hyatts in several American cities. He gives the exteriors an absolute geometric image, parts of which in mirrorplate flash reflections like overblown jewels. The planning is reminiscent of the megalomaniacal schemes of Boullée.

tect became at embellishing such buildings (and of course they were working at a distinct disadvantage, having previously equated "ornament and crime"), the more the anomaly appears. A jewel is a jewel; it is not a fitting object for great architecture. The banality of content will not go away.

Architecture obviously reflects what a society holds important, what it values both spiritually and in terms of cash. In the pre-industrial past the major areas for expression were the temple, the church, the palace, agora, meeting house, country house and city hall; while in the present, extra money is spent on hotels, head offices, restaurants, shopping malls and all those commercial building types just mentioned. As we will see, with the rise of Entertainment Architecture launched by Disney Corp in the mid-eighties, commercialization even sidetracked the careers of two eminent Post-Modernists, Michael Graves and Robert Stern. As Rem Koolhaas intoned quoting others, "shopping is the terminal condition of mankind." Architecture reduced to signs clipped on buildings became ersatz. Public housing and buildings expressing the public realm suffered the cutbacks. Buildings representing consumer values generate the investment. What John Kenneth Galbraith said of American Capitalism became a global condition, it results in private wealth and public squalor.

Several Modern architects, and even a few Post-Modernists, in a desperate attempt to cheer themselves up,

have decided that since this is an inevitable situation, it must also have its good points. Commercial tasks are more democratic than the previous aristocratic and religious ones; "Main Street is almost all right" according to Robert Venturi, and commercial signs should even be stuck on to sheds to produce dissociated architecture.

When these commercial design tasks first emerged into consciousness, at the turn of this century, they were celebrated by the Futurist, Sant' Elia, with a glee and moralizing tone that were later to become common. He contrasted the new building tasks, given over to commerce and energy, with the previous ones devoted to worship – the nineteenth-century dynamo versus the thirteenth-century Virgin:

> The formidable antithesis between the modern world and the old is determined by all those things that formerly did not exist…we have lost our predilection for the monumental, the heavy, the static, and we have enriched our sensibility with a taste for the light, the practical, the ephemeral and the swift. We no longer feel ourselves to be the men of the cathedrals, the palaces and the tribunes. We are the men of the great hotels, the railway stations, the immense streets, colossal ports, covered markets, luminous arcades, straight roads and beneficial demolitions.[10]

Look at that list closely. You find the social activities of a middle-class tourist wandering from railway station to hotel along wide super-highways dotted with bulldozed sites and lit by glowing neon signs. With slight modifications, Sant' Elia could be describing the glitter of Las Vegas, or, less fashionably, the main street of Warsaw. Whatever the country, whatever the economic system, such secular building tasks became the important ones since 1900, and so much Modern art and architecture tries to celebrate this fact. "The heroism of everyday life," that notion shared by Picasso, Leger and Le Corbusier in the twenties, was a philosophy which tried to place banal objects on a pedestal formerly reserved for special symbols of veneration. The fountain pen, the filing cabinet, the steel girder and the typewriter were the new icons. Mayakovsky and the Russian Constructivists took art into the streets and even performed one grand symphony of sirens and steam whistles, while waving colored flags on top of factory roofs! The hope of these artists and architects was to reform society on a new class and functional basis: substitute power stations for cathedrals, technocrats for aristocrats. A new, heroic, democratic society would emerge, led by a powerful race of pagan supermen, the avant-garde, the technicians and captains of industry, the enlightened scientists and teams of experts. What a dream!

Indeed, the managerial revolution did occur, and socialist revolutions happened in a few countries. But the dream was taken over by Madison Avenue (and its equivalents), and the "heroic object of everyday use" became the "new, revolutionary detergent." Societies kept on worshipping at their old altars, with diminishing faith, and tried to incorporate the new values at the same time. The result? Ersatz culture, a caricature of the past and future at once, a surreal fantasy dreamed up neither by the avant-garde, nor the traditionalists, and abhorrent to both of them and most people as well.

With the triumph of consumer society in the West and, for seventy years, bureaucratic State capitalism in the East, our unfortunate Modern architect was left without much uplifting social content to champion. If architecture has to concentrate its efforts on symbolizing a way of life and the public realm, it is in a bit of a fix when these things lose their credibility. There is nothing much the architect can do about this except protest as a citizen, design dissenting buildings that express the complex situation and, as will be argued in conclusion, look to new values emerging both in science and art. Because Post-Modern global culture has ushered in, and been partly created by, the information age, there are a host of new opportunities and building types that have emerged which have more than commercial potential. Above all the museum has emerged as the cathedral of our time, with an inadequate theology it is true, but still as a new and fitting focus for the urban public realm.

But even working in a commercial culture the architect can communicate missing values and criticize with irony, faint praise or negation the ones he dislikes. Several recent buildings have it both ways. Using methods advocated by Post-Modern writers such as Umberto Eco and Linda Hutcheon, he can send a double message of dissent from within. But to do that he must make use of the language of the local culture, otherwise his message falls on deaf ears, or is distorted to fit this local language. So it is to the idea of using architectural language to send complex messages that we now turn, and the linguistic analogy in architecture.

Part II
The Modes of Architectural Communication

Monsieur Jourdain, Moliere's *Bourgeois Gentilhomme*, was rather surprised to discover that he had been speaking prose for forty years – "without knowing anything about it." Modern architects might suffer a similar shock, or doubt that they have been speaking anything as elevated as prose. To look at the environment is to agree with their doubt. We see a babble of tongues, a free-for-all of personal idiolects, not the Classical language of the Doric, Ionic and Corinthian Orders (or even the coherent prose of the vernacular) (39). Where there once were rules of architectural grammar, we now have a mutual diatribe between speculative builders and bureaucratic monoliths.

Look at the prime site on the south bank of the River Thames in London (40). Where there once was a gentle discourse between the Houses of Parliament and Westminster Abbey, there is now, across the river, the Shell Building bellowing at the Hayward Gallery, which grunts back at a stammering and giggling Festival Hall — the whole boisterous shouting match now warily regarded by a Ferris wheel lost from the circus, London's misplaced Millennium Eye. It is all jabber and strife, and yet this invective is still language even if it is not very comprehensible or persuasive. There are various analogies architecture shares with language and, if we use the terms loosely, we can speak of architectural "words," "phrases," "syntax," and "semantics."[11] I will discuss several of these analogies in turn, showing how they can be more consciously used as communicational means, starting with the mode most commonly disregarded in Modern Architecture.

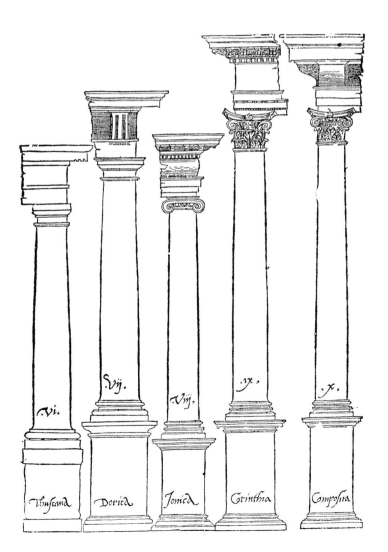

39 *THE FIVE ORDERS*: Tuscan, Doric, Ionic, Corinthian and Composite from Sebastiano Serlio's *The Book of Architecture*, 1611.

40 *THE SOUTH BANK*, London, 1976. With large chunks devoted to different functions: left to right: The Queen Elizabeth Hall, Royal Festival Hall and Shell Tower carry on their distinctive form of garbled conversation. Each chunk sends out a single, if muted, message that it is an important monument of some unspecified kind.

41 Top left: *CONCRETE GRILLES*, now the sign of parking garage, were first used on offices in America in the late fifties. They work here to carry the external loads and mask the cars. While the "cheese grater" is now no longer perceived as a metaphor, the precast grille is on rare occasions still used for offices. Whether it signifies garage or office depends on the frequency of usage within a society.

METAPHOR AND CODE

People invariably see one building in terms of another, or in terms of a similar object; in short, as a metaphor. The more unfamiliar a Modern building is, the more they will compare it metaphorically to what they know. This matching of one experience to another is a property of all thought, particularly that which is creative. Thus, when pre-cast concrete grilles were first used on buildings in the late fifties, they were seen as "cheese-graters," "beehives," "chain-link fences," while ten years later, when these forms became a norm in a certain building type, they were seen in functional terms: "this looks like a parking garage" (41). From metaphor to cliché, from neologism through constant usage to architectural sign, this is the continual route traveled by new and successful forms and techniques.

Typical negative metaphors used by the public and by critics such as Lewis Mumford to condemn Modern Architecture were "cardboard box, shoe-box, egg-crate, filing cabinet, grid-paper." These comparisons were sought not only for their pejorative, mechanistic overtones, but also because they were strongly *coded* in a culture that had become sensitized to the specter of 1984. This obvious point has some curious implications, as we shall see.

One implication became apparent when I was visiting Japan and the architect Kisho Kurokawa in 1972. We went to

42 Above: KISHO KUROKAWA, *Nakagin Capsule Building*, Tokyo, 1972. Forty boxes were driven to the site and lifted on to the two concrete cores. Each habitable room has built-in bathroom, stereo tape deck, calculators and other amenities for the businessman. The metaphor of stacking rooms like bricks or sugar cubes has re-emerged every five years or so ever since Walter Gropius proposed it in 1922. The overtones are ambiguous: to some they have always suggested regimentation, to others the unity in variety of the Italian hill town. (Tomio Ohashi).

43 *The DUCK-RABBIT ILLUSION*, read from left to right by duck hunters and from right to left by frequenters of the Playboy Club. Since this illusion is so well known we can now see it as a new animal with two heads. But note: you can only read it one way at a time depending on the code you choose to adopt. (E. H. Gombrich, *Art and Illusion*).

see his new apartment tower in Tokyo, made from stacked shipping containers which had a most unusual overall shape. They looked like stacked sugar cubes, or even more, like superimposed washing machines, because the white cubes all had round windows in their center (42). When I said this metaphor had unfortunate overtones for living, Kurokawa evinced surprise. "They aren't washing machines, they're bird cages. You see, in Japan we build concrete-box bird nests with round holes and place them in the trees. I've built these bird nests for itinerant businessmen who visit Tokyo, for bachelors who fly in every so often with their birds." A witty answer, perhaps made up on the spot, but one which underscored very nicely a difference in our visual codes.

The basic point is that codes of perception underlie the way we see architecture and value it. A well-known visual illusion brings this out: the famous "duck-rabbit figure," which will be seen first one way then the other (43). Since we all have well-learned visual codes for *both* animals, and even probably now a code for the hybrid monster with two heads, we can see it three ways. One view may predominate, according to either the strength of the code or according to the direction from which we see the figure at first. To get further readings ("bellows" or "keyhole" etc.,) is harder because these codes are less strong for this figure, they map less well than the primary ones – at least in our culture. The general point is that code restrictions based on personal learning and background culture guide a reading of architecture. In a global civilization there are multiple codes, some of which may be in conflict and this presents the basic starting point for the Post-Modern architect: how to deal with this plurality? How to balance conflicting meaning, which codes to prefer, which to suppress?

In very general terms, there are two large subcultures: one

44 JORN UTZON, *Sydney Opera House*, Australia, 1957–74. A mixed metaphor: the shells have symbolized flowers unfolding, sailboats in the harbor fish swallowing each other and now, because of the local code, high cost. As with the Eiffel Tower, ambiguous meanings have finally transcended all possible functional considerations and the building has become simply a national symbol. This rare class of sign, like a Rorschach test, provokes response which focuses interest on the responder, not the sign. It could be called the enigmatic signifier, because, like the ocean, it happily receives projected meanings from everyone. (New South Wales Government Office, London).

45 *CARTOON* presented by students when Queen Elizabeth officially opened the building. (From *Architecture in Australia*).

with the contemporary code based on the training and ideology of Modern architects, and another with the traditional or local code based on everyone's experience of normalized architectural elements. As already mentioned, there are compelling reasons why these codes may be at odds and architecture may be radically schizophrenic, both in its creation and interpretation. Since some buildings incorporate various codes, they can become mixed metaphors with opposing meanings: e.g. "the pure volume" of the Modern architect becomes the "shoe-box" or "filing cabinet" to the public.

One building just on the cusp between Modernism and Post-Modernism, the Sydney Opera House, provoked an abundance of metaphorical responses, both in the popular and professional press (44). The reasons are, again, that the forms are both unfamiliar to architecture and reminiscent of other visual objects. Most of the metaphors are organic: thus the architect, Jorn Utzon, showed how the shells of the building related to the surface of a sphere (like "orange segments") and the wings of a bird in flight. They also relate, obviously, to white seashells, and it is this metaphor, plus the comparison to the white sails bobbing around in Sydney Harbour, that have become journalistic clichés. This raises another obvious point with unexpected implications: the interpretation of architectural metaphor is more elastic and dependent on local codes than the interpretation of metaphor in spoken or written language. Local context guides the reading, and limits the metaphors to travel along certain routes, although very wide ones.

Some critics insisted that the superimposed shells resembled the growth of a flower over time — the unfolding of petals; while the architectural students of Australia caricatured this same aspect as "turtles making love" (45). From several points of view, the violent aspect of broken and smashed-up shapes is apparent — "a traffic accident with no survivors"; while again these same views elicit possible organic metaphors — "fish swallowing each other." Reinforcing this interpretation are the shiny, scaly elements of the tiled surface which are apparent up close. But the most extraordinary metaphor, and the one that Australians apply with a certain bemused affection, is "scrum of nuns." All those shells leaning over, confronting each other in two main directions, resemble the head-dresses and cowls of two opposed religious orders, and the wildly unlikely idea that this could be a scrimmage of mother superiors dominates the possibilities. "Wit" has been defined as "the unlikely copulation of ideas together," and the more unlikely *but* successful the union, the more it will strike the viewer and stay in his mind. A witty building is one which permits us to make extraordinary but convincing associations. This became a hallmark of Post-Modern architecture as we shall see.

The question obviously arises of how appropriate these metaphors are to the building's function and its symbolic role. Concentrating on this aspect and momentarily disregarding other things such as the cost (the Australians spent something like twenty times the original estimate for their mixed metaphor), we might come to the following conclusion. The organic metaphors are very appropriate to a cultural center: images which suggest growth are particularly apt for meanings of creativity. The building flies, sails, splashes, curves up and unfolds like an animated vegetable. Fine. Perhaps if the building were renamed The Australian Cultural Center (not the Sydney Opera House) and justified as a symbol of Australia's liberation from Anglo-Saxon dependence (which it has become), then its interpretation might be clearer. We could then see these extraordinary metaphors in their most positive light, as symbols of Australia's break with colonial conformity and provinciality.

But a few things cloud this interpretation somewhat. We know the building was designed by a European (not an

46 KONSTANTIN MELNIKOV, *Russakov Club*, Moscow, 1928. The wedge shape plus rectangular flytower became established as the "word" for auditorium in the language of Modern Architecture because of this building. The shapes follow, more or less, the volumes needed for the functions.

Australian) as an *opera* house — and one that works neither economically nor functionally in the manner it was conceived. Since such knowledge is an integral part of the code with which we interpret the building, our judgement cannot avoid being contaminated by this knowledge. Knowledge and seeing are connected, something that the duck-rabbit figure brings out: perception is shaped by codes based on previous experience. It is virtually impossible to perceive the building without knowing about the notorious "Sydney Opera House Case," the firing of the architect, the cost, and so forth. So these local, specific meanings also become symbolized by what are now seen as "extravagant shells."

Several Modernists criticized the Opera House for hiding a series of different functions under repetitive shells that had no relation to the interior spaces. The various theatres, restaurants and exhibition halls are hidden and equated by the shells, which is why it has been so annoying to those architects brought up as functionalists. They expect to see each function given a clear and separate volume, which ideally speaking, is an outline diagram of the use — such as the auditorium. They would have designed the building as a series of boxy fly towers and wedge shapes (the conventionalized "word" for auditorium in Modern architecture) (46). The building violates this code, as Classical architecture often did, by obscuring actual functions behind overall patterns. The debate then becomes whether the wit, exuberance and appropriateness of the organic metaphor justify such obscurantism. I think they do, but others would deny this.

AGAINST THE DECORATED SHED

One of them might be Robert Venturi, who also starts from the position that architecture should be looked at as communication, but comes to very different conclusions from mine. Because in his early work he was important for Post-Modernism, our disagreements are germane for both the debates on architectural language and understanding how the tradition has developed. Stemming from research that George Baird and I had published as *Meaning in Architecture* in 1969, Venturi formulated a theory of signs and symbols in *Learning from Las Vegas*, 1972. Where we had followed the semiotic theory that distinguished three types of signification — icons, index and symbol — he settled on a simpler opposition, between what he called "ducks and decorated sheds" (47).

The decorated shed is a simple enclosure with signs attached like a billboard, or the application of conventional ornament, such as a pediment symbolizing entry (48). These he promoted as being in keeping with the spirit of the age, with Las Vegas or, more prosaically, with advertisement on the ubiquitous American highway, Route One. By contrast, for him a duck is a structure in the shape of its function; his usage was inspired by a bird-shaped building, constructed in Long Island in 1931, that sold ducks — hence his strange nomenclature. Other examples of a "duck," he averred, were Modern buildings where the construction, structure and volume became the decoration. Clearly because the shell motif has dominated all other concerns Venturi would call the Sydney Opera House a duck. Furthermore, he would consign this mode of communication to the scrapheap of history arguing that, for one thing, the Modern Movement has overdone it and, for another, it is out of keeping with an electronic society based on signage. I would disagree with his historical judgement, and take even greater exception to the attitudes implied behind it.

Venturi, like the typical Modernist that he was criticizing in his seminal book *Complexity and Contradiction in Architecture*, is adopting the tactic of exclusive inversion. He is cutting out a whole area of architectural communication, duck buildings (technically speaking iconic signs), in order to make his preferred mode, decorated sheds (symbolic and indexical signs) that much more potent. Thus we are being asked to follow an exclusive, simplistic path not a complex and contradictory one. But just as clearly the environment needs all the modes of communication it can get and it is the Modernist commitment to architectural street-fighting that leads to such oversimplification, not a balanced theory of signification.

MULTIVALENCE AND THE ENIGMATIC SIGNIFIER

In any case, the Sydney Opera House does pose essential questions that have become particularly relevant to Post-Modernism, especially in its complexity phase today. While the organic metaphors are suitable analogues for a culture center, they are not reinforced by conventional signs that spring from the Australian vernacular, and therefore their initial meaning is erratic and surrealist. Like a Magritte painting "the apple that expands to fill a whole room" their reference is striking but enigmatic, evasive but suggestive. Clearly by piling on evocative connotations *our emotions are being heightened* but there is no exact goal towards which all the overtones — shells, sails, nun's cowls, orange peels, etc., — converge. They float around in our mind to pick up connections where they can, like a luxuriant dream following too much cheese and wine.

48 *SECURITY MARINE BANK*, Wisconsin, c.1971. The symbolic shed, one part communication of status and security, the other part function. Commercial pressures today naturally dissociate signifier and signified in this way, a destructive tendency for architectural symbolism which depends on a resonance of meaning. (Wayne Attoe).

47 ROBERT VENTURI, *The Duck versus Decorated Shed*. Venturi would prefer more decorated sheds, because he contends they communicate effectively, and modern architects have for too long only designed "ducks." The duck is, in semiotic terms, an iconic sign, because the signifier (form) has certain aspects in common with the signified (content). The decorated shed depends on learned meanings — writing or decoration — which are symbolic signs.

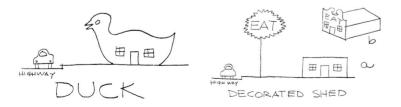

50 HENRY J GOODWIN. *Big Donut Drive-in*, Los Angeles, 1954. Originally there were ten of these giants, now there are, alas, three. The doughnuts sold are big.

49 *HOT DOG STAND*, Los Angeles, *c.*1938. Reinforced with additional signs such as oozing mustard, "Tail-o-the-pup" etc. This architecture would appear to be unambiguous, yet at the Architectural Association in London it is classified in the slide library as a "hamburger stand"! Once again, visual codes are mainly local.

They do however prove a general point about communication: the more the metaphors, the greater the drama, and the more they are slightly suggestive, the greater the mystery. A mixed metaphor is strong, as every student of Shakespeare knows, but a suggested and mixed one is powerful. In architecture, to name a metaphor is often to kill it, like analyzing jokes. When hot dog stands are in the shape of hot dogs, then little work is left to the imagination, and all other metaphors are suppressed: they cannot even suggest hamburgers (49). This is the problem of one-liners, or Venturi's signs stuck on decorated sheds. They are too easy to figure out. Like all signs they have a few, denotative meanings. Contrary to his theory, decorated sheds are not symbols; in fact they are the reverse of symbols which must, by definition, mediate between connotations, the known and unknown.

Yet even this kind of univalent metaphor, the hot dog stand in the shape of a frankfurter (or the Pop architecture of Los Angeles) has its imaginative and communicative side. For one thing, the customary scale and context are violently distorted, so the ordinary object, for instance a doughnut in one LA building, takes on a series of possible meanings not usually associated with this item of food (50). Defamiliarization, as the surrealists called it, has an important role to play in reinvigorating the cliché. When the doughnut is blown up thirty feet, built out of wood and sits on a small building, it becomes the Magritte apple that has stolen the house from the inhabitants. Partly hostile and menacing, it is nevertheless a symbol of sugary breakfasts and *Gemütlichkeit*. It is a double symbol and, on the vernacular level, an example of Post-Modern double-coding (albeit unintended as PM).

Secondly, an architecture made up from such signs communicates unambiguously to those moving fifty miles per hour through the city. In contrast with so much modern building, these iconic signs speak with exactitude and humor about their function. Their literalism, however infantile, articulates factual truths which Mies' work obscures, and there is a certain general pleasure (which does not escape children) in perceiving a sequence of them. Contrary to Venturi, we need more ducks; modern architects have not propagated enough.

One who tried was Eero Saarinen. Immediately after he selected Jorn Utzon's design as the winner of the Sydney Opera House competition, he returned to America and designed his own version of the curvilinear, shell building. The TWA terminal in New York is an icon of a bird, and by extension, of aeroplane flight (51, 52). In the details and merging of circulation lines, of passenger exits and crossways, it is a particularly clever working out of this metaphor. A supporting strut is mapped to a bird's leg, the rain spout becomes an ominous beak, and an interior bridge covered in blood-red carpet becomes, by implication, the pulmonary artery. Here the imaginative meanings add up in an appropriate and calculated way, pointing towards a common metaphor of flight – the mutual interaction of these meanings produces a multivalent work of architecture, a true symbolic architecture and one of the first Post-Modern buildings.

The most effective use of *suggested* metaphor that I can think of in Modern Architecture is Le Corbusier's chapel at Ronchamp in northeastern France (53). This, because of its suggestiveness, is a good candidate for the first PM building. It has been compared to all sorts of things, varying from the white houses of Mykonos to Swiss cheese. Part of its power is this suggestiveness – to mean many different things at once, to set the mind off on a wild goose chase where it actually catches the goose, among other animals (54–59). For instance a duck (once again this famous character of Modern Architecture) is vaguely suggested in the south ele-

51 EERO SAARINEN, *TWA Building*, New York, 1962. Designed after Saarinen judged the Sydney Opera House competition. Here the concrete shells are clearly recognizable as a metaphor of flight, although there are other animals suggested.

52 EERO SAARINEN, *TWA interior* with its viscous forms, a continuation of the avian metaphor.

vation (see illustration). But so too is a ship and, appropriately, praying hands. The visual codes, which here take in both elitist and popular meanings, are working mostly on an unconscious level, unlike the hot dog stand. We read the metaphors immediately without bothering to name or draw them (as is done here) and clearly the skill of the architect is dependent on his ability to call up our rich storehouse of visual images without our being aware it. Perhaps it is also a somewhat unconscious process for the designer. Le Corbusier only admitted to two metaphors, both of which are esoteric: the "visual acoustics" of the curving walls which shape the four horizons as if they were "sounds" (responding in antiphony), and the "crab shell" form of the roof. But the building conveys many more metaphors than two; so many, in fact, that it is over-coded, saturated with possible interpretations.

This over-coding explains why British critics such as Nikolaus Pevsner and James Stirling have found the building so upsetting, but also why others have found it so enigmatic. It seems to suggest precise ritualistic meanings, it looks like the temple of some very complicated sect which reached a high degree of metaphysical sophistication; whereas we *know* it is simply a pilgrimage chapel created by someone who believed in a natural religion, a pantheism. Put another way, the Ronchamp chapel has all the fascination of the discovery of a new archaic language. We stumble upon this Rosetta stone, this fragment of a lost civilization, and every attempt to decode its surface yields yet another coherent meaning which we know does not refer to any precise social practice, as it appears to do. Le Corbusier has so over-coded his building with metaphor, and so precisely related part to part, that the meanings seem as if they had been fixed by countless generations engaged in ritual:

something as rich as the delicate patterns of Islam, the exact iconography of Shinto, is suggested. How frustrating, how enjoyable it is to experience this game of signification, which we know rests mostly on imaginative brilliance. Frank Gehry has used the same enigmatic over-coding, as we will see, with his Disney Hall in LA and the New Guggenheim in Bilbao (289, 377). Through these and other buildings this type of enigmatic signifier has become the

53 LE CORBUSIER, *Ronchamp Chapel*, France, 1955. View north. The building is over-coded with visual metaphors, and none of them is very explicit, so that the chapel always seems about to tell us something which we just cannot place. The effect can be compared to having a word on the tip of your tongue that you cannot quite remember. But the ambiguity can be dramatic rather than frustrating – you search your memory for possible clues.

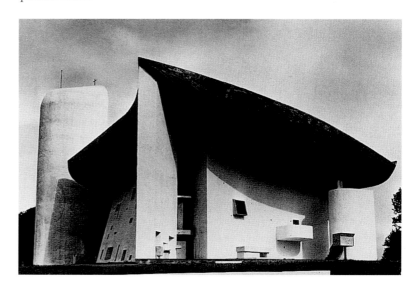

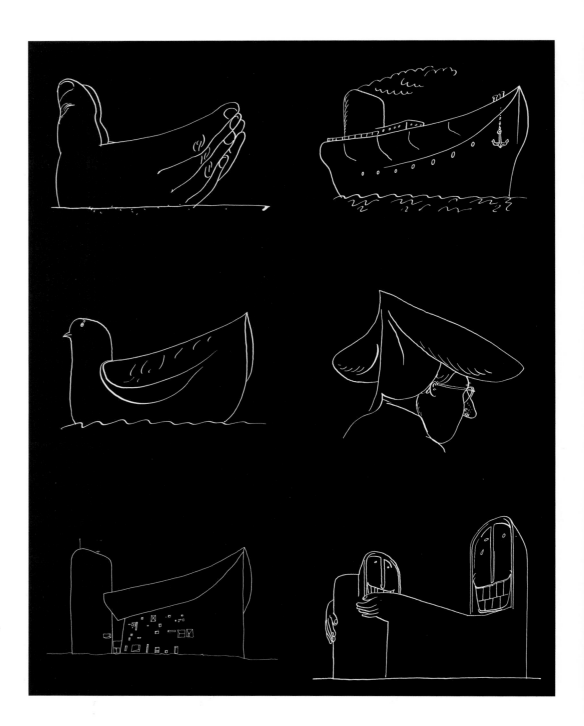

54–59 *METAPHORS* of Ronchamp, drawn by Hillel Schocken in a seminar on architectural semiotics at the Architectural Association. The mapping is amazingly literal when compared to the actual views. Compare with the New Guggenheim (377).

standard way a Post-Modernist handles the monument in a pluralist culture. It suggest many things and thereby heightens perception, allowing different taste cultures to read various meanings. Over time this multivalence provokes yet more interpretation, keeps the building alive, turns it into a classic. This Ronchamp has become the first open-ended, enigmatic signifier of our time.

Another early metaphorical building, which continued this tradition, was Cesar Pelli's Pacific Design Center — known locally in Los Angeles as "the Blue Whale" (61).

Opposed to Ronchamp and TWA, it makes use of rectilinear forms and a curtain wall of three different types of glass. But these familiar elements nonetheless call up unfamiliar associations because of their peculiar treatment: "iceberg," "cash register," "aircraft hangar," and most appropriately "extruded architectural moulding" (it is a center for interior decorators and designers) (60).

These metaphors can be mapped quite literally in terms of outline shape and section; not so the "Blue Whale" image which relates only in terms of color and mass. And yet this

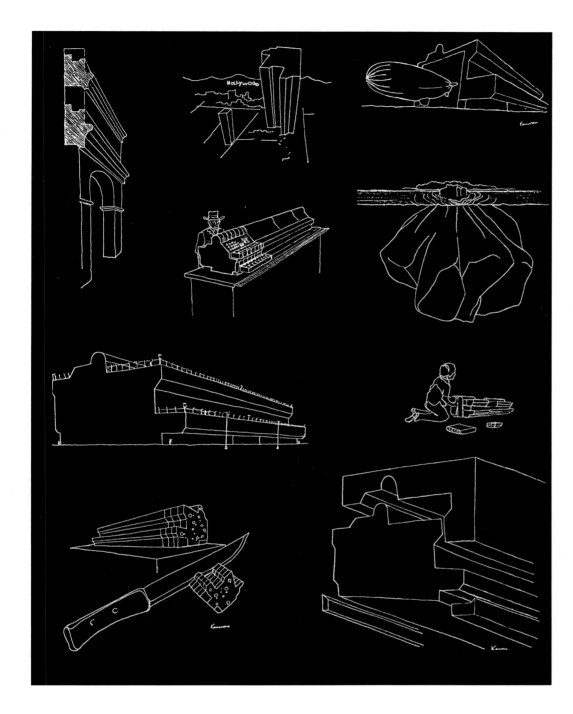

60 PDC metaphors seen in a seminar on architectural semiotics, UCLA, 1976, drawn by Kamran. The metaphors were voted on by the class and placed in the following order of plausibility: 1 aircraft hangar, 2 extrusion or architectural moulding, 3 station or terminal building, 4 model of a building, 5 warehouse, 6 blue iceberg, 7 prison, 8 a child's building-blocks or puzzle. The fact that so many metaphors turned out to be actual building types (e.g. "station or terminal") shows that the PDC recalls other architecture quite strongly.

61 CESAR PELLI, *Pacific Design Center*, Los Angeles, 1976. A long, high building which looks like an extruded moulding, among other things, because its section is projected throughout the building and on the end elevations. This metaphor is appropriate to its function, since the building displays the mouldings of interior designers (among other products). Its blue exterior, in translucent, transparent and reflective glass, gives it a startling presence in Los Angeles; and because of its size, it is known as "The Blue Whale."

is the favored nickname. Why? Because there happens to be a local restaurant whose doorway is a large blue whale's mouth, and the building is recognized as a leviathan in its small-scaled neighborhood swallowing up all the little fish (in this case the diminutive decorators' shops). In other words, two local pertinent codes, the large scale and the connection with the nearby restaurant, take precedence over the more plausible metaphors of the building, the aircraft hangar or moulding. Like Sydney's "sails," this is another good example of the way architecture is more at the mercy

of the local codes than, say, poetry is influenced by where it is read.

Architecture, as a language, is much more malleable than the spoken language, and subject to the transformations of short-lived codes. While a building may stand three hundred years, the way people regard and use it may change every decade. It would be perverse to rewrite Shakespearean sonnets, change love poetry to hate letters, read comedy as tragedy; but it is perfectly acceptable to hang washing on decorative balustrades, convert a church into a concert hall,

62 *MANUFACTURERS HANOVER TRUST*, New York, 1970. This kind of building on Park Avenue and elsewhere is often satirized by cartoonists such as Steinburg and Kovarsky, who will represent it as grid paper, bank account statement, or any number of economic graphs which rise and fall.

63–67 *The COLUMN as a "WORD"*, seen in different contexts, changes its meaning. At *ST. MARTIN-IN-THE-FIELDS*, London, 1726, it is seen on a portico with other columns of the same order clearly signifying "colonnade," "entrance," "public building" as well as historical associations. *NELSON'S COLUMN*, Trafalgar Square, 1860, shifts the semantic overtones towards commemoration, "victor," "politics," "standing alone" etc. The *COLUMN-SMOKESTACKS at BATTERSEA POWER STATION*, London, 1929–55, have entirely different associations because of their syntactic properties. They are placed above a massive base on four corners (incidentally, this is now the sign of power station), and so the building looks, from another perspective, like an overturned table. Smoke belches out the top – which has no capital or entablature – so the fluted columns have been "violated." Adolf Loos' *CHICAGO TRIBUNE COLUMN*, a competition entry for a newspaper, was a double pun on the word column ("newspaper column," "tribune," the name of the newspaper). Loos felt that the Doric Order was a most basic statement of architectural order and therefore fitting for a monument. Finally, the *KENTON COUNTY WATER TOWER*, Ohio, 1955, again shows the polyvalent aspect of this vertical shape, how it can be used on elevator shafts, chimneys, rocket launchers and oil derricks. Because of the column's positive associations with antiquity, it is often used as a disguise for new, prosaic functions.

and use a building every day while never looking at it (actually the norm). Walter Benjamin pointed out that architecture is often experienced inattentively or with the greatest prejudice of mood and will – exactly opposite to the way one is supposed to experience a symphony or work of art.[12] There are two implications stemming from these examples. If architecture is to communicate as intended it should avoid signs that have only one meaning and, secondly, it should be over-coded, using a redundancy of popular signs and metaphors to survive the transformation of fast-changing codes, and codes of the locale.

Surprisingly, many Modern architects continue to deny the most potent, metaphorical, level of meaning. They find it nonfunctional and personal, literary and vague, certainly not something they can consciously control and use appropriately. Instead they concentrate on the supposedly rational aspects of design – the cost, function, space and packaging. The result is that inadvertent malaprops take metaphorical revenge and kick them from behind: their buildings may end up looking like metaphors of function and economics, and condemned as "rent slabs" (62). With Post-Modernism, however, the situation has changed. Social research and architectural semiotics have demonstrated the interpersonal, shared response to metaphor, journalists and the public have celebrated the highly charged, suggestive building, and the new tradition has emerged.

WORDS

Underlying much of what I have been saying so far is the notion of cliché – the fact that the architectural language, like the spoken one, must use known units of meaning. To make the linguistic analogy more complete, we could call these units architectural "words." There are dictionaries of architecture that define the meanings of these words: doors, windows, columns, partitions, cantilevers, and so forth. Obviously these repeated elements are a necessity of architectural practice. The building industry standardizes count-

less products and the architectural office repeats its favorite details in building after building over many years.

As in language, yesterday's creative metaphor becomes today's tired usage, a conventional word. I have mentioned that the wedge shape became a sign of the auditorium, and that concrete grilles – the cheese-grater metaphor – became a sign of parking garage ("office" is the secondary usage). Yet, there is a crucial difference between the "words" of architecture and of speech. Consider the case of the column (63–67). A column on a building is one thing, the Nelson Column in Trafalgar Square another, the column smokestack at Battersea Power Station in London a third, and Adolf Loos' entry for the Chicago Tribune Column a fourth. If the column is a "word," then the word has become a phrase, a sentence and, finally, a whole novel. Clearly architectural words are more elastic and polymorphous than those of spoken or written language, and are more based on their physical context and the code of the viewer for their specific sense. To determine what "Nelson's Column" means you have to analyse the social-physical context ("Trafalgar Square as a centre for political rallies"), the semantic overtones of Nelson ("naval victories," "historical figure," etc.), the syntactic markers ("standing alone," "surrounded by open space and fountains"), and the historical connotations of column ("use on temples," "Three Orders," "phallic symbol," etc.). Such an analysis is beyond the scope of this book, but an initial attempt has been made at analyzing the column in general, which shows how fruitful this can be.[13] We can make a componential analysis of architectural elements and find out which are, for any culture, distinctive units.

Modern architects have not always faced up to the implications of clichés, or traditional words. They have, by and large, tried to avoid the re-use of *symbolic signs* (the technical term for meaning set by conventional usage) because they felt these historical elements signified lack of creativity. For Frank Lloyd Wright and Walter Gropius, the use of historical elements even signified lack of integrity and character. An architect who used the symbolic sign was probably insincere and certainly snobbish – the Classical orders were a kind of pretentious Latin, not the everyday vernacular of industrial building and sober utility. From these latter building tasks, a universal language, they hoped, could be constructed, a sort of Esperanto of cross-cultural usage based on functional types. These signs would be *indexical* (either directly indicating their use, like arrows, linear corridors), or else *iconic*, in which case the form would be a diagram of its function (a structurally shaped bridge, and Venturi's duck). Modern architectural words would be limited to these types of signs.

However, the problem with this approach is that most architectural words are symbolic signs; certainly those that are most potent and persuasive are the ones which are learned and conventional, not "natural." The symbolic sign dominates the indexical and iconic, and even these latter depend somewhat on knowledge and convention for their correct interpretation. There was thus a devastating theoretical mistake at the very core of the Modern language. It could not work the way the architects hoped because no living language can: they are mostly based on learned conventions, on symbolic signs, not ones that can be understood directly, without training.

A good example of architects' mistaken attitude towards the symbolic sign is their treatment of the pitched roof, which conventionally signifies "home" in northern countries. The Modern architect disregarded this custom for

68, 69 LE CORBUSIER, *Pessac Housing*, before and after, 1925 and 1969. Ground floors were walled up, pitched roofs were added, the ribbon windows were divided up, terraces were turned into extra bedrooms, and a great number of signs which connoted security, "home," ownership, were placed all over the exterior, thus effectively destroying the Purist language. (Architectural Association, Philippe Boudon).

70 The *ETON HOUSE*, Ideal Home Exhibition, London, 1974. The facial metaphor is often present at the Ideal Home Exhibition, with two or three examples strictly symmetrical about the front door (mouth). Various signs of status are tacked on (such as the fiberglass Adam detailing), but the snobbism is more apparent than real: it is not meant to convince the neighbors that you sent your son to Eton, but simply to distinguish the building from council housing. This is perhaps the strongest social motivation, the distinction between us and them (those controlled by the government). Hence the Ideal Home styles are relatively permissive, including Swiss Chalet and American Ranch House. In fact for 1976, the Ideal British Home was Colonial, an unforeseen consequence of 1776.

functional and aesthetic reasons, to create roof gardens, more space, rectilinear form (Walter Gropius gave six rational reasons for designing flat roofs). Not surprisingly these flat-top buildings were regarded as alien, as insecure, even unfinished and "without a head." The houses had been decapitated. Many of the inhabitants of Le Corbusier's Pessac (68, 69) felt his stark white cubical forms lacked a proper sense of shelter and protection, so they shortened the ribbon windows, added shutters and more window mullions. They articulated the blank white surfaces with window boxes, cornices and eaves; and some put on the old Bordeaux sign of protection, the pitched roof. In short, they systematically misunderstood his Purist language and systematically redesigned it to incorporate their conventional signs of home. Ironically, at the end of his life Le Corbusier acknowledged the legitimacy of the people distorting his message when he said of the changes at Pessac: "Life is right, the architect wrong." Post-Modernists got the message and the result is that, as we will see, a whole tradition of face and body houses developed, the best of which coded these metaphors with other meanings, made them somewhat ambiguous, suggestive.

In spite of the many flat-roofed housing estates today, certain unreconstructed people still go on, in their incorrigible way, thinking that pitched roofs mean shelter and psychological protection. Many studies have shown this, and a major building society in England, recognizing the fact, has taken as its symbol an archetypal couple that walks arm in arm under a pitched-roof umbrella. Since this sign exists, and since repeated usage will create the symbolic sign, the architect might change his attitude towards these conventions. He might regard them as powerful meanings to be used normally in a straightforward way, if only to catch the attention of an audience he wants to convert and send unusual meanings.

If one wants to change a culture's taste and behavior, as do Modern architects, then first one has to speak the accept-

ed language. If the language and message are changed at the same time, then both will be systematically misunderstood and reinterpreted to fit the conventional categories, the habitual patterns of life. This is precisely what has happened with Modern housing estates: Pruitt-Igoe and Pessac are the two most celebrated examples. A more promising approach for the Modern architect, or social interventionist, would be to study the popular house in its variety and see how it signifies a different way of life for different taste cultures and ethnic groups. A major shift of Post-Modernism is to articulate universalizing categories — the people, the nation, society — into subcategories, while keeping alive the Modern or Enlightenment idea that there are still connections between all peoples.

SEMIOTIC GROUPS

Broadly speaking, social groups are classified in socio-economic terms by sociologists and market researchers, even though there is a lot of overlap and borrowing between groups, and there are other forces at work.[14] The class influence on taste is only one of several such influences. It seems to me more exact to speak of semiotic groups than class-based taste cultures, because those groups which share preferences of meaning have a life and continuity of their own, that is only partly colored by socio-economic background. Basically, semiotic groups are in different universes of signification and have different views of the good life. Three versions of the western popular house that spring from these different groups will be mentioned here and, of course, one should keep in mind that the meanings sketched are specific to the culture and the time when they were investigated, in the 1970s.

1. The ideal of many working-class families in Europe and America is to buy a small, detached house, a bungalow roughly similar to others in an area they know. The values expressed in these houses are security, ownership, separation (a freestanding building), and a kind of conservative anonymity (represented by conforming more or less to the norm of the area). Levittown in America, and the Ideal Home Exhibition in Britain (70), as well as most buildings in both countries, cater to this semiotic group. It could be called conservative or conformist, sensible or petit-bourgeois, depending on which values are stressed and who is doing the valuing, because all these aspects are very clearly signified in the language. The archetype is a two-storey house with a central doorway, a symmetrical displacement of windows on either side, a chimney and pitched roof – all of which vaguely resembles a face with two eyes (top windows), nose (entrance portico) and mouth (doorway) (71).

The band of planting in front of the house could be the shirt collar or moustache, symbolic "moat," or "forest," depending on what other signs are stressed. Since this group often wants to signal its new-found independence, meanings tend to support the old Anglo-Saxon maxim, "every man's home is his castle" – and the castle may be defended by a picket fence or garden gnomes. There is a stately avenue winding to the front door – the curved pathway; past sylvan forests – bushes.

2. The next semiotic group tends to take the previous values for granted, since it has not just left what is regarded as the teeming city. In America this group might be called middle-class fastidious, since the clipped lawns and status

signs of colonial provenance (nearly always false) harangue the passer-by like some Bicentennial orator in a fit of nationalism. Indeed, cleanliness and caution, hard work and discretion, prosperity and sobriety – all the images of WASP success – are there to brand this as the ultimate bourgeois dream. The only problem with this classification is that the appeal of these values reaches much further than the middle class.

For instance, the reigning style of movie star houses, those of Beverly Hills and Bel Air which sold in the 1970s for prices ranging from a quarter of a million to three million dollars, fall in this category (72, 73). The movie stars clearly are not middle-class, even if their tastes look it and they have come from this background. Are they slumming, or have they just adopted a previously existing semiotic tradition and then amplified it? Often they are called the "aristocracy of America," because their values and way of life have become the standard of emulation for the mass of the country. Films, and countless sightseeing bus trips going past the stars' houses (a minor industry since 1922), have made these buildings the most influential on popular taste. As my students from UCLA found when investigating, they tend to be in one of six styles: 1. Southern Mansion, 2. Old English, 3. New England Colonial, 4. French Provincial-Regency, 5. Spanish Colonial, or 6. Contemporary-Colonial Hybrid. These also mirror the six reigning styles of the popular suburban house. It is apparent that most of these houses are Ersatz. That is, few of them are serious, scholarly revivals, there is almost no pretence to historical accuracy or serious eclecticism. The styles are notional, signs of status and historical roots – but signs that recall the past, not convince you that the building is living in the present.

71 KEVIN FISHER, *English Popular House Analysis*, 1976. This synthesis of several reigning trends in the market shows how eclectic and permissive the popular English house is becoming. A pastiche of Japanese, American and English, modern and traditional, urban and rural. Few architects would dare use such a language because of its impurity, so the market remains open to the speculators. It is of course possible to use any language to send any message.

72, 73 JIMMY STEWART'S *House*, Beverly Hills, c.1940. A very fastidious mixture of Tudor and Japanese architecture with Swiss accents. The clarity of outline, the black and white alternatives, the very studied informality of massing and planting send out a clear message. Such houses, often exposed in films, have confirmed if not created our image of the American Dream House. Similar examples can be found outside every major city from Boston to Los Angeles, and since the norm is so invariable it almost constitutes a language without speech. Put another way, one could say the language does the talking and the designer is its mouthpiece. (Carol Barkin and Stephanie Vaughan).

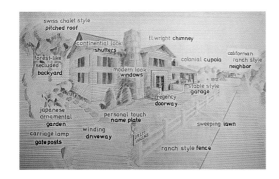

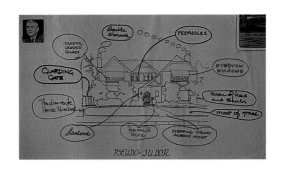

74 RICHARD MEIER, *Douglas House*, Harbor Springs. Michigan, 1971–73. The villa in nature, enclosed, protected, and yet standing out as a man-made element This Italian tradition, taken over equally by Le Corbusier and the upper classes, contrasts the raw and the cooked, the untouched and the finished. Here Meier uses a Corbusian syntax to represent the interior space, which is layered both horizontally and vertically through four storeys. (Ezra Stoller).

75 Right: *PORTMEIRION*, view up Battery Square and Pantheon, showing seaside architecture and Italian campanile. This stage-set architecture has, not surprisingly, been used in several films and commercials. This was the first creation of a formula that was later applied, in a cheapened version, to communities such as Port Grimaud, and ride-through parks such as Disneyland.

3. Another semiotic group distinguishes itself from the previous one by inverting these signs and values. A studied casualness is preferred to fastidiousness, a kind of seedy, unselfconscious comfort is preferred to blatant order and rectitude. The down-at-the-heels aristocrat and the intellectual, the drop-out and left-wing socialite all unite against what they take to be the vulgarity of the previous group's good taste. Even the Modern architect unites with them on this score.

Thus we find the emphasis on nature and naturalness, the building isolated and hidden in the actual woods (as opposed to bushes), which are not manicured to near perfection. They are allowed to grow almost freely, just cut back at certain points to reveal a gable here, a roof there, as if by felicitous chance. The attitude is close to the picturesque tradi-

tion, the celebration of the carefully careless and studied accident, in a variety of new clothes. These come in entirely different cuts. One is the white Modern architecture of the 1920s (74) (*Le Style Corbu* has actually become a popular status-badge when handled by Richard Meier and Charles Gwathmy). Throughout Long Island in the late sixties, and then across American suburbia, it became the equivalent of the white Classical villa of the nineteenth century. Second is the stick-and-shed style popularized by Charles Moore on the West Coast of America, again in the late 1960s. But by far the most popular of these upscale modes was the House and Garden style of the last seventy years, represented on a collective level by such resorts and communities as Portmeirion and Port Grimaud (75). This whimsical picturesque was flexible enough to accept any

contradictions, and thus it naturally appealed to the divergent family life of the late twentieth century.

Portmeirion, started in the early part of the last century, is a misplaced Italian hill town set on the lush Welsh coast, surrounded by two miles of rhododendron and other exotic overgrowth. Every vista is carefully composed as a landscape, each path wanders perfectly around every rock outcrop, each bush and flower relates miraculously to near and far buildings, and space ebbs and flows like water into small contained pools and dramatic, open cascades. *Trompe l'oeil*, phoney windows, buildings shrunken to five-sixths of their normal size, eye traps, calculated naivetés, whimsical conceits (a sailboat is turned into concrete, and thence into a retaining wall) – this sort of easygoing wit has proven popular with writers and tourists. The builder, Sir Clough William-Ellis, has cannibalized old buildings and preserved parts of them in his new confections.

This care for the old and traditional is very apparent and one may take it as a characteristic sign of this semiotic group. The ancient is valued not so much for itself, but as a sign of continuity between generations and a connection with the past. While the first guess is that such values and understatements appeal only to elite tastes, this does not turn out to be true. For instance, 100,000 visitors come to Portmeirion every year and it became the model both for Disneyland and Port Grimaud; furthermore, millions visit country houses in England, mostly because they have collected real historical associations.

These three semiotic groups, the conservative, the fastidious and the natural, hardly exhaust the plurality of taste cultures which exist in any large city. The urban sociologist Herbert Gans has further mapped this plurality into seven taste cultures and, as if this articulation were not enough, the science of geo-demographics has further articulated the field into forty clusters. In America, one cluster, the Main Street tradition, has been analyzed by Robert Venturi and

Denise Scott Brown as a series of signs, and England has its counterpart in the High Street.

Venturi, Scott Brown and their team have been instrumental in calling attention to this wide area of signification and in an important exhibition of 1976, "Signs of Life: Symbols in the American City" they presented some of the images that make up the popular American building (76). Their own design, when called for, incorporates these signs, but usually in ironic and esoteric ways (77, 78). While some critics deplored this work as unnecessarily banal, or condescending – that is, anything but popular – their deadpan approach was intentional. They wished to show that the modern solution was on a certain level already "ordinary and ugly," epithets that were used against them by the Modernist architect Gordon Bunshaft. Of course, an architect may use a language without sending the customary messages, and if he wants to signify the ugly and ordinary with this language he has a perfect right to do so. The Venturi team justified its approach as social criticism: they want to express, in a gentle way, a mixed appreciation for the American Way of Life. Grudging respect, not total acceptance. They do not share all the values of a consumer society, but they wished to speak to this society, even if partially in dissent. Post-Modernism as "resistance from within" found expression in this early work, and they deserve credit for opening the door onto the vitality of street life.

77, 78 VENTURI and RAUCH, *Tucker House*. Katonah, New York, 1975. The exterior exaggerates elements of the popular code, the overhanging eaves and picture window – while the interior uses the white, planar International Style as a backdrop for Kitsch and other objects. Actually, the fireplace with its round mirror is a miniature of the house, a very witty comment on the traditional idea of aedicules, miniature models and dolls' houses. (Stephen Shore).

Another reason for the mixture of their language was sensibility, their training in the language of Le Corbusier and Louis Kahn, the Modernist side of the Post-Modern duality. Because of this they did not use popular signs in a relaxed and exuberant way – on a level with the Las Vegas sign artists whom they admired. But, after being inspired by the writings of Tom Wolfe on Las Vegas, how could they possibly be unselfconscious? Besides, it takes years to master the unselfconscious *and* conscious use of a new language, and so these architects are, to use a phrase borrowed from the Futurists, "the primitives of a new sensibility."

It was the younger generation of PM architects who used the hybrid language with more confidence, its wide metaphorical reach, its written signs and vulgarity, its symbolic signs and clichés – the full gamut of architectural expression. Hans Hollein, Michael Graves and Robert Stern, at first, and then the LA School led by Frank Gehry and Eric Moss (79).

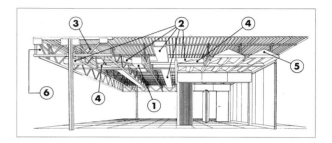

79 ERIC MOSS, *Gary Group*, Culver City, Los Angeles, 1988. Advertising turned into an expressive art.

80 EZRA EHRENKRANTZ, *SCSD* (Schools Construction System Development), California, 1960s. The syntax of architecture obviously relates to functional concerns, as this drawing shows. Six major elements: 1 mixing boxes, 2 rigid ducts, 3 flexible ducts, 4 outlets, 5 lighting, 6 roof plenum, show the air-conditioning requirements. These were combined with roof, floor and a partition system to give a flexible syntax that could be changed in several ways. (Drawing by Mary Banham from *The Architecture of the Well-tempered Environment* by Reyner Banham).

SYNTAX

Another aspect architecture shares with language is more mundane than metaphors and words. A building has to stand up and be put together according to certain rules, and methods of joinery (80). The laws of gravity and geometry dictate such things as an up and down, a roof and floor and various storeys in between, just as the laws of sound and speech formation dictate certain vowels, consonants and grammatical formations. These compelling forces create what could be called: syntax of architecture – that is, the rules for combining the various words of door, window, wall, ceiling and so forth. Most doors, for instance, follow the syntactical rule requiring a floor, necessarily flat, on both sides. What happens when this rule is constantly broken? The fun house at the Amusement Park, a tilt that takes advantage of the fact that the nervous system unconsciously knows the syntactical rules and thus enjoys having them broken from time to time. Delirious word salads, the speech of schizophrenics and poetry, all distort conventional grammar. It is obviously one of the defining characteristics of all sign systems used aesthetically. They call attention to the language itself by misuse, exaggeration, repetition, and all the devices of rhetorical skill.

Post-Modern syntactical play started in a modest way with the spatial ambiguities of Robert Venturi and Charles Moore, in the late 1960s. By the 1970s it had become the complex and layered spaces of Peter Eisenman and The Five Architects. By the 1980s, it had mutated into the deconstructed contradictions of Frank Gehry and Morphosis and, by the 1990s, the absolutely dense and frenetic cacaphonies of Coop Himmelblau and Daniel Libeskind (81). Syntactical elaboration became, in this sense, the *subject* of architecture, excessive form as the content.

At the beginning of this evolution, Michael Graves spoke about "fore-grounding" the elements of architecture (82). He turned columns on their side, or extended structures into

81 COOP HIMMELBLAU, *Rooftop office conversion*, Vienna, 1984–86. Post-modern spatial layering and lighting reaches maximum complexity with the work of Wolf Prix and Helmut Swizinsky. The interior is dissolved into an indeterminate explosion of angles and lines.(Gerald Zugmann).

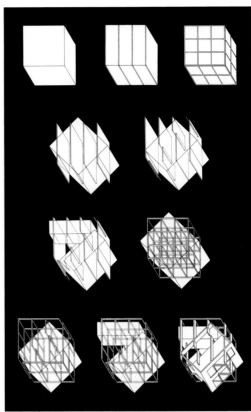

82 MICHAEL GRAVES, *Benacerraf House addition*, Princeton, 1969. A Cubist syntax is used to call attention to itself, This heightening of our perception of doors, stairways, balustrades and views from a terrace is complex and masterful. It is so rich here that one forgets to ask what the functions are (actually an open terrace above, and a playroom and breakfast room below). Note how the structure, sometimes unnecessary, is pulled away from the wall. Railings and cut-out wall planes also serve to define a net of rectilinear space. The front balustrade is conceptually, a column lying on its side — a play on syntactical meaning, as is the whole addition. (Laurin McCracken).

83, 84 PETER EISENMAN, *House III* for Robert Miller, Lakeville, Connecticut, 1971. Several of the drawings which generated the house show the main oppositions between two grids at 45 degrees (step 6), a conceptual cage of boxed space (step 7), a column grid (step 3), and wall planes in "shear" (step 5). Bridges and open volumes unite and divide the room functions. The façades mark some interior transformations — if you look at them with the diagrams in your hand and think for a long time. This architecture, like nineteenth-century programme music, demands a complementary text in order to be fully understood.

the landscape — holding nothing — like scaffolding awaiting an ever-absent load. Then he painted all this architecture like a Juan Gris still-life, fore-grounding the basic wall, soffit, stair and railing. His early houses are thus poetic distortions of a Cubist syntax, whose only fault in terms of communication is in the choice of a limited syntax and under-coding. You may need a reader's guide to appreciate that a blue balustrade is a column lying down; otherwise it is an exuberant play on a De Stijl house of the 1920s, a PM comment on a Modern building.

Elaborating this game even more, Peter Eisenman produced beautiful syntactic knots that dazzle the eye, confuse the mind, and ultimately signify *for him* the process that generated them (83, 84). He called this architecture that represented process Cardboard Architecture, a fitting title since the cardboard model was the ultimate signifier. How enticing; how banal. The spirit of process is supposed to lift

you heavenwards so you overlook the prosaic assumptions, and for the owner of his *House III* it did precisely that, (he wrote an article "I guess you win, Peter"). After living in the house for a while he began to appreciate all the voids, juxtapositions, rotations and syntactic violations — even the way they disturbed his daily breakfast and nightly sleep. He came to love the movement of light over white surfaces, the abstract Corbusian drama played with more completion, and abandon, than a Modernist would have ever allowed.

Semantically (a mode of communication that Eisenman was then negating), these buildings convey the sharp white light of rationality and the virtues of geometrical organization: the exciting "bridges to cross," surprising punched-out "holes of space," the framed "vistas," the Chinese puzzle of structure. In effect, abstract elements are being connected with associations such as the white architecture of the twenties, Protestantism, and the functions of daily use. In other

words, the realm of syntax tends to be incorporated into semantic fields and Eisenman's architecture only becomes more fully Post-Modern by the mid-eighties, when he recognized the legitimacy of semantics.

SEMANTICS

In the nineteenth century, when different styles of architecture were being revived, there was a fairly coherent doctrine of semantics that explained which style to use on which building type. An architect would pick the Doric Order for use on a bank because that Order and the banking function had certain overtones in common: sobriety, impersonality, masculinity and rationality (a bank was meant to look tough enough to discourage robbers, and sensible enough to encourage depositors). Not only were these semantic properties set by comparison, by looking at the Orders in opposition to each other and other styles, but so were a host of syntactic aspects: the size of the Doric capital, the column's relation to other columns, and its proportion to the cornice, frieze and base. Since these forms and relationships were used coherently, people felt able to pass judgement on their suitability. Decorum, appropriateness, *bienseance* were key words marking this semantic fit. The result was that architecture communicated its use and fine shades of meaning; a slight change in emphasis, a variation of proportion, meant a shift in function.

Of course, this is to idealize the situation, as only a small part of the community could make these distinctions. But at least some could do so, and this community (echoing the root-word "communication") kept the architect responsive to the enjoyable game of signification. He knew that if the semantic system were violently overthrown or became too complicated, then communication would be reduced to primitive gestures. Revivalist architects also justified their choice of style in terms of appropriateness, and this gave a degree of coherence to their formal choice. One architect, J. C. Loudon, proposed a theory of associationism based on the Lockean notion of "association of ideas," and went so far as to say that each house should convey in its manner the character and role of its owner (85).[15] If the inhabitant were a country parson, the house should be dressed in castellated Gothic or related clothing. Thus, as society became more differentiated, the environment would become more and more legible.

To a certain extent, this doctrine was followed in the nineteenth century, and we find that the introduction of a new style is assimilated into the appropriate semantic field. The Neo-Egyptian Style, popular in 1830 because of the Rosetta Stone and Napoleon's previous campaigns, was used sensibly on banks, tombs, prisons and medical colleges. The argument for its use might be based on either conventional or natural meanings, that is, either symbolic or iconic signs (see above). In the first case for banks, Neo-Egyptian was appropriate because the Pharaohs buried their treasure in

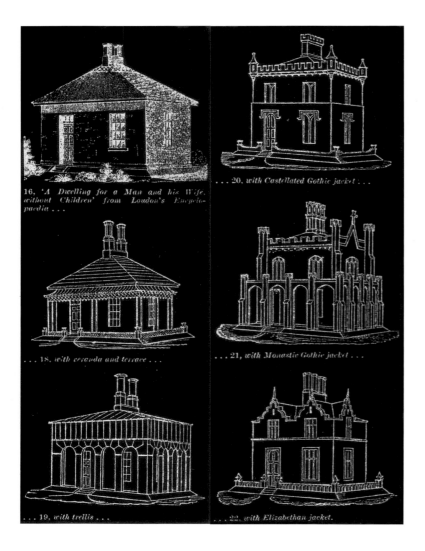

85 J. C. LOUDON, *How to Dress a Utilitarian Cottage*, sketches from Loudon's *Encyclopaedia*. A basic cube with hipped roof is transformed with verandah and terrace, with trellis, a castellated Gothic jacket, monastic habit and Elizabethan front. The style is chosen according to the owner's role and place of residence.

86 THOMAS USTICK WALTER, *Moyamensing Prison*, Philadelphia, 1835. The Egyptian style, with its battered walls, head columns and small openings, naturally signified a structure from which it was hard to escape. (HABS, Library of Congress, photo Jack E. Boucher).

temples of this style; and famous Egyptian doctors, healers and practitioners of medicine were sometimes also architects. Hence by the association of ideas, you could properly use the Egyptian style on treasuries and chemists' shops. Secondly, since the style had natural meanings of heaviness, with battered walls and small openings, it naturally signified high security, appropriate for prisons (86).

OPENING SEMANTIC SPACE: THE ARTICULATION OF DIFFERENCE

The importance of these issues for the Post-Modern goal of articulating difference is fairly obvious. Plurality, identity and locale, which had been overlooked by the universalist approach, could be represented by semantic differentiation. In the western past this was partly achieved by the Classical language of architecture, and it is worth pausing a moment to see how the Three Orders constituted a semantic system, because the lessons can be generalized to the more eclectic situation reigning today (87). Frank Gehry and Arata Isozaki, for instance, typically use contrasting materials and forms to exaggerate the different functions and characters of a building. And character suggests what it sounds like, the personification of dead form, turning it into a social being.

In the first century BC, Vitruvius characterized the Doric Order in human terms as bold, severe, simple, blunt, true, honest, straightforward, and in sexual terms, masculine. In part, this personification stemmed from the natural metaphors inherent in the form, but it also had origins in historical accident (at least, according to Vitruvius' account of the Doric Order's birth).

The Corinthian Order was, by contrast, delicate, dainty, slender, ornamental and, sexually speaking, a young virgin. As one would guess, the middle Order, the Ionic, was a kind of architectural hermaphrodite, a neuter — in fact for

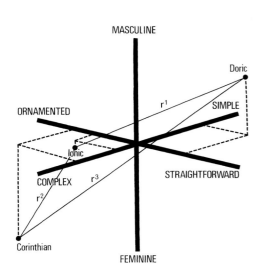

87 *The THREE ORDERS*. I have used these particular axes of Vitruvius for the sake of simplicity and comparison with the subsequent diagrams. But more interesting oppositions could be chosen, as long as they are semantically distinct enough to give different information from each other. For instance, "nature" might be opposed to "culture," "power" to "impotence," etc. Semantic meaning consists of oppositions within a system.

88 JOHN NASH, *Royal Pavilion*, Brighton, 1815–18. Nash threw into his soufflé a bit of Gothic, a bit of Chinese, a bit of cast-iron (palm tree columns) and his own version of a bulbous Hindu style. Ersatz, the first exuberant Kitsch building in England. Bad taste has been a positive creative force since then, reaching one high with the Victorian country house. All this obscures, however, the appropriateness of choosing the Indian style for an escape palace next to the sea. If you are designing a "pleasure dome" for the Prince who wants to get away from London sobriety, what better than the style of *Kubla Khan* (published 1816)?

Vitruvius, a matronly Order, because it was slightly more feminine than masculine (with elegant volutes). But these characterizations really only begin to make sense, as E. H. Gombrich has pointed out, when the Orders are put in opposition to each other:

The rigid orders of ancient architecture would seem to be a fairly recalcitrant matrix for the expression of psychological and physiognomic categories; still it makes sense when Vitruvius recommends Doric temples for Minerva, Mars, and Hercules, Corinthian ones for Venus, Flora, and Prosperina, while Juno, Diana, and other divinities who stand in between the two extremes, are given Ionic temples. Within the medium at the architects' disposal, Doric is clearly more virile than Corinthian. We say that Doric expresses the god's severity; it does, but only because it is on the more severe end of the scale and not because there is necessarily much in common between the god of war and the Doric order.[16]

Clearly there is nothing in common between warfare and the Doric except with respect to comparable things or elements: they each occupy equivalent semantic zones. In other words, if we map the Three Orders in a semantic space, it is the relationships (r1, r2, r3) which really matter, and not the natural meaning of the forms, nor the particular semantic axes we choose, whether Vitruvius' or our own. The important thing is that the axes are chosen far apart to articulate difference, because then custom and usage will set them in one semantic space and transform them into another.

We can see this transformation of meanings in the jump from the Classical language of architecture to eclecticism, and in the work of one architect, John Nash (88). The historian Nikolaus Pevsner summarized the way Nash used a different "style for the job":

[Nash] had a nice sense of associational propriety; as shown in his choice of the Neo-Classical for his town house and of the Gothic for his county mansion (complete with Gothic conservatory). Moreover, he built Cronkhill in Shropshire (1802), as an Italianate villa with a round-arched loggia on slender columns and with the widely projecting eaves of the Southern farmhouse (Roscoe's *Lorenzo Medici* had come out in 1796); he built Blaise Castle, near Bristol (1809) in a rustic Old-English cottage style with barge-boarded gables and thatched roofs (one is reminded of *The Vicar of Wakefield*, Marie Antoinette's dairy in the Park of Versailles, and Gainsborough's and Greuze's sweet peasant children); and he continued the Brighton Pavilion in a "Hindu" fashion, just introduced after 1800 at Sezincote in the Cotswolds where the owner, out of personal nostalgia, insisted on the style "Indian Gothic."[17]

Effectively, in the same semantic space we have used, Nash has substituted a revival style for each of the Three Orders

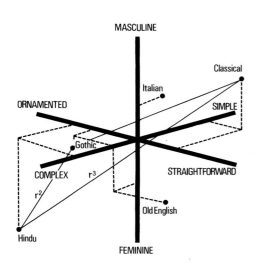

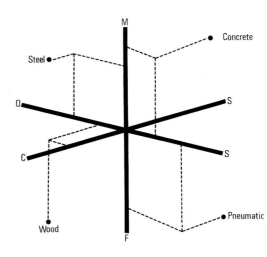

89 JOHN NASH'S *Five Styles* compared in the same semantic space as the *Three Orders* (87). The comparison brings out the fact that it is the relationship between styles, or Orders, which matters most in determining semantic meaning. The Corinthian, or Classical Order, has thus taken on its exact opposite meaning in Nash's system, because now it is more masculine, simple and straightforward than the Hindu style.

90 *BARBARELLA*, 1968, is always shown surrounded with viscous, shiny plastic and soft, hairy fur. (ALA Fotocine).

91 *FOUR BUILDING SYSTEMS*. Particular uses of each building system have to be established before these relationships can be plotted: e.g. the particular use of concrete may in fact be more complex and feminine than the use of steel. Then the functional aspects have to be mapped in the same semantic space, and the two mappings compared.

(89). Roughly speaking, Hindu replaced Corinthian, Gothic occupies the space of Ionic and Classical substitutes for Doric (the Old English and Italian styles occupy new niches).

And there is a surprise that makes an important point. A single form has taken on its *opposite* meaning in the system. The Corinthian (or Nash's Classical Order) has become what Vitruvius called "masculine, simple and straightforward," because now it is set against other formal elements. This inversion is a good illustration of the semiotic rule that it is relationships between elements that count more than their inherent meanings. We could find countless other examples throughout architectural history: the Picturesque aesthetic was "functional" in 1840 for Pugin and "anti-functional" in 1920 for the Modernists; simple, Platonic forms symbolizing "truth and honesty" in 1540 became "deceit and artifice" in 1870, and so on. Although the perception of form may feel straightforward and natural, it is influenced by an elaborate set of changing conventions.

It is the differences between juxtaposed elements that constitute one of the bases for their meaning and today this is often achieved by an exaggerated juxtaposition of materials. In an age where associations are not shared, materiality reigns. An architect will use a curtain wall for an office building, because glass and steel feel cold, impersonal, precise and ordered. These haptic qualities mirror the overtones of methodical business, rational planning and commercial transactions. Wood is intrinsically warm, pliable, soft, organic, and full of natural marks such as knots and grain, so it is used domestically or where people come into close contact with the building. Brick is associated by use with housing, and is inherently flexible in detail, so it is also used domestically. In spite of the fact that there are much more economic building systems available, the wood-and-brick hybrid still accounts for seventy-five per cent of speculative and council housing in Britain — a clear indication that semantic issues take precedence, in the public's mind, over technical ones.

What about new materials such as nylon, which make up pneumatic buildings? The inflatable system is pudgy, squashy, cuddly, sexual, volumetric and pleasant to touch, so it has naturally found a niche in the semantic space and is used appropriately on swimming pools, blow-up furniture, entertainment areas and other unmentionable places (90). Its occasional use as a church or office building brings out different, less dominant semantic overtones. These comparative aspects of building systems can be graphed in a semantic space similar to that already used, although axes other than the ones I have taken over from Vitruvius might be more relevant (91). Once again it is the relations between brick, pneumatics, concrete and steel that set up the semantic

92 PASSARELLI BROTHERS, *Multi-use structure*, Rome, 1965. The concrete and hanging vines classify the flats, the black steel curtain wall indicates office, and below ground, exposed concrete articulates parking. Termed "Schizo" by *Architectural Review* and attacked by Modernists for its impurity, the building none the less makes basic distinctions which are obscured in Purist design.

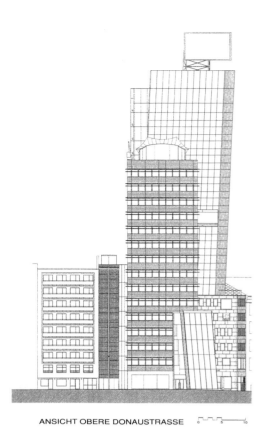

ANSICHT OBERE DONAUSTRASSE

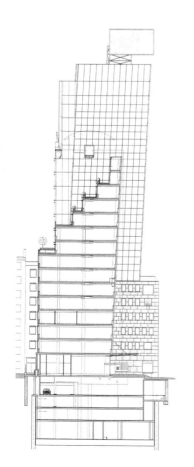

field, and this varies only slightly for each individual and particular usage employed.

When architects took the first, hesitant steps to contrast materials for semantic reasons they were heavily criticized by Modernists, both for cliché and schizophrenia. For instance, a multi-use structure in Rome completed in 1965 by the Passarelli brothers (92), employs at its base the conventional glass and steel forms for office space. Above this are the conventional signs for dwelling – hanging vines, broken silhouettes, picturesque massing and balconies. A third building system below ground, in monolithic, Brutalist concrete, is the parking garage. The standard joke was that each of the brothers designed a different part of the building and never talked to each other. Part of the criticism concerned the use of styles already more developed by Harrison and Abromovitz, Paul Rudolph and Le Corbusier, a telling point. But a deeper reason for the pique was the simple variety of material and structures. Architects brought up with the International Style were ingrained with the Purist notion that one aesthetic and structural system should be used on a entire building. Attendant ideas were the notions of harmony, the Classical ideal that a part cannot be added or subtracted without disturbing the integrated whole, and that each building had, Platonically speaking, one and only one best solution.

Furthermore, Le Corbusier had said, "the styles are a lie," Frank Lloyd Wright and Walter Gropius believed that a single style expressed the authenticity and sincerity of the architect, and Nikolaus Pevsner recounted the story of Modernism, in his influential *Pioneers of the Modern Movement*, 1936, as a revolt against adopting the style of the client.

There are two obvious problems with this single-style approach. First, as the Passarelli building shows; mixed styles are an aid to communication, and an architect must master at least three or four to articulate any complex building today, especially if he is to design the interior. Social pluralism, as the Post-Modern adage has it, must be recognized by formal pluralism. Secondly, and quite ironically, the "Masters of Modern Architecture" (I take the phrase from a series of books) have become like the consumer products Coca-Cola, Xerox and Ford, each with their own house style and corporate brand. Since the principal way of selling their reputation was to develop a single image purveyed through magazines and TV, their sign of authenticity and sincerity turned into a sign of commodification and sell-out. "Black is beautiful, buy Coppertone." The same thing happened to the image of Ché Guevara (and, of course, "Picasso" was cynically marketed as an automobile). Modernists once again, inadvertently, fought their revolution for Madison Avenue, for branding.

The result is an urban landscape dotted with integrated monuments to different brand images. Modernist sincerity has become good old hypocrisy and, one has to admit in this department, Post-Modernists have often followed their parents. In the 1990s, branding became a self-conscious strategy of architects such as Rem Koolhaas, and if there were any progress here it was, at least, in being admitted. Dirty Realism was one name for facing this pragmatic market-place directly.

On the other hand, there were also many Post-Modernists such as Hans Hollein, Arata Isozaki and Frank Gehry who modified the "style for the job" (93). They looked to context, function, history, and the taste of their clients for possible clues of difference. They could see the urban cacophony that resulted when every architect followed his own style rather than worked with the place and particular situation, that babbling confusion of London's South Bank with which the chapter opened. "Form follows function," the war cry of Modernism, had become "Form follows Brand." Post-Modernists, as we will see in the historical narrative that follows, developed urban and cultural strategies to resist these pressures.

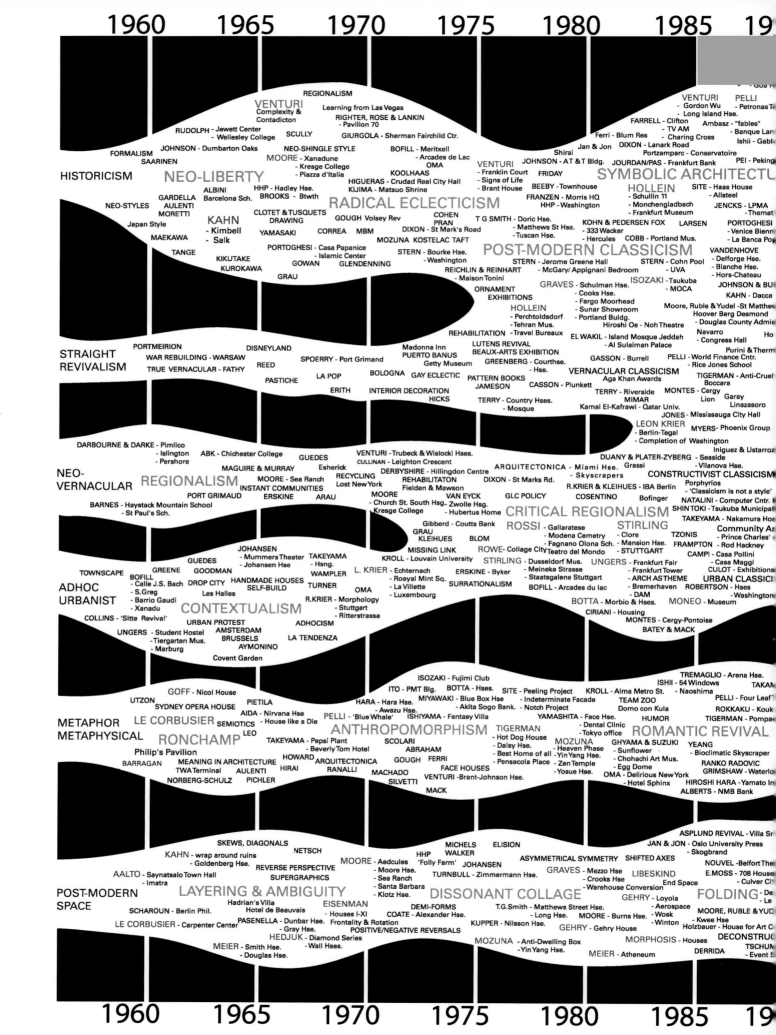

94–95 POST-MODERN EVOLUTION – EVOLUTIONARY TREE

Post-Modernists of all persuasions are committed to pluralism and this more than anything else unifies a disparate tradition. In fighting for heterogeneity, they combine the Modernist emphasis on universalism with the rights and values of the locale, ethnic group and individual. This evolutionary tree, and its six main classifiers (far left), shows the plurality of narratives.

In the 1960s Post-Modernism started with the counter culture and the renewed concern for urbanism. This created a series of movements – contextualism, participatory architecture, critical regionalism, among others – while a new interest in history and communication sparked off the tendency to radical eclecticism, symbolic architecture, ornament, and the vernacular. During the early 1980s these trends coalesced around Post-Modern Classicism, a formation that lasted about ten years, average for an architectural movement.

Then, as it became part of the establishment, a reaction set in and several Neo-Modernist movements dominated the 1990s, none of which is shown. But, stemming from Le Corbusier's Ronchamp and experiments in Post-Modern space, two other trends come to the fore. One, at the bottom of the diagram, develops the ambiguity and complex spatial layering – the skews, shifted axes and dissonant figures worked out by Venturi, Gehry and Eisenman in the 1970s. This leads into the movement of folding, blob architecture and Biomorphic design, all aided by the computer. The second trend, of metaphorical design, also is helped by computer production and the two movements merge together with the success of Frank Gehry's work at Bilbao. From this marriage a new convention is born, the enigmatic signifier, the grand, public building that suggests much more than it names. Eisenman, Libeskind, Coop Himmelbau, Miralles, Hadid, Alsop, Morphosis are some of its leaders, but this highly expressive tendency is more of a general trend than an organized movement. The warped and fractal architecture of the new paradigm cuts across several approaches though it does indeed stem from complexity theory and post-modernism.

Twenty-one trends and movements (red), five hundred buildings (black) and nine major architects (green) constitute this broad tendency, a critique and modification of mainstream modernism

Part III
Post-Modern Architecture

HISTORICISM, ONE BEGINNING OF PM

Post-Modernism as a cultural formation started, as mentioned in the introduction, at many points and times. It grew with the counter-culture of the 1960s, the rise of the post-industrial society first in America, the disenchantment with Abstract Expressionism in the art world, the growth of a global market and so on. By contrast, the First World War, Hiroshima and the Holocaust are all markers that philosophers and historians have seen as turning points, as creating the crisis of Modernity. In architecture a case can be made that the shift occurred when Modern architecture became mass-cult, the historic city was threatened by economic forces, and architects rediscovered architectural DNA, that is, the continuity of languages and historic types. This rediscovery created its own form of "crisis."

In the late 1950s, the question of what period of architecture might be plausibly revived was fiercely, and rather uncharitably, debated by the English and Italians. Reyner Banham and his teacher Nikolaus Pevsner launched quite different kinds of attacks on Italian Neo-Liberty and what they took to be a return to Historicism (not to be confused with Karl Popper's use of this term in politics). Professor Banham, calling the class to order, attacked "The Italian retreat from Modern Architecture" as "infantile regression," because it went back to a pre-machine-age style. Pevsner listed the other retreats from the faith and found shades of deviant "neo-Art Nouveau and neo-De Stijl," neo-this and neo-that sprouting everywhere like poisonous weeds. The English articles and attacks, lasting from 1959 to 1962, were meant to wipe out these heresies with a little critical weed-killer, but in the event the Italians fought back at this Puritanism, what they called "the refrigerator school of criticism."[18]

The kind of buildings that provoked this debate had vague or repressed historical allusions: Franco Albini's museums and Rinascente Store, 1957–62, were reminiscent of traditional Roman building. The Torre Velasca, Milan, 1957, looked somewhat like a medieval tower, Luigi Moretti used an actual rusticated base in the Casa del Girasole, Rome, 1952, while Lubetkin, in England, used, ironically, a caryatid *porte-cochére* as early as 1939 (96). One of the most convincing Historicist buildings of the fifties was Paolo Portoghesi's Casa Baldi 1, 1959–61, an essay in free-form curves definitely reminiscent of the Borromini he was studying, yet also unmistakably influenced by Le Corbusier (97). Here is the schizophrenic cross between two codes that is characteristic of Post-Modernism. On the one hand, the enveloping, sweeping curves of the Baroque, the overlap of space, the various foci of space interfering with each other and, on the other, the Brutalist treatment, the expression of concrete block, rugged joinery and the guitar-shapes of Modernism. The dates of this Italian historicism are given to set it against the slightly later emergence of the same thing in Japan, Spain and America (where critics sometimes claim it happened first). Although Eero Saarinen built his "orange-peel dome," the Kresge Auditorium and chapel, in

97 PAOLO PORTOGHESI and VITTORIO GIGLIOTTI, *Casa Baldi I*, Rome, 1959–61. Half Baroque, half Modern in its curves and materials. The wall planes curve to acknowledge windows or doors, or create overlapping foci of space. Unlike later buildings by the same architects, the forms are not entirely sculptural but keep semantic memories (e.g. cornice, building block, closed bedroom). (Oscar Savio).

96 LUBETKIN and TECTON, *Highpoint II*, Highgate, 1938. Because of local hostility to Modernism, the architects, half-ironically, incorporated casts of the caryatid removed from the Erechtheum. The Classical reference was perhaps fitting to their ordered, Classical geometries, but at this stage in time it is the presence of the human figure and the representational boldness, where it is appropriate – at the door – which are noteworthy.

98 EERO SARRINEN and ASSOCIATES, *Stiles and Morse Colleges*. New Haven, 1958–62. Wandering medieval spaces and the crude masonry of San Gimignano were partly sought because of the neo-Gothic campus of Yale. In retrospect the historicism seems diagrammatic, as homogeneous and scaleless as the Modernism it was criticizing.

99 PHILIP JOHNSON, *Kneses Tifereth Israel Synogogue*, Port Chester, 1956. A thin plaster canopy is stretched tent-like across the nave to break it up into vaulted bays. This use of a traditional compression form in tension, and back-lit, clearly recalls, as Johnson intended, Soane's amazing distortion of Classical grammar. (Ezra Stoller).

1955, and these were reminiscent of Renaissance and medieval prototypes, it was not really until his Stiles and Morse colleges at Yale, 1958–62, in "peanut-brittle Gothic," that overt Historicism arrives (98). Here we have a conscious medieval layout, picturesque massing, an attention to the local Yale context – in sum the beginnings of a sensitive urban place-making. The detail and massing may be diagrammatic, and slightly cheapskate, but this is part of the Modernist inheritance, and love for the diagram.

Semi-Historicism starts in America, in a big way, about 1960 with the major works of Philip Johnson and the more kitsch variants of Minoru Yamasaki, Ed Stone and Wallace Harrison. Yamasaki and Stone produced their sparkling version of what were termed Islamic "grilles and frills" in 1958 and then "almost-real-Gothic" in 1962. The latter is the date of Yamasaki's infamous instant arches awaiting their cathedral, in Seattle. The Historicism is attenuated, embarrassed, half-baked – neither convincing appliqué nor rigorous structuralism – a problem for many of the architects who left Mies setting out for decoration (and never quite arrived).

Philip Johnson is easily the most accomplished and intelligent of this group; indeed he probably thought about the problem of Historicism far sooner and longer than other architects. His first, tentative break with his mentor Mies van der Rohe was the Synagogue in Port Chester, 1956 (99). On the outside it was a startling simplification recalling those of Ledoux; on the inside it was reminiscent of the Soane Museum. These historical quotes are located within a black picture-frame of Miesian steel, and the absence of ornament and content mark it as Modernist; so Johnson –

like so many others – is looking two ways. But it was his writing, sensibility and support for the young that were far more important in contributing to Post-Modernism than his buildings.

In 1955 an essay attacking "The Seven Crutches of Modern Architecture" exposed some of the formulae behind which Modern architects hid, or tried to escape responsibility for formal choice: for instance, the pretence to utility and structural efficiency were two such "crutches."[19] Johnson later, in "The Processional Element in Architecture," 1965, also debunked the spatial rationalizations of the Modern Movement. Playing with traditional shapes (the redundant segmental arch appears in his Amon Carter Museum 1961 and Folie 1962) these arguments no doubt pushed the door of history open further. He advanced into this forbidden territory armed with laconic sarcasm:

> Mies is such a genius! But I grew old! And bored! My direction is clear; eclectic tradition. This is not academic revivalism. There are no Classic orders or Gothic finials. I try to pick up what I like throughout history. We cannot not know history. [20]

So, by 1961, we have a camp statement in favor of eclecticism. What keeps Johnson from developing this more seriously is not only his jocular tone, his preference for surface wit over deeper investigation, but also his Modernist commitment to pure form, ugly or beautiful – but pure form.[21] The Historicism of Johnson remains on the level of spotting the source, "sorcery," on esoteric codes rather than on more accessible and conventional ones. He thus never really creates an argument for ornament, regional suitability, or contextual appropriateness – three potential aids to his eclecti-

100 KIYONORI KIKUTAKE, *Tokoen Hotel*, Kaike Spa, Yonago, 1963–64. The "Japan Style" is evident in the constructional elements and the roof restaurant with its gentle curves. In addition the building is highly readable and broken into different semantic areas: board-rooms and conference rooms at the base, an open deck, and two levels of hotel rooms (on the inside proportioned by tatami mats).

cism that might have strengthened it.

If Johnson and Saarinen can be classified as semi-Historicist, or one-half Post-Modern, then so too can the "Japan Style," and the "Barcelona School" which developed at the same time, but toward a regionalist expression. The "new Japan Style," a phrase used by Robin Boyd, is best exemplified in the sixties work of Kunio Maekawa, Kenzo Tange, Kiyonori Kikutake and Kisho Kurokawa (100).[22] It incorporates nationalist and traditionalist elements within a basically Corbusian syntax. Thus, projecting beam ends, brackets, torri gates, gentle curves, beveled masts, constructional expression "all the hallmarks of Japanese architecture in wood" are translated into reinforced concrete and juxtaposed according to the method of "compaction composition." Le Corbusier developed this method of Cubist collage, and the Japanese, with their traditional Zen aesthetics of asymmetrical balance, frequently push it toward the refined and exquisite. While they use Brutalist materials and smash them through each other, they still end up with something as elegant as a Tea Ceremony Room (albeit in concrete). As with Johnson and Saarinen they remain hesitant about tradition, and wary of a full-blown eclecticism. As Kenzo Tange remarked in 1958:

> So-called regionalism is always nothing more than the decorative use of traditional elements. This kind of regionalism is always looking backwards…the same should be said of tradition,[23]

No one was prepared in the sixties to pose these questions in a radical or functional way, and so the Modernist suspicion of ornament and convention remained (while the practice slipped towards regionalism).

ROBERT VENTURI AND THE IRONIES OF MANNERIST PM

The first *Modern* architect to use traditional and ornamental elements (such as the doorway arch) in an ironic and semantic way was Robert Venturi (101). On the street façade, his Headquarters Building for Nurses and Dentists, 1960, has decorative moldings placed as exaggerated eyebrows over lower windows and, around the where one enters, a paper-thin arch bisected by diagonal struts which announces "public entrance" (102–104). Several ideas here proved influential, so it could be called quite appropriately the first anti-monument of Post-Modernism. Robert Stern was to develop the ornamental ideas and many architects, such as Charles Moore, were to learn from its surprising corners, inflected walls, and Post-Modern space (but more of that later). Suffice it to say that we have, finally, a building that was willfully traditional in some respects, while still partly modern. Going beyond the previous historicism, it could face the past both straightforwardly *and* with irony. With Venturi's dual message, one always hears, and sees, the "*and*" coming.

Like Baroque architecture this building was designed in terms of the urban context, the street line and flowing spatial requirements; like a Mannerist conceit it played tricks with scale, amplifying certain windows and doors, while diminishing others. Certainly its calculated disjunctions were Mannerist: the roof, is an ultra-thin cornice, the flatness of the wall and punched out shapes are a play on the International Style.

The New Paradigm in Architecture   55

101 Robert Venturi, born in 1925, worked in the offices of Eero Saarinen and Louis Kahn before setting up a partnership with John Rauch, in 1964, and his wife, Denise Scott Brown, 1967. The Modernist inheritance, particularly of the Philadelphia School, remained strong throughout their polemics against orthodox Modernism. Denise (*née* Lakofski, born in 'Nkana, Zambia in 1931) a planner with a social conscience, brought to the practice an interest in cultural pluralism and a commitment to honoring the different taste-cultures that make up this pluralism. For this and the polemics, the team were often attacked and misunderstood to be supporting Las Vegas and commercialism, especially by the Left and Kenneth Frampton.

Responding to other Modernist attacks on their work as "ordinary and ugly," they immediately adopted these epithets as slogans to carry into battle, thus inflecting their work in a mannerist and academic direction. The result is an aristocratic sort of populism, a very sophisticated style and set of attitudes. One has to look twice to get the real message, something that critics often fail to do, much to the everlasting umbrage of Venturi-Scott Brown. "Ultimately our architecture engages mannerism, an architectural approach that accommodates aesthetic ambiguity but also, in our time, creates ambiguity: In our time the critics don't get it — i.e. man-

This last typical tut-tut was recently written as an attack on Post-Modernism ("*A Bas* Post-Modernism, Of Course") in an issue of the *American Architecture* magazine devoted to "Post-Modernism" (May 2001). Here Venturi denies he was a PM, of course, and asserts his credo: "Remember it's not about Space any more, it's about Communication. *A bas* Space and Structure of then; viva Symbolism and Iconography of now!" This is the kind of exclusivist position that makes Venturi the typical Modernist. Space is out, Communication in, and in this reductivist stance he is definitely not a Post-Modernist or a pluralist. He employs the idea of the zeitgeist to exclude those interested in space and structure, that is more than ninety per cent of the architectural profession and, not stopping at this cleaning of the Augean Stables, he then promotes an "iconography of now" based on — "the Nasdaq sign and Times Square". These are, of course, signs not symbols.

In such unremitting attacks on Late, Neo- and Post-Modernism, Venturi-Scott Brown have solidified their position as a unique movement: of one team! Yet their early work had a profound influence on Post-Modernism, as great as that of Jane Jacobs and Rachel Carsons. Robert Venturi defined many notions and keywords of the movement in Complexity and Contradiction in Architecture, 1966: ambiguity, the phenomenon of "Both-And" in Architec-

Element, and, above all, the obligation Toward the Difficult Whole." These ideas, illustrated with historical examples and Venturi's early brilliant work remain a cornerstone of the movement.

While their completed work is often for museums and universities (at UCLA, Princeton and the University of Pennsylvania, among others) occasionally they receive roadside commissions where they can carry through the lessons learned from Las Vegas. The resultant decorated sheds can be startlingly appropriate supergraphics, as in the BEST showroom, or banal one-liners as in the Exxon Gas Station for Disney. The most convincing ornamented buildings are at UCLA and for the Hotel du Department in Toulouse, where the context and function become the pretext for well-constructed symbolism. Venturi's Thesis at Princeton, in 1950, explored such contextual thinking, one of the earliest recent explorations of the subject. To my mind the best contextual work of the Venturi Team is their addition to London's National Gallery. The Renaissance paintings on the inside, the relation to a complex site and the old Gallery were all part of a larger context taken up in the fabric and symbolism of the building. Just as it was completed in 1991 Venturi was justifiably awarded the Pritzker Prize for architecture of that year, Robert.

Venturi and Denise Scott Brown

Robert Venturi's polemics against Modernism concentrated, at the beginning of his career, on the question of taste, and then later, on symbolism. His first book, *Complexity and Contradiction in Architecture*, 1966, set up a series of visual preferences placed in opposition to simplicity and the integration of Modernism. Complexity and contradiction was opposed to simplification; ambiguity and tension against straightforwardness. Architectural elements, according to his canons, should be "both-and" rather than "either-or," or have a mixture of more than one function. Above all, the hybrid assemblage and messy vitality were preferred to obvious unity. All of these norms culminate brilliantly in an argument that the architect had an "obligation towards the difficult whole." As opposed to the Miesian method of suppressing functions for visual or structural consistency, the architect should try to include as much urban reality and variety as the building demanded. This opened the door to what became known as "inclusivism."

In addition to these stylistic canons, Venturi provided two more important contributions to what, by the middle sixties, was a growing argument: first was his interest in borrowing from disregarded historical work, such as that of the Mannerists and Edwin Lutyens (who became with Antonio Gaudi a paragon for Post-Modernists). Second was his plunge into Pop Art, then Main Street, Las Vegas, and finally Levittown. Along with Scott Brown, and his design team, Venturi looked at these hitherto snubbed manifestations of popular taste for their "Lessons in Symbolism." The results were collected in what could be appropriately called the first anti-exhibition of Post-Modern architecture, "Signs of Life: Symbols in the American City" ("anti" because it went against the conventional museum codes of displaying artifacts – see above page 39).

The major problem with their notion of symbolism based on decorated sheds, and the way they excluded a whole repertoire of codes has already been mentioned. They rule out not only "ducks," but also what they call "Heroic and Original" architecture, the grand gesture, the revival of the *palazzo pubblico*, and all the work they conceive in opposition to their decorated sheds.[24] They did this because of their Modernist notion of the *zeitgeist*. They claimed that today's spirit of the age "is not the environment for heroic

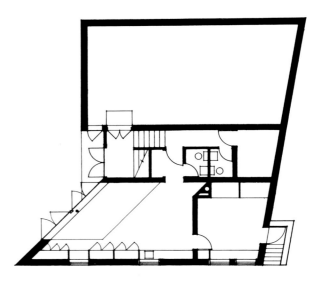

102, 103 ROBERT VENTURI and SHORT, *Headquarters Building*, North Penn Visiting Nurses Association, 1960. The arch, a sign of door, is contrasted with rectangular and diagonal elements to announce the public entrance. Traditional decorative mouldings are also distorted on the windows. This bizarre usage was nevertheless one of the first buildings to incorporate historical ornament in a recognizable and symbolic way.

104 VENTURI and SHORT, *Headquarters Building*, plan, is a distorted box which, on the outside forms an embracing court, and on the inside directs movement with its diagonals. The odd angles and skewed layered space of Post-Modernism developed from such plans.

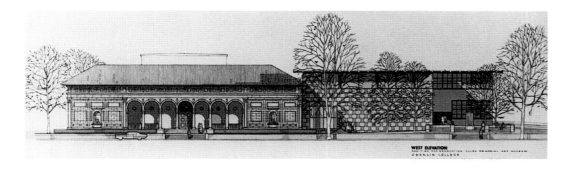

105, 106 VENTURI and BAUCH, *Allen Art Museum*, Oberlin College, 1973–77. This addition to an Italian Renaissance revival building of 1917 tries to harmonize and contrast with the previous building through its proportions and pink and red stone. Semantically, however, this "elegantly" decorated shed is more a gymnasium than a museum, and awkwardly, not gracefully, integrated with its neighbor.

communication through pure architecture. Each medium has its day." "Has its day?" This is a silly position to adopt in a global electronic age, as they call it, characterized above all by pluralism. The "heroic" and "pure" building flourished for the next thirty years, as much as any other type.

By adopting both an exclusivist *and* inclusivist approach they traced a zig-zag path which itself must be looked at with irony and nuance. The exclusivism meant that they cut themselves off from much heroic Post-Modernism,[25] that of Michael Graves, Aldo Rossi and Frank Gehry, and more importantly for their own arguments, the participatory design of those such as Lucien Kroll, Charles Moore and Ralph Erskine.

Participatory methods, as we will see, give the designer a respect for tastes that are not necessarily his own. On the other hand, the Venturi Team responded to some codes outside the usual architectural repertoire, especially those coming from the commercial strip, Las Vegas and Route 66. And here is a double irony that should be savored. Since most of their early work was built for a non-Pop taste culture – for professors or colleges or "tasteful clients" – it meant that Pop imagery (checkerboards, diagrammatic signs, flat graphics) had to be smuggled into the architecture with extreme good taste!

Thus the Oberlin College Addition, 1973–77 (105, 106), is a decorated shed of pink granite and red sandstone – "a

high school gym of the 1940s," as they call it, slammed onto a harmonious Neo-Renaissance building. The juncture, the texture, the roof and pattern are all calculatedly discordant. The justification is that "the artists don't want architectural heroics," they want a gym, or they want the industrial, background building that, for instance, Frank Gehry provided as the Temporary Contemporary in Los Angeles. This proved very popular. But at Oberlin, Team Venturi provide, not a gym, but a very subtle version of Lutyen's checkerboards, sliced at odd points to show they are mere appliqué. Furthermore, the flat window walls underline the wallpaper aspect, or the notion of signs stuck onto buildings. The grammar is exquisitely related to the context in color *and* completely out of context, both with a gym and the client's tastes. You can admire the subtlety of this Mannerism *and* hate it. Perhaps both reactions are intended?

In any case, their Brant House, 1971, makes a stronger argument for its coding by way of association (107). Since the owners have one of the great collections of Art Deco objects, there are various signs of this in the detailing. On the outside, two shades of green-glazed brick slide on the diagonal, and flat streamlines, in shiny metal, edge the surface. On the inside, taking cues from Lutyens, black-and-white marble stairs vibrate in opposition and the entrance sequence is punctuated by a series of shifts in axis and scale.

But arbitrary coding again enters at the back, which is "1930s Post–Office and Walter Gropius"! What have these references to do with Art Deco, the client's taste – or anything? Clearly the Venturi Team is slumming and enjoying the "ordinary and dumb" side of things. One more quote brings out the esoteric nature of the codes involved: they say the southern front "resembles a plain Georgian country house (except there is no central motif)."[26] Once this comparison is made, however, as with so many other Modernist buildings claiming historical overtones, it is the *non*-historical parallels that dominate. The bow front, and gigantic side porch, have expanded to the point that no Georgian would recognize them. The windows, coloring and details are all anti-Georgian in their Mannerized proportions. One can enjoy the building for its marvelous idiosyncrasy, for its careful distortion of codes, and its delightful wit – a nice green trellis jumps up the west side – but still wonder why the Venturi Team have to try so hard at being original in this esoteric way? It is as if their sensibility were still Modernist, while their theory were Post.

Two buildings that are more straightforward in their historical allusions and enjoy an easy-going, but interesting, commerce with the past, are the Trubeck and Wislocki houses, 1970, which use the Cape Cod vernacular in a conventional yet fascinating way, and the Franklin Court design, 1972–76, a Bicentennial homage to Benjamin Franklin (108). The latter uses something that would become a Post-Modern trademark: the ghost image of a building. In this case a stainless steel outline marks the profile of a previously existing mansion of Franklin's. Below it are the archaeological remains, which can be spied through various bunker-like slits thoughtfully provided above ground. A neo-colonial garden, laid out roughly on Franklin's description, is peppered with some of his morally uplifting slogans. Thus the Venturi Team has produced not a building, but a very amusing garden which combines meanings from the past and present in a way that is not excessively idiosyncratic. It is fitting to the urban context, and within both popular and elitist codes. It is ugly *and* beautiful and because it is successfully double-coded it could be called their first pro-monument of Post-Modernism.

Because Robert Venturi and Denise Scott Brown had to fight Modernists, such as Gordon Bunshaft, who called their buildings "ordinary and ugly" they adopted the epithets hurled against them and took on a more strident position than did their followers. They have made lasting contributions to the theory and practice of Post-Modernism, to mixing codes, to contextualism, ambiguity and, the best of their slogans, "the obligation to the difficult whole." *Complexity and Contradiction in Architecture* brought in the first stage of complexity theory, as did Jane Jacobs's writings, but because their taste was so Mannerist and their position so contentious, they were less successful in caring through the implications of pluralism that those such as Frank Gehry. Moreover, Robert Stern, who will be discussed later, has a kind of exuberant facility with the "Venturi Style," and the Barcelona School also turned it with ease to immediate purpose.[27] One group of Barcelona designers, Mora-Pinon-Viaplana, has taken cues not only from Venturi's formal ideas, but also from semiotics in general, to produce ironic juxtapositions of urban landscape.

Another Barcelona group, Clotet and Tusquets, amplified Venturian juxtapositions of the car and Classicism, machine and garden (109, 110). For a bedroom-pavilion, they placed a paper-thin trellis above an heroic order of piers. Within the piers and on the roof of the house is the place to park the car surrounded by a balustrade; finally, the piers, which come down to the ground, act as a screen behind which are rustic shutters and windows – out of phase with the piers. The syncopation of verticals is masterful, the layering of space a surprise, the contrast of meanings a delight. It is rather as if one composed a Classical building according to International

107 VENTURI and RAUCH, *Brant House*, Greenwich, 1971, southern exterior. The green-glazed brick in two shades and the metal strips are in tune with the Art Deco collection of the owners, but the intended references to country houses are so under-coded as to go unnoticed.

108 VENTURI and RAUCH, *Franklin Court*, Philadelphia, 1972–76. An open frame of stainless steel approximates Franklin's old mansion, the "surprise garden" houses his memorabilia, while the surrounding buildings have been restored – a convincing if modest knitting together of old and new.

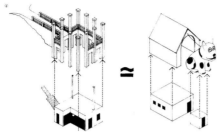

109 LUIS CLOTET and OSCAR TUSQUETS, comparison of their Belvedere and a Dog House in South Africa. The amplification of a surrealist sign so that it swallows the shed owes something to Venturi and Magritte.

110 CLOTET, TUSQUETS and PER, *Giorgino Belvedere*, Gerona. 1971–72. This-belvedere-bedroom is meant to relate to and contrast with the classical estate. You drive in – on the roof – between the temple's colonnade. Double-height space is set off against small-scale trellis and balustrade, and rustic wood shutters against white stucco, a grand irony of Post-Modernism.

111 RAYMOND ERITH and QUINLAN TERRY, *Kingswalden Bury*, 1971. Symmetrical temple front is placed in a recessed, diminished entrance. Very slight visual rhythms can just be detected in window bays, but the Palladian exercise lacks any strong underlying idea, or any extension of the Classical tradition.

Style aesthetics (or vice versa), a typical PM conceit.

With such a building then, finished in 1972, the Modern architect *almost* makes his peace with historicism and allows a direct traditional quote where it has a purpose (the building is on a Classical estate). The word "almost" is emphasized because these designers cannot go the whole way down this traditional road because they rightfully fear meeting interior decorators, and Reactionaries, coming back the other way. This road block stopped their full use of the past – the nostalgia boom, the continuation of reproduction architecture with its Reproduction Furniture, the Traditionalesque Style that never died and was mostly kitsch. The ex-Modernists did not want to be tainted, so when they made hesitant steps towards tradition it was always distorted enough to be recognizably anti-kitsch.

Thus, Post-Modernists distinguish themselves from the next group, those revivalists who never were Modern in the first place. The only reason they are included in this book is because of their influence on PM, the fact that they opened the expanding field to more options. Pluralism against all totalizing approaches, whether they are Modern or Traditional, but a critical pluralism, critical of straight revival.

STRAIGHT REVIVALISM AND THE POWER OF PARODY

Gothic architecture, it is surprising to think, survived in England through the sixteenth, seventeenth and eighteenth centuries right into the Gothic Revival. It never entirely died because people liked this "national style," and there were always a few cathedrals in need of repair. In like manner, the old way of doing things never really stopped. Rather historians stopped looking, except Henry Russell Hitchcock, who called one small chapter of his contemporary history "Architecture called Traditional in the Twentieth Century." Even he stops the account in the 1930s, and points out a problem:

[. . .] whatever life twentieth-century traditional architecture retained as late as the second and even the third decade of the century had departed by the fourth. Post-mortems on traditional architecture have been many – and often premature.

The causes of death are still disputable, but the fact of dissolution is by now [1958] generally accepted.

By the 1980s and the intervention of Prince Charles into the debate it became obvious that his dissolution certificate was also premature. Raymond Erith and then Quinlan Terry, Leon Krier, Robert Adams and others continued the Classical tradition with varying invention (111).

Are there moments when Straight Revivalism is appropriate, without any ironies? Conrad Jameson would argue "yes" when it comes to housing, particularly mass housing, where pattern books are called for.[28] The argument is that Georgian or Edwardian terraces work better than Modern mass housing, because a tradition – which ever one it is, as long as it is unbroken – contains more values, and well-balanced ones, than a Modern architect can invent or design (112). People enjoy these terraces more than new inventions. They are often cheaper to build than the system-built alternative, and they fit into the urban context, in language and scale. Thus, according to Jameson, one selects a pattern language suitable to the area and only modifies it piecemeal, if there is need for a new technology: a garage door here, or a refrigerator there. Otherwise tradition always gets the benefit of the doubt: architecture is a social craft, *not* a creative art.

While Jameson's arguments are plausible for mass housing, they are not as exclusive as he intends. His Radical Traditionalism is just one approach among many, and there is no reason an architect cannot use it also to send aesthetic and metaphysical meanings addressed to the few. Already in the early 1970s, when he was writing, one strand of commercial revivalism became a major industry: the popular house and speculator's development. Even more widely influential were the well-known pastiches of Portmeirion, Disneyland and their world-wide variants. This tradition developed most quickly in the Far East, Los Angeles and Houston where

Ersatz new towns, or at least vast housing estates, sprung up as fast as a plastic polymer gone berserk. In Europe, various Ersatz towns were created, especially by the seashore, such as Port Grimaud (113), La Galiote, Puerto Banus.

How did such Ersatz become a polemical force in architecture? Through straight comparison with Modernist new towns. Clearly these mass-produced fabrications were more humane, appropriate and enjoyable, hence their commercial success. Maurice Culot, a *soi-disant* Stalinist, even saw them as the answer for the communist future, a nice irony where the hyperactive capitalism of Port Grimaud would become the model for the working class.[29] Well, twenty years later it happened at the new towns of Seaside and Celebration in America, and across the country with what was called the New Urbanism, except it was built for the upper-middle class and placed securely within a contained field, if not a gated community (114). What starts as a serious argument ends as a backdrop for Disney Corp and films such as *The Truman Show*.

An American example of revivalism, which elicited all sorts of response from architects and critics in the middle 1970s, was John Paul Getty's Museum in Malibu, California (115, 116). This captured the debate for a moment because it was such a thorough going revival (of Herculaneum's Villa of the Papyri) and, like Port Grimaud, such a visible opposition to reigning Modernism. Architects predictably damned the building as "disgusting," "downright outrageous," "too learned," "frequently lacking in basic architectural design judgement," "fraudulent," "recreated by inappropriate technologies" and, of course, "too expensive" ($10 million – or was it $17 – a mere hors-d'oeuvre for Getty). These outcries were quickly rebutted by David Gebhardt, an historian who, unpredictably, was also a supporter of Modernism. He nonetheless found it one of the most important buildings for ten years, because of its obvious functional appropriateness and popularity:

As a functioning object, the Getty Museum appears to work as well as – or even better than – most recently built museums… [the designers] have evinced a far more sympathetic response to the needs of a popular audience than that expressed in any of the recently completed "modern" image buildings which have been constructed in the U.S.[30]

112 *Warsaw Old Center*, rebuilt 1945–53 in replica form based on old photographs, measured drawings and personal accounts of the people who lived there. The market place was rebuilt after the Nazi destruction as a symbol of Poland's rebirth, The interiors were, of course, remodelled in a new way, piecemeal, to suit modern requirements and plumbing. Embassy of the Polish People's Republic).

113 FRANÇOIS SPOERRY, *Port Grimaud*, 1965–69. Drive your sailing boat right up to the manicured lawn of a Provençal fishing village in reinforced concrete. No two houses are the same, and the variety of spatial experience is well above the Modernist counterpart, making this village the major model for resort centers around the world.

114 ANDRES DUANY & ELIZABETH
PLATER-ZYBERK, *Town of Seaside*, Florida,
1978–83.

115 DR NORMAN NEUERBURG *et al.*, *Getty Museum*, Malibu, 1970–75, inner peristyle garden. False windows, replica statues and wall paintings imitating first-century imitations of marble – unintended wit. (The Trustees of the J. Paul Getty Museum).

116 *Getty Museum.* The Villa dei Papyri was never quite like this since it lacked a parking garage, chlorinated water, and mechanized waxing, but several parts of this seaside palace have been replicated. Its transplantation to Southern California and a magnificent view overlooking the Pacific is appropriate especially as a museum for antiquities. Note the *trompe l'oeil* columns, garland and false marble. Several Pompeiian styles made a virtue of deceit which here is ironically more deceitful – for instance, contradictory shadows. (The Trustees of the J. Paul Getty Museum).

By contrast, another Modernist historian Reyner Banham, known for his sometime celebration of such Pop recreations, condemned the whole thing for its lifeless air, the "bureaucratic precision" of detailing:

> The erudition and workmanship are as impeccable, and absolutely deathly, as this kind of pluperfect reconstruction must always be . . . no blood was spilled here, nor sperm, nor wine, nor other vital juice.

The building became a lightning rod for such opposite opinion and thereby both over-praised and over-condemned. It is passably fair in its setting, and certainly delightful to experience as a good replica, like Sir Arthur Evans' reconstruction of the Palace of Knossos in Crete. Yet its relevance for the growing Post-Modern argument was neither its appropriateness nor quality, but rather its use of simulation techniques.

It accidentally raised the point that our time can indulge, like no other, in accurate historical virtual reality. Through reproduction techniques (xerox, film, synthetic materials) and specialized research (in this case archaeological and landscape specialists), with high technologies of air-conditioning and temperature control and new structural capabil-

ities (of putting the whole thing over a parking garage), there are possibilities beyond the nineteenth-century revival. We can reproduce the fragmented experience of different cultures and, since the media have been doing that since 1960, our sensibilities have been expanded. Thanks to color magazines, travel, and Kodak or, later, the computer and virtual reality, Everyman has a well-stocked *musée imaginaire* and is a potential eclectic. He is exposed to a plurality of other cultures and makes discriminations from within this wide corpus, whereas previous cultures were stuck with a smaller choice they had inherited. As Reyner Banham pointed out in arguing for a Pop architecture, Everyman had become a new type, "the knowing consumer." The point of this was to become progressively more important for Post-Modernism as Simulation City became both a computer game, and by the 1990s in Asia, a reality.

In the early seventies simulation started as a game of pastiche. It varied in intention from sarcastic deceit to the sly counterfeiting with pre-fab moldings, from humorous send-up to parodic satire of the rich and famous. The Gay Eclectic designers of Los Angeles – the interior decorators who went exterior on their "Bungaloids" (converted bungalows whose sex is changed from 1930s Spanish to 1970s Rococola) – were not criticizing the mansions of Beverly Hills when they shrunk them by nine-tenths and put lobsters in their pediments. They were just camping up establishment taste while affirming it (117).

By contrast, more serious Japanese architects, such as Mozuna Monta, consciously travesty the Modern Movement and the Renaissance, making an enigmatic art form out of parody (118). Toyokaze Watanabe weaves Le Corbusier's Villa Savoye and Aalto's Town Hall into one building, or builds a coliseum inside an Ottoman castle. Monta, who is the supreme ironist, a man who sees and feels all the cultural confusion of a Japanese living in Western dress – simultaneously in the twentieth and fifteenth centuries – has spliced various Renaissance prototypes. In one small house, Michelangelo's Palazzo Farnese is mixed with Brunelleschi's Pazzi Chapel and carried out in a black-and-white Modernist idiom. The results of such architectural cross-dressing have a certain formal integrity and interest; the game of architectural chess had these undiscovered forms of checkmate inherent in its rules. For a culture, like LA or Japan or Australia, which is always copying or essentializing trends a little bit after the fact, there is an exquisite sweetness to be enjoyed by making this time-lag into a conscious art of deviation.

Caricature of serious culture undermines its pretensions, just as the unconscious travesty devalues it. Yet the subversion may be only momentary, a short space of time before the latent humor asserts itself and establishes the caricature as a new kind of culture. The Monkeys Pop group aped the Beatles until their aping became a new

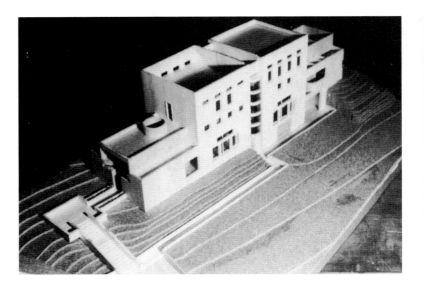

118 MOZUNA MONTA, *Okawa House*, project, 1974. "The renaissance of the Renaissance," with the outside of the Palazzo Farnese crossed with the inside of the Pazzi Chapel. Since the Japanese, like the Angelenos, re-broadcast culture and get it slightly wrong, artists such as Monta have taken this parody as their starting point and created serious works based on caricature. The result is sometimes an extension of traditional language.

form of authenticity. In the 1970s, Monta, Watanabe, Shirai, and to a certain extent Arata Isozaki and Minoru Takeyama, employed parody as a kind of mirror-image form of cultural confusion and criticism. As the writer Linda Hutcheon pointed out in *A Poetics of Post-modernism*, 1988, this turns into a major literary genre. Parody allows a double meaning to be conveyed at the semi-conscious level: "I may be sending up this object, but by doing so I confirm its worth, its significance." Affirmation and denial come in the same split second. Perhaps this is why PM parody is taken up by artists such as Cindy Sherman and the Japanese painter of religious and sexual impersonations, Yasamasa Morimura: they both mimic the popular icons that dominate the media. Those on the edge, at the margins of Modernism and western power, find it a very strategic place from which to undermine the center. Being ex-centric, as Hutcheon calls it, allows one to mock and mimic at the same time, a very PM place to be.

It is thus fitting that one type of Post-Modern urbanism should triumph as commercial parody. Not the mid-cult concoctions of the New Urbanism or those of Disney Corp – this is either Straight Revivalism or PoMo – but rather their first cousin: the shopping-urbanism of Jon Jerde (119). This LA architect managed to turn the 1960s formula for shopping centers, of Dumb Boxes surrounded by Parking Lots, worked out by Victor Gruen, into tight, urban parodies of Main Street plus Buck Rogers. His PM formula is certainly not high culture, but it is an improvement on the previous shopping wasteland: who said there is no progress in the arts?

117 *8834 Dorrington*, Los Angeles, *c.*1972? Bungalows re-styled in various neo-neo-modes by interior designers. The basic eighteen-foot box is extended in front by a fence, a hedge, and then a stuccoed or veneered façade with various exaggerated signs of status and entrance. But the Neo-styles are mocked with a certain creative wit: note the pediment monsters – lobsters – the disjunction in scale, and the violent contrasts in material. These scenographic tricks are highly readable, like all good caricature.

119 JON JERDE, *Canal City*, Hakata, Japan, 1996. A knowing pastiche of historical and Futurist ideas turned into a commercial urbanism. Jerde, almost alone among architects, has created many successful urbane places – at a price.

the communist world at the time, so Neo-Vernacular was reforming Modernism (that is, no too much – hence the irony).

Ever since Jane Jacobs launched her attack on Modern planning, there had been an increasing demand for mixed renewal, mixture of age, style and use. This was in 1961, about the time the architects Darbourne and Darke won the Pimlico competition in London against groups such as Archigram who favored comprehensive rebuilding. The Darbourne and Darke solution nicely illustrated several of Jane Jacobs' points. It incorporates old buildings such as the dark brick nineteenth-century church. It mixes various activities, such as corner pub, library, old age home and housing; it has a rich variety of spaces full of trees; and provides that quality which the concerned architect cared about, a sense of place. Finally, it used a "Victorianesque" aesthetic of chunky brick and thus established, if not invented, the Neo-Vernacular style.

In the seventies this style became, for an impoverished and ideologically uncertain Britain, *the* style to fall back on when there were no other clear directions. It was and remains acceptable to the majority of English people because it does not depart too far from the traditional family house (although Darbourne and Darke have added such

120 DARBOURNE and DARKE, *Pimlico Housing*, 1961–70. The chunky brick aesthetic and volumes treated as giant decoration. This scheme mixed various uses in relatively low-rise high-density, and also mixed new and old building, landscapes and masonry. The D&D projects always show a sensitivity to contrast which stems from the Picturesque tradition. G. E. Street's Church of St. James-the-Less has been preserved to become the focal point of the design. Brick was chosen partly for economic reasons, partly for associations which the inhabitants wanted: substantiality rather than flimsy – like panel construction.

NEO-VERNACULAR = MODERN REVISIONISM

Another response to the obvious failure of Modern redevelopment and comprehensive renewal was a return to a "kind of" vernacular. The inverted commas are necessary here (Ersatz is the age of quotation marks) because the vernacular was neither straight revivalist nor accurate reproduction, but "quasi" or "in the manner of" a hybrid between Modern and nineteenth-century brick building. The style, however, is highly recognizable: it nearly always has pitched-roofs, chunky detailing, picturesque massing and brick, brick, brick. "Brick is humanist," so the slogan goes, or gets caricatured. Indeed, it became *so* humanist that the ex-Brutalist architect Kunio Maekawa, a follower of Le Corbusier in Japan, used it on skyscrapers in downtown Tokyo. By the seventies, it could signify his ideological break with Modernism! It may seem surprising that the use of a mere material may carry so much ideological weight but as we will see, in this section, brick vernacular became a major way Modern architects dealt with the failures of mass housing. Just as Revisionism was changing

121 ANDREW DERBYSHIRE of ROBERT MATTHEW, JOHNSON, MARSHALL and PARTNERS, *Hillingdon Civic Center*, 1974–77. Decorative brickwork around the windows, a large bureaucracy fragmented into a village scale, a collision of several pitched roofs with Frank Lloyd Wright and "human values." The building is also curiously reminiscent of the large nineteenth-century resort hotels in America. The architects consciously attempted to design within the users' language. (Sam Lambert, *Architects' Journal*).

122 FEILDEN and MAWSON. *Friars Quay Housing*, Norwich, 1972–75. Picturesque layout and the North European merchant's house adapted to this historical site near the Cathedral Close. The steep pitched roofs, variety of colour, and semi-private space add to feelings of historical continuity. Bernard Feilden has been involved with major restorations at St. Paul's and York Cathedral.

un-English, Modern elements as streets in the air [120], quasi-Mansarding and staccato, rather than individual house-by-house massing). In an exhibition of this kind of work, from May–July 1977, Colin Amery and Lance Wright from the *Architectural Review* marked what they took to be the typical, if understated, mainstream of English architec-

ture. It ran from Pugin through Shaw and Ebenezer Howard to the Letchworth Garden Suburb:

[It] restates particularly English virtues of domestic architecture. At the same time as many local authorities were indulging in an orgy of inhuman system building, Darbourne and Darke quietly proved that some of the essentials of domestic life like privacy, small gardens and good landscaping could be provided at high densities in cities within a framework of vernacular materials . . . Then there is the side so developed at Pershore – which is concerned with bringing back traditional (and therefore genial) materials and forms – a brick arch over the front door, windows that are more vertical in proportion.[31]

A more radical traditionalist like Conrad Jameson would, of course, show how many quirky neologisms Darbourne and Darke have introduced. Most seriously they have abolished the traditional street and created instead a large housing estate – however fragmented in appearance. Thus this Neo-Vernacular was yet another half-way house, as the hyphenated appellation suggests, and not intended to be either Modern or traditional, but a bit of both.

Other English architects who worked in the method and style, again being acutely sensitive to scale and picturesque massing, were McGuire and Murray, Ahrends Burton and Koralek, Edward Cullinan, on occasion the GLC (Greater London Council), and interior designer/architects such as Max Clendinning. So strong did the approach become that, by 1975, it could almost be proclaimed as official British policy (although policies such as these are never official, and certainly not proclaimed, in Britain). An indication is the Hillingdon Civic Centre, 1975–77, in its higgledy-piggledy

Victorianesque of-course-brick, designed very much for, and within, the Welfare State by Andrew Derbyshire. He was explicit in justifying its intentions at the RIBA Conference:

> ... we set out in this project to design ... a building that spoke a language of form intelligible to its users (its occupants as well as the citizens of the borough) and used it to say something that they wanted to hear.[32]

There follows the claim that the building will break down administrative barriers and get everyone talking cordially with their elected representatives, as if the friendliness of the forms would suddenly induce a corresponding outbreak of hospitality in the neighborhood. Such claims, that architecture can radically change behavior, are Modernist ones, although the attention to user-reactions and actual social research are Post-Modern. Indeed the emphasis on the *language* of architecture and the codes of the various groups who might use the building is the argument being advocated here. But the assumptions are more literalist. "Pitched roofs," Derbyshire avers, "cover the steps of the wall section almost to ground level so that more roof — the protective, welcoming element — is seen than wall — the defensive, hostile element."[33] One form equals one straightforward meaning is the implication. The notion of multiple readings, and ones that change over time, is reduced to the singular, popular meaning: that pitched roofs equal "the protective, welcoming element" (121).

While one might commend the interest in actual codes, the impression is that they are subtly being limited to good taste, middle-class stereotypes. Indeed, work in the Neo-Vernacular sometimes suffers from a pervasive smugness. This piety may be preferable to the deserts of mass-housing, with which the architecture is invariably contrasted, but it is somewhat less than a close reflection of existing architectural taste cultures. Already the work of Venturi and Scott Brown had shown these to be richer than "Architect's Architecture" in brick.

The Neo-Vernacular made obvious and fitting connections with the trend towards rehabilitation and re-use that also became public policy by 1975. This program was proclaimed at the time of the European Architectural Heritage Year, and it became a major approach of the GLC. A firm such as Feilden and Mawson could divide its time between restoration of historic monuments, straight Modernism, and vernacular revival — like their brick housing in Norwich designed on the model of the tall North European merchant's house (122). These designs not only went back to old prototypes, but also adopted ancient city patterns, existing street lines, and the wealth of accumulated accident — or rather the specific historic facts that made a street bend here, a row of houses twist and angle there. These quirky picturesque odd-spots, a delightful hallmark of the medieval city, finally became design formulae in the 1970s work of Aldo van Eyck and Théo Bosch.

The importance of this switch for world architecture was that Van Eyck was a leader of Team Ten, a brilliant polemicist and philosopher-architect.

Their scheme in Zwolle, built between 1975–77, renovates many buildings in the old historic centre and adds to these a mixed development: twenty-one businesses and seventy-five new houses. These, narrow and high like the traditional Dutch prototype, also conform to the existing, bending street pattern. Thus diverse spaces emerge: short alleys, small streets with arcades, streets with external staircases leading to residences on higher levels, semi-public space with gardens. The dwellings truncate the gable roof at the top of the head, to show they are *not* traditional, but otherwise they extend traditional form in a marvelous ways. For instance, the interior spaces open through veiled loggias, where one may look over the semi-public gardens, or up into sun-filled, distorted attic space. This rich ambiguity is characteristic of PM space, as we will later describe (123).

Van Eyck was called in on this project during the seventies, in a typical protest of the time against inhumane city redevelopment. His arguments for renewal and infill housing, made in terms of a "snow image," can be taken as the toughest statement of a Modern architect just as he is becoming Post:

> What the snow image suggests in terms of the city is a careful adjustment, adaptation, modification and addition. Cities are chaotic and necessarily so. They are also kaleidoscopic. This should be accepted as a positive credo before it is too late ... Add to this the notion that no abstract norm imposed from above, or any other motive, sanitary or speculative, can further justify the wanton destruction of existing buildings or street

123 ALDO VAN EYCK and THEO BOSCH, *Zwolle Housing*, 1975–77. Diverse functions and renovation combined with a new scheme based on the narrow Dutch façade — only the gable has been lopped off. The curving blocks are knitted into the traditional urban patterns to keep the street lines and neighbourhood identity. Sixteen types of residences were incorporated, many with semi-private gardens looking out on the public space.

124 VAN DEN BOUT and DE LEY,
Bickerseiland Housing, Amsterdam, 1972–76.
Narrow, deep houses with oriel windows,
"lightyards" in the center, truncated gables
(compare with the seventeenth-century example) and semi-Brutalist detailing. This cheap
neo-vernacular housing saved the area from
being developed by outside commercial interests, much to the gratitude of the remaining
community. An example, like Zwolle, of urban
protest resulting in positive action.

125 Right: JOSEPH ESHERICK, *Cannery*,
San Francisco, 1970. Nearly every historic city
now has a converted area that has been somewhat pedestrianised to the great joy of shop-
pers. This middle-classification of Victoriana
robs it of guts, but supplies it with cash flow, a
Mephisphelean deal.

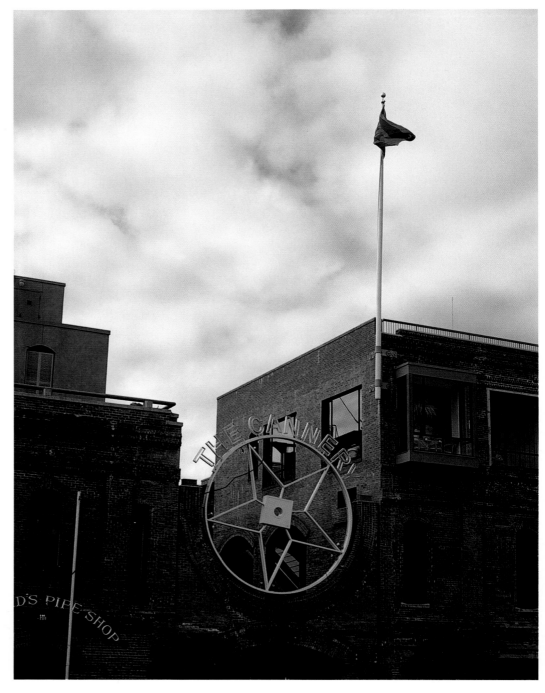

126 MARTORELL. BOHIGAS and MACKAY, *Santa Agueda*, Benicassim,
Spain, 1966–67, A serious version of popular vernacular housing done in a
picturesque way with pantiles and window blinds (that extend the living
room space). MBM, exemplary eclectics, modify their style to suit the job;
this is in one of their five current modes, which also include the
Industrial Style, Barcelona School Style, Pop Manner and Eclectic Mode.
(Xavier Miserachs).

patterns . . . Ultimately, the world today can no longer afford
such waste, nor can it afford to overlook the right of people to
maintain both the built form as the social fabric of their domi-
cile if that is their choice. Anything else is sociocide – local
genocide with only the people left alive.[34]

Another typical project that came out of the urban
activism of the time was the Bickerseiland renewal in
Amsterdam, where architects Van den Bout and De Ley also
worked with the local community to provide infill, vernacular houses (124). Again, these were tall, narrow and deep with
a Dutch head flattened off just above the eyebrows, raising a

question: if a Modernist could go this far backward, why could he not go the next step and get the remainder right? The answer is again linguistic in nature: "flat roofs" meant "still Modern," even if they were, like Revisionism in general, only half flat.

It is interesting, in this context, to compare the Neo-Vernacular of different countries, let us say Joseph Esherick's Cannery in San Francisco and MBM's (Martorell, Bohigas and MacKay's) Santa Agueda in Benicassim, Spain – both worked on in the mid-sixties (125, 126). The former is a transformed nineteenth-century warehouse with Modern graphics, where elevators shoot through and enliven a tarted-up brick vernacular. Curves and arches are accentuated, the old fabric is heightened by reducing the window mullions to a minimum and using strong, contrasting colors. The result is very popular with the middle-class shopper, which is why such rehabilitations were swiftly repeated from Australia to Canada. Nearly every downtown around the world had a shopping center carved into such old warehouses. What they lost in terms of authenticity was gained in terms of jollity, no doubt their economic saving and psychic curse. The past was saved at the cost of fumigating the corpse – and who would not make this Faustian bargain?

The same is partly true of MBM's traditionalesque housing with its picturesque pantiles and inevitable brick. Like tourist resorts and Port Grimaud, the aesthetic code is mostly a socio-economic formula, because such comfortable and cosy images appeal to the middle class. In fact, they also cut across many social lines and appeal to the rich and poor in different countries. It would be false to term this a universal taste, or more popular than its opposite, Neo-Classical terrace housing, but it clearly articulates codes of meaning that go deep. Friendliness is conveyed through warm mixtures of wood and brick, individuality and ambiguity conveyed through broken massing, familiarity with respect conveyed by the choice of well-known elements. If it never quite lifts you off the ground with its brilliance or originality, then it can be termed a success, because it was meant to be modest – not heroic. In summarizing this emergent strand of Post-Modernism at the RIBA Conference in 1976, I put together the following hodge-podge of a conclusion to define the consensus:

> [Housing] should be small in scale, incorporate mixed uses and mixed ages of buildings, be rehabilitated where possible and put more on a craft than high art basis. It might be architect-designed, or based on pattern books modified to the particular situation. Wherever possible, it would be dweller controlled and sometimes it would be even self-built out of garbage and built in a pseudo-vernacular, depending on the taste of the culture for which it was built. Housing signifies a way of life . . .[35]

No other architect came closer to this goal (without reaching it) than one occasionally committed to participatory design, Ralph Erskine.

ADHOCISM AND PARTICIPATORY DESIGN

Ralph Erskine, an English architect who settled in Sweden in the late 1930s, designed in several styles, including the Neo-Vernacular which he used with consummate wit at Clare College, Cambridge, 1966 (127). Here the small scale and domestic verge on the cloying, but the whole thing is saved by typical Erskinisms such as the cheapskate corrugated detailing, and jokes – twelve feet of cantilevered doorway, cantilevered in brick, three inches from a support! A similar odd mixture of modern cantilevers supporting traditional housing became a hallmark of the Dutch group MVDRV thirty years later, perhaps for similar reasons: an attempt to enliven the everyday by pushing technology to its limit.

Erskine turned such expedients into a form of adhocism, where his happy-go-lucky style is clearly recognizable. At

127 RALPH ERSKINE, *Clare College*, Cambridge, 1972, entrance showing brick cantilevered almost to a support, but then saved in time – all doors should have something odd about them. (The student holding it up, Ken Yeang, was to become the famous inventor of the Bioclimatic Skyscraper, 347).

128 RALPH ERSKINE. *Byker Architects' Office*, Newcastle, 1972–74, in a converted funeral parlour. The red, white and blue graphics rise as optimistically as the balloon on this office in the heart of the renewal. The designers were accessible to the inhabitants who had a say in their future location, neighbors, and type of apartment.

129 RALPH ERSKINE. *Byker Wall*, Newcastle, 1974. A mixture of materials used in a semantic way: brick in the lower two floors, corrugated metal and asbestos in the upper ones; semi-private deck in green stained wood, circulation in blue, and untamed nature at the base. These articulations break down a potentially massive wall, and give it a human scale.

Byker, outside Newcastle, he oversaw a community of working-class housing which ranks with the Modern Weissenhof Settlement in Stuttgart, 1927, in setting a new direction. First among its principles, and most important for the Byker community, is a degree of self-government, a certain local power to balance that of the central city. To support this, the architect set up his office on the building site and allowed the people being re-housed (9,500) to choose their location, friends and apartment plan (within a restricted budget) (128). This participation in the planning process helped form and continue the community, as much as did the preservation of the existing social ties. Since eighty per cent of the people remained within the area during the building, most of the old associations remained too.

Indeed, several important buildings were preserved: churches, a gymnasium and local buildings. Thus the resultant patchwork has a depth of historical association much greater than the typical new town. Classical elements, discarded building parts, and ornament from previous buildings were incorporated either as decoration or use – such as seats and tables transformed *ad hoc* from column capitals.

In the Byker renewal, Erskine allowed the multi-use of activities and corresponding multi-expression of function, although it must be admitted this articulation is more in his own *ad hoc* style than in the local codes of Byker. Every house, and seventy per cent are on ground level, has a private domain and is surrounded by semi-private space such as gardens and small walkways. Even the exterior apartment

corridors in the Byker "wall" are broken up and given local planting, so that this large block has the identity and safety so lacking in the old paradigm of Pruitt-Igoe (129). One reason the St Louis development failed was for lack of defensible, outdoor space, a deficiency here made good.

Erskine shows that, in the words of the urban theorist John Turner, architecture is a verb, an *action*, not just a set of correct theories or prescriptions. The Erskine office became immersed in the Byker community by setting up shop in a disused funeral parlor where they sold plants and flowers (an obvious popular activity in England). They also acted as the local lost and found, that is, they performed countless non-architectural tasks to get to know the people. Then the slow process of design and construction took place. Endless discussions and small decisions, were made so that the landscape, "doorway," color, history, idiosyncrasy and other non-commensurables could find a place. The success of the result, as both an amusing and humane environment, makes this a key PM project.

The pluralist language of Byker stemmed partly from the participatory process. "Participation in design" became, during the seventies, a respectable if loaded term that usually meant a one-sided consultation with those for whom one was designing. They might see the plans beforehand, but they did not have the expertise or power to propose viable alternatives.[36] Thus further methods of interaction were developed, the most radical of which developed out of May '68, *les evenements de Mai*, and the student movement around the world. The relationship of Post-Modernism with the counter-culture is most explicit here, and architecturally manifest in the work of a Belgian architect, Lucien Kroll. At Louvain University, he and his team took the process of participation as far as it could go in an anarchistic direction and, for a short time, it looked as if this *ad hoc* approach

130 LUCIEN KROLL and ATELIER, *Medical Faculty Buildings*, University of Louvain, near Brussels, 1969–74. An artificial hill town of various activities, articulated with different building systems. The large glazed area is communal, also the restaurant space. The other materials – wood, brick, plastic, aluminium and concrete – are also used semantically. Traditional signs are incorporated: greenhouses, pitched roof and chimneys signify the more private areas. The variety and detail simulate the piecemeal decisions which take place over time and give identity to any old city.

131 *Medical Faculty Buildings*, University of Louvain. View across the main Piazza showing builders' contribution to the design. The rocks grow up from the ground into brick and then tile. Participation and individualism have produced a witty environment.

might be the shape of things to come. The teaching and student community (or part of it) became deeply involved in design decisions.

Students were divided into flexible teams, and designed parts of the dorms and public spaces where they would spend the next four years. Along with Kroll, who acted like the orchestra leader, they shifted small bits of plastic foam around to work out an overall model (130). When disputes arose, or one group became too dogmatic and fixated, Kroll re-organized the teams so that each one became familiar with the other's problems. Not until a possible solution was in sight did he draw up the plans to make it workable. The resultant buildings show a complexity and richness of meaning, a delicate pluralism that reflects the codes of the inhabitants and builders (the contractors were actually encouraged to participate as well, hence such things as the undulating stone walls) (131).

The importance of Kroll's work at Louvain cannot be overstressed. It showed that participatory design and self-build

could work on a large scale, that it could result in creative architecture, that it could build in the kind of density of meaning that usually takes years to achieve, that is the result of many inhabitants making small adjustments over time.

But (one could hear it coming) there was a problem. The codes were so relentlessly personalized and picturesque that normal and Modern architecture was suppressed. Here at Louvain, if anywhere, the commitment of Post-Modernism to a more radical pluralism, including even competitive codes, might have been attempted. As seen in part two, architectural meaning consists in oppositions within a system, a dialectic in space or over time and, predictably, the next generation of students has not found their more conventional tastes recognized. Having said that, Kroll's example set a standard for future designers, such as Frank Gehry, to build on.

Nearby in Brussels, the group ARAU (*Atelier de Recherche et d'Action Urbaine*) used participatory methods in a more political way to stop large-scale redevelopment. This was quite a feat in the capital of the Common Market. By employing the model of Port Grimaud and combining it with a Brussels vernacular they created counter-proposals that stopped ITT and other multinationals in their tracks.

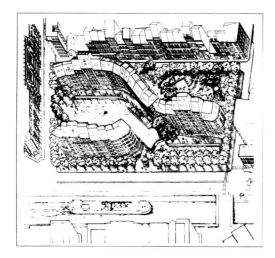

132 ARAU, *Brussels*, 1975. This group uses various counter designs to stop massive redevelopment, leaving it up to the community to choose which alternative, or combination, they want. Using pastiche, Port Grimaud, or here, Honfleur and Van Eyck as alternatives to Modernist redevelopment, they seek to confirm the underlying city patterns.

133 MOORE, RUBLE & YUDELL, *St. Matthew's Parish Church*, Pacific Palisades, CA., 1982–48.

The typical situation unfolded as follows. A large corporation would propose a monolithic scheme for a sensitive part of old Brussels. Then ARAU would challenge it with a counter-design, organize neighborhood support and call a press conference. With newspapers and media behind the counter-design, the initial scheme would either be shelved or redirected into a more suitable urban pattern. Using such methods, ARAU successfully fought dozens of battles and, once again, the architectural results were an *ad hoc* mixture of different urban types and styles (132). Maurice Culot, one of its members, underscored the hands-off pluralism:

> For ARAU members the city is a place where democracy could live – they reject any proposal that banishes inhabitants from the city... My mission is not to create new forms but only to explain the options and programmes being debated by ARAU. We do not force our own architectural tastes on people, but follow the advice of the people involved.[37]

Throughout the seventies, similar protests and counter-schemes stopped destruction in many large cities. For San Francisco, the Covent Garden area in London, parts of New York City and most capital cities in Europe, the intervention at the Nieumarket district in Amsterdam typified the architectural agit-prop, indeed even the use of the Venturian "ghost building" as a sign of destroyed fabric. Advocacy planning in America was also effective in stopping urban disruption, although it did not initiate development.

But there was another benefit. As well as slowing the indiscriminate destruction of the city, participatory design opened up architects to solutions they might otherwise not have imagined. This happened, on more than one occasion, with Charles Moore who collaborated with local communities and even audiences in a television studio. A case in point was his redesign of the Episcopal Church of St. Matthew in the Pacific Palisades, Los Angeles (133). This building replaced a previous structure that had burned down in one of those typically fast-moving LA canyon fires. When Moore confronted this congregation of Episcopalians, he found they were divided, ideologically and by taste, into several groups: the most basic split was between high and low church. So he and his partners, Ruble and Yudell, introduced methods of design that allowed the various sides to gain confidence in expressing their particular viewpoints. The first event was simply a slide show of various buildings and churches in many different styles; this opened the discussion of different types of layout and ways of conducting a service (134). Based on such precedents, some parishioners designed centralized layouts, others more formal Latin-cross plans, while most did informal layouts akin to their favorite church, Alvar Aalto's Imatra in Finland.

Four all-day workshops, spaced about a month apart, were set up. The first was devoted to picking the site, the next to making models of the church the parishioners wanted, a third to manipulating a kit of parts brought by the architects and a fourth to picking details and establishing an overall ambience. As with Lucien Kroll's procedures the process resulted in disagreement, but this very polarization of opinion became a spur for creativity. Moore showed how the two basic types of church could be combined *ad hoc* in a new synthesis that, in Venturi's words, would be complex and

136 FRANK GEHRY, *Loyola Law School*, Los Angeles, 1981–84. Gehry, working closely with his clients, juxtaposes Classical elements that some of the lawyers wanted, with vernacular and industrial languages. He has continued working closely with clients throughout his career.

134 Architects working with parishioners.

135 St. Matthew's intersection of central and longitudinal plans, a creative result of two opposing views of what the church should be.

contradictory but nonetheless a whole. For instance, the low ground-hugging outside reflected those who wanted a simple structure, while the large-scaled center reflected those who wanted a more formal cathedral-like space. The details also reflected oppositions. For instance, the dormer windows were round, like the traditional rose window, but their formality was broken by the penetration of simple vertical mullions, an echo of the wooden studs on the inside, and the typical stucco box of LA.

The most creative result of these contradictions, and the *architectural* vindication of participatory design, was the hybrid plan. This combined a half-ellipse, giving a centralized feeling and allowing parishioners as close to the altar as possible, *and* a modified Latin cross with long dormers for gables. Not only did this interactive process give the church a complexity of form, but it also led to the acceptance of the choices and, ultimately, the feeling that the building belonged to the parishioners (135). As a result they have looked after it well, a bonus that often occurs at the end of mutual design.

Participatory design and adhocism waned in the 1980s though, as will be seen, aspects of it were carried on, especially by Frank Gehry who was influenced by Moore (136). His *bricolage* and use of cheapskate materials stem from this LA background and also his desire to work closely with his clients, understanding their motivations. Like Erskine, Kroll and Moore, he actually feels empowered by constant interaction with those commissioning the building. In fact, Gehry would be unable to take the expressive risks he does without consultation. In this sense one of the great lessons of participation is that, with certain architects, it can liberate not hamper creativity.

CONTEXTUALISM AND COLLAGE CITY

The Modern Movement played a role in the deterioration of cities by supporting Le Corbusier's model of the city in the park, disurbanization and comprehensive redevelopment. These were largely anti-city policies, but apologists of Modernism would point out that the real villain was us, that is, consumer society, the motor car and the pull of suburbia. Whoever is convicted and with how many accomplices remains to be seen, but it is true that Modernists did little to solve the crime. Sometimes they made it worse. The nostrums of CIAM favored the megastructure, functional separation and the destruction of the street, and its followers had no political and economic theory of how a city thrives, or how civic virtues might be nurtured.

Post-Modernists, Lucien Kroll, Maurice Culot, the Krier brothers, advocacy planners and, in the late nineties, Richard Rogers took a different view of city life. They stressed the active, evaluative aspect of urban design. The planner, architect, mayor, or market researcher intervenes to bring about those goals he supports, but he does this within a political context where the values can be made explicit and debated. The proper place for much that now transpires as architecture and planning is the political forum, the neighborhood meeting or the meeting of elected representatives. While no adequate city forum yet exists to further this process, since the late sixties it has been put on the agenda, again and again.

One call was for a return to the public realm. In the past this meant the agora, assembly area, mosque or gymnasium – a place for people to debate their varying views of the good life, or assert their communality.[38] As an ideal the public realm returned as a major focus of design in the schemes of a European group loosely gathered under the label of the Rationalists. Because of a quite different 1920s movement with the same name, the appellation Neo-Rationalism is preferred here, but whatever the term the tendency was led in the seventies and eighties by Aldo Rossi, Matthias Ungers, Antoine Grumbach and the Krier Brothers. Only Robert Venturi, among the Post-Modernists, took a stand against the agora and *palazzo pubblico*, and he did this, as we have seen, because he was committed to a zeitgeist limited to the information revolution.

Rob and Leon Krier, in particular, celebrated the public realm in many of their design schemes and competition entries. Basically, they followed Camillo Sitte's nineteenth-century models. This treated architecture as forming continuous urban space as a negative volume, what was called "a positive figural void." These figural voids, usually Platonic shapes such as squares, rectangles, hemicycles and circles, were to flow through back streets and then reach a crescendo around public buildings. The marketplace, shopping arcade, square, or school might serve as the pretext for an agora. With such urban tissue the Kriers proposed a series of reconstructions of the European city, ideal plans that would patch together the fragmenting reality.

An early ideal scheme was Leon Krier's redesign for Echternach, near where he was brought up in Luxembourg (138). Here he inserts a traditional arcade and circus, using the existing morphology of the eighteenth century to create an identifiable spine to the town and a culmination of the entrance route at the existing abbey. Height, scale, silhouette and building materials are all compatible with the existing fabric, although accentuated to give a new emphasis to the public realm. Leon Krier adapts the traditional aerial perspective of tourist maps to stitch these forms together, and a master-planning concept whose grand sweep is reminiscent of Bath. However, at this time in his career, just after he left practice with James Stirling, such Historicist methods were combined with a Modern language of form. Le Corbusier, and his bi-plane, circle poetically over a town that is not allowed to sprawl. The organization and style of this work equates the contemporary and historical. Through this potent combination and his seductive drawings, Leon Krier managed to lead Post-Modern urbanism for the next fifteen years, until he tipped the balance towards Classicism, and Prince Charles. Alas.

In his entry for the La Villette Competition, he proposed a return to the intimate scale of historic cities by creating a urban block unit based on a collectivity of twelve or so families (139). These closely grained blocks are then used as a background fabric against which the more public buildings stand out along a center spine. The idea is a return to the historic city of Paris, and to an architectural language

137 *Rational Architecture Rationnelle*, under this title formed a group of European architects led by Leon Krier, Robert Krier, Aldo Rossi, Robert Delevoy, Massimo Scolari, and the painter Rita Wolf. Mixing a poetic reinterpretation of Classicism with a new urban typology, they fought for the reconstruction of the fragmenting city.

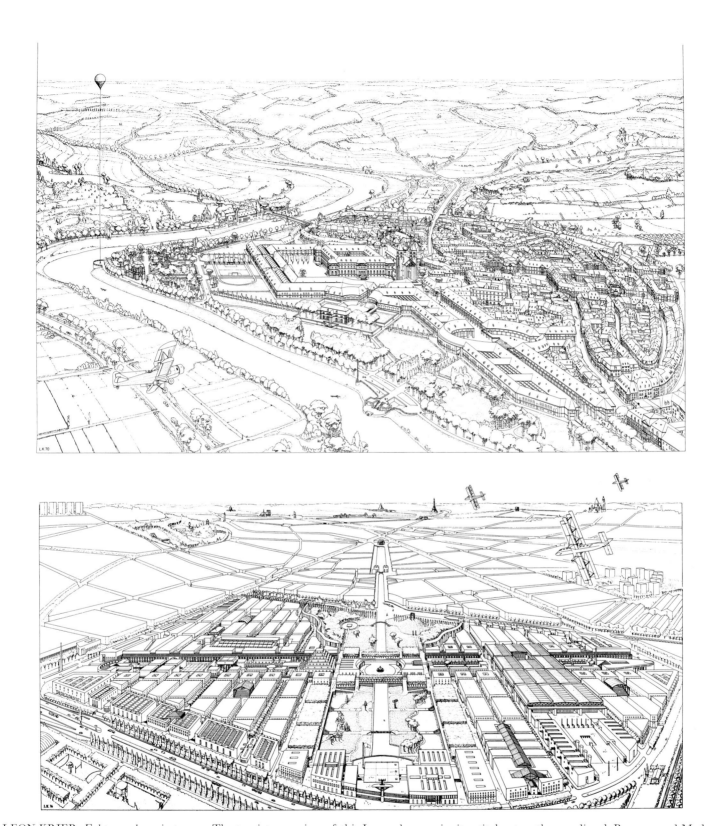

138 LEON KRIER, *Echternach project*, 1970. The tourist map view of this Luxembourgeois city stitches together medieval, Baroque and Modern elements. Circuses, grand avenues, and endless bay repetition are reminiscent of Bath and Baron Haussmann. Every city, Krier avers, should have its urbanist eyeview so that the public parts – squares, Streets, monuments – articulate its memory.

139 LEON KRIER, *La Villette Competition*. Paris, 2nd prize, 1976. Made up of small, community units of almost a dozen or so families which, Krier contends, would have local control, this scheme nevertheless appears homogeneous. A grand, public boulevard runs north-south (right/left) containing the Place Centrale, Place de a Mairie, and Square des Congrès. Rolling English parks create the other axis which focuses on historic Paris. The bi-planes are also reminiscent of Le Corbusier.

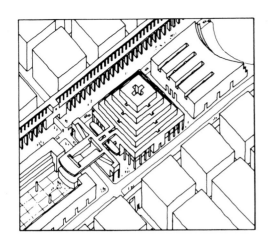
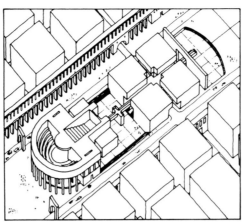

140 LEON KRIER, *La Villette typology*, of the Hotel and Cultural Center. The ziggurat is lifted from its historical context, and Ledoux's design for a barn is turned into a town hall. Krier's hope for a universal language that could be understood founders on the same misunderstandings that plagued Ledoux and Le Corbusier. The meaning of form is social and temporal, and cannot be established by fiat, especially when based on abstractions. It is curious that Krier, who attacks Le Corbusier for his urban insensitivity, should have such similar notions, but the theory of how architecture communicates is not widely understood.

based on socially recognizable types (140). The categories were, in his capitalized emphasis, The Theatre, The Library, The Hotel, and so forth. They were not to be understood as unique signs, as words in an esoteric language, but rather as an attempt to create a system of social and formal references that would make up the landmarks of a contemporary city. The intention of establishing a public symbolism and knitting this within the fabric of Paris was exemplary, even if the symbolism was abstract and hard to read. More convincing was the way he conceived city building as gaining significance from various dialectics: that between the private and public realm, the present and the past and the morphology of solid and void. These binary oppositions lead to the city of dialectical meaning and that idea takes us directly to the writings of Colin Rowe, a friend of Krier. From such interactions grew the practice known as Contextualism.

As an un-named movement it started in the early sixties at Cornell University with studies into the way cities formed various binary patterns of legibility. Alvin Boyarsky looked at Camillo Sitte's work for its implications, just as George Collins was doing at the time, and the most important binary pair emerged from Sitte's drawings: the opposition between solid and void, or figure and ground. By 1976 Grahame Shane could summarize the doctrine in an issue of *Architectural Design*, the British magazine that was to become a center of PM thought. He describes here the language of Contextualism as based on abstract dualities rather as if it were a digitized, computer language of 0s versus 1s. There are urban patterns of *regular* vs *irregular, formal* vs *informal, types* vs *variants, figures* vs *fields* (if effectively combined known as set-pieces), *center* vs *infill*, and *tissue* vs *boundary edge*.

Such a glossary could begin with the term *context*. By definition the design must fit with, respond to, or mediate its surroundings, perhaps completing a pattern implicit in the street layout or introducing a new one. Crucial to this appreciation of urban patterns is the Gestalt double image of the *figure-ground*. This pattern, which can be read either way — solid or void, black or white — is the key to the contextualist approach to urban space.[39]

According to this argument, the failure of Modern architecture and planning, very briefly, was its lack of understanding the urban context, its over-emphasis on objects rather than the tissue between them. It valorized design from the inside out rather than from the exterior space to the inside. By pondering hard on the large chunks of blackened areas in Sitte's drawings, and studying Nolli's seventeenth-

141 GIAMBATTISTA NOLLI, *Map of Rome*, 1748. Private building in gray cross-hatching is hollowed out by public space in white. The latter may be a street, piazza, courtyard, or church interior. The map gives an idea of semi-public space and how it mediates between the major antinomy, public and private.

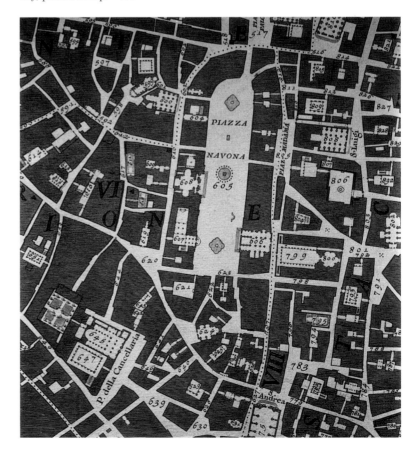

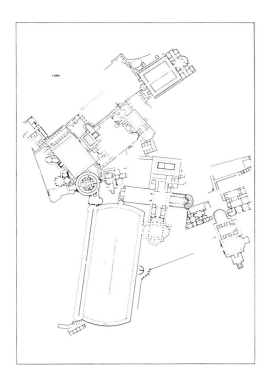

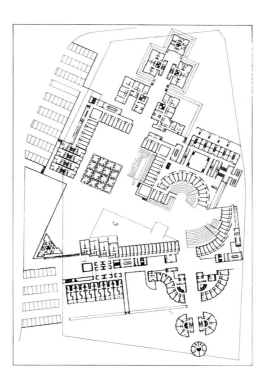

century map of Rome, the Contextualists found, as did Robert Venturi, a new respect for *poché* or left-over tissue building, the "ground" for any city's attractive "figures" (141)

Colin Rowe became the philosopher, figurehead and guru of this movement, though, because he was from an older generation, with James Stirling as one of his star pupils, he kept well ahead of his academic followers. A self-styled mandarin who had labored under the historian Rudolf Wittkower (as he told me), Rowe could hypnotize an audience with Gibbonian prose. Using examples from every period and culture, he wove the above binary pairs of the Contextualists into a spellbinding dialectic.

His article and then book *Collage City* (written with Fred Koetter) set up arguments between the mechanism of Enlightenment thinkers and the organicism of the Hegelians, the Olde Worlde fantasies of the Americans without roots at Disneyland, and the Brave New World of Superstudio with too much past in Florence. He contrasted the fixed, Platonic utopias of the Renaissance with the "utopia as extrusion" of the Futurists. The influence here was Isaiah Berlin and his distinction between the single, big ideas of the "hedgehogs" and the many, little goals of the "foxes." "Palladio is a hedgehog," Rowe announced, "Giulio Romano, a fox; Hawksmoor, Soane, Philip Webb are probably hedgehogs, Wren, Nash, Norman Shaw almost certainly foxes . . ."[40]

Such games, and analogical thinking, work most effectively when Rowe employs one side of his equation to criticize the other, and comes up with a compound that includes both antinomies. Thus his Collage City is based on the *bricolage* of many different utopias, or, because they are so small, what he calls "vest pocket utopias." The Swiss Canton, New England village, Dome of the Rock, Place Vendôme are characteristic examples. He pulls them all together in one eclectic composition and thus has everything both ways, with a beneficent vengeance. As he summarizes these mini-perfections, they allow "the enjoyment of utopian poetics without our being obliged to suffer the embarrassment of utopian politics." Total history becomes the potential repertoire for selection. Here is the equivalent, on a high level, with what we have seen on a low, "the knowing consumer." When Post-Modernism is attacked for ransacking the past, it is not just the MTV generation that is being impugned, but also the most learned of architects and theorists.

We can see this with the way that one building, Hadrian's Villa at Tivoli, became *the* prototype for PM urbanism, not just for Colin Rowe (142). Various architects and critics such as Louis Kahn, Charles Moore, Matthias Ungers and Vincent Scully saw it as the model to follow (143). For some, it is the richness of overlapping spatial foci which is the lesson to be learned. For others it was the eclecticism of sources (Egypt and Greece), or the palimpsest of meaning, or the Mannerism of sharp juxtaposition. For Rowe, Hadrian's Villa is the supreme instance of fox-like dialectic because it avoids the "totalizing" tendency that other Post-Modernists were attacking:

> For if Versailles may be a sketch for total design in a context of total politics, the Villa Adriana attempts to dissimulate all reference to any single controlling idea . . . Hadrian, who proposes the reverse of any "totality," seems only to need accumulation of the most various fragments . . . The Villa Adriana is a miniature Rome. It plausibly reproduces all the collisions of set pieces and all the random empirical happenings which the city so lavishly exhibited . . . It is almost certain that the uninhibited aesthetic

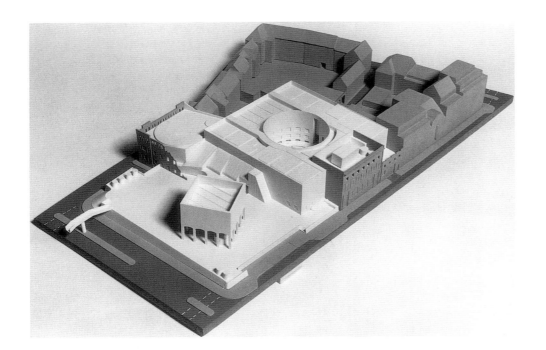

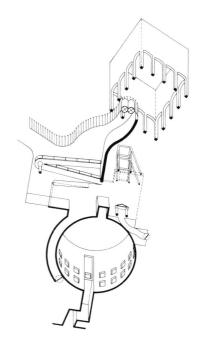

preference of today is for the structural discontinuities and the multiple syncopated excitements which the Villa Adriana presents ..., the bias of this [anti-hedgehog] argument should be clear, it is better to think of an aggregation of small, and even contradictory set pieces (almost like the products of different regimes) than to entertain fantasies about total and "faultless" solutions which the condition of politics can only abort.[41]

This argument for Collage City was, like that of *Adhocism*, based on the method of *bricolage* and the importance of memory in forming a base for prophecy and city design.[42] Rowe musters the examples of several historicists mentioned above – Lubetkin and Luigi Moretti – who juxtaposed past and present elements to gain a richer meaning.

Thus, a Post-Modern consensus had emerged by the midseventies. It was loosely centered on the urbanism entailed by many of the things we have looked at: Robert Venturi's Mannerism, the Kriers' and Aldo Rossi's Neo-Rationalism, the Contextualism and writings of Colin Rowe and Matthias Ungers and, above all, a worldwide eclectic practice that was growing fast. This paradigm, what could be called Complexity 1 (because the scientific theory of Complexity had yet to be formulated) is best represented by the Düsseldorf scheme of James Stirling (144, 145). Sadly it was never built because, had it been, Post-Modernism might have had a superb urban exemplar carried out by a brilliant architect.

At any rate it had the plans and models of this. So, by 1975, a leading architect uses *bricolage* as a technique to knit, and sometimes jam, the past and the present together, and mediate between that basic antinomy: the solid urban tissue and the void of the public realm. There are the obvious Post-Modern ironies. For instance, Stirling employs a wrap-around nineteenth-century façade on one side to fit

144 JAMES STIRLING, *Düsseldorf Museum Project*, 1975. A sensitive example of contextual infill, where the height, scale and masonry of the area are respected, but the symbolic elements are still allowed expression. The entrance cube inflects from the grid and is also a major focus for site lines which relate to other monuments. The nineteenth-century façade to the left is wrapped around part of the new museum. Glass sheeting, the only Modernist remnant, is appropriately used as public circulation and congregation area. (John Donat).

145 JAMES STIRLING, Dusseldorf up-axonometric showing the route as an organizational device that unites opposite monumental types – open/closed, square/circular, industrial/ornamented.

into the context, and crumbles it away on the other, to signal the fact that it is false, a knowing pastiche. He pulls a pedestrian route from the more dense urban fabric into a circular court and then inverts this, dialectically, into a square object (the ground has become the figure, the circle squared). This pronounced object is then inflected on its podium to acknowledge a major city axis and act as a focusing monument – becoming thereby one more in a neighborhood group. With its understated Classical references, this project crystallized the new stage in urbanism. It showed a Modern architect acting with the kind of sensitivity towards the historical context one would expect of a traditionalist, but with the freshness and invention of a Renaissance designer, a clear example of double-coding. While unbuilt, the project nevertheless became well known and thereby a stepping stone to the best Post-Modern work of the 1980s, especially Stirling's own buildings at Stuttgart, the epitome of this paradigm.

METAPHOR AND METAPHYSICS:
THE REVENGE OF THE MISSING BODY

Another motive causing architects to leave the Modern fold was its inability to pose general questions of architectural meaning. What was architecture "to be about," what subjects and metaphors would guide its generation? This question became especially pressing with the decline of belief in a progressive technology and the Machine Aesthetic. Architecture inevitably carries a signifying reference: the Renaissance had its Platonic metaphysics, the Romans their belief in Imperial organization – what, beyond a polite agnosticism, is our age to reflect?

We have seen that the failure of Modernism to communicate, as intended, its malapropism, was somewhat caused by not facing up to this question. But a few highly metaphorical buildings – Ronchamp, the Sydney Opera House, TWA, the Blue Whale – started to change the situation. These expressive and sculptural creations opened up a genre that was to become progressively more important over the next thirty years, the enigmatic signifier, the multi-layered building that suggested many more meanings than it explicitly named. This small movement of Post-Modernism, in the late 1970s, was to become its leading protagonist by the late 1990s.

It grew around meanings counter to mechanistic metaphors, especially ones related to body images and our continuity with the natural and animal kingdoms. The human body, the face, the symmetry of animal forms became the primitive foundations for a metaphysics that was immediate and relevant. This was not a neo-humanism; that philosophy had already been discredited by anthropologists, such as Claude Levi-Strauss, and Post-Modern thinkers, such as Thomas Berry, as too anthropocentric. Man is not, they argued persuasively, the measure of all things, as Greek and Renaissance architects believed, but rather a being typical of nature's self-organizing tendencies. As such he responds willingly and unconsciously to body images, the haptic metaphors of inside and out, up and down; that is, projections of his own internal body orientation. Even his description of architecture is colored by this imagery. Metaphors reveal these states. Buildings "lie on the horizon," or "rise up from it," have "a front" which is more acceptable than "a back" (just like living beings) and are "dressed up" or "plain."

The architects Charles Moore and Kent Bloomer analyzed such images in an important book of 1977, *Body, Memory and Architecture*, at just the time architects were designing anthropomorphic buildings. The authors claimed that body images and physical states form a fundamental model for the experience of the environment, and one not limited to the priority of sight.

> By combining the values and feelings that we assign to internal landmarks with the moral qualities that we impart to psychophysical co-ordinates, [right/left etc] we can imagine a model of

exceptionally rich and sensitive body meanings. It is a comprehensible model (because we "possess" it), although it is much more humanely complex than a mathematical matrix.[43]

For such reasons, the argument goes, the city is considered empty without its anthropomorphic organs, particularly a central "heart," or equivalent to the main piazza. The house has more such *foci*. We project onto it not only a heart (the hearth) but, as Carl Jung pointed out, the whole anatomy of the face and body.[44] In his example, an eighteenth-century Hebrew text, the turrets of the house are the ears, the furnace is the stomach and the windows, as usual, are the eyes. As previously mentioned, the house is often perceived as a face and found to be decapitated, as when Le Corbusier or Van Eyck gave it a flat roof.

During the Renaissance, such body images were conventionalized and incorporated into architectural dimensions (146). The human body was inscribed both into the plan and

146 MAISON DES CARIATIDES, 28 rue Chaudronnerie, Dijon, *c*.1610. Something like 37 heads decorate this house, perhaps too many even for a Mannerist. The mixing of architectural and human members is quite extraordinary in its ingenuity. Note, for instance, the careful asymmetries set against the ordered use of pilaster-people. Windows, doors, chimneys and other places of transition were celebrated with complex metaphors, quite appropriate for the erogenous zones of architecture.

elevation of churches, and the metaphor was taken so serious-ly that Bernini was even criticized because his piazza for St. Peter's resulted in a contorted figure with mangled arms.[45] Any doubt about the potency of body images is quickly dis-pelled by counting the caryatids, herms, terms and so forth that climb over buildings, or hold them up, throughout Europe. Aix-en-Provence is a veritable menagerie of funny faces and strange races, Vienna a children's ward (it contains an old apartment gaining support from ten-foot high, giant babies).

Post-Modern architects transformed this tradition, some-times at the scale of a whole building. Thus Minoru Takeyama's Beverly Tom Hotel, 1974, became shaped like a Shinto *tenri* symbol, that is to say a phallus — a symbol repeated throughout the hotel in the details, right down to the ashtrays (147). Why, beyond the Japanese convention, this image? It is clear that the vertical shape may have led to the symbol, and hotels are, in a sense, corridors of power; but neither rationalization sufficiently explains the form, which seems to be the abstract statement of primitive power meant to contrast with the industrial landscape. Thirty years later Jean Nouvel explicitly calls on this idea, as well as the fact that in some cultures, such as the Indian, it has been openly dealt with in a religious context. If previous societies can so openly celebrate sexual potency, why, Nouvel asks, can architects not make it something mysterious and beautiful, especially in a vertical building? And so he does, in Barcelona (148).

Stanley Tigerman also used explicit metaphors to gener-ate architecture: the Animal Cracker House, Hot Dog House, Zipper apartments and again a phallus-shaped building called euphemistically the Daisy House (149, 149a). Here the

147 MINORU TAKEYAMA. *Hotel Beverly Tom*, Hokkaido, 1973–74. Eighty rooms are syncopated in three-quarters of the cylinder: a restau-rant and roof garden are indicated by other syntactic changes. The phallic form is coded with other, functional meanings.

148 JEAN NOUVEL, *Torre Agbar*, Barcelona, 2001–3. Located on the main diagonal route, the landmark tower is a straightforward phallus, given a diaphanous skin that glistens in semi-transparency. Among other precedents, Nouvel invokes the Indian tradition of explicit sexual symbol-ism, among other precedents. (Nouvel).

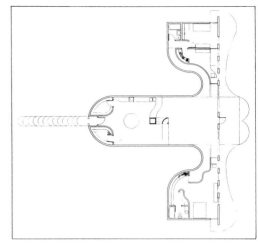

150 Below: *Gable Watching in Amsterdam*. The faces of these buildings are as different and engaging as those in typical portraits of Dutch burghers. Animals as well as the face and body are also present in the decoration.

149 Above and top right: STANLEY TIGERMAN, *Daisy House*, Indiana. 1976–77. The plan and parts of the elevation mapped with varying degrees of subtlety to well-known parts of the male and female anatomy. These shapes, partly due to the client's wishes, are again finished off with a series of oppositions: the flat, stucco wall versus textured cedar curves, the rectilinear window grid versus curvilinear viewing panes. One blank side is for public entrance and kitchen, the other flat side for viewing the lake. This last elevation is a transformation of the plan which visually implies that the phallus continues forward on to the deck and the windows go on into the ground. (Tigerman).

justification came from the client, who had seen the Hot Dog House and wanted something visually edible too. Various lubricious reasons led to the final form, perhaps the most printable being that Tigerman wanted to make his client laugh. At any rate, the point is not so much whether Tigerman's or Takeyama's similes are ultimately justifiable and profound, but rather that, unlike Modern architects, they realize the importance of the metaphorical plane of expression. The results may be raw, but the architect has *intended* to use this mode of speech, formerly confined to the commercial sector with its giant donuts and hot dogs. These buildings are not the misfired malaprops of Modernism, but the over-fired similes of PM in its first stage.

One of the most persuasive metaphors of the house has been the suggested face. Children often draw their home this way; it is normal to project, empathetically, human feelings and dimensions onto building. Other anthropomorphic parts have been represented in traditional architecture — a balance of supports suggesting legs, a bodily symmetry, a proportion suggesting human ratios of arm to torso — that have given it a familiarity and welcome disposition. The row houses of Amsterdam with their high, pitched gables, symmetrical visage and face-like orifices, stare out like so many prosperous burghers in a guild portrait by Rembrandt (150). This metaphor, a commonplace for centuries, is coded in such a way that the contradiction between competition and civic pride is directly portrayed. Each visage is given equal weight in these "cheek by jowl" façades.

Furthermore, the coding is mixed and ambiguous, unlike, say, the face buildings of the Italian Renaissance: the Zuccaro Palace in Rome, (151) and the faces at the garden of Bomarzo. These so over-code the forms that the face, as it is meant to, alienates, or mystifies.

The Japanese architect Kazumasu Yamashita has taken

151 FEDERICO ZUCCARO. *Palazzo façade*, Via Gregoriano, Rome. *c.*L592. The metaphor of windows as eyes is here dislocated to the mouth. The doorway grimaces, the windows smile. Note how pediments, keystones and cornucopia intersect the face. Is this the conventional entrance to Hades?

152 KAZUMASA YAMASHITA, *Face House*, Kyoto, 1974. You are swallowed by a scowl, the eyes bulge, the nose needs plastic surgery. Such literalism suggests a question – "Ah, but where are the ears?" (Ryuji Miyamoto).

this strand of the tradition to its logical conclusion in Kyoto. Here his Face House, with its round eyes and gun-barrel nose, scowls and yells and ultimately swallows the inhabitant (152). By mapping the forms so literally the metaphor becomes reductive: "home" it says, "is nothing but an inscrutable face." This reductivism, always a danger of simile, should be contrasted with the Amsterdam examples or the popular bungalows in America with their multi-projecting foreheads, or with the anthropomorphic creations of Bernard Maybeck.

A similar mixed coding is possible in several buildings where the image is not seen at first. A studio in Cape Cod has the normal pitched roof, while the mouth, teeth and eyebrows are more purely architectural in their suggestion, and even the explicit eyes and nose are here familiar enough architectural elements to seem merely arches and a plane (153). The face is then perhaps not immediately recognizable; at least it was intended to be subliminal and work as an extension to the architectural meanings, providing them with a penumbra of vague feeling. In London a curved archform above a stagger is used throughout the house. Because of its symmetry, curves and set-backs it maps onto a head and tree equally well. On the garden façade the mapping is still both literal and functional, part of opposite systems. Thus one can read the windows and arches at the top as children who overlook two parents, who stand at the base with shoulders, legs, and a belt of small windows; or, conversely, just see the white forms as large window walls that open and close (154).

Michael Graves, before his work became so explicitly representational, used anthropomorphism in a suggested way. He elaborated windows, doorways, and profiles, the erogenous zones of architecture, to call attention to their syntactical role (155). The intention was also to dramatize the everyday human experience of familiar actions, standing beside a window ledge, holding it and gazing out, noticing the visual juncture between the ceiling and sky (what he termed "the celestial soffit"). The bodily metaphors are here much more general and implied than they became in the middle eighties, the point when Graves became more completely wedded to Classicism.

In the late seventies, Post-Modernism touched a nerve in Communist countries, particularly those underground groups of architects in Czechoslovakia, Poland and Hungary under Soviet domination. One was the Group Pécs, from a city of that name in Hungary and another was led, in the same country, by Imre Makovecz. A common concern was the way buildings might express local meanings coming from the body and landscape. Like the Pécs group, Makovecz, the son of a carpenter, was producing extraordinarily expressive work in wood that continued natural themes like the shape of a hill, or the curve of the head (156).

At his mortuary hall at the Farkasret cemetery, the inte-

153 CHARLES JENCKS, *Garagia Rotunda*, Wellfleet, 1977. Symmetrical ends of pitched buildings often produce a physiognomic expression quite by chance. Here the face is partly in purdah, with the teeth basement hidden by shrubbery. The metaphor is somewhat veiled as a geometric pattern of arches and verticals.

154 CHARLES JENCKS with TERRY FARRELL, *Thematic House*, London, 1979–84. Veiled face and body motifs are tied with functional and natural elements: man, woman, two children and a dog. Such mixed coding is taken through the rest of the house.

155 MICHAEL GRAVES, *Plocek House*, Warren. New Jersey, 1978–82. The windows and details form an implicit image of the face.

156 Above right: IMRE MAKOVECZ, *Richter House*, Budapest, 1985. The head buried in the earth, a primitive and popular sign of house, is manipulated with functional and typological solutions – garage and double dome – to create a pleasing ambiguity.

157 Left: IMRE MAKOVECZ, *Cultural Center*, Sárospatak, Hungary, 1979-83. The face and eyebrows of an animal are hard to escape, and perhaps acceptable in a cultural center; but what makes his best work interesting is the way images flow from the constructional possibilities of wood and shingle. Compared to the latent metaphors of Ronchamp and the Bilbao Guggenheim – enigmatic signifiers – Makovecz's buildings are more explicit yet still multivalent.

158 Above: IMRE MAKOVECZ, *Cultural Center interior*, a mixed structural metaphor combining trees and coffers.

rior is shaped like a mouth, rib-cage, or animal stomach – depending on the view. The space is formed by thousands of curved slats, a tectonic use of structure and an undulating, anthropomorphic, or zoomorphic space. Many of his buildings are half-embedded in the earth, and are meant to be seen as emerging from the ground like a primitive animal. The motive of this half-buried architecture is to conserve energy and symbolize a continuity with nature. Where Peter

Eisenman will use a similar rhetorical device to signify a digging into the unconscious, Makovecz will employ it to suggest a ritual return to Mother Earth, even a burial mound. This, combined with a few historicist signs, led the Hungarian press to criticize his work for "reviving romantic rural ideas from the past." He tacitly acknowledges the

159 ERIC MOSS, *Hayden Tract*, Culver City, LA, 1993–94. A face with a
hat in black, a portrait of the owner, is combined with other metaphors
and architectural elements – stairway, railing and domed skylight.

point when referring to "this provincialism that characterizes our country," and his respect for folk architecture. But
he also transforms these sources within his own syntax of
undulating, forms in wood.

One can find the influence of Rudolph Steiner and
Anthroposophy in the domes and eyebrow motifs that punctuate his shingled, scaly figurations. For Makovecz, like his
mentors in the organic tradition, architecture does three
things: it relates a building directly to the site, it is based on
flowing, biomorphic spaces, and it promotes an empathetic
response. To these qualities he adds a fourth refinement
which he calls "canonic." By this means, a building will
have symmetrical axes, like the human body, but also have
asymmetrical additions or displacements where these are
justified by a special organ or function. Thus one has to perceive his compositions, like that of other Post-Modernists, as
based on the rhetorical figure of asymmetrical symmetry.

This can be seen in the rural buildings he has built since the
sixties – hostels, tourist camps, restaurants, department stores
and one of his few urban commissions, the Sárospatek
Cultural Center (157, 158). Fundamentally a U-shaped structure that culminates in a central "head," like a symmetrical
French château, the left "arm" of this building has an embedded rectangular restaurant that is skewed in plan and slightly
different in geometry from the flowing biomorphic forms.
These portray the character of a brooding, moving creature –
a slumbering animal to some, and a menacing crab to others.
Whatever the image, it is decidedly animalistic and powerful
with its hooded eyes fixed on the approaching visitor.

The exterior of the Cultural Center is again also reminiscent of farmyard barns and, oddly, Japanese temples with their
strong emphasis on the roof volume. Here dark slates roll over
head, shoulders and arms, all of which rest above an underbelly in light-colored concrete. Inside the space flows towards
the culminating auditorium, a dark-red, wooded forest of tim-

bers which reach up to support a gridded ceiling. Makovecz
wanted this central space to undulate even more, like the thorax of his mortuary hall, but the contrast between the generalized grid and the leaping struts is a welcome compromise. It
gives this meeting hall an appropriately mixed mood.

The most successful work that probes this territory of
metaphor is ambiguous, allowing architecture to assert its realities while, at the same time, responding to areas outside
the profession. An example of such veiled anthropomorphism in the nineties is Eric Owen Moss' work in Culver
City, Los Angeles (159). Renovating old warehouses here,
he has transformed the former utilitarian sheds into new
offices and mixed-use structures. One, with a characteristic
mixture of structural types, portrays the logo of a company,
the owner in a hat, below a fractured dome over the
entrance. The face motif in black is part of a weave of more
purely architectural elements and several languages mixing the vernacular, Pop and Modern. It is also the culmination of the type of labyrinthine space that has become the
hallmark of Post-Modern ambiguity.

POST-MODERN SPACE – THE LIMINAL

Modern Architecture often took as its main subject matter
the articulation of space, that is, abstract space as the content of the form. The origins of this go back to the nineteenth century and Germany when space, *Raum*, void etc.,
had a kind of metaphysical priority. Not only was space the
essence of architecture, its ultimate stuff, but also each culture expressed its will and existence through this medium.
Sigfried Giedion's "space-concepts" are the culmination of
this tradition, just as are the Bauhaus, the Barcelona
Pavilion and the Villa Savoye – these buildings illustrated
Giedion's ideas of transparency and "space-time perception." Another tradition of Modern space, perhaps stronger,
comes through the "rational" Chicago frame and its development by Le Corbusier in the domino block. Here space is
seen as isotropic, homogeneous in every direction, although
layered in grids at right angles to the frontal plane and floor
lines. The ultimate development of this warehouse space is
in the vast, enclosed halls of Mies van der Rohe and his followers. Besides being isotropic, it can be characterized as
abstract, limited by boundaries or edges, and rational or logically inferable from part to whole, or whole to part.

PM space, opposed to the Miesian version, is worth summarizing as a type. It is historically specific, rooted in conventions, ambiguous in zoning and transformational in its
relation of parts to whole. The boundaries are often left
unclear, the space extended infinitely without apparent
edge. Like other aspects of Post-Modernism, however, it is
evolutionary, not revolutionary, and thus it contains Modern
qualities – particularly the layering and compaction composition developed by Le Corbusier.[46] His La Roche house,

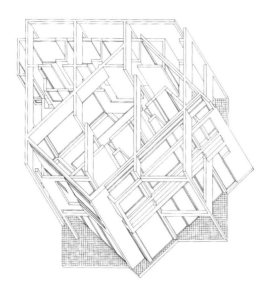

160, 161 PETER EISENMAN, *House III* for Robert Miller, Lakeville, 1971. A careful collision at 45 degrees of structure, volume, function, space, wardrobes, and what-have-you. Following through these collisions rigorously makes one expect the presence, or absence, of a diagonal – an architecture of implication. (Martin Tomallyay).

162 PETER EISENMAN, *House VI* for the Franks, Washington. Connecticut, 1975. The back of the house continues the theme of a large, flat plane placed frontally to the approach, and lesser motifs placed at right angles to the direction of movement. Note the column lines marked on the outside either as an extended pilaster, or a wedge of space between two volumes. The front door is around to the left, the main bedroom is on the first floor to the right, above the living room. Find the hanging column in the middle, if you can. (Norman McGrath).

1923, develops what would become several of the PM themes: back-lighting, punched-out screen space, and the implication of infinite extension created by overlapping planes. To these formal motifs Robert Venturi added the skew or distorted space, created by sharp angles that exaggerate perspective and, above all, ambiguous space. This last can be seen in the house designed for his mother, especially by the entrance. Here entryway, closet, stairway and fireplace all interact and interpenetrate giving a series of "both-and" readings. The off-axis, curved entry, a device that Lutyens often used, gives one a pleasant surprise since it contrasts with the large, axial archway overhead.

Both Venturi and Peter Eisenman vastly increased the complexity of Le Corbusier's compaction composition. The juxtaposition of a few bold elements produced a major traffic accident of collisions. Where before a few cardboard cutouts had existed, the walls were now carved up like paper-dolls, and layered on top of each other like a patch-work quilt. If Le Corbusier's space is a Cubist collage, then PM space is a Schwitters' *Merz*. Indeed, one could say it developed indirectly from Kurt Schwitters' great *Merzbau*, the column of memories that he constructed inside his house, and which was a literal accretion of every aspect of his life. Unfortunately the assemblage was destroyed by the Nazis.

With Eisenman's and Graves' early work, the spaces always keep a mental co-ordinate system, no matter how free-form and Baroque they become. The grid is implied as the reference plane. This means that the route through the building, or curvilinear elements, are related to a conceptual cage of space perceived frontally. This frontality and the

163 The absent column marching through ceiling, roof and floor divides the marital bed. Originally it opened right up into the living room below.

164 PETER EISENMAN, Two steps of transformation drawing for *House VI*. One can see the stairs, real and virtual, existing in counterpoint; the two reference planes, real and virtual; and the underlying presence or absence of the column grid. The general grid layering is kept throughout, thus continuing the movement in frontal and 90 degree turns. But there is a slight shift of reference planes on the diagonal, 45 degrees.

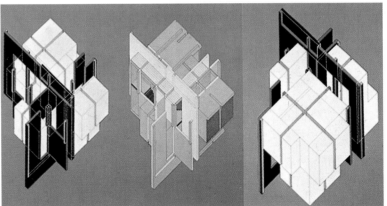

rotation away from it, as we have seen, was a hallmark of Eisenman's House III (160, 161).

His House VI, although ultra-Modern in its abstraction, employs certain humorous touches and a complex space that are definitely PM (162, 163). Not only does one staircase run upside-down over another, an Esher-like impossibility, but columns, instead of supporting, hang six inches off the ground. These playful conceits are carried out with remorseless seriousness, in order to underline the syntactic qualities of the building, and as often with the best jokes they are unintentional. Columns play their tricks with ruthless logic.

They are painted shades of gray and off-white – anything but a color – to indicate their load-bearing role, or their mechanical function, or their decorative use, or for no reason at all. Thus, as one explores the house one becomes sensitized to these variations, the column features as a redundant character in a very amusing and aesthetic drama. It may be in one of the four states mentioned above, or – and this is most extraordinary – its absence may be indicated as a rectangular cut in a surface or a volume (as the drawings show). This *absent* column cuts through the roof, wall and even floor, wreaking its havoc on domesticity (such is Eisenman's

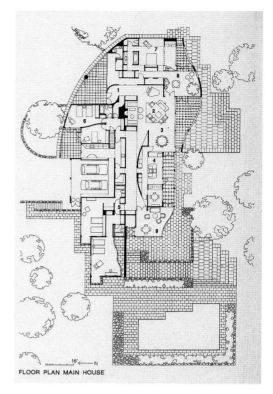

FLOOR PLAN MAIN HOUSE

165 ROBERT STERN and JOHN HAGMANN, *Westchester Residence*, Armonk, NY, 1974–76. Pool front with fragmented signs relating to Classical architecture, Frank Lloyd Wright and Tuscany (the light ocher paint is stopped by a thin, virtual cornice of two red bands). An odd scale and tension are setup with the woods and rusticated base: the stuccoed wall seems too small and thin for the base – as if it would be blown away into the woods. This fragility and delicacy is presented in such great contrast that it may be termed Mannerist, frustrating.

166 *Westchester interior*. Space is stretched along a major axis that connects the master bedroom (7) to the sun-porch (9). Parallel with this axis are five minor planes of space, also layered frontally to the entrance (1). The way space is brought in and out across these axes is delightful, if hard to read. The curving wall disappears into a colonnade and screen to then emerge again.

questioning of function). It divides a dining table, it even divides the marital bed of the Frank family in two (164). A false step or leap and one would land in the living room, or would have until the Franks glazed over the void cut by this conceptual ordering device.

The column has further revenge in the master bedroom as it transforms into a door. Ever seen a door as a column that rotates? And in three shades of gray and white? It is easy to imagine the problem. When the column is "closed," there is still about two feet of open space letting in all that noise, and the unwelcome guest. But there is another surprise. This Duchampian door (he also created a paradoxical one that closed while it opened), this pivoting column which is "not a door/door," is startling beautiful as a volumetric object and very playful in its context. As a single conceit it may be questionable, but as the transformation of a theme, well prepared for in advance, it is delightful and even sensual. One of the unlikely things about this building is that the internal coding, the consistent self-reference of elements, more than makes up for the lack of any external reference. While the Purist language of Eisenman may be Modern, his semantic and haptic use of it is very PM.

Robert Stern's early houses also have the linear, cardboard quality of the International Style behind them. They employ vast planes of pure white wall separated by primary colors and good-taste abstractions. By contrast with Eisenman, they defer to the context and popular-signs, because Stern believes in the importance of "inclusivism" (he was taught by Venturi at Yale).[47] His design for a residence in Westchester County continues the amusing spatial tricks we have seen, but combines these with a variety of Modern motifs (165, 166). Careful asymmetries slide across an off-white (light ocher) plane. There is an absence of sills and of decorative articulation where one expects them, except for the two bands of red at the top (is this a diminutive cornice, or a misplaced stringcourse?).

A further mannerism features the exaggeratedly flat fieldstone terraces, again without the copings and horizontal ornaments one would expect in a more traditional building. The interior carries on the mixed coding with bold splashes of color used to accentuate the volumes, Art Deco versions of a Le Corbusier interior, so pure, light and undecorated is it. The notion of fragmenting references becomes important to Stern, as it does to Graves, and here it leads to the unfin-

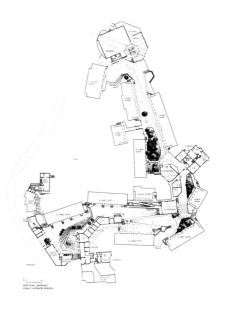

167 CHARLES MOORE and WILLIAM TURNBULL, *Kresge College*, 1972–74, University of California at Santa Cruz, L972–74. The two storey arcade and entrance stairs, are slightly exaggerated here in scale as are the conventional number plaques. Complicated rhythms are set up which run through the whole scheme like a Mannerist palazzo: here ABCBCDBAC. The porches which serve for sunning and street-watching are painted underneath in strong primary reds and yellows. (Morley Baer).

168 CHARLES MOORE and WILLIAM TURNBULL, *Kresge College*. A meandering route threaded through a redwood forest has defines each plaza with a monument. Many buildings set up their own rhythmical systems rather like Hadrian's Villa, but here on a linear L-route. The sense of place was further underlined by creating opposite activities at two ends of the scheme – Post Office and entrance arena at bottom, and assembly/dining areas at the top. Hence the street is well used and keeps students going from one side to the other. A complex water works and orange trees reinforce the Spanish image: a laundromat stands for the "village well," and telephone kiosks are turned into major archways. (Morley Baer).

ished form. For instance, the south façade is partially unified by broken S-curves and by broken string-courses and planes in sheer, that is to say, fragmented motifs lifted from the Baroque and Edwin Lutyens. The plan also contains half forms: that is, semi-circles, semi-ovals, semi-rectangles and a semi-spine of circulation, fragments that de-mand completion in the imagination.

The handling of such space is suggestive, complex and diffuse, without the obvious unities of Modern architecture. As all the plans shown here suggest, PM space is labyrinthine, rambling, without a definite goal, a liminal or in-between space that mediates between pairs of antinomies. By doing this it suspends the normal categories of time and meaning built up in everyday architecture, sometimes becoming thereby impossible to figure out.

Charles Moore adopts these ideas of liminal space but ties them to recognizable images of place. His Kresge College dormitories in California combine many historical memories that are only vaguely presented, mixing the Chinese garden with a tight Italian hill town (167, 168). The feeling of the Mediterranean village is more overt and reinforced by several cues: large white planes, a public, two-storey

arcade, and angular junctions between the volumes. But whereas the southern European village gives stability and a sense of permanence with stone, Kresge is made from cardboard-like wood. Thus a feeling of insubstantiality is created at the very point that the metaphor of enclosure is about to be consummated and, in like manner, the references to the Spanish Steps, the *Arc de Triomphe*, the cascades and waterways of the Alhambra – all memories Moore has absorbed on his many travels – call into question their present use.

Is this a kind of haute vulgarization, or pastiche? Perhaps the first. Moore has spoken, not pejoratively, about whimsy and nostalgia in architecture and this work has some of the virtues and vices of both. On the negative side, we can see how the insubstantiality combines with the bright supergraphics to elicit the student epithet, "Clown Town." But by and large these meanings are overtaken by the stronger metaphors of place, which he has intended.

Kresge College mixes the very personal scale of a village with the calculated surprise of a walk through a garden. The two-storey arcades have varying syncopated rhythms, combined with syncopated colors behind them, to increase the

169 FRANK GEHRY, *Santa Monica House*, 1978–79. A 1920s pastiche has been cut up on the inside and layered on the outside creating a series of disparate and aggressive readings between past and present, low and high life. Gehry here perfected the "unfinished building as finish."

170 FRANK GEHRY. The answer to Mies van der Rohe's problem of the corner – planes bisecting and sliding past.

171 FRANK GEHRY, Interior of the exterior. The kitchen-dining room eats the outside of the old house, while several volumes tumble through it. Light and space spill through all the additions and subtractions.

feelings of suspense and discovery. Since, in plan, the buildings pinch in perspective they heighten the sense of movement; as various "anti-monuments" punctuate the route – post office, laundromat, telephone altar, etc., – there is some content, however banal, to anticipate and pull students from one end of the site to the other. Moore has justified this low-keyed approach as fitting for the modest, egalitarian role of the student dormitory:

> All the inhabitants are students, there for four or five years together. So it seemed important to us to establish, not just a set of institutional monuments along the street to help give a sense of place to the whole, and a sense of where one was in one's passage up the street, but rather to make a set of trivial monuments. [To turn] things like drainage ditches into fountains, the laundromat façade into a speaker's rostrum, with garbage collection under...[48]

If we contrast this dormitory village with others built at the time its virtues are more apparent. As opposed to Mies van der Rohe's IIT, for instance, it is carefully set in its context. Thus the backs of the buildings, in wood painted ocher, are sympathetic to the forest, and the buildings slide this way and that to avoid existing redwoods. Opposed to the predictable spaces of rational architecture, there is always a twist and surprise; where different functions are abstracted in Modern building they are here accentuated with different colors and the presence of everyday objects.

At the end of the seventies, Frank Gehry, in a house he converted for his family, pushes PM space in a yet more complex direction. An old 1920s salmon-pink house in Santa Monica is wrapped and punctuated by corrugated metal and chain-link fences (169). These materials, even more cheapskate than those Moore used at Kresge, were used in the neighboring houses and it was Gehry's insight to see that he could take this repudiated vernacular and turn it to new ends. The neighbors were at first outraged at his making a high art out of their low reality, but as the building became one of the most celebrated *ad hoc* confections in America, opinion began to change. Like the Arte Povera movement, Gehry could take the mundane materials that people use to

incarcerate themselves and treat their neighbors like crimi-
nals, and then use them not only to keep his children from
falling off the roof but as flying wedges (170). Chain-link
doubled or overlapped could also create magical interference
patterns. Suddenly junk was sculpture.

Spatially the *ad hoc* reconstruction grew from the work I
have mentioned and Gehry's previous experiments. Various
parts of the conventional house were ripped away, its studs
and foundations exposed to indicate the reality of construction and bring this to attention. Windows are centered, and
the grid is warped to produce a perspectival diminishment.
On the prominent external corner, the place that Mies van der
Rohe had spent so much time trying to achieve an ideal meeting of two planes, Gehry stops one plane and lets the other
slide past effortlessly, mocking, as it were, the perfect solution.

The virtue of the space is its layering of surprising views.
New frames old, or vice-versa; high collides with low and

refinement with Punk. When outside the original house and
walking on black tar, it is surprising to find oneself really on
the inside of a new kitchen (171). Or, when looking through
the old living room, with studs now exposed, one is amazed
to find a sunken aedicule outside the old, but inside the new.
All boundaries are thus broken, borders transgressed, and
experience thereby slowed down and turned inside-out. It is
this transgression, and elision of elements, that is at once
mysterious and full of surprise, a kind of ultimate liminal
experience.

On paper, at least, these collisions, complexities and paradoxical qualities were pushed even further by Daniel
Libeskind in his series of drawings called *Micromegas*, of

172 DANIEL LIBESKIND, *Maldoror's Equation*, drawing, 1979. Although
more densely packed, many of Libeskind's later forms are evident here, a
liminal space taken to its limit.

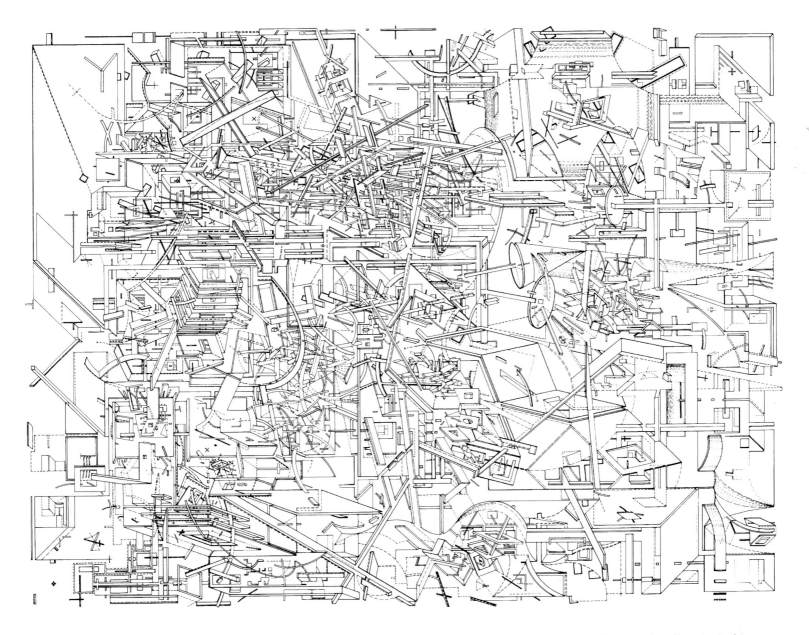

1979. Exhibited under the subtitle "The Architecture of End Space," they reveal his basic grammar of exploration. Their most obvious quality is the way they explode a normal space of measured dimensions and right angles. At first glance they defeat any attempt at decoding, an obvious intention in itself and one to which we must willingly submit in order to appreciate them. Their musical and thematic transformations swarm over the surface from one edge to another, eating up the available area as if they were stick-like bacteria consuming a host. In a poster for the 1979 drawings Libeskind even put a cross through the words "End Space," as if he wanted to terminate everyday space for good. Some of the drawings are based on suggestive contradictions: "Little Universe," "Vertical Horizon" and "Dream Calculus." The drawing "Arctic Flowers" is not so much an oxymoron as an implication that strange flowers – thin rectangular ones in this case – can grow in a very cold climate, like ice crystals.

What are the intentions behind these haunting words and dense complexities? Mystery, contradiction, confusion, endlessness, a new intuitive ordering, an open aesthetic? If one wants to get into this uncanny world of End Space, start with simple parts, such as the upper right-hand corner of the drawing called *Maldoror's Equation* (172). Study the elements (cross, reverse perspective, dashes, layering, cocktail sticks etc.,) until you understand the fractal, a small bit of the self-similar grammar. Then multiply it endlessly, rotate its axes, and increase its density in parts. The result is the fractal composition common to good music that, as many have pointed out, is a mixture of expectation and surprise. Libeskind, trained as a musician, follows the convention knowingly, and writes of "The conflict between the Voluntary and the Involuntary." Order and chaos, theme and variation, unity and variety, we have heard these formulae repeated in music and architecture from the beginning of each profession. So the basic method of Libeskind is common in aesthetic theory.

What is new, in his architecture and drawing, is the intensity and density of contradiction and the tilting of the ground plane. A basic right-angled geometry may underline the lines, and certainly defines the edges of his paper, but within this order there is liminal space, or his End Space. What is liminal space? If in architecture it is that of the labyrinth, then in society it is that of the theatre and ritual. When present at a transition in life, while attending a funeral or wedding, space-time looses visual co-ordinates and becomes liminal or endless.

It is quite obvious that Libeskind has different intentions from Stern and Moore in the semantics of this liminal space. There are differences of abstraction and reference as well, but these important distinctions should not blind us to the similar elaboration of a new type of paradoxical space. Beyond this is another similarity. As we will see, Libeskind finally started building this kind of morphology fifteen years later in many projects, particularly the Jewish Museum in Berlin. Here the content, or specific semantic meaning becomes the essential determinant of the form and it communicates well, at many levels and to many different kinds of people. In this sense the museum carries on the agenda of deriving a public language of architecture. Furthermore, its content is related to the many Holocaust museums under construction in the early 1990s, and facing up to the tragedies of Modernity remains, of course, a key motivation of Post-Modernism.

So, a tradition of exploration that starts with the skews and complexities of Venturi and Eisenman reaches a kind of culmination in the abstract, but evocative, paradoxes of Libeskind. These are given oxymoronic meaning to displace normal perception, to move it in a spiritual or psychic direction or, at least, "beyond the utterable." But, like Modernism before it, there were many strands to PM, and it is to others that developed in the 1980s that we now turn.

Radical Eclecticism

Between 1978 and 1981, Post-Modernism took off as a worldwide movement in all the arts, especially architecture. Jean-François Lyotard gave this movement impetus and direction with his *La Condition Postmodern*, 1979, and thus started a debate internal to the field that has continued to the present, a dialogue of difference that has helped not hurt its development. Along with other French philosophers such as Jean Baudrillard, Lyotard stressed the negative aspects of the condition: the scepticism towards all belief systems, the relativism and anything-goes eclecticism. These strictures had their point when aimed at the *condition*, but by contrast, I was defending a nascent *movement* — a much more focused change — and the possible evolution of an eclecticism that was not weak and just consumerist, but thoughtful and radical. Radical Eclecticism would speak to a plural audience in many tongues; it would adopt appropriate ornament to represent function, and it would "eclect," or "select," quotes and use them in ironic ways to signal our present predicament. Radical Eclecticism started to emerge just as Post-Modernism exploded onto the world stage.

What changed the architectural scene? The shift of three major architects in a Post-Modern direction: Hans Hollein, Aldo Rossi and James Stirling. The turnabout of large American practitioners in New York and Chicago, SOM and KPF, leaving their previous faith in favor of the new creed. An international exhibition at the Venice Biennale launching the common direction. Finally various *success de scandales*, such as Charles Moore's design for the Piazza d'Italia, Michael Graves' for the Portland Public Services Building and Philip Johnson for the AT&T in New York. Negatively, these three media events branded PM in some people's minds as Pop Classicism, a stereotyping that reduced the plural movement to a single strand (and then to PoMo). Postively, they put it on the map (or at least the cover of mass-market weeklies). A movement, started to deal with the problem of communication, itself began to exemplify the problem.

At the same time several architects such as Philip Johnson and Helmut Jahn began to zig-zag between Late and Post-Modern design in successive works, further confusing the public.[49] The Late-Modern buildings exaggerated such concerns as the technological image of a building (its circulation, logic and structure) whereas PM architects, in their desire to communicate with a plural audience, double-coded their buildings, that is produced an eclectic mix of local and Modern codes. A good example of a young architect mixing these codes in a very self-possessed way is a member of the group known as the Chicago Seven, Thomas Beeby.[50]

Significantly he worked out this synthesis for a row of different houses, a solution-type that became the PM alternative to the superblock. In a town house project for Chicago,

Beeby discovered an almost inevitable conjunction between Neo-Palladianism and Neo-Mies that was elegant in its crisp detailing and structuring of space (173). As one house in a row of varying contextual buildings, it mixed Modern structural grids with traditional aedicules and barrel vaults. The Classicism inherent in Mies is so close to Neo-Palladianism that when they are forced to meet in Beeby's work the conjunction seems an inevitable consequence of Palladian rules being followed in reinforced concrete and steel. Beeby also mixes iconography in a thoroughgoing manner so that the grotesque face of Hades in the basement grotto seems at home with the polished chrome dragster on the ground floor. The strength of this work is its sure handling of structure and complex spatial rhythms that read horizontally and vertically in syncopation. Each internal façade becomes a variation on the previous one and on the front Serliano. The ornament, such as it is, results directly from constructional elements — particularly the mullion, and in this way provides another bridge between Modern and traditional practice. It is as if Mies had gone Post-Modern, or at least back to his Schinkel period (and Beeby went on to produce countless larger buildings in this idiom).

Perhaps the most important aspect of these town houses is that they return to the American street tradition by combining individual variation within an overall street morphology. This tradition (which exists notably in San Francisco, Chicago and New York) was broken by Mod-

173 THOMAS BEEBY, *Townhouse Project*, Chicago, 1978. Based on Palladio's Villa Poiana, like lsozaki's Post-Modern work, with archetypal circles, rectangles and flat decorative detail, this townhouse also incorporates a Miesian structural logic on a five-foot module. A sequence of varying spatial character is defined with barrel vault, a dome over the stairs and subterranean grotto. (Thomas Beeby).

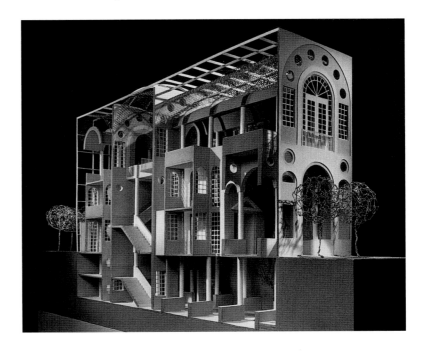

traditional language and requirements; the stereotypes are used in a relatively straightforward way, as stock as the London brick with which it is built.

But then, on further inspection, there are esoteric meanings more directly accessible to the architect, or the inhabitant who cares to search for them. Once again we find that favorite PM type, the physiognomic visage, the suggestion of a face, which is appropriately made by the front door (or rather the combination of two front doors over the traditional stoop). This face is also another preferred image, an aedicule, a "little house," the signifier of domesticity that had such a long history in the West since its first use in ancient Greece. Dixon masterfully repeats the aedicule form at different scales – in the windows, roof profiles and entrance gates – to unite a complex array of formal quotes (176). These vary from the Neo-Vernacular brick to the Dutch gable with its crow-step articulation, from Art Deco

176 JEREMY DIXON, *Self-Portrait as Face House*, 1980, makes explicit the implicit code.

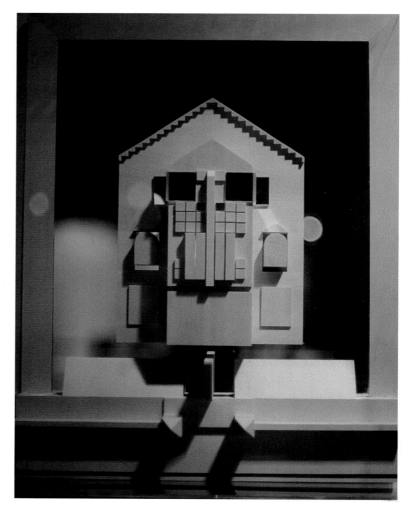

175 JEREMY DIXON, *St. Mark's Road*, London, 1976–79. Twenty-four houses and twenty flats placed on a tight site pick up the existing Edwardian street pattern and scale. By doubling the houses in a single, visual unit the appearance of a large house is kept; the angled plan, while an economic use of the site, produces odd internal conditions.

ernism. The Chicago town houses, variants of which were built everywhere, showed an elegant handling of stripped Classical detail and ornament that re-established an urban grain and incident. It was a small, but important step in the direction of personalized mass housing (174).

In Europe, similar types of scheme evolved with less individual expression for each house; in London, an early version of this infill architecture was completed in 1979. Jeremy Dixon designed a scheme that fitted into the nineteenth-century urban pattern both in plan and detail. Accepting the street lines and traditional layout, the bay windows of adjoining houses and their emphasis on the front door, the scheme manages to be both acceptably familiar and inventive (175). The inhabitants can recognize their ziggurats to Rationalist grids. Particularly ingenious is the way the aedicular gate-post becomes a cover for garbage cans on the house side.

In one respect, this scheme epitomizes the PM search for a rich, flexible language that stems from the locale. The language is eclectic, as mixed as the Queen Anne of a century ago and as responsive to particular cultural conditions. The attempt to derive such a language was also made by other architects in Amsterdam and Vienna, notably by the group called Missing Link (177). These young designers have undertaken empirical studies of pre-existing urban signs – the towers, gates, doors, street corners and court-yards of Vienna. Elegant line drawings are made of these recurrent motifs – "words" of the Viennese architectural language – and a new set of typologies is derived from them through a process of abstraction. Perhaps their design results do not yet completely forge the hoped-for "missing link" with the past, but their analyses show one way of proceeding towards that goal.

177 MISSING LINK (Otto Kapfinger and Adolf Krischanitz), *Vienna Studies*, 1977. A series of elegant line drawings of typical Viennese buildings. Here the Wohnhöfe (the public housing of the twenties), abstracts recurrent aspects of the local language – towers, gates, corners, court-yards, etc. From these studies a new eclectic whole is created which relates to the past. (Missing Link).

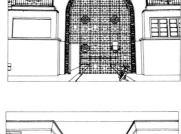

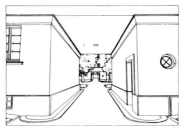

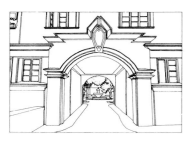

178 LEON KRIER, *Rome project*, Rome, 1978, for the Via Condotti and Via Corso. An international center and aeroport terminal are among the functions projected for this monument to a new public realm. Krier, as other Rationalists, both uses and distorts the existing language and morphology of the city, producing heroic images of a yet unborn society. The mixture of primitive construction and sophisticated technology is as striking as the contrasts with Piranesi. (Leon Krier).

All of this work was a loose part of Contextualism, and it is worth emphasizing that this movement did not seek merely to fit in with, or complete, the urban context, but also to contrast with and disrupt it. In some respects, Contextualism was always complex and contradictory. The goal was acknowledgement, not reproduction, of the past. Such distinctions become clear if one looks closely at Beeby and Dixon's housing, or the leader of Contextualism at this time, Leon Krier. His designs for Rome, and the other schemes produced for the show "Roma Interrotta," of summer 1978, are both contextual *and* disruptive; that is, based on the Nolli plan of Rome *and* opposed to its grain (178). Krier has, in typical Rationalist manner, reinvented the "primitive hut" of columns and triangular roof truss. It is, however, anything but primitive: each column is the size of an eight-storey tower! And the pyramidal roof encloses an awesome public realm, a cross between a train-shed and an open-air market. As if these disruptions were not enough, he has returned St. Peter's Basilica to its origins – a Roman Bath. The drawings, when seen collaged into the Roman perspectives of Piranesi, actually stand up to these grand and disturbing images. The public buildings have the breadth of scale and heavy gestural quality typical of the Roman tradition. They are meant to support a local form of civic organization, the *rione*, an alternative to the centralized bureaucracy and state. Each one would have restaurants, clubs, rooms for games and large top-floor studios for artists who would fabricate the syndicalist imagery.[51] The idea, as Krier describes it, is to revive the *res publico* and create new civic institutions which can support it, ones on a par with the seventeenth-century churches of Rome. For a short period, until Krier and others went over to a more straight Revivalism five years later, this collage of new and old was the preferred method. It was also like Colin Rowe's *Collage City*, a radical mixture of small political types: utopian syndicalism, neighborhood autonomy, and state intervention. The hybrid position characterized European Rationalists in Brussels, Barcelona, Paris and Italy generally.

A few scattered fragments of the idea were realized. Georgia Benamo and Christian de Portzamparc completed a small urban scheme, the Rue des Hautes-Formes, on the edge of Paris (179). This inevitably recreated the street, the square, the urban place but at greater density than in a traditional city. Tower and slab blocks of Modernism were combined and given a PM formal treatment of cut-out screens *à la* Moore, false hanging arches to signify entry *à la* Venturi and a variety of window treatments *à la mode*. The last is further justified as a method of breaking down the scale and reducing the feeling of being overlooked by a thousand eyes – something that would have resulted from an all-window version. If there are doubts about the scheme they concern the leaking space, the small size of the piazza and *res publica* and the neutralized relation of solid to void, urban poche to monument (the scheme lacks monuments). But these criticisms could be made of other PM schemes of the time: there was not the political will to realize a complex urbanism, as it was being taught by Rowe and others. That remained a dream.

Japanese Post-Modernists, however, supplied one way of dealing with the missing urban focus, and they did it with amusing metaphors and metaphysical conceits. Monta Mozuna and Hiroshi Hara used themes of the mandala and what they called "centered space" similar to those of Charles Moore and James Stirling. Hara wrote at the time: "Homogeneous space tends to atomize human relationships …if you agree that homogeneous space is negative and undesirable, then we must somehow regain control of the Post-Modern spatial order…a house…must possess a strong independent centre. This creates a regular order that is opposed to the surrounding homogeneous space outside."[52] His work, like the others', makes use of strong enclosures, repetitive grids, axial symmetries, mirror images, Palladian motifs and a religious handling of objects. Interior volumes are arranged as so many altars, hieratically fixed on an axis

of light that runs down the spine of the building, the "body image and heart" for which Charles Moore had called.

More Historicist in his metaphysical conceits is Kazuhiro Ishii, an architect who was trained under Moore at Yale. His "54 Windows," a house for a doctor, uses popular signs and color codes which he argues are regional in nature. And his Naoshima School transforms the Renaissance colonnade into a PM syncopated paradox (180). Here he actually leaves out columns, thus dealing with the Renaissance "problem of the corner" (that also exercised Mies) in an ironic way. But, unlike Mies, he indicates these problems with Mannerist jokes (hanging capitals of steel bars) so that the reference can be appreciated by non-architects.

The use of architectural humor was suddenly acceptable, if it made a public point. "Where is the front door?" was a question that plagued Modern designers. The group SITE responded with several large shopping centers that had odd twists, such as a front door that crumbled apart every morn-

179 GEORGIA BENAMO and CHRISTIAN DE PORTZAMPARC, *Rue des Hautes-Formes*, Paris, 1975–79. Hanging arches, a thick wall with various window types and a plan which acknowledges the street and central public realm.

180 KAZUHIRO ISHII, *Naoshimo School*, 1977. A colonnade and other traditional forms mediate a modern shed space behind. The complicated rhythm of the colonnade (A, B, A, C, A, B, 2A, C, A. C, A, B, 2A, C, A, B, A, C, 2A, C) syncopates Renaissance examples, while other historicist comments include "missing columns" (indicated by hanging capitals). (Ishii).

ing to announce the opening. Arata Isozaki designed a country club in Japan with a Roman barrel vault that ends in a Palladian motif and round green dot (181). The ensemble forms a giant question-mark, posing the metaphysical (and social) question: "why do the Japanese play golf?" Indeed, why? Implied answer: "because, like the Classical quotes, they help settle deals with the West."

Quotation and irony, the ability to send two opposite meanings at once, became the PM approach. Umberto Eco argued that this generic double-coding stemmed from the condition of living in an age of lost innocence, when everything had already been said. He explains our plight with an amusing example:

> I think of the postmodern attitude as that of a man who loves a very cultivated woman and knows he cannot say to her, "I love you madly," because he knows that she knows (and that she knows that he knows) that these words have already been written by Barbara Cartland. Still there is a solution. He can say, "As Barbara Cartland would put it, I love you madly." At this point, having avoided false innocence, having said clearly that it is no longer possible to speak innocently, he will nevertheless have said what he wanted to say to the woman: that he loves her; but he loves her in an age of lost innocence.[53]

In other words, to labor the point, if architects are going to use past conventions, as they must do in order to communicate, then they have to signal the already said. This signalling gives their forms and ornament a subversive meaning counter to the revivalists, that is it subverts tradition from within it.

181 ARATA ISOZAKI, *Fujima Country Club*, 1975. A barrel vault twists into the form of a metaphysical question-mark and it ends with a version of Palladio's Villa Poiana. It asks — why Palladio in a Japanese country-club, why do the Japanese play golf? (M. Arai, *The Japan Architect*).

By the early 1980s there were many exhibitions, conferences and magazines on the subject of ornament, not to mention countless projects and completed works.[54] This return presented certain problems for those brought up in a Modernist tradition where "ornament and crime" were equated by Adolf Loos. Auguste Perret, the famous engineer-architect, had laid down the party-line: "ornament always hides a fault in construction," and it was often equated both with immorality and falsity. To counter these dicta, Post-Modernists made straightforward arguments in its defense: it gives scale, depth and proportion to large, bureaucratic monoliths. It provides symphonic variations on themes stated elsewhere in the building and brings them to an enjoyable crescendo. And, as we saw, it gives semantic identity and weight to a building, telling you how to use it. All these were sensible points, but it was really the witty use of ornament, Umberto Eco's lovers, that clinched the argument. And, by the end of the 1970s, three architects had

Born in Vienna in 1934, Hans Hollein studied both here and in Chicago and Berkeley and his wide background is reflected in his work. Beginning with his tiny candle and jewelry shops, and learning from Viennese Rococo and Modernism, as well as artists and visionaries, his sensibility is thoroughly eclectic and sophisticated. His earliest work was a leading part of the visionary tradition in Vienna. Photo collages of an aircraft carrier in a wheat field implied a city of the future; a sculptural contraption resembling a plumbing trap implied an urban node; an erect phallus was conceived as a skyscraper. Such images were supported by manifestoes proclaiming "*alles ist architectur*", a position underlined by the way Hollein transgressed boundaries between art, consumer society and architecture.

Indeed, he is a tireless promoter of the new in art and architecture. Although a professor in Vienna and part of the establishment, he has supported the young and the avant-garde.

His first large scale building, opening up the discussion of the museum as a new building type, was at Monchengladbach, West Germany, 1976–82. Part landscape design, part acropolis, it was also an industrial shed, office building – with his signature erosions – and a labyrinth of space. Some of the art was even Hollein's. Later work, including a few skyscrapers, shows the same breadth of reference and commitment. On the one hand, there is an attention to detail and luxurious materials, reminiscent of Adolf Loos, that is rare today. On the other hand, it incorporates traditional emblems amid commercial signs, in a way that goes beyond the Pop collage or decorated shed. One might see Hollein as the most inclusive architect practicing in Europe. Two buildings completed in 2001 go beyond American Post-Modernism by combining signs and craftsmanship, contextual reference and dissonant collage. The Interbank tower in Peru and the Generali-Media Tower in Vienna are the most accomplished essays in this mixed genre.

Such work strides across the categories illustrating his credo, "all is architecture." This "all" now includes several underground buildings, a project for a Volcano museum, furniture, silverware, fabric design, exhibitions, utopian drawings, sexual symbolism and anything that can be built. The fact that Hollein also teaches at various universities and is Dean of Architecture at the University of Applied Arts in Vienna further underlines his status as the ultimate polymath. The result of this accomplished diversity is to reconcile positions that are customarily opposed: particularly important is the divide between craftwork and mass-production. Hollein spurns such oppositions as he patiently invents curtain walls, expensive marble details and electronic signs – with equal commitment.

I first met Hans Hollein at a Meeting of Team Ten in 1966, and along with Kisho Kurokawa the three of us were not exactly welcomed onto this revisionist-modern Team: we were considered heretics and apostates. Of all the Post-Modernists, when he is one, Hollein designs and builds slowly, with care and thought. His work as an artist-architect thus demands a corresponding slowness in deciphering its deep subtleties. Sometimes the humor is so sophisticated it is hard to know whether it is intended, but the occasional flash of a grin suggests that it is.

183 HANS HOLLEIN, *Perchtoldsdorf Town Hall*, renovation, Austria, 1975–76. The wavy decorative lines in blue and chrome mediate between the ceiling, table and floor ornament while the stylized vine and grapes provide visual distraction during interminable debates. A sympathetic collage of old and new which has a semantic justification. (J. Surwillo).

184 HANS HOLLEIN, *Austrian Travel Agency*. Placed under the cool white light of a Secessionist barrel vault are various signs of foreign travel: a bronze Lutyens dome for India, palm trees for exotic places, ruined columns for Greece and Italy.

turned ironic appropriation into *the* PM method for using ornament: Hans Hollein, Charles Moore and James Stirling.

Hans Hollein, in his renovation of the Perchtoldsdorf Town Hall, near Vienna, produced a grand, ornamental use of chrome and furniture elements to intensify the existing ornament (183). His problem was to keep the portraits of the previous mayors, some who had been slaughtered by the Turks, and keep the heraldic emblems, while letting his audience know that he knew they knew he was not a revivalist. He achieves this balancing act with an undulating blue line edged in chrome. This divides the wall into two basic parts: above is the traditional dado line that accentuates the portraits of the previous mayors while below are his rippling panels. Over the side entrance doors, otherwise

unarticulated except for handles, the waves invert to allow headroom and signal a change of function. This contextual use of ornament (reminiscent of Viennese Rococo) signifies a positive functional choice Hollein made when confronted with the difficult requirement of adding to the size of the council chamber. He decided that rather than build a new chamber, he would crowd all the councilors into the old one and thereby preserve their historic link, because the room had great emotional overtones. The crowded ornament not only half frames the elders, but also half frames the crowded councilors seated below, and thus acts as a metaphorical link between the two groups. The latter are squashed tight against each other in thin, Art Deco chairs that just fit into places allotted at the table. On the floor in the centre of the

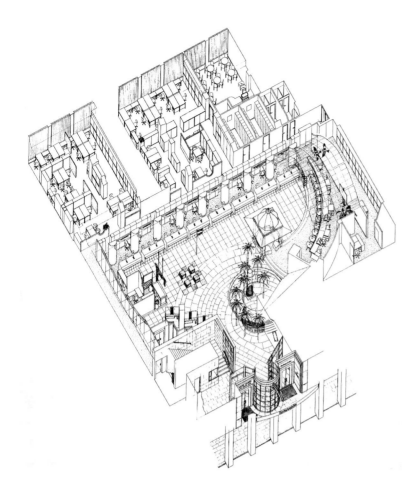

topee, theatre tickets by a stage curtain, air travel by birds. Ironically, the place where one paid for it all, the cashier's desk, was signified by the outlines of a Rolls Royce radiator grille (186). All of this was sheltered under a light-filled vault reminiscent of the local Post Office Savings Bank, the magnificent Modern space Otto Wagner built in 1906. In effect, it said: "to be a tourist you don't even have to leave Vienna." Local reference is set against stereotype, existing urban fabric against infill. Hollein was thus speaking to a wide commercial audience and using its clichés (something of a necessity in a travel bureau) but with a wit and care unusual in mass-culture.

How far could such eclecticism go, without becoming a bore or whimsical? Charles Moore, in the Piazza d'Italia in New Orleans, pushed the approach to its limits producing a dazzling cocktail that only just avoids banality. The bravado works here because each typology and trope is selected for a particular purpose: the urban context the building fits into; the particular form and ornament for each function; and the way the overall style suits the inhabitants for whom it was designed, the Italian community. Three justifications, three choices, deepen the eclecticism and underline the strange dialogue between present taste and past architecture.

The Piazza is set in a mixed area of New Orleans. To one

185 HANS HOLLEIN, *Austrian Travel Agency*, Vienna, 1976–78. The axonometric, shows the symbolic centers collaged onto an abstract grid of space. Continuous open space is thus dramatized, as opposed to Late-Modern, isotropic space.

186 HANS HOLLEIN, *The cashier's desk*, a Rolls Royce Radiator set amidst luxurious details.

oval is a stylized vine and bunch of grapes. This, Hollein said, is to entertain councilors when debate becomes dull, and symbolize the main product of their town, wine. The fact that the grapes are gold is one more sign that he knows that they know that he knows it is embarrassing to speak about money. But he must, in an age of lost innocence.

Hollein's most adept collage of quotes was for a small office of the Austrian Travel Agency right in the heart of Vienna, a brilliant design, now sadly gone (184, 185). It consisted of an ornamental series of giant furniture-pieces set in opposition. On the exterior the neutral, gray urban fabric was preserved and yet the new function was subtly cued by the introduction of polished bronze which gleamed out from the gray. On the inside, the various tourist fantasies and stereotypes became the excuse for an eclecticism that could would once again be termed radical. Each element had a semantic appropriateness: ruined columns impaled by chrome shafts signified travel in Greece and Italy; desert travel was communicated by bronze versions of the palm columns at the Brighton Pavilion; India by a bronze solar

side is a Modern skyscraper, whose black-and-white graphics are taken up to generate a graduating series of rings. This circular form, at once a Modern bull's-eye and Baroque urban form (Place des Victoires, Paris), percolates out into three streets giving a cue to the passer-by that something unusual is going on behind the existing buildings (187). The circles are partial discs, screens of columns that spin asymmetrically on the diagonal of movement towards a culmination point, an archway, in fact a Modern *Serliana*. This diagonal is reinforced by the cascade of broken forms – the boot of Italy – that focuses on the highest plateau, the "Italian Alps." Thus we have a clear organization of form and content. As Italy rises towards the Northern Alps, so too do the Five Orders of Italian columns, and they culminate in a new

sixth order that frames the future restaurant, the "Deli Order" (188). Neon necklaces around the neck of these columns further indicate the present day, and that commercial bad taste is very much a part of it. Moore has a liking for architectural whimsy and puns (he calls the watering metopes, "wetopes") and it is a credit to his teamwork that these calculated vulgarities do not get the upper hand. They are part of a rich mix of meanings.

Some of these, coming through participatory design, led to relevant knowledge: the importance of the annual St. Joseph's festival which became the rationale behind the fountain and piazza. It turned out that once a year in New Orleans, the Italian community comes to the fore to celebrate its presence by selling Italian specialties and local con-

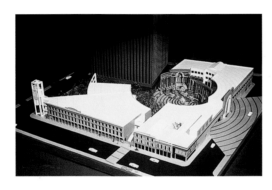

187 CHARLES MOORE (with Allen Eskew and Malcolm Heard Jr. of Perez & Associates and Ron Filson), *Piazza d'Italia*, New Orleans, 1976–79. The aerial view shows the piazza (circle) set into the urban tissue (rectangle) like a mandala which announces its presence by various cues: a pergola, a campanile and archway or the rings of paving. This scheme, like many Rationalist ones, reinforces the historic urban fabric while at the same time changing its meaning. (UIC).

188 *Piazza d'Italia*. Columnar screens and flying arches lead up to one focus, the future German Restaurant with its "Deli Order" of neon and the modern Serliana with raised keystone. Note the reflective glow of the neon. The dark, flat imposts look like an architect's rendering of a cross-section. (Norman McGrath).

coctions (muffalattas, salami, cheese, etc.,) on the day of their patron saint. Since the stated purpose of the design was rhetorical, to give identity to the Italian community in a city where other ethnic groups dominate (the French and Spanish, the Blacks and Anglos), there was good reason for some historical reference and explicit content. What was the content? "Italianness" clearly, as symbolized by the echoes of the Trevi fountain, the Five rather than Three Greek Orders, the strong earth coloring, the Latin inscription ("This fountain was given by the citizens of New Orleans as a gift to all the people"). Most obvious is the plan of Italy (with the Adriatic and Tyrrhenian seas represented by moving water). Since the community is made up mostly of Sicilians, this island occupies the centre of the bulls-eye, an emphasis that is increased by another focus, the black-and-white podium. This can function as a speaker's platform on St. Joseph's day when the piazza works as a *res publica*, a social content that gives the rhetorical forms a credibility they would otherwise lack. But, it is a rhetoric that extends across many taste-cultures.

For the architecturally aware there are references to the Marine Theatre of Hadrian and the triumphal gateways of Schinkel; for the Sicilians, echoes of archetypal piazzas and fountains; for the Modernists there is an acknowledgement of skyscrapers and the use of current technologies (the neon and concrete); for the lover of abstract form there are cut-away imposts finished in speckled marble and a most sensuous use of polished stainless steel. Column capitals glisten with this material as water shoots out of the acanthus leaves: or the stern, squat Tuscan columns are cut from this material leaving razor-sharp "paramilitary" images, the silhouettes of Greek helmets.[55] The overall impression, finally, is a sensuous and rhetorical one, overemphasized, no doubt, because the background context was not, most unfortunately, built. Had it been the scheme might have recommended itself to those calling for a public architecture, and those Modernists who damned it ("Charles Moore puking out water" was one of the ways they saw his water bust). But conceptually at least it is an example of radical eclecticism because it fits into and extends the urban context, it characterizes the various functions, symbolic and practical, with various styles, and it takes its cues for content and form from the local taste-culture, the Italian community. Moreover, to repeat the intention of some Post-Modernists, it provides this community with a "heart."

The problem for the designer where there is no clear client community, such as the Italians in New Orleans, is how to recognize differences without, at the same time, favoring one group over another. For the PM philosopher Jean-François Lyotard the answer was to recognize the different identities, the language games of a culture, avoiding thereby a totalizing solution. As has been reiterated, this resulted in the double coding of forms, a mixture of language systems. For Colin Rowe the same problem results in collage; for Venturi it pro-duces complexity and contradiction. No building summarized these overlapping propositions more than James Stirling and Michael Wilford's *Neue Staatsgalerie* in Suttgart, built between 1977 and 1984 (190). Its impact was felt well before completion and, because it culminates the whole drive towards radical eclecticism, and the first phase of PM collage, it concludes this section of the book.

The new galleries are a carefully balanced mixture of opposite codes, basically local, Modern and traditional. Around the back are references to the Modernists, in particular to Alvar Aalto and the 1927 Stuttgart Exhibition. This is a pertinent recollection because that was the time and place where Modernism went public on a broad front, and so through quotation Stirling acknowledges the legitimacy of that moment. At the same time his scheme picks up formal cues from the existing context, in this case the height and grain of adjacent buildings and the basic axial relationship to the main street. In effect then neither the 1927 Internationalists nor the local context completely controls the agenda – they are given equal weight.

This basic opposition is deepened by further dualities. There is the contrast of rectilinear and rotational elements, circles and squares, rectangles and diagonals, and in terms of style, a Modernist vocabulary collaged onto a Classical base. The irony of this last duality is then played in surprising ways. Where one would expect Modern elements to be used in functional ways they are used symbolically – as entrance canopies and highly colored railings that direct movement – and where traditional architecture is employed it turns out to be highly functional – the Classical podium. These ironic inversions are amusing but also part of Stirling's deeper message. In effect he is showing that an eclectic approach can solve complex problems, especially when elements are used in a fresh way.

For instance, the U-shaped *palazzo* of the old gallery is amplified to accept the larger scale of new art, and then it is set back on a high plinth, or "Acropolis," above the traffic. But this Classical base is not just a contextual gesture: it holds a very real parking garage, one whose grim necessity is indicated by several further signs, some of them beautiful, others amusing. The sandstone and heavy blocks of transitive have been punched out of the wall, ironically, and have fallen, like ruins, to the ground (191).

The resultant holes show the *real* construction – not the thick marble blocks of the real Acropolis, but a steel frame holding stone cladding that allows the air ventilation required by law. One can sit on these false ruins and ponder the truth of our, and Umberto Eco's, "lost innocence"; that we live in an age which can build with beautiful, expressive masonry as long as we make it skin-deep and hang it on a steel skeleton. A Modernist would of course deny himself and us this pleasure for a number of reasons: "truth to materials," "logical consistency," and the ever present drive to purge and purify.

189 Born in Glasgow in 1926, James Stirling became a disciple of Le Corbusier under the tutelage of his friend at Liverpool, Colin Rowe. His first important works, with James Gowan, particularly the Leicester Engineering Building, 1964, reflected a poetic interpretation of the functionalist tradition, and in the 1960s because of such highly expressive work he became the leader of Late-Modernism. His production was small, but influence great because he combined so many architectural and outside influences into a unique synthesis. Historical types, Pop quotes, functional inventions and ironic inversions were pulled together, often using the axonometric drawing technique. This allowed bird's eye and worm's-eye views of his work to be seen as pure organizational types, in the manner of Le Corbusier. Key Late-Modern buildings were the Cambridge History Faculty Building, 1968, and Oxford Florey Building, 1971, both which had functional shortcomings but were nevertheless spectacularly logical artefacts. Always struggling with provincial arbiters he had several houses turned down for aesthetic reasons. The silliest ignominy was being forced to change the color of his 1972 Olivetti Extension, located in the woods, seventeen times — because it might frighten the birds! As a result of such encounters he took a dim view of the guardians of official taste.

British commissions dried up for ten years and partly because of this Stirling's opinions started to change. The reasons were various. Important was the influence of Leon Krier who worked in his office in 1969–70 and prepared many of the Le Corbusier-like drawings for his monograph of 1974. Urban contextualism entered his corpus both through Krier and Colin Rowe. At the same time, I had extended discussions with him on the role of metaphor and the way his architecture communicated which may have influenced some of this shift (we exchanged letters and two articles were published on the semantics of his buildings). Furthermore, Stirling collected Thomas Hope furniture in the early seventies and, after seeing an exhibit on Neo-Classicism, his taste started to absorb more traditional codes. He now mixed all of these influences with the previous Pop and technical images. By 1975, and the Dusseldorf scheme, his collage contextualism made him a global leader of Post-Modernism, on a par with Robert Venturi. This approach he developed through Stuttgart, a science library in California, and campus buildings at Harvard, Rice and Cornell. It culminated at Stuttgart and his No.1 Poultry Scheme, in London, of 1987.

Unfortunately, this project was attacked by Prince Charles as looking like "an old 1930s wireless" (i.e. radio set). Although the comparison was absurd, the design was subject to a protracted public inquiry because it necessitated the destruction of some Victorian buildings. Finally given approval in 1991, it was built after his untimely death in 1992.

"Big Jim," as he was known was different from the other famous architects in Britain, an alternative to the reigning High-Tech school. The continuous struggle with opponents, and even friends, made Stirling a welcome, outspoken presence on the architectural scene. With the support of his wife, Mary Shand, he created a convivial center for discussion in his London home.

In the last years, after Post-Modernism had been debased under Thatcherism, he changed style again and returned to a monumental functionalism evident in the Braun Headquarters Building, 1986–92. Sometimes contrary, always a dialectical thinker, he criticized Le Corbusier's move away from orthodox Modernism — only to follow it himself. His best work such as at Stuttgart, is brilliantly inventive, tough, amusing and eclectic. Stirling also analyzed a key factor behind the most successful buildings. They were a result of his oscillating between dualities — abstraction and representation, modernism and vernacular, monumental and informal, tradition and High-Tech — oppositions he sought to confront and sometimes reconcile.

James Stirling with son Ben, at their Belsize Avenue home, London, c.1970.

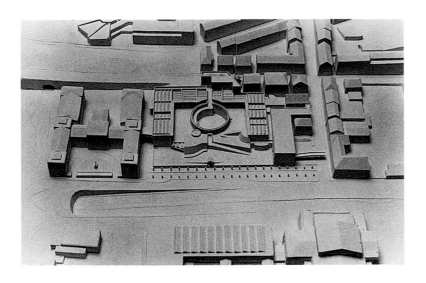

190 JAMES STIRLING & MICHAEL WILFORD, *Neue Staatsgalerie*, Stuttgart, 1977–84. The new u-shaped building to the right nestles into the context, and unites the pedestrian routes across the site. The layout relates to various buildings around it and the high-speed traffic – a masterpiece of PM urbanism.

By contrast Stirling, like Eco's lovers, wants to communicate more and different values. To signify the permanent nature of the museum he has used traditional rustication and Classical forms including an Egyptian cornice, an open-air Pantheon, and segmental arches. These are both conventionally beautiful *and* distorted, because of the use of a Modern material such as reinforced concrete. They say: "We are beautiful like the Acropolis or Pantheon, but we are also based on concrete technology and deceit." The extreme form of this double coding is visible at the entry points, a steel temple outline which announces the drop-off point and the Modernist steel canopies which indicate the entrance to the public. These forms and colors are reminiscent of de Stijl – that quintessentially Modern language – but they are collaged onto the traditional background. Thus Modernism confronts Classicism to such an extent that both Modernists and Classicists would be surprised, if not initially offended. There is not the simple harmony and consistency of either language or world view. In effect Stirling is saying that we live in a complex world where we cannot deny either the past, and conventional beauty, or the present, and technical reality. Caught between this past and present, unwilling to oversimplify our situation, Stirling creates an art and ornament out of the predicament.

This extends throughout the site which carefully mixes and confronts opposite codes. The focus of the museum epitomizes these contrasts; the circular sculpture court is a "domeless dome," an inside-out space, the room towards which one moves to find oneself, paradoxically, *outside*, cut off from urban noise and in touch with sculpture or the sky. The ideas behind this, the mandala, the "dome of heaven –

the sky," another "heart of the city" and, like Moore's, a circular *res publica* (191, 192). I spent a day at Stuttgart with Stirling and while we were there we saw it being used in countless different ways: as a fashion backdrop, and as an intimate place for lovers who slid down the railings. School children hung colored streamers across the court and performed a theatrical event, while at the end of the day a few older citizens set up easels and painted it. When I interviewed some of these groups I found the teeenagers saw the building as youthful High-Tech, the pipes reminded them of the Pompidou Center; the *plein-air* painters saw a Schinkelesque background. For me the "domeless dome" was reminiscent of Hadrian's Villa and a secret garden in Verona, a sacred space surrounded by a masonry wall and topped by trees.

The new museum thus articulated these opposite experiences and interpretations, spread out different groups, accommodated differing tastes, carefully avoided one grand synthesis yet was unified geometrically. Its eclecticism was radical in a sense that might even satisfy Lyotard: no totalizing vision, but rather a confrontation of language games that reflected current pluralism. It is true that German Modernists were initially outraged by what they took to be something close to Albert Speer, thus forcing Stirling's angry riposte: "Hitler did not ruin Schinkel for all time." But they, like other critics, came around to the building after a while. I found the museum shocking and awkward on first glance, but after several hours on the site the idiosyncrasies started to feel inevitable. The clash of color, the green hyperbaloid set against the banded masonry, such juxtapositions gave relief to what, because of its scale, would have been an oppressive monolith had it been completed in one mode. As I have said, no other building or group of structures balanced heterogeneity so precariously and beautifully as this scheme. It summarized as a high art Rowe's idea of Collage City and my ideas of radical eclecticism. Frank Gehry, Robert Venturi and others continued to develop eclectic collage in different directions and then by the mid-1990s another idea for dealing with heterogeneity emerged, but this building epitomized the first stage of Post-Modernism in much the way the Villa Savoye and Barcelona Pavilion summarized early Modernism.

192 *Neue Staatsgalerie*, the heart of the scheme, the sculpture court, is a cosmic space open to the sky, and circled by shrubbery.

191 *Neue Staatsgalerie*, the didactic void as PM ornament. Venting the parking garage was a necessity, so Stirling knocked out some stones and they sit, like ruins, revealing the real steel construction on the inside. This and the thin slits between the stones became the method for making an architecture out of the distinction between truth and falsity, function and artifice.

193 *Neue Staatsgalerie* the opposition between various codes, the classical one used for
functional reasons, the modern one for
semantic and ornamental roles – some ironic
reversals.

194 *Strada Novissima*, Venice Biennale, 1980. The notions of the façade and street return, with most of the façades in a Free-Style Classical manner. From the left are the façades of Krier, Kleihues and Hollein. (Venice Biennale).

POST-MODERN CLASSICISM

As Post-Modernism grew, was named in this book and coalesced into a movement, it also came together as a style practiced around the world. This was both fortunate and problematic. The virtue was a new Post-Modern Classicism. This, as the evolutionary tree shows (above pages 50–51) brought together many strands and made architecture once again a public, comprehensible language of design, one of the goals of the movement. The vice, as will be seen, is that success had its usual revenge. As with all movements of art and architecture that became dominant since 1800, commercial acceptance soon led to cliché and loss of direction – here to PoMo. But for a short time the situation looked full of hope, as if the most creative Modern architects would embrace the new paradigm, as if participation and pluralism would lead to an architecture that communicated with a broad public. In this chapter the positive aspects of the synthesis will be looked at first, leaving the critique for later.

For a short period, roughly 1980–84, designers began to use a full repertoire again – metaphor, ornament, polychromy, convention, irony, sensuous materials – to reach a wide audience. This synthesis amounted to a consensus, like the International Style of the Twenties, but one with a difference. Whereas the Modern Movement had come to fruition, in Nikolaus Pevsner's infelicitous phrase of 1936, as a "totalitarian" style, this one coalesced, in Lyotard's phrase, "as a war on totality." Universalism versus pluralism, the two motivating ideas made the synthesis of each quite different.[56]

In the case of Post-Modernism it meant a Free-Style Classicism that had several distinct oppositions as well as the general notion that meaning consists partly *in* opposition: the significance of form depends on a system of difference, as seen with the semantic space.[57] Hence a surprising development. At the very moment a worldwide consensus occurred within Post-Modernism it fractured into different positions. The common territory was disputed, a debate started between the Americans and Europeans (among others) and PM Classicism developed different moods, theories and modes. The three basic positions will be looked at here: one based on constructional and thematic types, mostly a European development; a highly representational one, mostly American; and an abstract one less tied to a culture.

THE NEW TUSCANISM –
THE FUNCTIONAL MODE

The synthesis of current trends first appeared in the public realm with the 1980 Biennale in Venice. Organized by Paolo Portoghesi and a committee that included Robert Stern, Christian Norberg-Schulz, Vincent Scully and myself, the Biennale's real subject was Post-Modern architecture, although its actual title was "The Presence of the Past."[58] This phrase unfortunately bent the meaning of Post-Modernism towards historical reference, but it did bring the movement to a large audience. The public responded to the display of façades and the streetscape of difference (194). Over 2,000 visitors came per day and that, at the time, was a large number for an architectural exhibition. Furthermore, a version of the exhibit was reassembled in Paris and San Francisco while the attendant books and catalogues spread the message. Part of the publicity was inadvertent. Modernist critics, such as Bruno Zevi, sought to kill off the movement with multi-media venom (thereby assuring its notoriety), yet the majority of non-architectural writers supported what they saw as a fresh departure.

If architecture is defined as the public art, then the 1980 Biennale vindicated the public part of the definition, It reached the broadest audience of Italians through television and newspaper coverage. For those hostile to the show it was mere puffery: a "Potemkin's Village" of cardboard screens that would blow away with the next fashion. But for the seventy-two architects taking part it was a chance to experiment on a small scale and see what happened when inhibitions were dropped (Portoghesi subtitled one section "The End of Prohibitions").

A leading contributor, Aldo Rossi, was a friend of Portoghesi – something that partly explained his primary place in the exhibition, designing the entry gate and the floating *Teatro del Mondo* (196). This last combined a Classical organization with vernacular construction, a hybrid that shared with Venturi's buildings an interest in the archetypal: the square-mullioned window, the flat, cheap, plainer façade. This floating "theatre of the world" was pulled through the canals of Venice and, as it bobbed in the water near the Santa Maria della Salute and the golden dome of the Custom's House, it seemed like a cheerful, flag-topped tower cut out from a Carpaccio painting. "The Presence of the Past" indeed, even the color had affinities with Bellini blue. Historical memory and the associations of art were themes that preoccupied Rossi.

His most important project, under continual but slow construction for many years – and thus an embodiment of time – was the Modena Cemetery (197, 198). This is both a giant mausoleum and an urban landmark. Laid out as a series of primary elements organized on a grid, its primary axis focuses on "the House of the Dead" and a stark cone-shaped funnel, both memorable images of finality. Here black shadows replace windows to evoke a burnt-out ruin. No details, no mullions or window sills, no base or top distract from the haunting metaphor of death, the timeless, democratic, universal fact of life. A roof over the top, a pane of glass, or any countervailing element is shunned. One can

195 Born in Milan in 1931, Aldo Rossi was a force in architecture from the time of his writing *L'architettura della città*, 1966, until his untimely death in 1997. In 1959 he graduated from the polytechnic university in Milan and he continued to teach here, as well as in Venice, Switzerland and the United States. Writing for *Casabella-continuità* in the early 1960s he founded the movement of Rational architecture which referred back to that of the 1920s and Adolf Loos. From this he developed with others the so-called "Tendency" and "New Figuration," a cross between abstract representation and historical reminiscence. A sometime dour Marxist who would on occasion defend the Stalinist architecture of East Berlin, he could also be playfully ironic and design tea sets in the shape of buildings. His gift was to transform monumental building into something hauntingly unfamiliar by making it at once vernacular, abstract and poetic. Drawing and writing were the keys to his analogical thought, his ability to feel the associations hidden behind farm buildings, highways and little cabins by the sea. Childhood memories are evoked by his childlike colored drawings and thus his stern, Marxist reductivism is tempered by uncanny associations.

Some of the early buildings are minimalist to the point of deprivation — such as the Gallaratese housing outside Milan — but by the 1980s Rossi became more explicitly classical and lyrical. A haunting presence of the absence still pervades this architecture, as it did the work of De Chirico, a clear influence, and in this sense Rossi can be seen as the counterpart of the painter, a Metaphysical Architect. Curiously for a Marxist, he insisted on the autonomy of architecture, its type-solutions independent of time and culture — a reason his work has such power, as well as influence on architects such as Peter Eisenman. Like Euclid's elements, his postulates and deductions started from simple, regular solids. Cubes, cylinders, pyramids and stepped polygons are the predominate elements. Propositions deduced from them are then given unusual proportions, combined and colored in strong opposing hues to bring out the identity of each part. Such forceful contrasts keep the simple and obvious from becoming banal.

He called his work "timeless and universal" but actually its haunting quality stops time. Surprisingly for an architect committed to socialism and the public realm, he attracted spec developers and mercantile clients. By the mid-1980s all sorts of commercial buildings were being commissioned around the world including airports, shopping centers, hotels, art galleries, gas stations, city centers and, for Disney, an office complex in Orlando, Florida. Some of this verges on pastiche, depending on how well it is detailed and built by associated architects. The best of it, like the Bonnefanten Museum, or even his mass-produced watch, are PM classics.

He credits suffering an auto accident for making him compare the city of the living to that of the dead, the cemetery, and his first monumental poetic work resulted from this: for the Modena Cemetery. Repetitive forms in the House of the Dead give it an eternal silence, as indeed do all his repetitive figures. His polemic in favor of preserving city memory made him, with the Krier brothers and figures like Jane Jacobs, one of the great resistance fighters of city destruction. He saw the point of extending and completing city fabric, but with repetitive striking monuments. Often prophetic about his own life, its ending in a car crash near his home by the Lago Maggiore may not have surprised him.

196 ALDO ROSSI, *Il Teatro del Mondo*, The Floating Theatre, Venice Biennale, 1979–80. A Classical four-square geometry centering like the domed churches of Venice on a lantern and globe. The blue decorative elements relate to the context, while the wooden construction relates to the vernacular.

197, 198 ALDO ROSSI, *Modena Cemetery*, 1971– . The "House of the Dead" in the foreground is a haunting image, with the windows blown out and the roof non-existent. An empty street leads toward the towering common grave, unfortunately coded as a crematorium funnel. Whether a cemetery should be so remorselessly deadly is open to doubt, but beyond question is the monumental presence, the image of architecture as public memory and symbolism.

criticize the remorseless singularity of the meaning – after all cemeteries are for the living, for celebration, and are not meant to frighten people with the idea of eternal nullity (except perhaps in some theologies of damnation) – but nowhere else will one find it put with such poetry and directness.

In this scheme Rossi also works out his typology for "the City of the Living" and again it is based on the reduction of functional types to simple elements, and constructional reality to repetitive rhythms of solid-void. The architecture of shadows thus merges with an earlier idea of Adolf Loos' that "architecture resides in the monument and the grave" and both these types depend on their power for evoking images of death for life. The monument is still, silent, timeless; the grave, when effective, has a fundamentalist presence. Both sear themselves so strongly into the mind they are unforgettable. This Rossi's work manages to do with frightening and childlike images, a clear example of the way Post-Modernism, like the Baroque, is motivated by the desire to communicate. He will even hint at the image of a bomb or missile, and employ a military repetitiveness, to further the overtones of fear. Like de Chirico and Frances Bacon he uses dread to further his message. This would seem to push him in the direction of Brutalist architects and yet it does not: his work retains a childlike buoyancy, freshness and optimism even when obsessed by death, an uncanny transformation of the uncanny. Hence his popularity and the way he successfully reintroduced the notion of the enigmatic monument into Post-Modernism (199).

Aldo Rossi had previously formed the school of Neo-Rationalism in the late 1960s, *La Tendenza,* which influenced, in turn, the synthesis of Post-Modern Classicism.

199 ALDO ROSSI, *Bonnefanten Museum*, Maastricht, 1995. Combining classical and industrial forms and breaking them with odd but functional shapes, Rossi continued to provide the monumental building with a disturbing and dignified presence.

From Rossi, and others such as the Krier brothers and Mario Botta, it gained aspects of controlled repetition, urban propriety and the notion of type-forms. Above all it employed a restrained mood which, because it related to the undecorated Doric style, could be called "the New Tuscanism."[59]

Quite independently Oswald Matthias Ungers and I employed another term for this trend, the New Abstraction, in order to contrast with the New Representation and refer to design concerned with abstract architectural themes. Rossi, in his influential book *L'Architettura della Città,* 1966, had emphasized the polysemic nature of architecture, how structures such as a Roman arena could be transformed in various cultures and re-used as housing. Following this Matthias Ungers, in his book *Architettura come Tema,* (Architecture as Theme) 1982, generalized the notion to the point where building themes became autonomous characters in architectural history. They combine and give birth to new versions of themselves. House-type marries arcade-type and their offspring have affairs with hotel-type and stadium-type. Autonomous architecture is thus born, but the combinatorial types remain identified as hybrids. Whereas when we exchange DNA our characteristics are merged and blended, the results of the New Abstraction keep a clear record of their many origins. Furthermore, cultures come and go, but the abstract types go on transforming themselves forever:

> The New Abstraction in architecture deals with a rational geometry, with clear and regular forms in plan as well as in elevation…Emotion is controlled by rational thinking, and this is stimulated through intuition…[An architectural concept is something] which does not change at all, which is permanent, and which only proceeds through continual stages of transformation. The New Abstraction means exactly that – the transformation of ideas and concepts in the course of history.[60]

A transformational grammar based on universal archetypes became his method of combining opposites, what he called *coincidentia oppositorum* after the medieval philosopher Nicholas Cusanus (1401–64). Cusanus, understanding the contradiction between an infinite, unknowable God and our finite, growing knowledge, postulated the coincidence of opposites as a way of dealing with this unbridgeable gap. Intuition plays the key role in bringing opposites together, both for Cusanus and Ungers, but it is one that works with rational types, or ready-made ideas and forms. Hence its parallel with methods we have already discussed, collage and adhocism.

After teaching at Cornell, along with Colin Rowe, Ungers came onto the German scene in the early eighties with a sudden burst of several important buildings. His social housing in Berlin illustrated the transformation of the perimeter block type around an interior courtyard (200). One can easily read off the architectural themes: hanging trellis, balcony type, front door, courtyard entrance etc. His Frankfurt Fair

Hall and Galleria combined other purified themes: the glazed arcade, the red warehouse space and the stepped platform. Cypresses on the roof where the cars are parked combined the Convention Center type with the Isola Bella type, a weird but refreshing opposition (201). This illustrates a virtue of the New Abstraction: it forced one to think across functions, to get away from the stereotypes of normal production, to invent the mixed urban use that those such as Jane Jacobs had called for. Where Modernism and commercial development stressed functional separation and monoculture, this approach stressed the hybrid and polyculture. Furthermore, because of abstraction it lent itself to mass production and, like Rossi's work, the repetition of a single module set on a grid.

One little masterpiece was Ungers' German Architectural Museum, a conversion of a nineteenth-century house beside the River Main in Frankfurt (202). This conjunction of types centered on the notion of "a house within a house" and combined it with the garden and arcade types, all within a white, gridded abstraction. Its opening in 1984 featured an exhibition on Post-Modern Architecture, a collection of drawings and models put together by Heinrich Klotz that formed part of a growing, permanent collection. Like the Venice Biennale of 1980 it summarized the state of the international movement at that moment and, fittingly, illustrated the European position through its own architecture.

The New Abstraction, with its emphasis on the autonomy of architecture, meant that one could gain further control over it as an art. And this increased control allowed Mario Botta, the Neo-Rationalist from the Italian part of Switzerland, to turn the modest concrete block into the basis

200 O. M. UNGERS, *Perimeter Block*, Schillerstrasse, Berlin, 1978–82. The street line is kept and the basic Berlin apartment type is transformed around a courtyard to permit a variety of use and a lively, musical façade. (Waltraud Krase).

201 O. M. UNGERS, *Frankfurt Fair Hall and Galleria*, Frankfurt, 1979–82. A giant arcade, like those of the nineteenth century, connects one hall to another. Ungers' housing is like Rossi's, a repetition of a structural bay crossed with another type: the stepped platform, a kind of Isola Bella with cypresses and parked cars. (Von Hoessle-Frankfurt).

for a reduced Post-Modern aesthetic. It is as if Ungers' notion of the type had been shrunk to the size of a single constructional element. Having studied under both Louis Kahn and the Atelier of Le Corbusier, Botta developed the late styles of these masters toward a primitive Classicism. Recognizable in his work, although in distorted form, are such features as cornices, columns, rustication and the all-important pedimental skylight which can be seen as either an amplified fanlight or a diminished arcade. This last element gives a mythic quality to all his buildings, contrasting the sky with the weight of the masonry, sign of the ground. Such a traditional opposition between heaven and earth roots the buildings in a very primitive way.

Four houses, produced from 1979 to 1981, show him carrying out such archetypal ideas with modern materials. The Pregassona House, in the Ticino part of Switzerland where he usually builds, has a Classical cube with a nine-square Palladian plan. This is violently fractured on two sides to allow in light and articulate the space and view (203). The tiny glass-and-steel skylight contrasts aggressively with the white-gray box, just as the uncompromising geometry does with the site. The chiaroscuro is as extreme as the other Mannerist contrasts, as one perceives the flattest of façades gouged out by the darkest of voids. Intentional Mannerism might be denied by Botta since he explains his buildings as necessary and inevitable, a consequence of constructional reality. However, forceful shapes and disproportionate contrasts tell their own story. Moreover the semantics are Mannerist: these houses look like heavy rusticated bases awaiting a *piano nobile* and roof. Conceptually they are all foundation or bottom floor (204).

202 O. M. UNGERS, *German Architectural Museum*, "the house within the house," Frankfurt, 1982–85.

Nowhere is this clearer than at Massagno where he has constructed another one-family house with banded rustication of light red and gray concrete. Here the "foundation-house" has a miniscule skylight contrasting with a huge round window of the late Kahnian variety, the whole building perfectly illustrating the oxymorons: giant/midget, voided/solid, open/closed and round/square. When the diagonal glass mullions slide apart, the "eye of the camera" focuses on the dramatic view, while on the "back/front" of the house two tiny portholes provide the inscrutable visage. Here the opposition is similar to Japanese houses of the period.

More relaxed is the house at Viganello, a little temple with its giant fanlight and sunken keystone (205). These Classical distortions again order the view over the Swiss hills and are in closer proportion to one another. A centrally placed giant column in gray block gives a social rootedness to this mini-fortress while the same block skewed at forty-

203 MARIO BOTTA, *One Family House*, connecting earth and sky, Pregassona, Switzerland, 1979.

204 MARIO BOTTA, *One Family House*, the view and tree motif break through the wall, extreme contrasts of his Mannerist grammar. Massagno, 1979.

five degrees adds scale, and at the top becomes a refined cornice. It is a measure of Botta's control of his minimal means that he draws every salient constructional element in plan, section and axonometric so the fabric is rendered totally familiar. This knowing control makes his Classicism reminiscent of that of Kahn and Mies, but what distinguishes

205 MARIO BOTTA, *House at Viganello*, Ticino, Switzerland, 1980–81. A monumental temple/bunker contrasts with the mountainside and greenery. Botta achieves further Mannerist effects by enlarging the fanlight, diminishing a dentil frieze, and cutting out voids in extreme chiaroscuro. Note the absolute symmetry, voided keystone and decorative use of concrete block. (Alo Zanetta).

him from his predecessors is the explicit Mannerism. Where Modernists underplayed their Classicism behind a technological imperative, Botta lets his develop freely into a primitive symbolism. For instance, the constructional blocks in his Casa Rotonda fan apart to become a capital, or stagger at forty-five degrees to become a dentil frieze.

Strong contrasts, the use of chiaroscuro, the violent holes cut in the masonry wall are all signs of disquiet and tension. Perhaps it is his query of the new world to the old, the challenge of Modernism with traditional culture. In a sense the subject of Botta's Mannerism is concerned with this challenge, a collision of opposites. Like Stirling's work at

Stuttgart, there is no attempt to smooth over the difference or opt for a facile reconciliation of competing systems.

Botta's work – like that of Rossi, Ungers and other Neo-Rationalists – is in the New Tuscan Style partly because this is an inexpensive genre based on the simple repetition of walls and voids, and partly because the manner is both aristocratic and proletarian (206).[61] Like the Modernism Tom Wolfe satirized in *From Bauhaus to Our House*, the austere style is wonderfully ambiguous: it is both non-bourgeois and bourgeois.[62] Like designer blue jeans, it celebrates a sophisticated poverty, an elegant abstinence. It is also the easiest mode to detail or, as the case may be, leave without detail. In the Renaissance, Sebastiano Serlio recommended the plain Tuscan style for use on prisons, fortifications and harbors: rough, heavy functions close to everyday life and the soil. It is these virtues, and the nobility of the peasant, which recommended the manner to austere European architects.

It also led to passionate disputes, whether architecture is or is not implicated with style. Demetri Porphyrios threw

206 MARIO BOTTA *Casa Rotonda*, Stabio, 1979–81. The cylinder is ordered as a Palladian nine-square solution oriented to the view. The masonry is violently torn apart to dramatize the view and light. Every constructional block is drawn and understood. The primitive column unites earth and sky. The austere New Tuscan Style is impersonal, dignified, inexpensive, and appropriately used on modest houses. (Mario Botta).

down the gauntlet with a definite pronouncement, "Classicism is *not* a Style."[63] This polemic, published in 1982, asserted that the current spare Classicism developed solely as a morality concerning construction, what he termed the "mimetic elaboration of the constructional logic of vernacular Classicism." One could see what he meant, historically. The Doric Order, elaborating and symbolizing wooden construction, was a good example and no doubt it had a few contemporary parallels with Neo-Rationalist work. Porphyrios, somewhat predictably, juxtaposed this morality to what he saw as the waywardness of American representational architecture. And this position became a

standard point in the much publicized "Great Debate: Modernists versus the Rest," which took place at the Royal Institute of British Architects in London, in 1982.[64] For many ex-Modernists the only way forward was via constructional logic and, for the critic Kenneth Frampton, any use of symbolic or decorative detail was in danger of becoming kitsch. Such was one opposition that divided Post-Modernists. My answer in this dispute was the old point of semiologists, that all usages are turned into signs, and then styles, of usage. Thus the constructional fatalism of Porphyrios was inevitably conventionalized as a New Tuscanism, whether architects cared to admit this social reality or not.

Furthermore, this style could be defended as a genre of communication. It had all the beauties of simple prose. For instance, in Japan where the same movement was underway, Takefumi Aida's Toy Block Houses were as easy to understand as the child-like blocks from which they were built (207). Basic constructional elements, forming a thick-wall pattern in various hues, are stacked and surmounted by Platonic solids – pyramids, or extended pediments. The result is inevitably temple-like, a Free-Style Classicism that recalls the unadorned Tuscan style as well as Shinto temples. When analyzed further they revealed complex formal asymmetries reminiscent of De Stijl and Modernist aesthetics – thus becoming a typical PM hybrid.

Many Japanese designers started work in the same mode because it was so basic and close to the Shinto aesthetic. Among the most convincing designers who combined it with a Minimalist High-Tech were Toyo Ito and Minoru Takeyama. Although differing in other ways, they shared a similar commitment to using pristine industrial materials formed into Platonic shapes – the inevitable semi-circular arch, the archetypal pediment and the window-wall of grids (208). At first glance it may seem surprising that so many Japanese architects should embrace a Western Classicism. But, on reflection, the causes seem obvious. Japan is quick to pick up and transform foreign influences and has been doing this for thousands of years: also the archetypal nature of the Classical language lends itself to cultural borrowing. In the hands of one Japanese architect, Toyokazu Watanabe, this system takes on an almost demonic aspect. His concrete houses resembled the Modena Cemetery of Aldo Rossi. They were frightening graves, monumental bunkers that looked burnt-out, leaving stark shells with gruesome black voids (209). Only on second glance does the beauty and logic of the architecture overcome its fearsome quality. Solid Tuscan wall and window voids create the expression in a very logical way. Floors are stepped back, like a ziggurat, for the artists' studio above, and in order to let in light from many sources the clerestory windows are doubled. Here and in other buildings, this doubling of small panes makes the space appear twice its size. Like Adolf Loos' work, which Watanabe has studied, the simple logic of Classicism can

207 TAKEFUMI AIDA, *Toy Block House 111*, Tokyo 1980–81. Large elemental blocks – both construction and structure – are stacked sometimes as bricks, sometimes as post and lintel. This basic Classical compositional method is then contrasted with De Stijl asymmetries and overlapping units of space. The decoration results from the joining of blocks, as it often does in the Tuscan Style. (T Aida).

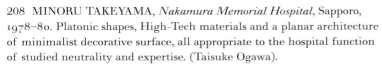

208 MINORU TAKEYAMA, *Nakamura Memorial Hospital*, Sapporo, 1978–80. Platonic shapes, High-Tech materials and a planar architecture of minimalist decorative surface, all appropriate to the hospital function of studied neutrality and expertise. (Taisuke Ogawa).

209 TOYOKAZU WATANABE, *Sugiyama House*, Osaka, 1980–81. For Adolf Loos, who influenced Watanabe, architecture resided in the monument and the grave. Nothing is more powerful than these monumentally haunting images, made more fearsome by the tricks in scale. Whether it is appropriate for housing is debatable, but it is certainly sublime and logical. (Hitoshi Kawamoto).

210 ROB KRIER, *Ritterstrasse Apartments*, Berlin-Kreuzberg, 1977–78. The eroded figure marks the public doorway as a Classical caryatid would, but becomes more a comment on the ruins of Berlin than a public figure. The flat Tuscan Style with symmetrical window voids is used in housing here to define urban space and the street. (Gerald Blomeyer).

lead to some beautiful and humorous propositions. Loos stacked his black-and-white cubes into ziggurats of housing and amplified a Doric column into an entire skyscraper. Watanabe, like Eisenman, has columns hanging in space – necessary for formal logic, unnecessary for support. Both Loos and Watanabe get a wry pleasure from the paradox inherent in Classicism.

The New Tuscanism became a dominant genre in parts of Europe such as Germany, Italy and Spain, and was used as one of several modes by Post-Modern Classicists. It is, as Serlio prescribed, most suitable on impersonal, rough and functional buildings, today the hospital, factory and street arcade. It did not stop kitsch commercialism, as some hoped, but it did create an aristocratically restrained mode. Understatement and cool probity are its virtues, brutalism and shoddy detailing are its occasional vices. In the hands of Robert Krier it became the departure point for a PM urbanism that was to transform Berlin during the 1980s, the subject for a later chapter. However, his first essay in this manner was created earlier, the Ritterstrasse apartments (210), and they even incorporated something anathema to the European hard-liners, ornamental sculpture symbolizing the entrance to social housing. The debate on construction versus symbolism may have divided Europeans from Americans, but as these apartments show both sides were also learning from each other.

THE NEW REPRESENTATION —
FLATNESS OR FULLNESS?

As a new language of architecture began to develop in the 1980s, it became ever more important to ground it in at least two areas: society and technology.[65] Modernism, with the International Style in the 1920s, made just such a double-barreled argument so it is not surprising that again these determinants came to the fore. Robert Venturi and Denise Scott Brown continued their polemic based on Las Vegas, Mannerism and mass-culture and pushed it, in 1982, to its logical conclusions. The idea was that the new architecture would be ornamental, based on signs that could be easily read; but, because of cheap, quick construction, it would also be appliquéd, stuck on:

> In the progression of our ideas about appliqué, first as spatial layerings, then signboard, and then ornament, we came to appliqué as representation in architecture – manifestations of this approach to symbolism in architecture are essentially two-dimensional and pictorial… In our time, economy and industrial standardization, on the one hand, and lack of craftsmanship, on the other, justify this simplified, repetitive and depictive approach to ornament.[66]

The validity of this argument would be disputed, as we have seen, by Rossi, Ungers and Botta, and further PM positions divide up the field even more. Ricardo Bofill, at the time, showed the potential for mass-produced concrete that could be crafted, cheaply, and (the argument of this book from the beginning) there was always the potential for com-puter-aided design. So, as an *exclusive* argument, this one of Venturi and Scott Brown could not be sustained: there are, indeed, many valid routes through the PM jungle.

Nevertheless, as a partial insight the idea of two-dimensional ornament is an interesting and provocative one. It asserts unambiguously the representational role of architecture. Furthermore, Venturi's flat ornament is both original and enjoyable for its flatness, while being stereotyped at the same time. For instance, his Gordon Wu Dining Hall uses Early Renaissance stereotypes on a Princeton campus, a version of the ABA *Serliana* motif (211). Where in the early 1900s revivalist architects had used such forms straight at Princeton, Venturi employs them in an obviously crooked way. The ultra-flat forms are cut off, slit at the top, or guillotined at the base. They become graphic devices stretched taught or stenciled across the picture plane – anti-tectonic, non-constructional – the very reverse of how Rossi or Bofill would handle them. Above the Gordon Wu entrance the one-inch thick black and white marble hangs precariously as if it were about to slice the entering student in half. Its similarity with the flat patterned brick and flat Modern windows emphasize the message – flat, flat, flat. (Modern abstract painters, twenty years earlier, were also emphasizing the flatness of the picture plane.)

Polemical flatness based on industrial necessity, or clever pastiche, done with irony to mark the front door (and much else besides)? As usual with the Venturi Team it was a bit of "both-and," "High-Low" and we might agree, that the cut-out patterns have their own inherent strengths of rhythmical opposition. Strong dark and light areas give a striking

211 VENTURI, RAUCH and SCOTT-BROWN, *Gordon Wu Dining Hall*, Princeton, New Jersey, 1981–83. Serlian ABA motifs hang symbolically to announce an entrance and contrast strongly with the flat ribbon window. The billboard approach of the sixties is still being used ironically on a campus with other Free-Style Classical revivals, but these are of a more naive kind. (Venturi, Rauch and Scott-Brown).

212 VENTURI, RAUCH and SCOTT-BROWN, *Brant House*, Tuckers Town, Bermuda, 1976–80. View of cut-out Ionic columns which give a rhythmical white dance over the dark blue sea, a rhythm which is syncopated in the arches below and beam ends above. (Venturi, Rauch and Scott-Brown).

213 ROBERT STERN, *Cohn Pool House*, Llewelyn Park, New Jersey, 1981–82, Palm columns glisten, Secessionist tiles bubble, fat women dance as quoins on the side, while the shades of blue and gold shimmer with the utmost luxuriant pleasure. (Norman McGrath).

steady beat like cut-out silhouettes. The visual logic of paper-dolls and stenciled patterns is to be supported when, as in this case, time and creativity have gone into their invention.

The same is true of the Ionic colonnade on the porch of their Brant House in Bermuda: it is paper-thin (212). Here the flatness indicates the non-structural role, while the Order indicates the major view over the sea. Here, real structure and applied ornament are in clear opposition. Elsewhere in the house, craftsmanship and careful detailing are evident. Finally, the white silhouette rhythms of the cut-out forms make a delightful foamy dance against the dark-blue water. Thus flat appliqué is vindicated by contrast and becomes a successful use of ornamental symbolism.

By the early 1980s the handling of ornament grew around the world in volume, if not in understanding. America led the rush to decorate and it produced a lot of colorful results of varying quality. There were exhibitions and commercial competitions on ornament and a slick book, packaging *Ornamentalism* as a movement, was given its intellectual launch by Paul Goldberger in 1982.[67] A host of West Coast architects, influenced by Venturi and Charles Moore, produced a highly iconic decoration. Thomas Gordon Smith, a group called ACE, the San Francisco archi-

tect Hans Kainz and many others, all mixed Classical, vernacular and decorative motifs in a free-style way. Inevitably, Robert Stern summarized many of these tendencies in his design for a Pool House – a sybaritic commission that pushed the edges of brazen expression. It is full of dazzling colors that enhance the delight of bathing (213). Glistening bronze and stainless steel "palm columns," based on those of Hans Hollein in Vienna, provide wet-look décor. A staccato beat of ornamental tiles represent foam splashing: columns and quoins represent bathers. It is all slightly heavy, like an overblown Lutyens fireplace, on which it may be based. The Secessionist and other quotes are a bit obvious. But, as a hedonist temple for bodily pleasure and regeneration, the flash detailing is, well, suited. Suitability, appropriateness, decorum – these were the catchwords of the Vitruvian canon. And Stern's proportions were clearly ironic and non-canonic: the Tuscan Columns, for instance, were as squat as they could be in order to hold a window-wall. But when representational Classicism gets this up-front, like the PoMo work of Jeff Koons, it raises other issues of decorum, beyond suitability for swimming.

What is an acceptable face to a building in the city and in the public eye? The 1980 Venice Biennale, as mentioned, and the many modest additions to urban streets that followed it raised this sort of question. Harry Cobb, for his Museum in Portland, Maine, produced, in 1982, a well-mannered Classicism with large voids cut out at the top, and understated brick and stone piers at the base. This sort of PM Classicism became the hallmark of large firms to be used on

214 I. M. PEI, *Hotel in the Fragrant Hills*, Peking, 1979–83. The large interior lobby is a grand Modernist space with a stylized decoration midway between Early Renaissance and stylized Chinese patterns. The courtyards and wall architecture are also extensions to the Chinese vernacular tradition. (I. M. Pei).

prestige commissions. Edward Larrabee Barnes, like Cobb a recent convert from Modernism, employed a restrained version on his Asia House in New York. And I. M. Pei, another Modernist trained under Walter Gropius, produced an understated mixture of Chinese and Renaissance design for his hotel on the edge of Peking, also finished in 1982, (214).

For Pei the experience was quite significant because it was the first time he used tradition in a representational manner. Appropriately enough, his switch of allegiance was prompted by a return to his home country, something that really engaged his architectural commitment. Of all his buildings it is the most rooted in culture, with the strongest sense of place. Although elsewhere committed to Modernism, Pei acknowledged the necessity of using ornament and symbolism in this building. Like Kevin Roche, who also took tentative steps in this direction, he remained fundamentally committed to abstraction and seeing architectural problems in terms of the large sculptural gesture. Like SOM, who actually held seminars on Post-Modern design, he followed the change, but only in a small percentage of commissions. Cobb, Pei, Barnes, Ulrich Franzen – one after one the Modernists tentatively stuck their toe in the boiling waters of ornament. This raised a big and dangerous question for Post-Modernism. If the tradition of ornament had died, and if a deep philosophy of ornament had not developed, can the results be anything but hesitant? And perhaps kitsch? Was Kenneth Frampton right?

Books like *Ornamentalism* did not give much aid, beyond presenting a selection of largely American examples. The only profound book to appear on the subject at the time was E. H. Gombrich's *The Sense of Order*, which came out in 1979.[68] This elucidated ornament, or more generally pattern-making, from a psychological, historical and constructive viewpoint. It showed how ornament has visual logic and musical life. It leads the eye and mind forward to look for certain expectancies – a change in rhythm, a culminating theme, a beginning and end to an architectural idea. It makes sense of a building's function, it sets the moods and orchestrates the feelings. Above all it has its own internal necessity, rules and limitations. It is as autonomous as a discipline as Ungers' types, Botta's construction and Venturi's flat stereotypes. Alas, architects never read it, and it was not until the 1990s that a superior form of ornament returned, in the work of Eisenman and Libeskind.

In the meantime, however, representational ornament developed piecemeal, building by building, and there was the odd building in Japan that deployed its rhythmical use. Kazuhiro Ishii, who studied with Venturi and Moore at Yale, made use of his American training in the Gable Building, an inexpensive office building in Tokyo (215). Here several formal motifs order the tall profile. The stepped gable culminates the vertical movement set up by the side edges and central balconies. These last white elements lead the eye up

215 KAZUHIRO ISHII, *Gable Building*, Tokyo, 1978–80. The Dutch gable and Japanese Minka roof are mixed, as Ishii states in a tablet inscribed for the passer-by. The entrances to the offices and Sushi bar are announced by the eroded arches. (Katsuaki Furudate).

216 PHILIP JOHNSON and JOHN BURGEE, *AT&T Building*, New York, 1978–83. This, the media-event of Post-Modernism, has become, in the event, an urban landmark when seen from a distance. The pink granite sheathing is also a welcome change from its repetitive neighbors.

towards a broken semi-circle and split pediment – Venturian motifs – and thus the impression of a thin skyscraper is created within the overall tower. This visual movement is rather Baroque, since arches at the base are broken and the balconies are given slightly different articulation: the eye is kept moving up and down to where one expects a strong resolution. The expected Classical theme – base, shaft and capital – is partly fulfilled and yet partly denied since the usual Platonic forms are present, but eroded by dark voids. The stilted arches at the base are each cut on their inside edge to hang in space, a visual joke with a functional reason since they allow two entrances. But there is a perceptual logic to this joke as well, for it takes the cliché of the stilted arches and turns it into a new figure, a conjoined U-shape, which also reinforces the vertical movement. Thus Post-Modern Classicism revives one of the oldest stereotypes of the skyscraper, the tripartite elevation, in a fresh way.[69] These sort of towers were to grow, indeed multiply.

They did as Post-Modern Classicism became a media event in America in 1978, with Philip Johnson's AT&T

(216). This building was news for three reasons. It was meant for a multinational company that had more stockholders than any other in the world, it was set against all the New York flat-topped skyscrapers, and it was designed by the Modernist who established the International Style as a brand in 1932. Johnson, like the other Harvard graduates of Gropius, was indoctrinated in one movement and then left it for another. His switch of allegiance, however, caused more of a stir because he was *the* power-broker of new movements. When he changed direction *Time* magazine took note and put him on the cover. *The New York Times* did likewise, and the global media followed suit (in Britain, Hong Kong and South America). The building, not completed until 1984, was not quite as interesting as the media event was for architecture. This "tower of power" placed a dignified broken pediment above rows of windows and a base borrowed from Brunelleschi's Pazzi Chapel. It employed kitsch details, such as the Golden Boy of AT&T, and placed him on the High Altar behind this Pazzi Chapel. It imagined that smoke-rings would blow out of the top circular void, when the mechanical equipment and temperature were just right, a funny version of the *Lucky Strike* add in Times Square. It had nicely upturned ears on the top, giving it a lift. Smiling, knowingly, it captured the market, just as AT&T had done. The Post-Modern movement that had been a slowly flowing river for five years suddenly, with this Rossian gravestone, became a flood.

I well remember getting wet. I had just given an evening lecture at Yale University on the Death of Modernism/the Rise of Post-Modernism. The next day, on 31 March 1978, at precisely 7.46 am in the morning, that is 2,086 days after Pruitt-Igoe had been blown up, five architectural students burst into my hotel room, woke me up and thrust a copy of *The New York Times* in my face. On the front page was a photo of Johnson's new foray into Post-Modernism and, inside, an article by Paul Goldberger proclaiming it (wrongly of course) to be the "first monument" of the movement. The students enquired of this monolith (from one perspective it looks funereal) "Is Post-Modernism Dead?" The logic of their question was compelling. If Modernism failed because it got too big and corporate, then this structure to one of the world's biggest corporations must be the movement's kiss of death. Success had once again taken its toll, as in the nineteenth century, littered with the corpses of changing styles that could survive every persecution, cope with any situation, except the loving embrace of a commercial society.

I almost agreed with this diagnosis as a glance back at the diagram, "Crisis in Architecture," will reveal (above page 11). Perhaps, however, one building by Johnson would not so much kill it as make it middle-aged.

Many designers were joining a movement to which they were only partly committed. Some of them followed the Venturi formula for producing a tough, industrial realism:

its opposite, an Arts and Crafts individuality. This team produced several hybrids of concrete, wood and steel, mixing, of all things, traditional domes and geodesic lanterns. Like the work of Imre Makovecz in the same country, theirs is suggestive of regional craft and local symbolism, such as the trefoil taken from wooden Hungarian grave markers. But they combine this national expression with metaphorical forms adapted from nature, that is, the flowering blossom and, surprise, the latest technology (218). This example, like others from within the former Soviet orbit, showed that while Post-Modernism was an international movement it could lead in different directions. There was no single zeitgeist, except in architects' minds and the fashion industry. My purpose in mentioning this is to again underline how important it was for PM ideology and its "war on totality," especially with fashions of its own making. After all the pernicious notion of the zeitgeist was a Modernist snake, particularly in the hands of Marx and Hitler and, if it could be slain, then perhaps it would be by PM globalism itself, the plural mongoose.

There is a tendency for all architectural cultures to look inwards, to celebrate only their own national élites. But at the same time there are many international trends and much contact between architects at the global level. Thus when Post-Modern Classicism became a world movement it was inevitable that some architects, in countries where craftsmanship and production methods were at different

217 TERRY FARRELL, *TV-AM*, London, 1980–82. The central, public space culminates in a sunburst stair that acts as the focus of studio life. Eastern and Western images, Shinto Shrine and ziggurat, are set off against Hollywood. On the exterior, shades of industrial gray are used ornamentally with a cool sophistication. Farrell's exploitation of current technology on a decorative level is always fresh and pragmatic. (Richard Bryant).

218 GYORGY CSETE and JENO DULANSZKY, *Cave Research Station*, Pécs-Orfu Hungary, 1971–78. A geodesic dome is supported by a floral "petal" in wood and a concrete base: the metaphorical equivalent of nature research is thus symbolized in the volume and stylized volutes and trefoils. A mixture of modern fabrication and hand-crafted ornament, nationalist and Celtic decorative motif, (Group Pécs).

flat, brash, repetitive ornament – stylized and distorted – with signs stuck on. The Houston group called Taft extended its use in all sorts of inexpensive buildings, and Terry Farrell in England manipulated it with High-Tech details, again with ingeniously cheap methods of building. His television studios in London managed to recall the exotic glamor of TV settings – Japan, Mesopotamia and Hollywood – with thin, industrial materials (217). Perhaps the content was a bit trite – egg decorations are turned into giant finials because this is a *breakfast* television station – but Farrell exploited available techniques in a way that captured the site, the cars, and the fast-moving ephemera that is the media. After this building radio and television studios became PM stage sets, everywhere.

There were at the time, however, entirely other attitudes towards representation that resulted in a different kind of ambience. A group in Hungary called Pécs (from that city) combined the Venturian, flat stereotyped use of motifs with

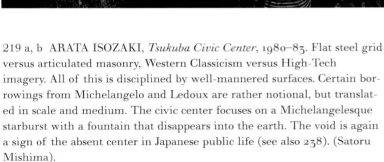

219 a, b ARATA ISOZAKI, *Tsukuba Civic Center*, 1980–83. Flat steel grid versus articulated masonry, Western Classicism versus High-Tech imagery. All of this is disciplined by well-mannered surfaces. Certain borrowings from Michelangelo and Ledoux are rather notional, but translated in scale and medium. The civic center focuses on a Michelangelesque starburst with a fountain that disappears into the earth. The void is again a sign of the absent center in Japanese public life (see also 238). (Satoru Mishima).

stages, should produce their own versions of the style. In Japan, Spain and France a more robust representational ornament was developed, more nuanced than the American variety, more three-dimensional. It was closer to the Classical masonry of the past, except carried out at larger scale and in unmalleable materials, such as reinforced concrete. Arata Isozaki, ever the eclectic, combined the Venturian flat ornament in metal with a more sculptural approach, and appropriately mixed these modes for a public building, the new civic center in Tsukuba (219a, b). His love of western architecture was expressed as a series of quotes

from past and present architects, a veritable encyclopedia of references. On this communal center he borrowed the heavy quoins that Ledoux had used, but turned them on the diagonal to emphasis their sculptural mass. Broken pediments, Apollo chasing Daphne through the garden, Moore's Piazza d'Italia, Graves' pergola, Michaelangelo's Campodoglio, Hollein's museum and ten more references were collaged into this quotation machine. Part of the idea was to mock the public realm at the very time it was asserted. The reason? Japan was trying to buy democracy and inventive science at Tsukuba, as if these things could be packaged and sold like any other product. Isozaki, by suppressing the communal space at the center, by pushing down Michaelangelo's sign of the heart of Rome, could send his double message: yes, we in Japan need this public meeting place, but no the social reality does not yet exist. At the center of the heart he put a hole, a vortex where all the water from the garden drains out, a Zen sign of absence. Here multiple signs and symbols are used for a point.

The case of Isozaki's radical eclecticism is interesting

between continents, expresses more than any other architect the potential heterogeneity of reference today. His work is the counterpart of the knowing consumer previously mentioned, that is, the knowing producer on a world stage.

If PM Classicism is employed by Isozaki to represent the public realm that does and does not exist, then Ricardo Bofill uses it for more associational and surrealist ends: to recall ancient stadia, engineering works, Soviet palaces for the people and, he sometimes hopes, giant non-sequiturs. Unfortunately the surrealism is not as controlled as the production methods and Bofill occasionally falls under the kind of malaprops I have been criticizing, but as for his mass-produced ornament it is extraordinary and exemplary

221 RICARDO BOFILL and the TALLER DE ARQUITECTURA, *Les Arcades du Lac*, St-Quentin-en-Yvelines, 1974–81. The heart of the scheme is a circular pedestrian piazza focusing on this enigmatic temple, another example of the Taller's mass-produced urban furniture in a Free-Style Baroque. The surrounding arcades are actually very small, while the end tower/columns are huge. The scale of pedestrian space will be more comvincing when the trees are fully grown.

220 ARATA ISOZAKI, *Art Tower*, Mito, Ibaragi, Japan, 1986–90. The museum, left background, adapts Palladian and Soanian motifs in an essentially Classical layout that contrasts with the fractured helix of steel triangles. More Japanese elements, such as the garden rock hanging above the water, are collaged onto this gray, Western background. Isozaki like Kurokawa accepts hybrid Japanese culture as both a rupture with the past and a seamless continuity. (Yasuhiro Ishimoto).

because it also reflects that of Post-Modern literature and philosophy. Influenced by the deconstruction of Jacques Derrida and the wider movement of "deconstruction from within," he plays with his own love-hate with the west, and allows the contradictions to come to the surface. Thus his buildings borrow from John Soane and Palladio, where there are semantic and structural reasons to do so, but they send clear signs that these thefts are gratuitous as well: Japanese versions of western solutions, combinatorial collages that have no deep cultural roots (220). All art and poetry is, to a degree, inbred, a reworking of previous solutions one loves. Isozaki, *the* global eclectic always travelling back and forth

222 TALLER BOFILL, *Theatre of the Palace of Abraxas*, Maine-la-Vallée, 1978–82. A ten-storey amphitheater is evenly divided into three visual storeys. Tuscan columns shoot up three storeys and are paired, giving a pleasing rhythm between windows; the vertical circulation is behind the fluted columns. The large vs small Order was a Michelangelesque motif; Bofill has been known to compare himself to this architect.

223 TALLER BOFILL, *Arch and Theatre of Abraxas*, all for low-cost housing. Glazed columns – living rooms – shoot up to three levels of planters and culminate in cypress trees, an ironic version of Le Corbusier's rooftop living.

as finish, as materiality. More to the point in this chapter it challenged notions of what construction can be. Ricardo Bofill and his Barcelona office, the Taller de Arquitectura, showed that current industrialization may lead to stereotypes, but they need not be flat and they can achieve very high precision. Indeed, concrete under quality control can sculpt the light as well as the best stone. Bofill, and then his countryman from Valencia, Santiago Calatrava, pushed concrete technology so far that it became a new form of sculptural material.

The first big scheme of the Taller in this genre was near Versailles and called Les Arcades du Lac (because it borders an artificial lake). It mass-produced arcades, window walls, broken pediments at triple the usual scale, that is, about one storey high. New functions are poured into old forms. An end column might be a stairway, or bathroom core. And a positive urban space is formed with this new constructional means, a pedestrian circus, or circular center (221). Once again there is a return to the notion of the heart of the city, and even a monument is placed there although, like Isozaki's "absent center," Bofill and the community had no particular idea of how this structure might be used. An existentialist temple to nothingness? The fact that this new town area is well-scaled, well-liked and repeated again and again was something of a challenge to modern mass-housing. Paradoxically, the work carried out certain ideals of the Modern movement: social housing for the masses at affordable prices. Sometimes

Bofill's work is commissioned by socialist mayors, sometimes it is loved by the inhabitants; and always it is mass-produced concrete of high quality. Together these ironies force unwelcome truths upon us. Before considering them other schemes should be mentioned.

More provoking than Les Arcades, because of its scale and symbolism, is the Palace of Abraxas, also on the outskirts of Paris (222, 223). Here again modern concrete is used to perform heavy Baroque tricks; again urban space is nicely molded to create an enclosed "theatre" that steps down to a large "arch" and densely planted *arbre*. But the handling of the Classical language and technology is more accomplished and the more interesting for being outrageous. Nine-storey fluted glass columns alternate with nine-storey pilasters of masonry. And they carry a triple capital of planting surmounted by a cypress tree! Is this a New Corinthian Order? Will giant, hormone-injected acanthus leaves shoot out of the six-foot high planters? In case these surreal, inhabitable glass columns are not exaggerations enough, there is a ten-storey, live-in *Arc de Triomphe* (in fluted Doric concrete) and a nineteen-storey *Palace of Abraxas* (named after that magician who gives us the celebrated nonsense known as abracadabra). It is a stimulating paradox, fitting for an architect who comes from the land of Don Quixote. Like Salvador Dali and Bunuel, from whom Bofill also learned, there is realism involved in these fantasies. They appeal to those they do not repulse: they remind the French that their Classicism can be the most proud, hard-edged and militaristic there is; they lend drama to everyday life and above all give an interesting image that is not just another metaphor of a machine.

Herein lies the unsettling message: mass-production is

224 TALLER BOFILL, *La Place du Nombre D'Or*, 288 apartments, shops and restaurants constitute a new French *place*.

not tied to any language of form, to Le Corbusier's machine aesthetic, or Venturi's flat appliqué, to archetypal universals, or anything. The notion that the fabrication process must lead to an inevitable style is shown to be a half-truth. In matters of style and metaphor the architect has a degree of choice, and responsibility. Organic, technological, Free-Style Classical, sculptural, ad hoc – and many more options are possible. The Taller not only mass-produced new towns in a monumental Classical style, but also small individual villas, the popular house. They made links with large French construction companies, such as Phoenix, who churn out industrialized Palladian temples by the thousands. This "Technological Classicism," as Peter Hodgkinson calls it, is quite different from some of the historicism we have looked at and as he says, "Much of Post-Modern Classical revivalism is a fad pretending to relate to the past. The Marne-la-Vallée complex relates to the future. It is the Cape Canaveral of the Classical space age, the return to a people's ritual."[70] As mass-housing La Place du Nombre D'Or in Montpelier is an alternative to the informal, non-place that is the norm (224). The pediments may seem heavy and mechanical, the pilasters and columns stereotyped, but the urban space is contained, pedestrian and appropriately shaded for Mediterranean life. These monuments may be a trifle bombastic, they may suffer from too much architecture, they may not be perfect in detail, but like the Brighton Pavilion, it is enjoyable to have them around, especially as options in a reductive age. They show that three-dimensional, constructed ornament can be put together with harmonic proportions and form positive urban space, modest but important goals.

225 Right: MICHAEL GRAVES. *Environmental Education Center*, New Jersey, 1980–83. Vernacular forms of wood and stucco construction are abstracted and given a monumental form: the square piers have an almost Egyptian stateliness to them. Note also the entrance truss, a transformed arch and pediment. (Acme Photo).

ABSTRACT REPRESENTATION – MEMORIES SUGGESTED

While straightforward communication remains a goal of Post-Modern architecture, as a poetic art it also employs idiomatic levels of discourse that are more suggested than named. This avenue of exploration, opened up by Ronchamp and the Sydney Opera House, was pushed in a Classical direction by Michael Graves, James Stirling and Hans Hollein.[71] Representational themes are abstracted and stylized to the point that their denotations are barely recognizable. Owen Jones, in the nineteenth century, showed how natural patterns became stylized in historical architecture, and endlessly transformed like musical themes.

In his work of the early 1980s, Michael Graves employed this suggestive method of transformation. For instance, at the Environmental Education Center, or what he called less pompously the "Frog Museum," he abstracts the square window, the aedicular or temple form, the square pier and round capital ornament and then constructs these shapes with very primitive means (225). The result, reminiscent of Leon Krier and Aldo Rossi, also recalls both vernacular and Classical architecture and the flat appliqué of Venturi. Graves' virtue at this time was to synthesize these sources through his drawings and paintings and give them seminal expression. Indeed for a moment the Graves Style became *the* hallmark of PM Classicism. The Frog Museum, as an abstract representation of various sources, is more effective than a literal quotation, because the memory is engaged in an active manner, it is forced to work over the material until its latent meanings are revealed. For instance, one only understands the point of the strange entrance arch, or "trellis-pediment," as a bridge when one sees its site-specific meaning: the museum is located overlooking a stretch of water near lower Manhattan where there are many highway bridges. And the primitive nature of the forms only becomes

meaningful when one relates them to their local function: as serving for a wild-life center dropped into a marsh. Beyond these hints and suggestions, this work was one of the first to carry out the idea of pavilion planning, a method of design that was to become important in the later synthesis of small-block urbanism. Treating a large scheme as a series of separate volumes, in contrasting materials, was further developed by Frank Gehry and the LA School.

For a library in San Juan Capistrano, Graves abstracted a similar grammar, but one based on the Spanish Mission Style since that is the local California vernacular. Here again the forms are heavy, reminiscent of Egyptian proportions and such things as obelisks, but in a general way. Partly this suggestion is achieved by crossing two related grammars, the Spanish Mission Style and the Hispanic architecture of South America, in particular the semi-curves of the former and "light monitors" of the latter (226). The village quality of this building also springs from such mixing and morphing, a quality which is playful without being trite, and one quite appropriate for dividing up a municipal library into semi-private places for reading.

Graves' ability to transform sources springs from his ability to draw. His notebooks are filled with many quick sketches, referential drawings of historic and vernacular buildings, which are abstracted and then combined in new ways. In a sense, he creates by elaborating pre-existing motifs until they look fresh, and fitting to the new context, but they always carry over some memories of the past. The dual nature is what gives his work such wide reference, it can call up the historical and the familiar without seeming hackneyed. This is particularly true of the Humana Headquarters Building, (227, 228) one of the most provocative skyscrapers built in recent years and a seminal work of Post-Modern Classicism, much more accomplished than his Portland Public Services Building because Graves was given a free hand and an adequate budget. The twenty-seven-storey structure relates both to its Modern and nineteenth-century neighbors, quite a feat since they are so different in scale and appearance. To one side, the older street scale is held with a low frontage while, to the other, the huge, black Miesian box is acknowledged in material and abstraction. Abstract representations of several local structures are sug-

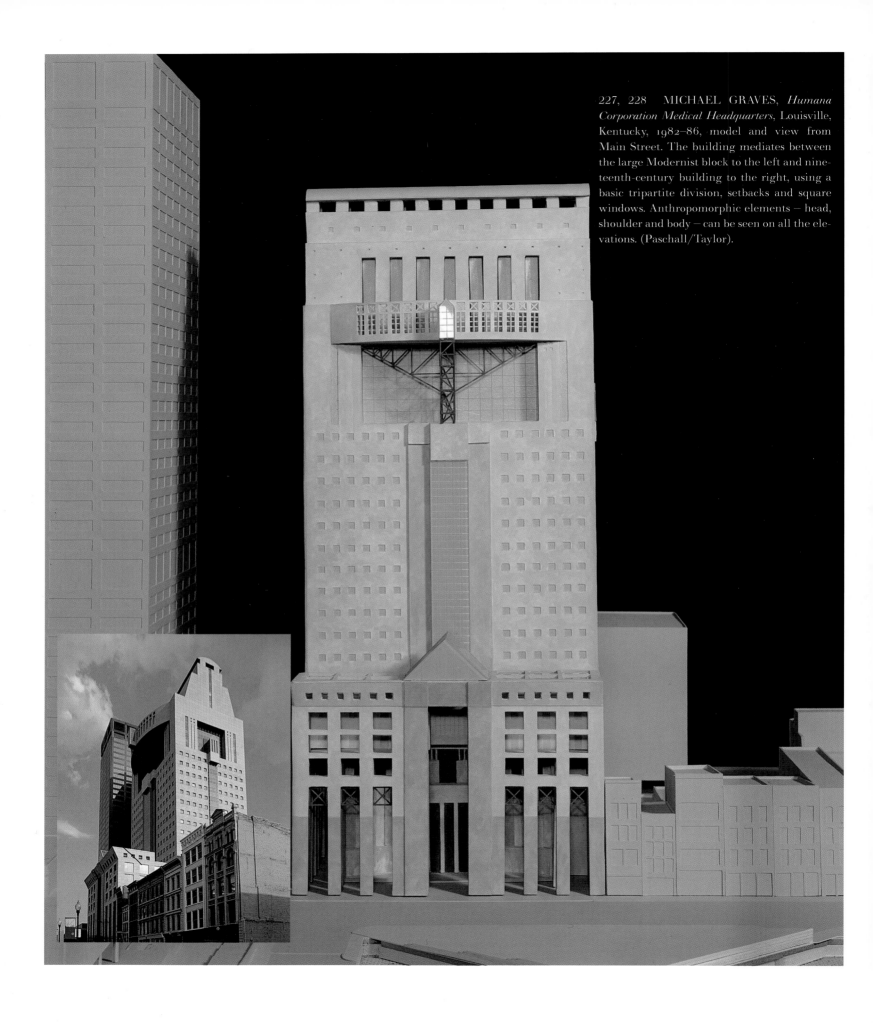

227, 228 MICHAEL GRAVES, *Humana Corporation Medical Headquarters*, Louisville, Kentucky, 1982–86, model and view from Main Street. The building mediates between the large Modernist block to the left and nineteenth-century building to the right, using a basic tripartite division, setbacks and square windows. Anthropomorphic elements – head, shoulder and body – can be seen on all the elevations. (Paschall/Taylor).

229 JAMES STIRLING, MICHAEL WILFORD and ASSOCIATES, *Clore Gallery*, London, 1982–86. This "garden building" with its pergola, pool and trellis, adapts the Classical grammar of the Tate and brick vernacular of an adjacent building to become a complex mediation of its context. Mannerist touches can be seen in the "hanging brick" (right) and the fact that the building changes material and rhythm not on the corners, as expected, but half way down one facade and on the diagonal. (Richard Bryant).

gested, not explicitly named. The bridges of the Ohio River are recalled by the cantilevered trusses on the twentieth floor, the 1930s Louisville dam is recalled in the topmost semi-circular crown and the pervasive industrial Classicism is generalized in the square windows, large moldings and tiny temples that mark the four horizons.

Such contrast of Classical shapes was taken up by many large firms, such as Kohn Pedersen Fox, to become an urban formula, but rarely carried through with such force as at Humana. The building recalls Le Corbusier's definition – "architecture is the masterly, correct and magnificent play of volumes in sunlight" – but here the juxtaposed volumes are given an urbane elegance. They also suggest, when looked at frontally, that PM standby, the symmetrical body or anthropomorphic figure. In the Louisville building this human presence confronts the river, giving scale and dynamism to inert material. The Humana Corporation becomes, as it were, an abstract representation of the humanist figure with its tripartite divisions – legs, torso and head. Graves also suggests a metaphor of the healing process by providing sun rooms with views over the river and water. Fountains meant to recall purification rites and, again, the

nearby Louisville dam further elaborate the idea. All in all it is a multivalent building which resolves into a tense whole the building task, anthropomorphism and urban landscape of the past and present.

James Stirling, since his Dusseldorf Museum scheme of 1975, continued to work patiently and slowly in a more understated form of Free-Style Classicism. It took him seven years to complete the Stuttgart Museum, and four to finish the Clore Gallery in London (229). Hans Hollein took ten years to realize his museum at Monchengladbach.[72] The slow pace meant this work could be carried through with a depth of thought not possible in the fast-build climate of America. And during these years an important social trend was more and more evident. The museum became the leading building type of the time, "the museum as cathedral" became a cliché with all the problems and opportunities this entailed. Art as a public religion, artists as priests, the art market as an engine of urban regeneration were ideas that raised questions that could not be escaped. The fact that they had no clear answers posed the basic problem for architects. It meant a building type with an inescapable role for architectural symbolism, but without a clear consensus on how this was to be handled. This remained a key challenge to which we will constantly return.

At the Clore Galley in London, an extension to the Tate, Stirling adopted a radical contextual approach to the museum. On the inside, where the Turner Collection was to be housed, he created the usual monumental route punctuated by incident and strong colors. Unfortunately the curators censored the deep red background for the paintings and turned the walls into an unassertive beige, something that drains the work of energy. On the outside, however, opposite colors and materials are used to heighten the experience of difference. Green windows slice through a background grid and provide a momentary glimpse into the garden. The entrance and the join with the old Tate employ a matching masonry. Next to an existing brick structure the grid is broken, on the diagonal, and takes on this coloring. Around the back, service side, the chameleon changes again taking on the color and texture of its environment. Because the site varies so much, Stirling transforms its façade five times, a precedent for PM contextualism that was to be followed by Robert Venturi in his London museum extension for the National Gallery. But again it is a contextualism that does not just repeat or fit in with its surrounding. The green grid of the entrance, the red pergola, the collage of trellis work, and the morphing of all of this into a pronounced hybrid are meant to challenge all sides of an equation. As at Stuttgart Stirling is insisting on the eclectic nature of the museum, the way it is a repository for opposite views of the good life. No grand synthesis is possible, beyond a collage within a grid.

Hans Hollein, a friend of Stirling, takes this pluralism in a different way in his museum at Mönchengladbach, towards a more labyrinthine plan. Originally designed in 1972, it was constructed from 1976 to 1982 and the time-lag

shows in its lack of pronounced ornament and symbolism, elements that were to become more explicit later. Fundamentally the museum is an acropolis,[73] a group of temples and warehouses of art, set on a hill enclosed by a public terrace, almost a Greek *temenos* (230). Undulating brick forms spill down the hill, conceptually vineyards in front of the acropolis, but they contain luscious plants not grapes. On top of this is the main propylaeum in marble with its honorific column in stainless steel. Then to one side is the main administration building – less of a temple and more of an office building with eroded undulations that echo the brick walls. Further buildings to left and right are a lecture hall and galleries. These are housed in still other forms and materials, so the effect of a complex collage is, as in Stirling's work, omnipresent. And the abstraction of themes is subtle enough to be occasionally missed. But, what is being represented here is a sacred enclosure of related but different temples. They may not have pediments, but their material and treatment mark them as special. The grid of sandstone and polished-aluminium facing, especially the way the mirror-plate window catches the reflection of the cathedral opposite, all mark the intention. It is a celebration of art, the local context and the significance of building types.

If, on the outside, the museum is being equated with the Acropolis and set as the twentieth-century equivalent of the adjacent church, then, on the inside, the meaning of art is given a different significance. For here a complex Post-Modern space allows the viewer to travel through the collection of Modern art in four or five routes. The implication is that there are various ways to interpret the destiny of Modernism: not one *zeitgeist* and story, as it used to be taught, but a plurality of meanings. But this again is only a suggestion of the plan and space. It is an abstracted labyrinth, not given a single label marked pluralism (231).

230 HANS HOLLEIN, *Städtiches Museum* Abteiberg, Mönchengladbach, 1976–82. The enclosed piazza in the air, or "temenos," connects the "propylaeum" left, with the city. The administration and galleries are to the right.

231 HANS HOLLEIN, *Städtiches Museum*, the interior with many routes through the labyrinth of art.

232 ARATA ISOZAKI, *Museum of Contemporary Art* (MOCA), Los Angeles, 1982–86. A curved Palladian window surmounts the library, while a diagonal pattern on green sheet steel indicates the administrative block. Indian red sandstone unifies most of the museum in this understated use of Classical sources. These subtle forms are used to create a constantly changing route full of gentle surprises, something that does not overpower the art.

Arata Isozaki, who has written on Hollein and Stirling, quite naturally follows a similar paradigm in his museum buildings. His temple for Modern art in Los Angeles, MOCA, is an eclectic mixture of western sources with hidden eastern references, all abstracted to the point of extreme ambiguity (232). Pyramidal galleries, a Renaissance garden, a diagonal trellis motif in steel (shades of Michael Graves), and the Palladian motif above the entrance gate are clearly western, while the sunken courtyard entrance, Indian sandstone and yin/yang circulation patterns are not so evidently eastern. There may be no great logic in the choice of lan-

guages or imagery, but the juxtapositions of styles and motifs again signify a generalized pluralism and the notion that art must today reflect this heterogeneity.

More single-minded is Gae Aulenti's conversion, along with French architects, of the Gare d'Orsay in Paris (233). Here an old fruity railroad station of 1907, in very Late Rococo, is transformed into a museum of nineteenth-century art. Egyptian motifs and proportions are abstracted to produce, where the trains used to move, very heavy walls and tight spaces that one might find in a Nile temple. The Egyptian style is only present as an abstract representation – there are no solar discs or lotus columns – and it is fairly suitable as a stable background for viewing sculpture and paintings. It also contrasts effectively with the ornate Beaux-Arts architecture and filigree of structure and top lighting. Like her conversions of the Pompidou Centre, the new Musée d'Orsay abstracts a generalized Classicism to calm down an over-voluble structure.

These interventions have been criticized for being too

233 GAE AULENTI and ACT, *Musée d'Orsay conversion*, Paris, 1980–86. A gently rising nave space contains nineteenth-century sculpture while different schools of painting are located behind the abstracted Egyptian forms in small spaces which are delicately layered, beautifully lit and subtly detailed in related forms of masonry.

234 *Musée d'Orsay*. Sculpture, painting, train shed and interior architecture placed in meaningful contrast. Jean-Baptiste Carpeaux's *Ugolin*, Thomas Couture's *Les Romains de la Decadence*, Victor Laloux's coffers and arches, and Gae Aulenti's masonry walls and frames – in ironic, but respectful, conversation.

Egyptian and reminiscent of Michael Graves for competing with the nineteenth-century building. But, it seems to me, such criticism entirely misses the point. The heavy forms provide an appropriately peaceful background for small paintings. They also allow countless framed views through tight apertures, and these reveal many interesting contrasts of the nineteenth century. And this creates a narrative the critics seem to miss or misunderstand. Up the left aisle of this cathedral/station, the avant-garde is given its sequence of rooms; up the right aisle the Academy has its *petits salons*; and up the middle a grand nave includes mixtures of avant-garde and reactionary art. The mixture is what has unnerved those who want to find their categories clearly distinguished. But again this misses the point, for they are separated *and* mixed. The argument that Aulenti and the curators are making assumes distinctions, but rather than repeating them, as every textbook does, they are confronting oppositions. They are taking the major building types of the nineteenth century – the power house, cathedral and museum – and forcing their meanings into close juxtaposition. It is not the usual Modernist isolation of movements, not the wide cube and the decontextualization of art, but a confrontation with our pluralist predicament.

Every now and then the space opens up on a surprising set-piece that forces one to face the horrific and contradictory beauty of the previous century. As one reaches the main transept of the nave one finds a somewhat kitsch product of academia that is used as a comment on the role of the museum today. The placement of *The Romans of the Decadence*, by Thomas Couture (how appropriate a name), is a nice piece of curatorial wit and the way it is framed and set up by the architectural promenade supports the design as well (234). And it all culminates at the high end of the train shed/nave. This focuses on an altar and shrouded model of Charles Garnier's Paris Opera House, something that can also be walked over, because Aulenti has sunk a model underneath a glass floor. "Paris capital of the nineteenth century," Paris a premonition of the twentieth? In effect art as spectacle, art as social religion, art as subliminal economic warfare are already themes a hundred years ago.

It is the quality and liveliness of the spaces that here heighten our perception of meaning. Small-scaled spaces, contained like closed rooms, are punched apart to reveal parallel movements and contrasts. As in Hollein's museum there is the possibility of both linear and comparative history, a sequence of schools and opposition of movements. This museum handles such contradictions very well, particularly that between small, domestic art and large-scale public works. By adapting the conventions of PM space – its layering, surprise and historical associations – Aulenti has been able to control her medium. And by turning these means to a symbolic programme that faces art as religion, she has engaged the basic question of the time. It was not to be addressed so clearly until Frank Gehry took it on ten years later at Bilbao.

POST-MODERNISM BECOMES A TRADITION — THE BLURRING OF PAST, PRESENT AND FUTURE

By the mid-1980s Post-Modernism became a widespread tradition with many large offices producing huge works at great speed: Philip Johnson, SOM (when they eschew Modernism) and KPF (Kohn Pedersen Fox). As the reader will recall from the chart on pages 53–58 success produces its usual problems. Modernism suffered from over-production and the vulgarization of its language, and there is no reason to suppose the new tradition would not also succumb to these same pressures. Already there was enough kitsch PoMo for some to declare the movement moribund, so the few large-scale buildings that evade this death sentence are especially relevant. They survived not because of their innovations or personality, but because of the quality of their construction and the thoughtfulness with which they carry through the new ideas. In this chapter we are looking at the ambivalence that comes with success, large commissions and commercial practice. Direction and creativity are sacrificed for the realization of ideas, the oldest of trade-offs. But then these ideas can be understood more impersonally for their implications, irrespective of personality.

KPF, the most commercially successful PM firm, have produced thirty or more skyscrapers using contextualist arguments. For the Procter & Gamble Headquarters in Cincinnati, they abstracted an Art Deco language of truncated pyramids and stepped octagons (235a). These forms are placed at a key juncture of the city where the expressway meets downtown. To mark this urban gateway, they designed two rather squat towers sheathed in white-and-gray masonry (235b). This language continues that of the pre-existing building, then subtly bends it towards more urban ends, forming a park-like setting on the city side. The interior carries through the grammar of octagons, white marble and stainless steel with a precision and consistency that is rare in a large building. Predictably there are no surprises and little individuality here — it is Procter & Gamble after all — yet the professionalism commands respect. Who else but a large integrated firm could achieve a consistent quality at such a scale and down to such detail? At the same time the idea that contextualism is both a continuation of and a challenge to the context is lost. Venturian and Rossian irony are missing, there is no resistance to the context, no collage or collision city, no raising of consciousness, no deconstruction from within. For these reasons the scheme is more a straight revival of the context than a Post-Modern intervention. The softening of focus is characteristic of all large-scale work in general, a blur that can be positive if it is understood and featured as such.

Contextualism has provided an acceptable excuse for the return to historical forms and thus it emerged as a major argument for those former Modernists committed, as they were, to a rationalist aesthetic. Cesar Pelli and Tom Beeby are such recent converts and their architecture reminds us that the best Post-Modernists still keep one eye focused on their former training. Pelli, whose office is nearly as productive as KPF, will adapt practically any visual grammar based on the local context, but he treats it as a thin curtain wall that reveals — for those who care to look — the reality of the steel construction underneath. Thus his work on the Rice campus in Texas takes the pre-existing Romanesque Style, rendered in red brick and white masonry, and gives it a contemporary jazz of staccato horizontals and ribbon windows. The rhythms of shape are emphasized by a change in material, from brick to steel to glass, and are underlined by a

235b KOHN PEDERSEN FOX ASSOCIATES, *Procter and Gamble Headquarters*, Cincinnati, 1982–86. Two truncated towers mark the city gateway to one side and contain an urban park on the other side. An octagonal geometry rendered in white, silver and gray ties the old building with the new.

235a KOHN PEDERSEN FOX ASSOCIATES, *Procter and Gamble Headquarters*, Cincinnati, 1982–86.

236 CESAR PELLI & ASSOCIATES, *Rice Jones School*, Houston, Texas, 1983–85. A contextual skin is hung on a steel frame to reveal the underlying construction. Both the diaper pattern of bricks and the lines of the thin walls are emphasized and thus the historical language is given new rhythms and meaning. (Paul Hester).

change in color, from pink to Burgundy red. On the end of each of the two long wings is a diaper pattern of bricks punctuated at random and with the side walls sliding by, visually separated. This punctuation and immaculate separation underline the point that the cladding is a thin veneer, not a real Romanesque structure of stone. So, as with Stirling's Stuttgart, both the truth *and* falsity of construction are expressed, made into an ornamental detail.

This may seem a subtle and didactic point, but it is what distinguishes Post-Modern contextualism from straightforward veneer, a point as we shall see, not germane to Michael Graves. For Pelli, however, the artifice of construction becomes a subject, consciousness is heightened. Furthermore, these signs become the pretext for inventing new rhythms and proportions in an old language. Thus while the context provides the rationale for the chosen grammar, the structure and construction provide the cues to how it is articulated. This keeps Pelli's buildings fresh and honest and also, as Frank Lloyd Wright called such work, flat-chested.

Pelli, like James Stirling, takes particular pleasure in showing the logic of construction and this may result in a truncated top, as at Rice (236), or a brittle surface that accentuates flatness. Most of his Modernist work achieved an exaggerated tense quality – like the Blue Whale – because it developed the thin skin that elided glass wall and mullion. This "membrane aesthetic" has now been pushed in a PM direction with the introduction of complex ornamental patterns and polychromy. The resultant mixture is unusual enough to deserve a new name – "High-Tech Contextualism" – and it can be seen in the addition to Carnegie Hall in New York (237). Here the pre-existing Renaissance grammar is shot upwards to sixty storeys and

flattened out in a crisp grid of well-proportioned rectangles and areas of contrasting colors. The spiky structure at the top, which carries window-cleaning equipment, becomes the contemporary equivalent of a cornice. Pelli, in effect, is looking for new uses and proportions for old forms.

Kisho Kurokawa, the Japanese architect, often achieves a similar blend and blur, what he calls an "architecture of symbiosis." Past, present and future are consciously synthesized into an ambiguous whole and the results can be beautifully enigmatic. One is never quite sure whether the synthesis is, in the end, incongruous or limpid. In either case, it is masterfully done, harmonious and just a bit facile. Whereas Stirling will confront past, present and future as if there were no question of peaceful coexistence between them, Kurokawa blends them together into a seamless web. His Wacoal building, for a major lingerie manufacturer, looks directly at the Emperor's Palace in the heart of Tokyo. As is

237 CESAR PELLI & ASSOCIATES, *Carnegie Hall Extension*, New York, 1986. The familiar Post-Modern treatment of a skyscraper is enlivened by the rigorous use of a thin skin and the re-interpretation of traditional motifs. The cornice serves to suspend window cleaning equipment. (Cesar Pelli).

238 KISHO KUROKAWA, *Wacoal Building*, Tokyo, 1982–85. Kurokawa's eclecticism resolves an unusual array of styles and motifs within a gray aesthetic. The scale of this large headquarters is broken down by a tartan of small grids which are punctuated by advertisement and signs of the Edo Period. They are absorbed into a totality without conflict or irony. (K. Kurokawa).

239 *Wacoal Building*, executive reception room in shades of gray mixes traditional sliding screens and brackets with a Free Style Classical Order, in the center, which has a dissolving capital and weightless mirror base. The "symbiosis" of East and West, high-tech and tradition. (K. Kurokawa).

often observed this palace and emperor cannot be seen, they are the absent center, the presence of the absence that Isozaki sought to represent in the void at the heart of Tsukuba.

Thus with Wacoal a potentially fraught and ironic situation. The eye of fashion, women's panty girdles and so forth, is focused directly on this missing center of Japanese tradition and power. Commerce confronts culture, the ephemeral dominates the permanent, at least in scale and visibility (238). Kurokawa is intensely conscious of such oppositions, but unlike a Westerner he chooses to smooth over the differences. Therefore, in the Wacoal Building, the emblematic "eye of fashion" is both a telescope looking into the future of *haute couture* and a somewhat traditional rising sun, with signs from the Edo Period, looking at the Emperor and the past. A Roman barrel vault is rendered in a newly

invented glass material which emphasizes the slickness and sensuality of the surface. Indeed Kurokawa, drawing on Delueze and Guattari's notion, describes the structure as a "pleasure machine" and one can find many parallels between the inherent sensuality of the product "skin-hugging lingerie" and the quality of the finish. In one place an artist has impressed the nude female body onto the glistening steel façade. On the ninth floor, in a reception room, polished and reflective surfaces in various shades of gray again convey the hedonistic mood of luxuriant sensuality (gray for Kurokawa is the color of ambiguity, the "both-and"). But this space is more than an up-market boutique: an integrated kaleidoscope of heterogeneous meaning (239).

The doorway is adapted from the work of the Renaissance architect Giacomo della Porta, the walls have

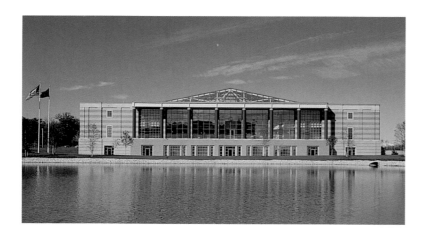

240 HAMMOND, BEEBY AND BABKA, *American Academy of Pediatrics*, Elk Grove Village, Illinois, 1984–85. A set of Classical types is cleverly combined and hung on a steel frame which is symbolized in the brick pilasters and illusionistic pediment. The robust coloring recalls nineteenth-century theories of polychromy. (Tom Beeby).

Japanese brackets and sliding screens and the columns are a new Order with mirrors top and bottom that dissolve their weight. This mixture, to distinguish it from Pelli's, might be called High-Tech Eclecticism, yet the "symbiosis" is complete enough that one might well overlook the differences in mood and meaning. With such smooth ambiguities Kurokawa comes close to conveying the homogenized variety of an information society, the way it will incorporate all contradictions into a total ideology or lifestyle. Some will fault this as consumerist and argue that it suppresses experience and dissent, as did Modernism. But like the Baroque style, with which it shares totalizing motives, it can actually enhance experience and choice when done well.

There have been many calls for a synthesis of technology and cultural expression, which amount more to statements of intent than announcements of success. Cesar Pelli, Kisho Kurokawa, Mario Botta and others are trying to reach this middle ground. The desire for synthesis is real and it is not just confined to architects; but it remains on the horizon. Through the abstract representation of themes, the opposite poles of technology, on the one hand, and history, context and anthropomorphism on the other hand, are brought into a tenuous form of union. Tom Beeby, previously in the Miesian tradition like so many other Chicago architects, pursues such a synthesis. His American Academy of Pediatrics shows the typical Post-Modern formula of banded masonry contrasted with steel structure, closed and permanent forms set off by more open and light-hearted ones. Basically, on the lakeside elevation, the building is an octastyle temple front crowned by the white outline of a steel pediment (which is cleverly the half-conic section of an atrium in the back), with palazzo book-ends and a rusticated base. The plan shows the same freestyle mixture of

Classical precedents that call on Mies and Palladio equally (240). The restrained gravitas of the whole building might have appealed to both of Beeby's exemplars — except for the robust coloring. With this building, Post-Modernism returns to the knowing game of constructional representation where brick pilasters divide up the surface into well-proportioned rhythms and every other one signifies the actual steel construction inside. But, whereas Palladio or Mies would have confined himself to the use of homogeneous materials and structure, Beeby uses brick cladding, limestone trim and steel-plate columns and cornice — the last two painted in strong colors. As a result the building manages to be both serious and lively, background and foreground. It takes on a series of "both-and" antinomies, just as Venturi recommended, which mediate between the extremes of technical necessity and cultural expression.

The blurred dualism of Kurokawa and Beeby becomes even more blended in the work of the Belgian Charles Vandenhove. So subtle and complete is his interweaving of past and present that one can look at his building as the architectural equivalent of the duck-rabbit figure. Seen volumetrically it is fifteenth century; seen structurally it is twentieth; the more one looks the more it flip-flops between periods like one of those hybrid morphed photographs blending the features of Margaret Thatcher and Julius Caesar. Vandenhove is an architect who, like Beeby, departed from an earlier Miesian approach based on constructional purity. His work has developed patiently in a direction that uniquely combines technical and semantic aspects, using constructional elements such as the precast column to carry specific contextual meaning. These virtually constitute

241 CHARLES VANDENHOVE, *Renovation in Hors-Château*, Liege, 1978–85. Sixteenth-century *hôtels* restored with a new polished concrete Order (left) and apartment building with its prefabricated grid of post and beams (right). This new/old fabric contains the Place Tikal, a square with several sculptural monuments including Tikal by Anne and Patrick Poirier. (C. Bastin & J. Evrard).

242 CHARLES VANDENHOVE, *Portico to Place Tikal*, Hors-Château, Liège, 1980. The entryways and important points of Vandenhove's buildings are articulated with invented Orders, both beautiful and technically current. (C. Bastin & J. Evrard).

243 CHARLES VANDENHOVE, *Le Salon Royal*, Renovation in the Théâtre de la Monnaie, Brussels, 1986. Guilio Paolini's sculpture is rotated in opposition, connected by thin bronze wires and fragmented on the ceiling; the floor stripes are by Daniel Buren; a running frieze, blank windows and icy marble complete this surreal installation by Vandenhove. (Charles Vandenhove).

a new Order of architecture, something that ties Vandenhove directly into the Western tradition. Instead of parodying or copying the Doric or Ionic Order, Vandenhove will imitate their spirit using contemporary technology.

Furthermore, he gives artists a primary role in articulating a building or urban space. One of his most convincing works is the reconstruction of a small part of Liège, Hors-Château, which consists of single-family dwellings grouped around a tiny pedestrian square (241). For this he has invented the "Liège Order," a post-and-beam system in concrete, that articulates the most significant entries with an amusing but beautiful version of the Ionic Order, with its bull's-eye volutes. In the background he uses the more appropriate and understated version of the Doric, with T-capitals and stepped architraves (242). Cast-iron window boxes repeat the steps in a different key, and the sculpture, by Anne and Patrick Poirier, which gives the new square its name, rings yet another change on the motif, turning it into a totem-like ziggurat. The texture of this rehabilitated *Place Hors-Château* recalls that of the past since the new post-and-beam structure is comparable in scale to what existed; but because the Order so successfully fuses an ornamental and constructional logic it avoids anachronism.

In his other work, Vandenhove has continued to mix approaches and cross disciplines. For the sixteenth-century Hotel Torrentius, where he now lives and works, he has grafted square geometries and a Secessionist vocabulary onto the former Renaissance building to produce an inclusive whole that combines various periods of art as well. For the Opera in Brussels, he worked with the artists Sol LeWitt, Sam Francis, Daniel Buren, and Giulio Paolini to redesign several key spaces, including a paradoxical marble chamber that reverses expectations. On the ceiling hang sculptural fragments, on the floor are suggestions of wooden beams, while Paolini's sculpture is duplicated in reverse at either end. In such interventions, his control of constructional elements complements the art and the pre-existing building. Classical precedent underlies these structures, but so too does a Modern sensibility (243). In this way, Vandenhove is something of a missing link between the past and present. His existence poses a nice evolutionary puzzle. What would have happened to the twentieth century if, instead of a rupture with the past, architecture had transformed itself gradually, step by step? There would have been seamless continuity, an interweaving of meaning, a more humane discourse, an uninterrupted urban fabric. It did not happen.

One goal of Post-Modernism that runs like a thread throughout this diverse movement is the notion of inclusion, including all of society. But this is a problem. For if society is a layer-cake and boiling pot of difference, not a totality called "the people," then architecture should reflect this plurality by calling on different languages and profes-

244 CHARLES JENCKS, *The Cosmic Oval, Thematic House*, London, 1984. Entryway with architecture, painting and words relating various cosmic narratives.

245 CHARLES JENCKS, *The Sun Stair* with 52 steps, radiating elements, sun, earth and moon spiraling through space over a black hole (by Eduardo Paolozzi).

sional codes. The idea is to nurture the multi-voiced discourse, as it is termed in PM literature, or keep an obligation towards the difficult whole, as Robert Venturi set the ideal for an inclusive architecture. This means, among other things, employing differing building arts and making them work together on common ideas. If some themes are shared then construction, ornament, furniture, signs and works of art can play together. This integration recalls the *gesamtkunstwerk* of previous times, the total work of art and architecture, except now the totalities are dissonant wholes, a mosaic of parts whose themes overlap. It is the relationships that form the unity.

By the mid-eighties I began to understand why such an approach was essential for Post-Modernism. The movement had already started to degenerate into a weak eclecticism, anything goes, "ornamentalism" as the American book called it, where lipstick on the gorilla meant to humanize the beast only made it more grotesque. Without some rhyme and reason to ornament, without some theme and content worth expressing, architecture – especially under Reaganite and Thatcherite capitalism – was turning into the kind of unthinking pastiche that Modernists had always feared. Venturi and Scott Brown had proposed the notion of the decorated shed as an answer to the social and economic forces at

work. By now it was clear this did not produce a symbolic architecture, as they hoped, but rather something I called "signolic architecture"[74]: that is, signs stuck on minimum structures. The result was the opposite of symbolism, a dissociation between signifier and signified, form and content. Symbolism, by contrast, only results when sign, ornament, space, structure and the entire building task are related. Relationships are the key, they produce the ambiguities and resonance of the symbol.

This was the idea behind a polemic I wrote, *Towards a Symbolic Architecture*. It featured a building I worked on for five years, with artists and architects, the Thematic House, an attempt to show how a resonant symbolism could emerge when construction was guided by a series of iconographic programmes loosely organized around the themes of time and contemporary cosmology. Common themes – the sun, earth, moon, the seasons, galaxies and asteroids – furnished one set of programmes, while more esoteric and private ones – black holes, windows on the world, London weather – supplemented these (244). The content, although not equivalent to the great meta-narratives of the past, was at least more significant than what commercial society was throwing up. Univalent content, criticized in Part One of this book, could be challenged if architects looked to the themes emerging in contemporary science and philosophy. So the Thematic House brought together the plastic arts around a narrative conceived as celebrating the cosmos and our place in it. Symbolism, where we were lucky enough to achieve a fusion of signs and meanings, was the result of multiple-coding. For instance, the spiral staircase, the sun stair with its fifty-two undulating steps, is surrounded by spiraling railings (245). These hold globes – sun, earth, moon, aster-

and gestural. The fundamentalist Classicism of Mario Botta is typical of this last partial shift. It mixes basic stepped forms with brick construction, a primary-shape grammar (circles and squares) with vestigial moldings, and the extreme mannerist contrast of interior technology erupting through an exterior envelope that looked permanent (246). Green sprouts, sign of the impending ecological crisis, surmount his offices and churches, primitive markers of the First Tree.

The Mississauga City Hall, by Ed Jones and Michael Kirkland, is also characteristic of this trend, a type of proto-symbolic architecture that stops short of an iconographic programme, but one that nonetheless resolves function,

247 ED JONES AND MICHAEL KIRKLAND, *Mississauga Civic Center*, 1982–87. The view from the southeast reveals the opposition of primary building types: colonnade, amphitheater, pediment building, campanile, tower and rotunda – an object lesson in small-block composition reminiscent of Leon Krier's School for 500 Children. (Robert Burley).

248 The plan reveals the architectural promenade from the south public area to the north governmental area, and the two secondary cross-axes. The section shows the sequence through high and low volumes connected by The Great Hall; the office tower and Council Chamber are both connected by forced perspectives.

246 MARIO BOTTA, *Office Building*, Lugano, Switzerland, 1981–85. A Platonic geometry, with brick used in ornamental patterns, is eroded to reveal a stern, high-tech interior. Botta achieves many Mannerist contrasts including an overall "big-smallness," here realized by adopting a simple, small figure and using it at gigantic scale. (A. Flammer).

oids – that spiral down to a black hole, designed by Eduardo Paolozzi. The other way they spiral up to the light, energy and, when it's out, the sun. When you look at any of these forms it is not possible to tell whether they are designed for functional, ornamental, or representational reasons: they resonate between these frames of reference, as do symbols. Signs, by contrast, have more definite and singular meanings and, my argument was, we needed a symbolic not signolic architecture.

Not many PM architects pursued this line of thinking. A few young designers such as NATO, led by Nigel Coates, began to work with artists and artisans on a narrative architecture. Frank Gehry and Michael Graves integrated art into their work, but it was not content-driven. Public art programmes around the world and collaborations between artists and architects became more prevalent in the 1980s, but their approach rarely went beyond a collage of oppositions. Symbolic ornament, when it did occur, tended to be primitive

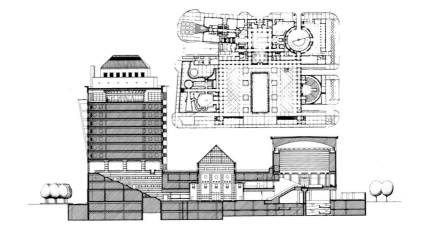

249 The Council Chamber rotunda with its paired Tuscan Doric columns and a frieze of sconces has a dark-blue fresco by Sharon McCann. This combines the constellations with images of Indian legends. (Robert Burley).

image, technology and sign (247). In that sense it becomes resonant and symbolic. This city hall, in search of its city, combines various influences – the small block composition of Leon Krier, some formal motifs of Aldo Rossi, Rob Krier and James Stirling – and it makes them fitting for a public building located in an unlikely place. It sits in Canadian suburbia, midway between urban Toronto and a farming community. Hence its mixture of a civic and vernacular language.

A clock tower, one of Rossi's cheerful blue *cabanons*, is the high-flyer meant to be visible from the highway. It is held aloft on steel cross-bracing above abstracted pediments and a rotunda. The signs are complex yet conventional enough to root the building in the community (248). Like a medieval city hall the belfry and palace block dominate the front of the *res publica*. We approach an open square shaded on three sides by colonnades. Basic functions are placed within Platonic solids clearly marked: mayor and adminis-

tration, office tower, and cylindrical council chamber (249). Further cues underscore the importance of these spaces. For instance, the banded masonry increases in scale, color and emphasis as one walks through the sequence to its final culmination in the rotonda. Here once again is the PM circle as heart of downtown (or at least its hope). All this is carried through in a sober yet dynamic language that can speak coherently of place, function and history.

One of the attractions of the Civic Center is the way it becomes a variegated fortress set in an open landscape. From a distance the massive solids in wheat-colored brick contrast with the big sky and flat prairie, rather like a medieval citadel done in Cotswold stone. Cream colors are set against blue and green following a well-proven formula. This is only slightly marred by the eclecticism of the campanile which never makes up its mind whether it is a Romanesque tower, engineering structure or blue *cabanon*. The positive intention is to recall local industrial farming. If there is one obvious hiccup in this exemplary discourse it is in the height of the cylindrical Council Chamber, which surely should have risen above the pediment-building of the councilors' suites.

Surely the acts of political life should dominate over the administration of things.

Nonetheless, in Mississauga the basic approach of small block planning and collage of Classical solids is particularly dynamic, especially when approached from the south-east where each volume sets off the next in a sequence of contrasts. Square pavilion, semi-circular amphitheater, broad pediment, campanile, tower, cylinder and rectangle – a basic typology of urban forms are juxtaposed on an axial plan and "architectural promenade." The focus for a democratic architecture in the Greek and medieval past was the agora and public square. Here, in suburbia, a clever transformation of this idea is achieved by extending porous "arms," the colonnades, into the landscape. Thus much larger assemblies are possible, ones that have both a city outdoor room and a prairie lawn. Civic hope *and* suburban reality. Cook-outs, car rallies, spectators at a pop festival are all absorbed into this inclusive architecture.

One enters the representational institution from the north through a great hall surmounted by a glass pyramid. This building type developed from Ed Jones' former scheme for the Northampton County Hall, 1973, and it amounts to one more giant northern atrium, a protective space for the long winters. The bands of black and green marble now play the exterior theme in a more sensual key, an appropriate intensification – except that it makes the culminating bands of the Council Chamber look rather bland by comparison. The atrium again repeats the motif of the rostrum over an arch and the small square window in different rhythms, a formula of many Post-Modern Classicists.

From this point the architectural promenade forks, one way up a perspectival stair to the office tower, the other way up an escalator to the rotunda. Here one reaches the Holy of Holies, the Pantheon with its dark blue ceiling of constellations and child-book Indian legends, its paired columns, sconces, lettering and rusticated bands. This space looks reduced in height from eleven to seven bands and, as mentioned, it might well be bigger on the outside. But if this is a bit of an anti-climax it is due in no small measure to the competence of what has occurred before. For the overall planning is a tightly organized sequence of axes and cross-axes, forced perspectives and culminating halls, low spaces set against high, square against circle, and one building type against another. It always holds our interest while at the same time dividing government into a village of workable blocks. The building thus represents many of the most cogent ideas and motifs developed by PM Classicists by the middle 1980s and shows the level at which they have gelled into a paradigm for a developing tradition.

Unfortunately, as we will see, this approach lost intensity and direction at the very moment it became a new international style around the world. Success and commercialization claimed another victim.

POST-MODERNISM BETWEEN KITSCH AND CULTURE

An architectural movement often finds it easier to survive persecution than success. Widespread acceptance not only diffuses the aims of a tradition, because so many followers get them partially wrong, but it also confuses the leaders. Single-minded and strong in opposition, they lose direction when they become the focus for mass culture and adulation. They may confuse their own success with a deeper change in society or the profession of architecture: or their message may be co-opted by large firms in a way that betrays its essential meaning. Such things happened to Post-Modern architecture by the late 1980s as it became successful, middle-aged, part of the establishment and taught in the academies.

Every movement has its inherent weakness. That of Modernism was mass-produced boredom, the machine aesthetic repeating itself endlessly; that of PM was Ersatz, the sign and image replicating themselves endlessly. High on the Post-Modern agenda was the idea of speaking to a pluralist society, the notion that architecture should cut across high and low taste cultures with a double coding that still holds the integrity of different voices. The inherent danger? That each voice is compromised, the blur of the last chapter becomes a pudding. In the 1950s Dwight MacDonald and other literary critics damned such mixed gruel as Mid-Cult – neither high nor low culture but a parody of both. This is the constant danger for Post-Modernists in every area, especially the most commercial ones: film, TV, music, the popular novel and architecture. The Post-Modern novelist John Barth identified this problem in literature, where writers were searching for an audience wider than that sought by the Modernists, "the Early Christians: professional devotees of high art." Post-Modernists may be constantly tempted to simplify their message, edit out its irony, critical stance and double coding, and appeal to the largest group with the falsely consoling idea of an integrated culture.[75]

This oversimplification betrays the basic goal of the movement, which is to enhance pluralism and cultural difference while remaining committed to society as "a difficult whole." Totalization, by contrast, was often the goal of traditional culture and Modernism, especially in the 1930s. Then Walter Gropius, Mies van der Rohe, Giuseppe Terragni and Le Corbusier, among many others, made their placating overtures to the centralizing states of the time – the Nazis, Fascists and Petain's government.[76] Modernists today prefer to forget these revealing slips, especially since their movement is often portrayed as anti-establishment and pure. But these lapses coupled with inadvertent praise should make them look again. As mentioned, in 1936 Nikolaus Pevsner defended the new architecture as "totalitarian" (in *The Pioneers of the Modern Movement*) and one

250 MICHAEL GRAVES, *The Dolphin and Swan Hotels*, model from the north, 1987. The volumes have a flat monumental quality like Boullée's diagrammatic drawings. The Scaleless Sublime. (W. Taylor).

251 MICHAEL GRAVES, *Swan Hotel*, Lake Buena Vista, Florida, 1987–90. If one overlooks the diagrammatic tents and underlooks the clichéd emblems, there is some rather sophisticated ornament and architecture in between. Lapping turquoise waves play a nice game of camouflage with the window patterns, and the long sweeping curve of the roof is a fresh gestural shape that Graves has added to his repertoire. (Steven Brooke).

can find similar remarks by these same pioneers. Their halo has always been a bit tarnished. The "universalist" tendency of Modernism was always an inducement to compromise with power, and remains so. Post-Modernists, with their theories of pluralism, have produced a new form of compromise – sending different groups or taste cultures different messages – and not trying to resolve the implications for society as a whole. To repeat: there is a downside to all traditions, especially evident when they are most successful.

DISNEY GIVES PM THE KISS

In 1985 Michael Eisner, head of the Walt Disney empire, set up the Disney Development Corporation and decided to develop theme parks, resorts and convention hotels as an integrated package. In this he was enormously enterprising, transforming a $1 billion per year turnover into $5 billion, revenue which was most dependent on parks and resorts, not films.[77] Euro-Disneyland, which opened in 1992 outside Paris, is a $2.3 billion, 4,800-acre resort/theme-park and what-have-you, with Grid Building by Frank Gehry, the Happy Trails Motel by Antoine Predock and other themoids by Antoine Grumbach, Michael Graves and Robert Stern. James Stirling, when asked, refused to play the game. Disney World in Florida, on 28,000 acres, is already a mega-park of specialized fun. This is perplexing, Why millions of people like to congregate together in one fantasy ghetto to undergo a strict regime of entertainment escapes me, but it is a secret on which the Disney corporation has thrived for years. Apparently it succeeds because of safety and control: the whole family can have an outing where thrills are pre-

dictable, danger is simulated and real problems – crime, drunks, accidents – never occur. The formula of controlled ride-through parks, Ersatz and mechanized experience appeals to the masses as much as it does to the multinationals and, as I pointed out at the beginning of this book, it led to "the crisis of Modern architecture." Fifteen years later it struck Post-Modernism.

Robert Stern designed Michael Eisner's parents' Manhattan apartment in the early 1970s so it was predictable that Eisner would consult Stern for architectural advice. This led to a meeting with Michael Graves and the transformation of Disney, as Paul Goldberger put it, into "the IBM of the Post-Modern age."[78] Not only did this conglomerate commission well over a billion dollars of work from Post-Modern architects, but Eisner asked Graves and Stern for strategic advice in transforming his empire from what was a mass-cult enterprise – when Walt Disney died – into something more up-market. The results can be seen in the two hotels by Michael Graves in Florida (250, 251).

The first point is too obvious to mention, but from it everything follows: Graves' structures are big (253). The Swan Hotel, with its twenty-eight-ton turquoise birds, has 758 bedrooms. The Dolphin Hotel has 1,510 and together

252 MICHAEL GRAVES, *Dolphin Hotel*, Lake Buena Vista, Florida, 1987–90. The amplification of Classical elements, following Bofill's example, results in a twenty-eight storey pyramid, two-storey columns and two-storey urns. Las Vegas was soon to trump this pyramid with rooms hanging out on the diagonal.

253 MICHAEL GRAVES, The Dolphin Hotel next to The Swan missed an opportunity to play off the inherent incongruities – one giant confronts another, and the inhabitant. (W. Taylor).

254 MICHAEL GRAVES, *Swan Statue*, the deep structure in steel and plywood. The 46-foot birds have plywood ribs fastened to a steel frame on which a fiberglass skin is fixed. These beautiful, underlying structures might have been partly re-vealed by a Post-Modernist such as James Stirling or Robert Venturi, and the giant swan could have become a real fantasy room from which to view the monuments in the swamp.

these artificial mountains cost more than a third of a billion – $375,000,000. The average huge hotel built during the London boom in the early seventies had 500 bedrooms and, as I also point out in the first chapter, "creates a disruption in scale and city life which amounts to the occupation of an invading army – a role tourists tend to fulfil." Here, in the reclaimed swamps of Florida, ironically it is the hotels the tourists come to see. They are slightly more culturally challenging than what is found in the ride-through parks.

This "entertainment architecture," as Eisner has christened his new policy, has more references to European culture than a scholar could spot in the entire Magic Kingdom. The quotes show this, although they are less blatant borrowings than the Bernini swans: water cascade from the Villa Lante, sailboat bridge and central pyramid from Ledoux, stepped massing from Zoser's famous pyramid, and the layout from the nineteenth-century École des Beaux-Arts. Such Euro-delights rev one up for more sorcery on the inside (thirteen restaurants, one themed as a fish, the next as the Palio race-course, etc), The ride-through park has now become the walk-through cafeteria with menu by Sir Bannister Fletcher, comparative western architecture on the digestive method.

Most of these delights were run up in a year or two when Graves, like Disney, had an enormous boom. In April 1990, his office had just completed eight major projects – such as the Newark Museum Renovation at $17 million, or the Crown American Corporate Headquarters at $27 million – and had sixty-four more under way (252). Most were hotels, offices and commercial buildings, but others included five large private houses and five museums, bringing the total amount of work to over a billion dollars. Such figures may be misleading, but it is of interest to compare them with those of Philip Johnson who, at the height of his profes-

sional success in 1985, had thirteen mega-projects in hand and $2.5 billion worth of work.[79]

Perhaps with a hint of competitive spleen Robert Stem dubbed Graves "the Paul Rudolph of PM," because so much of the work was signature-stamped rather than context-specific: it said more about who designed it than where it was. But closer to the mark would be "the SOM of PM," because like this large firm, Graves churns out architecture of a generally high standard. The question then might be "But isn't it all really *Modern?*"

Mechanization, quick speed of production, massive scale of building, and stereotyping are all hallmarks of the Modern Movement, especially in its latest alienating phase, as pointed out in "The Death of Modern Architecture." But the related question also has to be asked, when it comes to designing entertainment architecture: "How big is too big?" Here one finds divergent answers. As functioning hotels the Swan and Dolphin are not much better or worse than the average, gargantuan Sheraton which is their equal in cost and type: impersonal, efficient and bland in service. But as stage sets, which is the more proper comparison, they are on the scale of Cecil B. DeMille and quite appropriate for circuses and the slaughter of the Christians. The critique thus might be one that Reyner Benham levels at the Getty Museum: "no blood was spilled here." Blood is no more likely to flow at the Swan or Dolphin, given the super-controlled Disney ambience. The problem then is less that the hotels are too big than that the everyday activity is too small. One needs grand functions for the grandiosity to feel right, something like the naval battles staged on false lakes that the

255a MICHAEL GRAVES, *Walt Disney Headquarters*, Burbank, California, 1988–90. This Tuscan style palazzo has seven 19-foot dwarfs – 133 feet of midget – holding its front door. Michael Eisner, who commissioned it, said: "When I come to work I want to smile." The dwarfs leader, Dopey, smiles back. Above all this is a round tempietto, a Hadrianic "hinge" that is just as notional. (Maureen Sajbel).

255b MICHAEL GRAVES, *Walt Disney Headquarters* from street intersection. Red sandstone and cream stucco divide the building, while the four executive pavilions are marked by the large Ledoux/Mickey curves and a dignified symmetry of massed elements.

Romans and Florentines used to put on behind their similarly Herculean palazzi.

All the problems of scale, size, detailing and conception are well symbolized by the simpering birds that dominate the swamps for miles – Bernini's swans. These are inflated nine times in volume and displaced from their old perch near the Palazzo Barberini in Rome. They now loom forty-seven feet above the awed hordes, to simle and twaddle. Even Jeff Koons (who no doubt studied them) could not have made them as sweetly nauseous. But hold, it is not the kitsch or zoomorphism or ornamental gestures that are wrong: it is the fact that nothing more is done with these signs. Imagine building *two* fantastic structures to support these forty-seven foot swans: the angular one in steel, and a curved one over this in plywood. Then (look at the drawings) imagine *not* revealing these underlying, beautiful truths (254). Imagine creating two Statues of Liberty and not allowing people to walk up through the structure and look out. Perverse, stupid, unliberated, wasteful, aiming hard to miss the great opportunity?

What a chance it was to have it both ways, to raise consciousness and send a double message. To create large emblems of our connection with nature *and* make habitable rooms – a multivalent symbol. Remember Umberto Eco's parable of the lovers; or Stirling and Hollein's creating an architecture from the difference between truth and artifice. By missing this opportunity, and treating the sign as a consoling cliché, Graves reveals that he is fundamentally not a Post-Modernist. He misses the whole point of crossing boundaries, mixing codes and deconstructing from within.

What conclusions can one draw from this stage of Graves' career and its intersection with the fortunes of Disney? Some

of his work is produced slowly and remains well-controlled, like the Newark Museum conversion, whereas an equal amount is produced quickly, like the Momochi apartment building in Japan, a caricature of his style. Perhaps another third is both creatively integral and yet still flawed in parts, like the Youngstown Museum. This has an interesting massing that is ultimately dissatisfying because of its heavily proportioned backside and notional details. Looked at from the angle of fast-build, the sixty-four projects he has under way are noteworthy because of their high average quality. This is, oddly enough, a point the Modernist Aldo van Eyck would appreciate: although the self-confessed enemy of Gravesian Post-Modernism, he does preach the "quality of quantity" rather than the much easier quality of small-scale production. However, judged solely in these last terms, those of pre-industrial handcraft, the buildings are diagrammatic.

The balance of contending judgements could continue endlessly, culminating in the Disney's entire oeuvre. Looked at in terms of the corporation's past, the new "entertainment architecture" is obviously one step better than its old Cinderella's Castle. This was a sugary pastiche of Ludwig II of Bavaria's pastiche of *Les Trés Riches Heures'* exaggeration of a real Gothic castle. But in terms of PM development most of the work is regressive. This is particularly true of Graves' design for Disney's headquarters in Burbank California, and its façade that features the Seven Dwarfs (255a, 255b). This phase in Graves' work has been called "hokey-tecture"

256 ROBERT STERN, *Casting Center*, Walt Disney World, Lake Buena Vista, Florida, 1987–89. Venetian Gothic diaper pattern blown up and played against an airfoil door held in tension. Some baby-blue Mickey Mouse scuppers, and a couple of clown hats *a la* Rossi. Never has the decorated shed been so clearly decorated, and shed-like. (Peter Aaron, ESTO).

because its tongue-in-cheek fakery is so knowing.[80] The attempt, as in kitsch, is to succeed through excess; but when it is this calculating and obvious, one wonders. "I've tried to walk the line between the whimsical and the jokey," Graves has said, "or to navigate between the chasm of the cute and the abyss of easy irony." The question is, what positive terrain exists between these four trifles?

When looking at the Dwarf caryatids, one thinks of Mannerist and Baroque fantasies, those of Giuliano da Romano and the fountains of Rome, which had an equally explicit imagery. Or the papal symbolism dominating Catholic structures; or even iconic roadside architecture, the Hot Dog Stand (above page 30). Each of these, in different ways, is equally literal with its signs, so why are they more acceptable? Perhaps craftsmanship in the first case, the actual content in the second, and the surreal brazenness of the third. In three hundred years, might the Seven Dwarfs turn into mysterious icons and look interesting? Perhaps.

As it is, Dopey, the central Dwarf caryatid a mere nineteen-foot midget looks for the moment only like Dopey. Unlike Michael Graves' earlier sketches for sculpture — notably "Portlandia" for the Portland Building — there is no ambiguity, abstraction and transformation of the content and image. The whole façade becomes a "signolic," not symbolic architecture.[81]

Robert Stern's work for the corporation varies more widely, from the revivalist beach-resort hotel to the crazy decorated shed that is the Casting Center for Disney, in Orlando, Florida (256). This latter confection has the real vulgarity of roadside architecture. It is definitely aiming at what Herbert Gans, a theorist of Post-Modernism, would call the "lower middle taste culture," those suburbanites who cruise the edges of Houston and Los Angeles looking for cheap real estate which still has royal pretensions. Bald-faced deceit this brazen becomes sublime. The diaper pattern meant to evoke the Doge's Palace and the Grand Canal has, indeed, Gothicesque windows, but like the airfoil entrance canopy [*sic*], it belongs very much in The Age of Metal. Two little golden peaked finals (*gratis* Aldo Rossi) hold this airplane wing in place, while a truly grotesque lantern giggles between them.

Just so no one could possibly take any of this seriously, the images are collaged out of phase and their flat insubstantiality is exaggerated by paper-thin layering. Blue Mickey Mouse ears further punctuate the pretence, and Mickey Mouse's head is, appropriately enough, empty — the perfect visual void. (One is reminded here of Stern's masterful satire of the Best discount store and its caryatids with their empty heads shaped like TV sets.)

The view from the roadside spells C A S T I N G in giant gilt letters. One goes into this decorated shed to get a job as an imagineer, or some other engineer of fantasy, and is delighted to find the Disney icons played with as well as put on pedestals. Through his shifts in scale and violent confrontations of good and bad taste, through his collage of gen-

res, Stern, of all the architects, has come closest to re-using the Disney iconography for his own whimsical purposes.

The effect of Entertainment Architecture on Post-Modernism was to exaggerate its fault lines. Some Post-Modernists, such as James Stirling, declined Disney commissions because, as he said: "To me [the theme idea] seems demeaning and trivial and somehow not profound or important. It's overly commercial. In England, we're subjected to it in a gross way — the parading of the guards, the dressing up at the Tower of London, and Madame Tussaud's. Maybe we invented the bloody thing."[82] Robert Venturi, Charles Moore, Aldo Rossi and Hans Hollein, leading Post-Modernists, were all considered for jobs. Arata Isozaki's "Time Building" in Florida is the most dignified and interesting of the themed structures. Its collage of quotes, including the ubiquitous Mickey Mouse ears, is colorful and abstract. A central cone, used as a sundial both inside and out, is engaging both in content and form, perhaps because it has nothing to do with Disney and adopts a cosmic theme.

So there are exceptions to Gresham's Law, the bad does not always drive out the good. But certainly the evil empire tries: as the saying goes, "no one ever went broke underestimating the taste of the American public." Cynicism and entropy triumphant. The net effect of Disney on PM is to have exaggerated its commercial tendencies and brought this side of the movement to an end, to be the kiss of death of PoMo. From Orlando to the Disney Celebration New Town a few years later and then Las Vegas this trend continued to undermine the movement and make it appear silly and Ersatz. Modernists, who predicted this turn and made collages of Graves' Portland Building blowing up — like Pruitt-Igoe — must have cheered to be proven right (257). But there were other aspects of both a more ambiguous and critical nature that continued to develop, to which we now turn.

257 *Michael Graves' Portland Building Blowing Up*, the demise of PM, collage by Cervan Robinson, 1984.

URBANE MEGA-BUILD

Post-Modern urbanism, as interpreted by large developers and civic authorities, was mixed in quality but at least a notch above Disney. The early 1980s saw the widespread acceptance of Jane Jacobs' critique of modern planning and the good sense of her primary message. Economically viable cities should be built on mixed uses, mixed ages of building, mixed social groups. Mixture and pluralism – the two PM tenets in all fields – replaced functional zoning and the *tabula rasa* approach. Most cities in the West adopted a version of Jacobite planning lore, but unfortunately scaled it up to huge size, thus in a sense canceling one of her chief points: that growth should be piecemeal. The reason for this inver-

258 Faneuil Hall (lower left) and GRAHAM GUND & ADRIAN SMITH (SOM), *75 State Street*, (center), Boston, Mass., 1987–89. A 31-storey tower surmounts an urban ensemble created by Gund and other architects in the refurbished Faneuil Hall Marketplace. Adopting the Post-Modern formulae of Jane Jacobs, the Rouse Corporation has turned this area into one of the more urbane places in America.

sion, as might be expected, was quick profit. In London the Covent Garden district, Broadgate in the City and the massive Canary Wharf area of the Docklands received the PM formula, often distorted by large size: urbane mega-build was the oxymoronic result.

In America the Rouse Corporation carried out a slightly more yuppified version of the genre, notably in New York, Baltimore and – to my mind the most successful application of the formula – Boston's Faneuil Hall marketplace area (258). Here they were aided in urban place-making by the considerable experience of Ben Thompson and the infill buildings and towers of Graham Gund and Adrian Smith of SOM. The mixture of functions and new and old structures, the carving out of positive public space, the contextualism and ornament of the architecture are all of a generally high standard. A certain debt in pleasing the crowds is, ironically, owed to Disneyland where corporate street theatre was first formulated, but of course Disney himself learned this Main Street formula, in turn, from successful European cities.

Furthermore, like the mega-developments of Battery Park City in New York and Canary Wharf in London, there was even a positive social policy introduced that supported the visual pluralism. Hiring a minority workforce, reserving a certain percentage of employment for the black community, women and the disadvantaged, and encouraging small businesses have led to a social diversity that is the essence of urbanity. Enlightened planning everywhere in the eighties was based on a similar mixture of public and private co-operation that transcended the either/or categories of socialism or capitalism. A central planning authority might lay down the ground rules, supposedly provide most of the infrastructure and then let different private developers

259 MOORE, RUBLE & YUDELL, *Tegel Housing*, IBE, Berlin, West Germany, 1980–88. The perimeter block is Classical on the front and picturesque here, on the enclosed garden side (which has a view to the river in back). This housing is popular with the residents and unpopular with the Modernists in Berlin.

build and reap the profits. Such a Post-Modern mixture might be called "socipatalist" to underscore its hybridisation as socialized capitalism.[83]

Name it what you will, this synergetic enterprise was responsible for the most successful urbanism. Particularly important was the IBE (International Building Exhibition) in Berlin, a project of town building that continued over a decade, from the late 1970s to the late 1980s. In addition to the aforementioned formulae of mixing functions there was a particular emphasis in Berlin on perimeter block planning – that is, pushing the building right up to the street edge on four sides of a city block to allow maximum shelter for the backyards and the recreation of city street life (259). As Jane Jacobs pointed out, this life is essential to the functioning of a city, and as Leon Krier added, it provides the basic visual and circulation logic. Also the policy of choosing several architects for a site was emphasized, so that the city might once again have the visual variety and typological diversity that has always been its strength. Broadgate and Canary Wharf in London and Battery Park City in New York followed IBA's example in carrying out these principles, albeit with less sensitivity.

Another significant strategy the Berlin authorities adopted, under the guidance of Josef Paul Kleiheus and Rob

260 ALDO ROSSI (with C. BRAGHIERI), *Social Housing*, South Friedrichstadt, Berlin, West Germany, 1981–88. The street side of this perimeter block shows a strong industrial Classical façade of Jaguar-green steel, banded brick and curious, steep-pitched roofs – all of which gives great character to mass housing.

261 ALDO ROSSI, *Apartment House*, drawing, showing Filarete's Column on the corner and other associations important to him, 1981.

Krier, was to set up a competition system that selected some of the most creative international architects. This resulted, negatively, in a certain number of signature-buildings and, positively, in an equal number of we ll-designed housing layouts perhaps as much as thirty per cent of all the schemes over ten years. Two of the best projects were designed by the California-based team of Charles Moore and the Italian-based team of Aldo Rossi, and in both cases the architects were spurred to perform above their average for the natural reason that they were placed on the center stage of a major city along with their international peers. Moore, Ruble and Yudell's housing was Schinkelesque in front and picturesque on the garden side, whereas Rossi's was industrial Classicism on both sides of the perimeter

262 POUL INGEMANN, *Social Housing*, Odense, Denmark, 1987–88. Concrete and aluminium Classicism in the northern Scandinavian mode defines, in a very loose way, the street and garden sides with three forms: a tower, temple and terrace.

wall. In appearance it captured that elusive quality of Rossi's best works. A green-metal industrial language, based on a dark Jaguar green, alternates with banded brick and the corner punctuation of a mysterious white cylinder – Filarete's column, as it is called, after a similar one in Venice (260, 261). The ordinary repetition of window walls broken by the peaked hats of the stairway exits makes this perimeter block into both a monument and normal housing. Along with the work of O.M. Ungers it was probably the most successful of this period in Berlin.

In many ways IBA represented the high point of PM urbanism and it has become the model for other cities such as Frankfurt (where a central district has been developed) and Odense in Denmark (where these types of new housing are being evaluated by sociologists) (262). This is all very worthy, but if the projects have an obvious fault it is that housing alone cannot make a city either functional or urbane. Planning authorities in Europe do not appear to have the power or political will to commission a really rich mixture of public, commercial and domestic building. Paris, of course, is one exception where its *grands projets* are predictably all civic, public and imperial in scope. No doubt these were realized only for the last reason: because French presidents, in the manner of Louis XIV, have a tradition of leaving behind large objects that mark their reign. Is it a surprise that this memorializing urge has resulted for the most part in Late- rather than Post-Modernism? Could it be

that monuments on this scale, without any great social idealism, *have* to be abstract?

Another exception is Barcelona where the mayor Pasquel Maragall, a self-styled Post-Modernist, and the group of architects, MBM, led a ten-year drive to renew the nineteenth-century Cerda plan. They were helped by the injection of money for the 1992 Olympics. The result was a PM policy of diverse renewal: over a hundred parks were constructed to enhance the different districts (263). Cerda's unfinished urban structure was joined up. Areas such as the old harbor and working-class district were improved and transformed on a piecemeal basis. Infrastructure and new housing and monumental buildings were designed by different Post-Modern architects such as Enric Miralles and Oscar Tusquets. In effect then, a whole city was catalyzed by architects, politicians, the Olympics and European investment and, fittingly, it was given the RIBA Gold Medal for architecture in 1999, the first time a large community received it.

But Barcelona was the great exception: a more balanced urbanism eluded other cities. In America and Britain, where the political orientation favors market-led solutions, the developer played a larger role than the planning authority. When the conditions are right, when there is an economic boom and a street-wise entrepreneur, this can lead to whole tracts of a city undergoing immediate urban transformation. The Los Angeles-based Jon Jerde partnership characteristically finds itself simultaneously re-designing twenty or thirty hearts of a city that had suffered cardiac arrest in the sixties and seventies as the combined result of Modernist planning and the flight to the suburbs. Jerde

263 *Barcelona Park sculpture by Beverly Pepper*, 1991. One of over a hundred mini-parks for different districts. The mayor, Pasquell Maragall, along with architects led by Oriol Bohigas, transformed Barcelona into the PM city of the 1990s.

regenerates these old centers, again with the Jacobite remedy of mixed uses, mixed ages and mixed types of buildings: and his injection of public space, street theatre and commerce make it work economically. Whenever a central district needs regeneration, such as downtown San Diego, or whenever a sixties sprawl needs tying together, such as the suburban shopping mall, Jerde provides his medicine: shopping arcades, pedestrian space, and lots of street activity *à la Rouse* and Disney. As architecture the results are dayglo Michael Graves: as urbanism they are sensible versions of street planning (264). The missing factor is, again, the public realm of real civic buildings. Commerce, as the single urban generator, is only marginally more effective in creating the city than housing.

The most ambitious urbane mega-build in America is Battery Park City. This "city within the city" is located in downtown New York near Wall Street and next to the former World Trade Center destroyed in the attack of September 11, 2001. Here on a 92-acre landfill site on the Hudson River, a state agency teamed up with several developers including the largest in the world, the Canadian group Olympia and York, to produce urbanity at a massive and, it has to be added, lumpish scale. Planned again on Jacobite and PM principles by Cooper, Eckstut Associates, the scheme consists of two major residential areas north and south of the World Financial Centre (WFC) (265).

This complex of four squat skyscrapers contains seven and a half million square feet. To comprehend this figure imagine combining three Empire State Buildings. Six million square feet of this space is given to office workers who

264 JON JERDE, *Westside Pavilion*, Los Angeles, 1985–86. The shopping center and retail, in Jerde's hands, becomes the means to re-create a convivial urbanism. Gravesian architecture holds the street line very effectively and shields it from the parking lot in back, thus overcoming the bane of Los Angeles.

265 CESAR PELLI, *World Financial Center Towers*, 1982–87 and (left) CHARLES MOORE, *Housing, Battery Park City*, New York, 1985–87. A Classical urbanism set the guidelines and enforced the street patterns and elevations. The urbanity would be more urbane if it were not so dense.

beaver away for giant corporations (inside are the headquarters of American Express, Merrill Lynch and Dow Jones). Surrounding these 30,000 workers are 40,000 upper-income residents. The figures, like some of the repetitive architecture, can be fatiguing.

The WFC cost over $1.5 billion while the whole scheme is reckoned to have cost $4.5 – although these sums were 1986 estimates and may be higher.[84] Even more money was being spent by Olympia and York and others in the London Docklands. When one thinks of the figures, in the context of Disney, Graves, Philip Johnson *et al.*, the conclusion is reached that the billion dollar development has become as common to Post-Modernists as it was to the Modernists (even if a billion dollars is not what it used to be). One does not have to be a Marxist to believe that *all* this development has enough in common to make its stylistic and philosophical differences of marginal importance. Too big is too big, whatever the approach.

Nevertheless for Paul Goldberger and many astute critics "Battery Park City is a Triumph of Urban Design," because it mixes public and private values in about equal measure.[85] The public amenities include a riverside esplanade, lots of open space filled with site-specific, commissioned art works, and Rector Park. This open space Goldberger calls the best of its kind in New York since Gramercy Park. Also it follows the general aesthetic guidelines concerning massing, cornice lines, masonry materials and tripartition (most buildings have a defined base, middle and top). This creates the unity with variety that is the hallmark of urbanity. As for the private sector and contribution, this includes not only the housing as a function, but the fact that more than fifteen developers own the properties. So public and private values do interact synergistically in some ways.

Architecturally the results are impressive but flawed

266 CESAR PELLI, *WFC*, interior circulation rotunda. Corporate executives hurtle through these Classical spaces like the punched-card imagery of the dome – randomized, anonymous, beautiful and cut-up, where necessary.

because of the size. Like Graves' work for Disney, and the monstrous London hotels, they recall what I have termed "The Ivan Illich Law of Diminishing Architecture" (above page 11). "For any building type there is an upper limit to the number of people who can be served before the quality of an environment falls." QED 40,000 inhabitants plus 30,000 workers, placed in an environment run up in ten years results in, well, wallpaper architecture.

Given these limitations Cesar Pelli has produced very intelligent and sensuous wallpaper. For one thing his towers set back and thin out and change their window/wall ratio as they rise up to fifty storeys. Thus the visual bulk is reduced. For another thing the granite at the base decreases in quantum jumps just as the reflective glass increases, thus creating the interesting illusion of a building within a building within a building. This can also be read as another new idea, "the peeling building." These squat-scrapers also share similar granite bottoms and related copper tops. It is true the distinctive hats – stepped, pyramidal and domed – do not symbolize anything important and are thus only a superior form of wallpaper, but at least they are visual culminations.

For the inside Pelli has designed elegant domed spaces which transform the wallpaper into flat repetitive patterns that are cut across to accentuate their applied thinness (266). At these points the double coding is explicit and masterful: we know that he intends the sign of insubstantiality to be an essential part of the morality and aesthetic because the cuts are so abrupt. The center of the whole scheme, indeed Battery Park City's "heart," is the vaulted Winter Garden which now wraps the theme of the exterior skin into a series of telescopic folds. These repeat in section the stepped layering of the towers and thus conceptually bring the whole scheme into focus.

If Battery Park City is one of the better versions of urbane mega-build, then it shows this genre still has a long way to go before it constitutes a balanced fabric. No city hall or church or museum graces this city within the city. There is just the typical over-concentration of offices and housing, the over-specialization that distorted Modernism and still plagues its offspring. This situation is so ubiquitous that it now escapes comment, and there seems little political will to do anything about it. The application of Jacobite principles to mega-planning may be progress of a kind, and the reality the west is willing to pay for, but it is still, of course, no substitute for real urbanity.

VILLAGE PLANNING AS MODEL

The big cities of the world have expanded into huge regional megalopoli relatively recently, mostly in the last thirty years. The growth of the Boston to Washington megalopolis ("Bosh-Wash" as it was called in the late sixties) is typical and has its counterpart in Europe, Japan, Mexico and the

Greater London region. Like all these communicational sprawls, this runaway growth has too many interlinked causes to analyse here, but a point can be made. No society is politically or economically equipped to deal with this inflation on the macro-scale, and so imbalances in fabric will continue to occur. Lucky is the city that can just keep its transportation system up to date, never mind its overall plan, or balance in structure.

Chaos theory and self-organizing theory, worked out by the Nobel laureate Ilya Prigogine and the Santa Fe Institute, are being put forward as proper ways to deal with this runaway growth – for instance the anarchic beauty of Tokyo.[86] As we will see in subsequent chapters the new paradigm has forged new models, such as the fractal city, to picture these emergent patterns. But architects who must, perforce, deal with the micro-scale of city fabric need more explicitly formal models, and for this the idea of small block design, or village planning, came to the fore in the later 1980s. It constitutes one of the ways Post-Modern precepts overlap with, but do not quite match, traditional ones.

Designing a city of small blocks is a goal that has appealed to three entirely different urban theorists – Jane Jacobs, Leon Krier and Christopher Alexander – no doubt for different reasons. But the three agree on its suitability because of one point: it allows a piecemeal growth that is economically and aesthetically desirable. Small block planning lets feedback work, whether it concerns investment, or a functional or visual decision. For this the model of the Italian hill town, or "organic village" as it is also known, is a stereotype well appreciated. The force of the idea gains weight not only because of this popular and variegated acceptance "by three different schools of design" but also because of a recent fourth and fifth. Leon Krier, Prince Charles and those known as the New Urbanists who have joined the consensus, and the ad hoc designers, led by Frank Gehry and Hans Hollein, who have carried out several pilot schemes. With Gehry the notion has grown out of pavilion planning where a large superblock is broken up into a series of clustered pavilions, and he more than the others has made a new art form out of this heterogeneous planning.

It is worth noting, however, that the consensus contains an important contradiction with which we will start. The village model has been applied where one might least expect it, to the huge office building and multinational bank. The probability was that these Leviathans would continue in the modern corporate mould of building highly visible tributes to their might. They have followed this practice since the 1870s, with one freestanding monument trumping the previous one: the Woolworth Tower, the Chrysler Building, the AT&T, the Hong Kong Bank and, needless to say, New York's Trump Tower. One does not have to be Freud to know what is going on here. But there is now a feminine response to all these upright members: the groundscraper has arrived, the undulating body building

267 ANTON ALBERTS and VAN HUUT BV, *NMB Bank*, Amsterdam, The Netherlands, 1984. Ten brick pavilions snake around the side providing various anthropomorphic and animal images – horses' heads. Pentagonal sun collectors surmount each horse and provide light to the interior court and street. This was the most ecologically advanced office of the 1980s.

that hugs the earth, and tries to be green.

In Holland the architect Ton Alberts has broken up the mammoth NMB Bank – with its 2,400 employees – into a cluster of ten brick "blobs." These chunky "pavilions," as they are also known, snake around the site in an irregular, choppy curve thus providing a unique set of profiles from any one place (267). Gone is the image of the bank as a stiff Classical erection. Gone too are the images of bureaucracy and monotony; and back is the image of a medieval village, taller than usual, covered all over with perhaps too many "Dutch" bricks (3.5 million of them) and full of odd animal and organic metaphors. The architects are dedicated followers of Rudolf Steiner and his Anthroposophical method of design, one that stresses ecological sense, passive solar heating and all sorts of humane qualities. While the NMB Bank is not notable as high architecture it is certainly popular and sensible, especially because it breaks up a large volume and introduces the notion of the street and square into the building (which does, of course, subtract them from the outside world, where they belong).

A few other large corporations – the Centraal Beheer in Appeldorn and the Colonia Building in Cologne – have attempted a related concept and we could say the "office as village" may soon become an accepted model for the future. After all, sixty per cent of the work force in the First World is destined to spend their lives in these post-industrial factories, and each year this captive population demands more and more amenities just to keep on the job. If the corporation does not provide acceptable spaces and services then, as in Los Angeles, the electronic collage may start to become a more pressing challenge to the central office – at least for a few days each

268 HIROSHI HARA. *Yamato International*, Tokyo, 1984–87. Aluminum forms step up and billow to the right. Not only does the architecture resemble cloud forms (which are also stylized in the ornament), but also a village hung from a rock face. The small-block architecture manages to house the production and distribution functions of a fashion company.

week. In 1990 the London Telecom system estimated that perhaps twenty per cent of the population would soon be telecommuting. So social pressures, as well as architects, are pushing forward the new model of the office as village.

In Tokyo the architect Hiroshi Hara has designed an exquisite High-Tech office as village for the international fashion company Yamato. This has a "big/smallness" that is uncanny, a big volume that is broken up into so many small parts that it looks like a bubbly Italian hill-town of the future. One cannot tell quite how large it really is. The room-size forms are layered back and stepped to the right as they rise, as if tiny buildings were clinging to the face of a canyon (268). The reality is as charming as the photographs suggest, creating, for a change, a corporate world that is pleasantly subdivided and semi-private in parts.

One approaches under a large gate/bridge into a piazza with a flat reflecting pool. The paving-stones are so highly polished that one cannot divine the transition between water and masonry (269). Lighting standards here and elsewhere vary between the abstract and representational. Throughout the stacked village a series of abstracted themes repeat in a transformed way — clouds, shore-lines, geodesic structures, birds and trees — to create a very consistent ornamental programme (270). These images are not insistent one-liners, as they are in the Disney Kingdom, but much more subtle variations on a set of natural and cultural signs. They are often made of an industrial material — sheet metal, etched glass — and layered in flat, horizontal planes like the building itself. This correspondence between parts and the whole gives both a delightful resonance. Moreover, because one ornamental group is a repeated fractal pattern it makes one see the entire metallic building as a wafting cloud.

In sum, this office as village is successful because the architect has adopted a mixed grammar of curves and straight lines and played them at such an intricate scale that he has managed to symbolize the interpenetration of nature and culture. We begin to believe the impossible, that a giant fashion company can work like an organic community: all the functions from design to manufacture and distribution are housed here, and the image of interdependence looks so convincing. But is it a real community, as Japanese corporations like to claim they are? I haven't a clue.

A convincing Western example of the corporate village is the Landeszentral bank in Frankfurt, completed in 1988. It nestles so effectively into the urban fabric that many people would overlook its presence altogether. But when they ascend to one of the many surrounding towers — typical modern shafts of corporate potency — and look down, they will discover an exception to the tough urban roofscape (271). There below is not the usual collection of mechanical boxes, but a wild garden of hardy plants — herbs, junipers, polychromatic heather and cacti — all held within a discipline of gray steel tracks, the window cleaning equipment (272). Here is the typical double coding of Post-Modernism, and the greening of the industrial landscape.

271 ALBRECHT JOURDAN MULLER and BERGHOF LANDES RANG, *Rooftop of Landeszentralbank*, Frankfurt, 1982–88. The greening of the post-industrial landscape. During lunchtime the employees come out onto this roofscape which is a sensuous, herbal garden framed — Mondrian-like — by window cleaning tracks.

272 AJM and BLR, "Houses," grouped around a hanging garden that combines French topiary, diagonals and computer imagery.

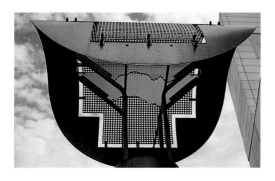

269 HIROSHI HARA, *Yamato International, Tokyo*, 1984–87, exterior light. Cut metal clouds and computerised ornament ring changes on natural and geometric themes.

270 HIROSHI HARA, *plaza entrance*. The water imitates the highly polished stones; also note the Secessionist lighting standards.

273 AJM and BLR, *Landeszentralbank*, the garden "face" or "tree" trellis. Steel, stone and nature are carefully intermeshed in an architecture that tries to overcome contradictions of period, material and style. (Waltraud Krase).

274 AJM and BLR, *Central Piazza*, again with the steel trees and masonry skin placed in rhythmical alternation. (Dieter Leistner).

The Landeszentral bank actually has six "hanging gardens" as well as the growing roofscape, and all six are in a different style. Some are modifications of the traditional French garden and set dark-green topiary against a fat-white-pebble background. Others combine the English romantic garden with wandering patterns based on the computer circuit-board. But the point is that each of the six, one floor above ground level, acts as a focus for the cluster of offices that surround it on three sides. These are conceived as houses grouped around a common green court.

Thus the large corporation, a central bank for others in the region, is broken down into units at a village scale. Instead of these units being stacked vertically, as they are in Norman Foster's Hong Kong Bank, or scattered about rather wastefully, as in the NMB Bank, they are grouped in an urbanistic pattern that visually welcomes in the rest of the city and reinforces the existing street grid.

The building is convincing not only because of its layout and gardens, but also because of its constructional symbolism. The difference between the underlying steel structure and the visible surface of stone blocks becomes the pretext for the characteristic PM type of symbolic ornament. Instead of the load-bearing construction of traditionalists, or the curtain wall of modernists, we find the "hung and peeled" façade of stone slabs, which are exaggerated in their layering to emphasize their non-structural, but urban role. The intermediate layers of construction are shown because of the peeling process, and the fact that the stone is non-structural is revealed by the cracks between them and their beveled edges. Thus the ornament derives directly from revealing the truth of construction, as it does in Stirling's work at Stuttgart, Pelli's in Texas and elsewhere.

A steel motif in the shape of a T, or tree, or face is repeated in several ways throughout the building, changing its shape to suit the particular context. When the T-shape is on the outside it works as a giant trellis so that growing plants can shield the hanging gardens (273, 274). Here it is surmounted by a delicate, tapering curve appropriately creating the profile of the crown of a tree. On the inside the T-shape is painted in shades of green and the natural imagery is made even more explicit in the piazza where the T-piers are accompanied by potted trees.

If a large corporation is to embody the true urbanity of a village, then it must instantly fabricate the variety of spaces and moods that the urban realm creates over time. This the bank does by employing different designers, artists and craftsmen to work on a set of related themes, many of which concern, inevitably, the making and losing of money. This is a welcome surprise, especially in a conservative institution that lends money. One enters the lobby to find murals depicting the story of Dr. Faustus and, after absorbing the irony of this attack on selling one's soul, one comes upon three large golden balls suffering various kinds of distress. The cleanest of these sculptures is the Deutschmark as the bank would like it, whereas the other two, with their erosions and protrusions, represent the two great fears of money lenders the world over: deflation and inflation. Throughout this five-storey village artworks point up the space, or else the banking function. The accent on variety extends also into the boardrooms, each of which is given a different character. For instance, the breakfast room from John Soane's house in London, or the Café Aubette of Theo van Doesburg are slightly transformed by the architects into their grammar of layered planes. But still the image is distinctive and recognizable, the mood made *different*. If we must build large chunks of the environment quickly, then it is only right that they incorporate a heterogeneity of taste and represent the pluralism of time.

The most impressive space in the building, and the culmination of the route, is the grand central piazza. This forms a spine of circulation that connects the six "houses of the village." Here would be an actual public realm, if only the bank were public and one end of this space opened to the city. The irony is that the Landeszentralbank has created such a good simulacrum of urban architecture that they should sell it to the authorities and make it actually work. This urban village should lower the drawbridge and welcome in the city.

TOWARDS A SUBTLE URBANISM

In the age of Disney and hype, of skyscrapers that shout corporate power, it is hard for clients and architects to resist the one-liner. Understatement may mean oblivion, completing the urban fabric may be an unappreciated expense. But, as well as the corporations I have mentioned, there have been a few museums and art centers that have shown the way.

275 JAMES STIRLING and MICHAEL WILFORD, *Center for the performing Arts*, model, Cornell University, Ithaca, New York, 1984–89. Nine small-block volumes are tightly packed on the edge of a gorge. The magnificent view is framed by steel and masonry piers whose cut signals a floor line, among other things.

Again the shift towards village planning may not represent a large trend, but it does indicate a change in paradigm. Three cultural centers, built in the late 1980s, show the shift: those by James Stirling, Kisho Kurokawa and Antoine Predock. Each is a multi-use art center and a convincing piece of urbanism in its own right. Each heralds the development of Post-Modernism towards a more nuanced elaboration of symbolism and historical reference; all three make a virtue of small-block planning. They may not be great buildings, but they point in a positive direction.

Stirling and Wilford's Center for the Performing Arts at Cornell University divides up a very complex mixture of functions into nine chunky blocks and then crashes them together very tightly because of a precipitous site (275). It teeters on the edge of Cascadilla Gorge. The scheme is in a fragmented Classical style for several reasons. One might be its location in a quasi-Mediterranean context. "Cascadilla" is Spanish for "little cascade," the site is Ithaca and the campus already has faint memories of the arcadian tradition. A second reason is the architect's previous use of this language, but there is yet another and surprising source for their grammar. It harkens back to Stirling and Gowan's Leicester Engineering Building of 1963, where small volumes were also juxtaposed and elided in a very compact way. In the past they may not have been given the kind of Classicizing ornament that the architects are now employing, but their deep structure is the same. It relates to the small grammatical units that can be found in any urban settlement in the ancient world, a comprehensible way of handling lots of space. Stirling has continued this method of articulation throughout his career, even if, from time to

277 Below: JAMES STIRLING and MICHAEL WILFORD, *The Loggia overlooking the gorge*. The marble is cut in an industrial manner and the crisp black voids not only symbolize this, but also the fact that it is hung from steel.

time, he has resorted to the modernist megastructure. In a sense his whole oeuvre is a complex dialogue of the method of compaction composition with modern requirements.

At Cornell the volumes of the performing arts building huddle around a central campanile, rather the way they do in any *ville perché* in the Mediterranean (276). This has led visitors to a first quick reaction – "Ah, an Italian hill town, I can see the gable-end of the church, the octagonal baptistery and the adjacent loggia."[87] But as always with Stirling, there is more to it than historical allusion, and as usual the old forms turn out to mean new things. In this sense the Center for Theatre Arts is an artful piece of theatre, and a supreme example of second-glance architecture. The "baptistry" is really, at its base, a public bus shelter, and above this it is a private office. As a whole urban form it is actually a gateway to the spectacular gorge, the main element that defines the "piazza" on the public front. One volume thus equals one historical reference "baptistry" but in addition, four different meanings.

Next, the "campanile" indeed has a melancholic Romanesque quality because of its lone, dark arch on each face, as if it had survived as a ruin from some abandoned village. But it is not a bell tower. It works as a lift shaft (though, it has to be said, its central position clearly plays a visual role, anchoring the very restless forms). The pitched roof "nave" of the "church"? Actually this shelters both a theatre and a dance studio, the latter jumping through the gable end to proclaim itself with a diagonal window – which also shows the dancers off to good effect on the street. Two functions are compressed into one volume which has, on second glance, subtle articulations that express this combination. However, if you approach the center from the public piazza side you expect not only an ecclesiastical function, but also a single nave interior. There is thus a certain pleasure in discovering that the two readings of the form – a historical allusion and real function – are each carried through with determination, producing, for instance, a dancer where a rose window might have been.

This anticipation and surprise continue around the site and into the details. The stone and steel loggia is, as you would imagine, a doubly-coded sign of the past and present – meeting each other halfway in cultural stalemate as it were. But it is also a sign of another duality: the fact that there are two, parallel loggias under one roof. One is glass-enclosed for the winter and the other is open to the view over the gorge (277). The mixed meanings of the rugged setting are also articulated in this dual structure, since the rock outcrops and landscape are at once violent and domesticated,

278 KISHO KUROKAWA, *Museum of Contemporary Art*, Hiroshima, 1988. This museum will form part of a huge cultural center as village, but already the small-block planning is clear. The tripartite code is established here with a base symbolizing the past, Edo construction. The middle, in white tile, represents the present while the top, in aluminium, signifies the future.

279 KISHO KURQKAWA, *Entrance Rotunda*, The flash of the A-bomb is created by cutting the cross-section of the Edo storehouse motif.

Finally, close up, the effect of gray-and-white Vermont marble recalls the rusticated bands of Siennese buildings. But if you get very close and examine the cracks you find the, by now, standard PM non-joint joint. The sharp black voids, the cuts, tell you clearly: "we are not stones that stand on each other, we hang from a steel frame." Ornament as truth-telling.

In effect, Stirling and Wilford are interweaving two separate languages to enhance each other, and they are doing this with enough subtlety to keep one step ahead of the viewer. Of course their use of a relatively popular code is appropriate – "cultural center = Mediterranean hill town" – and it allows the visitor to take in the overall use quickly. Furthermore the typology allows the mass to be broken up into small, grammatical blocks. But then there is the second, contemporary reading of realistic functions, which are allowed to speak in their utilitarian language, their stucco surface and box-like shape. These create dignified but tight spaces for performers and an audience which is there as much to see the gorge as the drama. The Classical and functional languages are given equal weight, suggesting that neither should dominate today.

We are back with ambiguity, the blur and the strong contrast between different voices, ideas that have characterized Post-Modernism for ten years.

They also typify Kisho Kurokawa's Museum of Contemporary Art that is carved into a hill overlooking the city of Hiroshima (278). At first glance we might think this is a Neo-Modern complex because of its glistening metallic surfaces, and it is only on second glance that we discover the historical subtext. Thus it inverts the emphasis Stirling gives his two texts and adds a third one, the future. Past, present and future are very clearly interwoven in yet another "village on a hill." From afar one sees only the mute, pitched outlines of the museum – sixty per cent of the mass is sunk out of sight into the small mountain – and these roofs are proportioned like traditional sixteenth-century Edo storehouses.

Would anyone grasp this reference? Perhaps not at first because the shapes might be understood as ubiquitous, the common pitched forms. But after a while, as one sees the same shape used in profile again and again – twelve times – it begins to play an iconic role, haunting the memory like an old tune that will not go away. In some cases the pitched form is played straight, in others with a little ornamental flourish, and in the heart of the museum – the entrance – it is curved into a circle and sliced apart with a silver slash. This could be an innocuous, functional necessity, just the section projected on the elevation.

But it is a flash of light, the sun's energy increased by the polished metal, and in this city the suggestion of an explosion is very potent (279). One feels the presence of the absence of the A-bomb in every old building that survived, and every new one that has sprung up in this thriving and apparently cheerful city. For a foreigner, especially an

280 KISHO KUROKAWA, *Sculpture Court*. The references to different cultures and periods are lurking, masterfully, below the surface to keep peace in this magical space.

281 ANTOINE PREDOCK, *Fine Arts Center*, Arizona State University, Tempe, Arizona, 1987–89. Night view of the roofscape with the small-block volumes cascading about to create a virtual world set apart from the chaotic city. (Timothy Hursley).

American, the experience of this bustling happy enterprise is unnerving, it drives in all the more the unnamable and unspeakable. And, of course, according to Lyotard and other philosophers, it is such things as Auschwitz and Hiroshima that usher in Post-Modernity. So how one treats or acknowledges this unwelcome truth, the rationalized mass-killing of modernity, becomes an essential question for architects as for everyone else. Overstatement or melodrama would be as obscene as denial. To Kurokawa's credit he has steered a subtle course between explicit and implicit representation. Many cues just increase the controlled ambiguity. Are the v-shapes just voided keystones, or signs of an explosion?

On the one hand, the circular entry space as seen from the air can be imagined as that ominous and familiar image, the mushroom cloud. This interpretation is further suggested by the discovery of stones scorched by the blast which are set by the entry-way. Everyone in Hiroshima is, of course, constantly reminded of the city's history, so the references to the blast are bound to be assumed in any building as significant as a museum. On the other hand, the wrapped circular form of columns is also the sign of community, a veiled reference to the embracing arms of St. Peter's in Rome and a natural sign of unity, of coming together. And the framed void from its centre, the view of the sky, is a sign of the cosmos, as it is in the oculus of the Pantheon. So we are free to read this circular form in at least four ways: as a functional entrance, a mushroom cloud, a sign of community and the conventional view of the heavens. Like Stirling's "baptistry" it is coherently multivalent.

Throughout the museum one meets more explicit signs of East and West. For instance, the crackling stone patterns of the traditional Edo castle and the light canons of Le

282 ANTOINE PREDOCK, *Entrance*. Saguaro cacti form the ritualized entryway, like sphinxes in front of an Egyptian temple, and then they turn into purple-gray concrete piers, again of an Egyptian muteness. Straight ahead is a trussed bridge and high wall for projecting images. (Timothy Hursley).

Corbusier. But these are just incidents that punctuate a more general language of past (masonry base), present (tiled middle section) and future (metallic top). This codification of time is carried through with consistency and subtlety. The most magical space, where all three ages mesh in a seamless manner, is the sculpture court (280). This reminds one at once of the raked pebble garden of Ryoanji, the airfoil door of Le Corbusier's Garches, the PM columns and keystones of

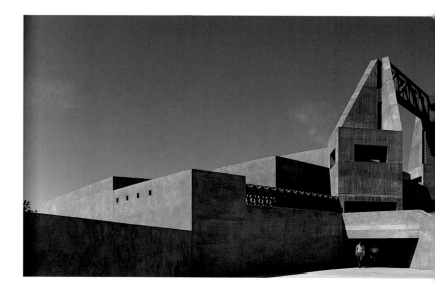

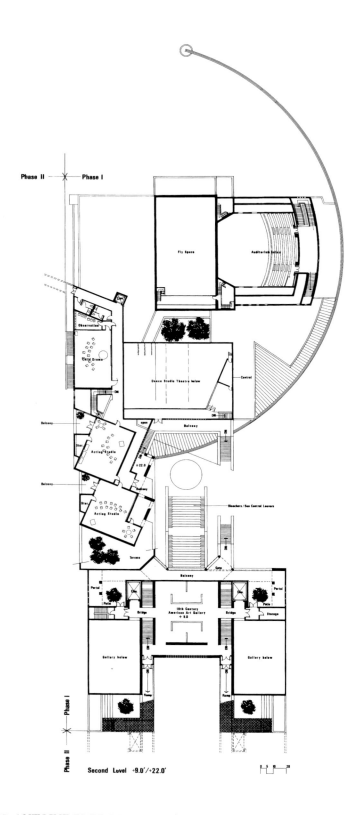

283 ANTOINE PREDOCK, *Plan of the Center*. A symmetrical entrance leads up and own to skewed studios and then the culmination, an auditorium set at right angles to the movement pattern.

284 ANTOINE PREDOCK, *The Roof forms* – pyramid, tower, bridge, void and a space full of promise. (Timothy Hursley).

Michael Graves and the sleek aluminium fuselage of a long UFO. None of these images is explicit, they are only hints.

Here we return to an idea broached in the second section of this book, the power of suggested metaphors to capture the imagination and send it off, running in coherent but divergent ways. The example was Le Corbusier's Ronchamp chapel, a building that is over-coded so that it alludes to many things, but abstract enough to avoid reduction to any one of them.

The third cultural center as village, Antoine Predock's Fine Arts Center for Arizona State University, also has this suggestiveness (281). Like most of his work, it hints at a regional location. Here in the southwest this is a landscape of rock outcrops, buttes and parched desert, masonry forms that find their equivalent around the site. They are most pronounced at the entrance-way, where rows of Saguaro cacti transform into freestanding columns cast from a purplish gray concrete (282). This mixture is an actual desert color. It is appropriate to be explicit about the code here, where people first meet the building, but how many of them could decipher it? The complex is understated and ambiguous enough to require patient analysis, even architectural cryptography. If cactus = concrete column = color of desert stone, then what about the roof-top maze one traverses? Do the divided pyramids = mountains, and the terraces = buttes? So much for the murmurs and hints of a desert landscape, they are no more than this (284).

Other meanings, lurking below the surface, are the two high points, a trussed gateway to the main entrance side and a blank concrete wall facing it. Functionally these serve all sorts of minor uses such as a bridge, projection booth and large screen on which images are cast at night. This wall also marks the fly-tower of the auditorium. But what do these rhetorical shapes mean? They certainly suggest more than their relatively unimportant uses. Here, perhaps, we can borrow another code Predock established in a previous

building, the Fuller House. In this desert complex, or *faux village* as Kurt Anderson has called it, there are two enigmatic shapes that also book-end a pyramid.[88]

At the east end is a pavilion for watching the sunrise, while on the west there is a slightly different one for watching it set. While the two dominating forms of the art center do not entail an activity as specific as this, they certainly evoke it. In mood the roofscape is a cross between a Mayan temple of sacrifice and an eighteenth-century Indian astronomical observatory. Here one feels part of some brooding cosmic spectacle where the planets and stars must be consulted to ward off feelings of existential angst. Perhaps that is rather a heavy load to drop on austere concrete forms. Their emptiness does suggest a slight melancholia, but this portentous note is never finally struck; the architecture just manages to avoid slipping into the bathos it so clearly tempts, the New Age, sci-fi "altered atmospheres" that the architect mentions as a motive for his work (283).

Partly this is because it is so abstract as to discourage explicit interpretation and sentiment. And partly it is because there are other allusions to some of the forms – the very small windows, the metalwork railing and the red arcades. These last, for instance, relate to the red curves of the adjacent building and strike an entirely new note: that of a pergola and refined European galley. Without such occasional divergent signs the building would sink back into that mute Modernism from which it is perhaps derived – the wall architecture of Luis Baragan.

There is no question that as a Post-Modernist Predock is a minimalist. He confines himself to one or two materials to create a virtual all-over world, a lunar landscape. The purple-gray concrete follows one almost everywhere, from the art-gallery lobby to the dance theatre and auditorium, although it is punctuated by slight articulations and details which define different parts of the area with a specific character. This is place-making of an allusive sort, like Ronchamp an enigmatic building with no specific interpretation that unlocks its secret, but many different keys that work on parts.

Ronchamp again, that seminal work opening up Post-Modernism and continuing to do so into the future. During the late eighties when much Post-Modernism was becoming too literal, Predock's work re-confirmed the truth that the most effective architecture is one which strikes a subtle balance between direct and implicit communication. Like Stirling and Kurokawa, he handles symbolism with a benign restraint – lets it grow from the site and function, and like them, produces an articulated world of small-scaled parts set in tense opposition. Whether these three cultural centers and the offices as village constitute a major paradigm for the 1990s remains to be seen. The urban and economic forces of concentration make this problematic, but not impossible. The traditions of Late- and Neo-Modernism, that favor huge scale, repetition and abstraction, go against it. But if it is unlikely to dominate the profession in this age of garrulous pluralism, at least it will concern those minorities who care for an intimate and convivial urbanism. After the orgy of success, and after being declared dead because of it, a leaner, tougher, more chastened tradition of Post-Modernism has emerged.

285 FRANK GEHRY, *Der Neue Zollhof*, Dusseldorf, 1994–99. Diversity within the major downtown building type. The large, speculative office building – often the bane of urbanity – is here broken into three curved volumes with staggered massing that further fragments a monolithic commission. Red brick, mirror-polished stainless steel and white plaster give still more identity to these blocks, facilitating leasing. The software program CATIA was used to rationalize the curved surfaces and these undulations are contrasted by the angular window units, prefabricated and dropped into place. A sculptural unity with variety is achieved by the trio, and the only obvious area where this heterogeneity fails to take root is in the flat, monolithic landscape. (FOG/A).

The Heteropolis

Over the last ten years, two developments have modified the direction of architecture. Pluralism, the keynote of Post-Modernism, has become a positive global movement as well as a chronic world problem; and the sciences of complexity, aided by the computer, have become an essential part of a new cultural paradigm. Both events are really larger-scale forces outside the domain of architecture and ones that will continue to modify the field irreversibly into the future. Both raise issues that were first engaged in the 1960s, and in this sense their intensification and coming into focus also represent the fruition of Post-Modernism, its maturity.

Yet this climax exacts its irony, like reversals of fortune at the end of a comic opera. Just as multiculturalism and the Internet became global engines of change, as predicted thirty years previously, Post-Modern architecture – as we saw in the last chapter – lost focus and fell out of fashion. Furthermore, various types of reaction set in. First was a fundamentalist Classicism led by Prince Charles and his countryside courtiers. This in turn created a Neo-Modernist backlash that gave new life to an ailing tradition, and a Neo-Minimalism occasionally focused on boutiques and prestige museums, and several other movements shown on the evolutionary chart, above page 50–51. Some of this reaction was genuine, creative and validly directed against PM excess. But the fundamental truths behind the Post-Modern condition continued to deepen. This chapter concentrates on the explosive growth of multicultural cities, a runaway inflation beyond anyone's ability to contain, and the way architects developed an heterogeneous architecture to deal with it, while the next two chapters treats the beginnings of a new complexity architecture.

CONFRONTING PLURALISM: THE HYBRID AND THE ENIGMATIC

The cosmopolitan city of traders, with its different ethnic groups and economic sectors, has long existed. Examples include Alexandria, Rome, Shanghai and New York with their polyglot of cultures competing and working together, melting pots and boiling pots. But, under severe pressures, the old cosmopolis mutated into the new heteropolis. The growth of edge cities and suburban sprawl, the increase in global communication of all kinds, the collapse of the Soviet Union (a Post-Modern event in itself) and the expansion of mass migration. In America during the 1980s eight million migrants arrived, the largest number for a single decade since 1900–1910. They settled mostly in Florida, California, the New York conurbation and Texas where the percentage of foreign-born rose anywhere from 5 to 20 per cent of the local state population.

In one heteropolis alone, Los Angeles, a million migrants arrived, most of them hispanics from Mexico. But LA underwent a mutation and became a new type of metropolis for more reasons than ethnic diversity. It was the increase in the variety of variety that made it an heteropolis, the fact that no single group or class or economic sector or cultural formation defined it – as they had in the past. Identifying characteristics: none – except heterogeneity itself.[89] With eighteen village cores, 132 incorporated cities within its orbit and thirteen major ethnic groups competing with over 100 minor ones, this ex-urb became a regional condition rather than a customary city. Forty different lifestyle clusters, defined by marketeers trying to figure it out, divided it up into consumption types, more than eighty different languages were spoken in the schools. Economic diversity added to the differentiation. By the 1990s, LA had the largest manufacturing base in the USA, the greatest concentration of high-tech industries amid, paradoxically, the greatest density of artisan industries such as jewelry-making, furniture, clothing and movie production. Urban sociologists, geographers and economists studied this run-away diversification of what they called the quintessential post-modern city, and showed it had the greatest "diversity index" of any population.[90] Unstudied in 1993, when I wrote my *Heteropolis – Los Angeles, the Riots and the Strange Beauty of Hetero-Architecture*, was an equal diversity of flora and fauna. Because the Colorado River was diverted through this rich desert climate, the landscape bore out the adage "anything can grow in LA given enough water." And the nomadic population imported the greatest variety of plant life: of the sixty major species thriving, only six were local. Small animals flourished amid this bounty, and even two kinds of coyote competed, with the edge given to those that learned how to open multiplying garbage bins.

Inevitably this diversity led to competition and discord, most notably the riots of 1992, when the black community directed its rage at an unjust verdict of the court. They struck out against contiguous groups, particularly the Koreans. For five days retail shops in Koreatown burned; Hispanics in the neighboring Barrio, or Little Mexico, prepared for struggle. It looked for awhile as if the city would fall into civil war, as it did later in other multicultural cities such as Sarajevo. Indeed, in August 1992 low intensity warfare was greater in LA than it was in Bosnia, which was also falling apart at the time. That month 260 people were killed, a higher death toll than in the former Yugoslavian province. The melting pot of America became the boiling pot, hyphenated-Americans lost their hyphen and were retribalized.

Such events accentuate the negative aspects of the new global heteropolis, but what about its positive qualities and architecture? Designers, as we have seen, had been formu-

286 FRANK GEHRY, *Chiat/Day/Mojo Office*, Venice, Los Angeles, design 1985, realization 1989–91. On the exterior a collage of abstract representational forms include a white boat (fish), coppers trees and binoculars, the last which focuses the car entrance to a garage, holds an interior boardroom and, symbolically, alludes to Pop architecture in LA and the function of the ad agency.

287 *Chiat/Day/Mojo interior*. The converted warehouse became the new informal space that changed offices around the world, a kind of interior city street – here including a conference room in the shape of a fish, a red Mini, a basketball backstop and other convivial places to work and relax. En-formality, urban life turned inwards and into an art form.

288 *Chiat/Day/Mojo Conference Room*. A space set apart, with sound insulation made from corrugated cardboard, has an oculus which like the dome of the Pantheon casts a sacred light around the paper coffers.

lating an hybrid architecture for thirty years and, inevitably, this became one way of acknowledging diversity. Political multiculturalism meant recognizing minorities, forming a rainbow coalition of separate identities. Radical eclecticism was its architectural counterpart, and none was stronger than the LA School led by Frank Gehry, Eric Moss, Frank Israel and the group Morphosis (285). These architects formed a loose approach based on mixing everyday materials in an informal and striking way creating thereby the architectural equivalent of a rainbow coalition. Gehry's Artists' Studios in the Venice part of LA, 1981, typified this adhocism, as did his Aerospace Museum of 1984, Edgmar Farms, 1987, and, above all, office design for the Chiat/Day/Mojo advertising agency, conceived and built over a long period, between 1985 and 1991. Here the collage method, or the confrontational type of post-modernism where opposite systems converge, reaches a climactic dissonance (286–8).

Variety is celebrated, difference is enjoyed, juxtaposition of mood and material is turned into a high art, the clash of cultures transformed into architecture, the heteropolis admitted as a positive condition, not just a place of war. On the inside of the office informal monumental structures – rooms made from metal, corrugated paper, or in the shape of a fish – are contrasted with a grid of open space contained in a warehouse. This sensuous interior environment was

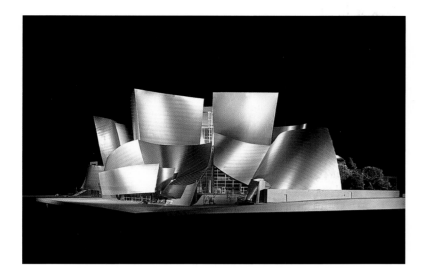

289　GEHRY, *Walt Disney Concert Hall*, Los Angeles, first design 1987, redesigned 1992, final design, 1998. A limestone base holds a garden that surrounds a stainless-steel flower with huge, fluttering leaves. This enigmatic signifier creates more ambiguities as the internal reflections make the surface glow from within. The building, and its metaphors of growth, may come to symbolize hopes for a multicultural Los Angeles. (Whit Preston).

290　*Disney Concert Hall*, 1999–2002. Although still covered, the stainless-steel skin can be seen hanging like clapboard siding in curved strips over an insulating layer and interior steel frame. The richness of these contrasting layers is revealed around the entry areas and windows. Beyond this structural opposition, the building is expressionist not critical. (Whit Preston).

particularly convincing for an office space at the time. It influenced the informal workspace of countless startup companies that characterized the Dotcom frenzy of the 1990s. Indeed, the LA style, what could be called en-formality, was adopted by this generation of entrepreneurs generally. Gehry's play with curvilinear forms centered on the main boardroom that, on the outside, became a pair of binoculars framing the entrance to the parking garage.

Spyglasses as an icon? This amusing bit of PM representation, recalling other Pop buildings in LA, had a further justification beyond showing people where and how to park. It signaled the function of an ad agency, just the kind of institution that was studying those forty lifestyle clusters of LA, on computers, if not eyeing them through binoculars. To its left was an abstract, white boat – sign of the water nearby – to its right, a faint allusion to copper trees (and LA had its rows of plastic trees planted a few miles away). But the ad agency was more explicitly representational than most other work of the LA School and Gehry's other buildings. The majority of these structures dealt with heterogeneity by analogy. The hyphenated-American felt at ease and at home in these workplaces because of their understated en-formality, their mixture of materials and odd shapes that did not recall *any* particular ethnicity.

Indeed, Gehry also showed the other main way of dealing with cultural difference. Instead of producing an eclectic mix of diverse signs and shapes that represented the different taste cultures – the method Stirling had turned into a high art at Stuttgart – he developed the PM method stemming from Le Corbusier's Ronchamp, that is, the enigmatic signifier. Competing against Stirling and other international designers, he won the prestige commission for the Disney Hall in 1988. This was the first large-scale version of his vermiform (or worm-like) grammar we will look at in the next chapter, but it is mentioned here because of its date and the fact that it was the first large public building that used the alternative strategy (289–90). When faced with a frac-

tious migrant population that shares very few symbols and values, it may be best to give them something they cannot recognize or even imagine, something completely other. The Disney Hall does this in extraordinary ways and now, nearing completion after twelve years of struggle, it has picked up the kind of suggestive metaphors that grew around Le Corbusier's Ronchamp. The enigmatic signifier accretes positive and negative epithets like the Berlin Wall picked up graffiti. Those who disliked it at the outset saw it as "wet cardboard," "a pile of broken crockery" (recalling Julian Schnabel), "LA after The Big One" (an earthquake), "a fortune cookie gone beserk," "an emptied waste basket," and "deconstructionist trash" (Deconstruction was the leading architectural movement that year).[91] Its defenders saw the inside, like Scharoun's Philharmonic Hall in Berlin, as vineyards for spectators, the outside like a galleon with billowing sails or, my favourite, a burgeoning plant. Other metaphors of growth and movement, of waves and flowing lava, of natural processes of change are perceived. From many angles the forms seem to reach and soar and play in antiphony, in obvious support of its musical function.

Gehry mentions how he wanted to create something "in tune with the relaxed sensibility of Los Angeles" and "avoid an air of cultural intimidation . . . It should prick the curiosity even of those Angelenos who might never attend a performance."[92] This it is bound to do, even for its detractors. The gently swooping forms in stainless steel, a material forced on the architect after his success with titanium at Bilbao, will catch internal reflections making the huge masses dematerialize and glow from within – a soft-hardness. Paradox, surprise, sensuality. The curiosity Gehry mentions has now become a motive in PM public architecture, a counterpart to Surrealist poetics of seventy years previously. The uncanny has become conventional, as we will see, imagination is forced into the public realm to do the reconciling and communicating that politics cannot achieve. Of course architecture does not change the facts of a competitive, multicultural society, but it can invent new strategies for dealing with pluralism.

Mass migration obviously is the biggest cause of the new heteropolis and this is on the increase though statistics are unreliable because much of the immigration is illegal and governments, though they want cheap labor, are loath to admit it. In 1992 the United Nations put the figure of those on the move at over one hundred million while China alone admitted to such a number in the late 1990s – and then halved it when inconvenient. Hypocrisy, inability to count, hard to define what a migrant really is? All this leads to the ambiguity, but what is clearer is that these nomads are attracted to the global centers of power, not just any large city. The heteropolis is a place where the headquarters of the world's biggest companies reside. As sure as exercise creates sweat, multinationals create multiculturalism – not by intention but as a byproduct of economic growth. Hence the major ones are those twenty or so financial powerhouses: New York, Los Angeles, Chicago, San Francisco, Seattle, London, Berlin, Frankfurt. Amsterdam, Rotterdam, Vienna, Toronto, Melbourne, Singapore, Tokyo, Hong Kong, Shanghai, Moscow, Mexico City, and so on. The implication of this continued influx, over the years, is that such cities will become like LA and have no clear majority culture but, like the world as a whole, become an aggregation of minorities.

Imagine for the future thirty heteropolii that resemble each other more than they do their host nation, global mixtures spread out over an area of one hundred miles. Should they be designed in one style as Lutyens laid out New Delhi, Le Corbusier did Chandigarh, and Niemeyer and others formed Brasilia? Obviously such harmonious models are inappropriate, even were they possible, which they are not except for the mid-size city. Moreover many people no longer seek cultural integration but are happy to exist on the margins of a pluralist society. The hundred-mile city is a polycentered sprawl, its peripheral rim is a place of growth, and those who have the ability and sensibility enjoy being "ex-centrics," outside the center, taking their meaning by opposition with an assumed establishment.[93] Taking advantage of heterogeneity is a matter of choice, desire, training and the style of life that celebrates difference. Hence the

role of architecture in furthering this taste. Three schemes of the early 1990s summarized this position as a refined art, by Stirling, Venturi and Hollein.

James Stirling and Michael Wilford managed to build a low-level block in the heart of the City of London, after much opposition from conservation groups and the Prince of Wales (291). Their No. 1. Poultry, replacing one of the last Victorian office clusters, took up medieval street patterns, a surrounding Classical grammar, the morphology of a triangular, corner site, and combined aspects of these contrasting forces with the requirements of a modern office block. Beyond this the building provided a roof garden and a circular, public realm set off from the street in a dense part of London where such open space is most welcome. The resultant grammar is a syncopated hybrid playing a checkerboard theme: large-windowed offices step back and forth above large volumes of banded masonry also stepping up and down. But the syncopation of these big sections break down the scale in a way that is far superior to the continuous monoliths of Lutyens, Baker and the Classicists around it. Stirling, perhaps learning a lesson from Leon Krier who was in his office fifteen years previously, shows how the multinational office leviathan can be heterogeneous *and* grammatical.

However, Prince Charles, not getting the point and trying to stop the scheme, damned the design as an "old 1930s wireless," although it hardly looks like an early radio set. He also attacked Stirling publicly several times. Inevitably this criticism took its toll and Stirling told me, over one of the infrequent lunches we used to have, that if he were to win the Disney Hall competition he would emigrate to America. As we have seen he lost this contest to Gehry with the result that he remained in Britain and became somewhat disillusioned with his relatively marginalized position (relative to the later Lord Rogers and Lord Foster). Stirling continued to debate the Prince through the press, granting that there was much truth in the future monarch's crusade against insensitive modern building, but he lamented the undemocratic tactics with which this campaign was pursued. Soon thereafter, in another change of fate, he was knighted by the Prince's mother and then, in the most tragic and freakish circumstance, died as the result of a medical accident. I mention this conflict because it was important to British architectural politics and because it illuminates the discord at the top of society, the way an heteropolis may differ from a more integrated culture.[94] The establishment in a true democracy must internalize difference in its primary institutions and among its leaders, or else one mode of thought tends to dominate. It is of interest that many of the designers we are considering here – Gehry, Koolhaas, MVRDV and ARM – are, like Stirling, both insiders and outsiders. Although they work within the power structure, their commitment to diversity has led to frequent conflicts with the establishment. It tends to prefer symbols of integration to heterogeneity.

JAMES STIRLING, MICHAEL WILFORD, *No. 1 Poultry*, London, 1987, revised 1988–91, constructed 1994–7. The large office is broken down into a checkerboard of glass and masonry units, hollowed out in the center for an urban rotunda, and surmounted by a roof garden. Contextual references are transformed with great sculptural sophistication – the most urbane recent office in London.

Stirling and Wilford's design was, like their Tate addition five years previously, partly a chameleon that transformed the elements of its surrounding. Contextualism took its next step with Robert Venturi's addition to London's National Gallery, finished in 1991, another sensitive building controversy in which the Prince intervened and tried to influence events. For the gallery the functional requirements were themselves radically hybrid, since museums were becoming mixed building types at the time. Not only were top-lit galleries needed, but so too a restaurant, large gift shop, auditorium, interactive data bank, administrative space, and a large entrance for the three million back-packers who would arrive by bus. This variety of functions, as well as the site that differed on each side, was a perfect opportunity for Venturi to prove his theories of complexity and contradiction, and he rose to the occasion brilliantly (292). The inside adopted a grey and white Renaissance grammar fitting for the art, and modified it in subtle and art-specific ways, while the outside addressed the varied contexts of Trafalgar Square, back streets, alleyways and the Clubs of Pall Mall.[95]

Each façade had a different use and asked for a slightly different expression. The superiority of Venturi's solution over others competing for the job, including James Stirling, was that it recognized these differences while still keeping "an obligation to the difficult whole." The grammar holds together and slightly transforms around its five façades, even as the galleries stick their head above the parapet and the dark entrance void open below to let in the thousands, like a stadium entrance. Here the grammar even morphs around the site, as it is to do with later schemes of young computer designers. For instance, the ghost pilaster and blank window pick up the existing National Gallery, then fade out and then end with the crescendo of an engaged column. This inventive use of Classicism was, needless to say, damned by both Modernists and Revivalists, though it was also well appreciated by the public and the curators. Heterogeneity could be acknowledged *and* smoothed together seamlessly, an important point for those of the next generation, as we will see.

Hans Hollein adopts a version of the chameleon-solution on another important site in yet another heteropolis, Vienna (293). Here however the transitions are more abrupt, the different grammars of each street summarized with greater contrast. It seems at first as if there is no obligation to the whole of the building, difficult or otherwise. But as one looks closer at the way the curved plan pulls together the two streets some unities start to appear, continuities of cornice line, window rhythms and volumes. The breaks from these, especially the cylindrical wall that juts out over the entrance, are set up to acknowledge and reflect the cathedral diagonally opposite. One justification for this glistening shape, another example of the enigmatic signifier, is that it mirrors the old fortifications, another that it

292 VENTURI, SCOTT BROWN & ASSOCIATES, *Sainsbury Wing*, National Gallery Addition, London 1987–91. A new Classical grammar is morphed around five façades of a site. Picking up cues from the old Gallery to the right, the addition intensifies the grammar with ghost pilasters, that are turned into a half-engaged column; the blank window slowly fades out, and the mass entrance opens up in black, below. These forms are then transformed sequentially as the building moves to a more private street and square in back.

293 HANS HOLLEIN, *Haas House*, Vienna, 1988–90. The corner building takes cues from all sides, and even the cathedral diagonally opposite, that it reflects. These forms and cornice lines are then abstracted and played with a grammar accentuating difference. The interior shopping space within expresses itself without as a bulging, shimmering geode: contextualism meets self-assertion.

turns the corner. But the most apparent reason for its emphasis is that it becomes a contemporary contrast to the succession of oppositions in the center of Vienna. Here we find distinct units strung out on a line: Gothic, Baroque, nineteenth-century, 1910, 1950s modern and now one more exception. As they accrue in number all these styles and

types, like the population as a whole, are becoming proportionally more of a minority. But they all follow the urban morphology. In effect the gleaming cylinder emphasizes this architecture of difference: its sparkle says "look at me looking at the cathedral." Its extraordinary cantilever and little temple at the top proclaim commerce (for this Haas-House, as it is called, contains upmarket boutiques). Shopping, which Hollein has previously turned into an art form, finds its apotheosis as a twentieth century ritual and this typology further differentiates the urban tissue. In dealing with its various requirements, the building employs both methods of dealing with pluralism that had become standard by this time, the hybrid collage and the enigmatic signifier.

THE SUPERPOSITION OF URBAN FIELDS — REM KOOLHAAS

Other strategies towards pluralism than these two were developed, functionalist ones that simply presented diverse requirements without comment or expression. Among those that championed this approach was Rem Koolhaas and he did so while being very strongly engaged with issues of the extra large commission, and themes of bigness and the generic. Of particular relevance was the question of repetition versus differentiation. Is the global environment becoming more the same everywhere, as many people perceive, or more various, or perhaps both at once? The strategies of radical eclecticism and collage city that characterized Post-Modernism since the 1970s argued for the desirability of differentiation, but there are many economic and social pressures that increase standardization. Rem Koolhaas, of all the architects involved in this debate, takes a curious position at either end of the argument, at the extremes. His writings, notably *Delirious New York*, 1978, and *S,M,L,XL*, 1995, restate the resultant paradox in differing ways. Moreover, through these amusing polemics Koolhaas influenced architecture in a way that recalls both Le Corbusier and Robert Venturi.

A whole generation of Dutch architects, branded as *Superdutch*, followed his notion of design based on the pragmatics of the program, the generation of architecture by summarizing emergent functions and their organizational possibilities. He and then they constructed statistical maps or what one group, with typical digital zeal, called datascapes of information. These virtual diagrams of rules and sociological data could be turned into a flowing landscape of blobs on the computer screen and thereby given a certain inevitability, like a force of history. This method of statistical diagramming Le Corbusier initiated in the 1920s and in the 1960s groups like Superstudio and Archizoom turned into a method of global planning. Like Venturi the functions Koolhaas considered often concerned the new global media and popular activities. In his design for the Parc de la Villette, for instance, he used the generic grid – ultimate abstraction – as the backdrop for five organizational types layered on top of each other (294,5). No one knew what the functions of this urban landscape in Paris would be in detail, but the statistics generated a datascape of five different assumptions. These were then superimposed and the random overlap created chaotic diversity on a uniform grid. A method of functional invention thus became *the* model for many subsequent architects, and it mixed repetition and differentiation at their extremes.

Delirious New York, Koolhaas called "A Retroactive Manifesto for Manhattan," and it argued for a culture of congestion along the lines of New York City. Here 2048 almost identical blocks, placed on a grid, are each used for a variety of changing functions, and each block has its own internal "mania" and/or defining identity. The delirium comes from the unlikely juxtaposition of functions: one Koolhaas scenario depicts nude prizefighters eating oysters with their boxing gloves on one floor of a skyscraper, while it is business as usual on another floor. If Jane Jacobs showed that mixed use was the essence of urban culture and economics, then Koolhaas took this variety even further and argued that culture should be positively *congested* with difference. His message was supported by Surrealist examples, and the paranoid critical method of Salvador Dali, and emphasized how the architect was made both impotent *and* empowered by the urban situation.

In his second book Koolhaas reprinted parts of the first with the message of chaos and paradox emblazoned across it in red: "The permanence of even the most frivolous item of architecture and the instability of the metropolis are incompatible. In this conflict the metropolis is, by definition, the victor; in its pervasive reality architecture is reduced to the status of a plaything, tolerated as a décor for the illusions of history and memory. In Manhattan this paradox is resolved

294, 295 REM KOOLHAAS, *Parc de la Villette*, Paris, 1982–83. The urban landscape is conceived as an artificial ground, as it is in Holland, for the superposition of one organizational type on top of the next. Five layers – bands of planting, confetti of small furniture, circulation systems, existing and new buildings – are distributed and placed over each other to form a rich congestion. This became a model for a later heterogeneous urbanism and city park.

296 **REM KOOLHAAS** was born in Rotterdam in 1944, and spent part of his youth in Indonesia where his father, a poet, was also part of the Dutch civil service. After a brief stint as a scriptwriter and film-maker (two films completed) he left Holland to apply his narrative interests to architecture and studied at the Architectural Association in London, from 1965 to 1972. His thesis set the tone for later work, *Exodus or the Voluntary Prisoners of Architecture* – a black-humored scenario of the way a hedonistic architecture could overcome adversity through eliciting desire. In 1975 Koolhaas formed an office with his wife Madelon Vriesendorp, and Elia and Zoe Zenghelis. Called OMA, the Office for Metropolitan Architecture, it emphasized a continuing position of his practice: that architecture, always in danger of triviality, is rejuvenated by larger, urban concerns. This found expression in his first major publication, *Delirious New York*, 1978, "a retroactive manifesto" by the self-styled ghost-writer to the city, and one illustrated largely by Vriesendorp's magic realist paintings. These revealed the secret life of New York sky-scrapers, not only the illicit love-affairs and hedonistic activities that featured in *Exodus*, but also the secret of a good city: the Culture of Congestion and the mania of each city block. This mania, or "Manhattanism" taken to an ex-treme, made each of 2048 city blocks into a purified expression of separate ideologies and styles. Thus, because each block excluded the values of the others, maximum pluralism led to maximum para-

noia. Indeed, in *Delirious New York*, Salvador Dali's paranoid critical method was applied to architecture and it became another main theme of his work.

The architecture of his first period was Miesian and minimalist, but his writings and projects, inspired by narratives and unusual programmatic activities were more radical. Koolhaas, like Le Corbusier, understood the pleasure of combining new social requirements into novel organizational types. These culminated in his entry to the Park de la Villette competition, 1982, a scheme influenced by the Russian Suprematists, Leonidov, Superstudio, his student Zaha Hadid, and Cedric Price. The importance of diagramming unpredictable urban activities now became another Koolhaas method, a procedure that was to influence a generation of students and Dutch architects. If one could not predict what the city of the future would need in detail, one could at least postulate some statistical probabilities and then superimpose and weave them through each other. The fast-growing, contemporary city, such as Atlanta, was out of control. To deal with this, the architect must become a surfer and align himself with the chaotic waves that break continually over its surface. As if to prove the point, in 1989 the Flemish city of Lille commissioned Koolhaas to design a masterplan, the highway system, the TGV interchange, the biggest parking garage in Europe and much else besides. It was as if "your parents asked you to play with fire." Once the decision to start the wave had been made by

Mitterand, Kohl, Thatcher, bankers, the mayor of Lille and the Culture of Congestion, no one could stop it. "We had no time to stand back and reflect on our hypotheses…the dynamic from hell produced a very desirable condition of unconsciousness." It also produced some very large urban chunks some of them designed by "The Flying Dutchman," as Koolhaas started to be known (for his constant air travel).

Typical of the scale and delirious activity of the Lille commission was an event organized like a *film-noir*: 5,000 Mazda dealers would watch the new model being demonstrated. Then the walls of the hall would pull back, and the salesmen would march towards their own new car and drive out the back of the building — the ritual over in thirty minutes. Surfing such mass-requirements, many of them made up at the last moment, delighted the agile designer who dragged a Dirty Realism from such programs. The budget was so small that Koolhaas was forced to use corrugated plastic and other cheap materials. Learning from Frank Gehry about the virtues of the unfinished building, and the poetry of the botch, he even used chain-link fencing as acoustic reflectors. Hedonism and desire, for the Voluntary Prisoners of Architec-ture, was supplied in other ways including a dazzling stairway in crinkled mirrorplate.

Two small houses in France were Dirty Realist gems that continued the lessons learned from Gehry: they combined fragments from Mies, Corb, High-Tech, Ando and the Age of Plastic into a

surrealist Exquisite Corpse. Many projects, discussed in the text below, influenced the architectural world, especially when collected in the tome *S,M,L,XL*, 1995. At the moment of his greatest success OMA started to go bankrupt and had to form a strategic alliance with the conglomerate, the Royal Haskoning Group. To supplement his income and extend his interest in "what used to be called the city," Koolhaas trained up a generation of Harvard students and produced a further series of heavy tomes on Exopolis: *The Harvard Guide to Shopping*, *The Pearl River Delta*, *Mutations of the City* and *Lagos*. Fortune changed again by the late 1990s as the tide came in, commissions from Prada, the Guggenheim, Microsoft, the Whitney Museum, etcetera; the surfer grabbed his board and steered his architecture along the edge of a very large collapsing wave.

(Sanne Peper/OMA).

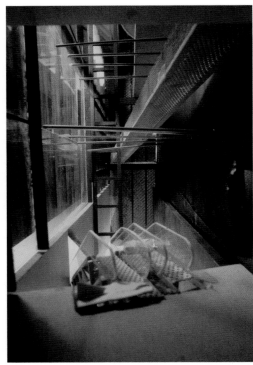

in a brilliant way: through the development of a mutant architecture that combines the aura of monumentality with the performance of instability. Its interiors accommodate compositions of program and activity that change constantly and independently of each other without affecting what is called, with accidental profundity, the envelope. The genius of Manhattan is the simplicity of this divorce between the appearance and performance; it keeps the illusion of architecture intact, while surrendering wholeheartedly to the needs of the metropolis. This architecture relates to the forces of the *Groszstadt* like a surfer to the waves."

Surfing is his metaphor for negotiating the contradictions: permanent envelopes versus fast-changing content; or an abstract grid of 2048 blocks – a generic city – versus the dynamism of a global economy that mass-produces difference. The contradictions for Koolhaas are acute. On the one hand, the marketplace is well defined as founded on goods that create, in Gregory Bateson's definition of information, "the difference that makes a difference." On the other hand, he and so many designers in Holland, have been brought up with a suspicion of consumerism and wealth. Koolhaas' sensibility, formed as it was by Mies van der Rohe, Minimalism and Dutch Calvinism, favors repetition, anonymity, abstraction and the generic. This aspect of his work is well expressed, as we will see, in his essays on Bigness and The Generic City, reprinted in *S,M,L,XL*, the book supported by Dutch subsidies, that became the most influential in architecture by the late 1990s.[96] The Dutch, as Simon Schama so famously demonstrated in *The Embarrassment of Riches*, 1987, were conflicted about their wealth in the Golden Age of the seventeenth century. As Bart Lootsma so ably argues

in his *Superdutch*, they remain so today with their new prosperity – particularly architects.[97] For both ecological and moral reasons they are committed to understating this affluence behind a cool anonymity. The group called *Droog Design* (Dry Design) typifies this sensibility, but it is Koolhaas who turns it into a method and style.

Following the example of Frank Gehry's "cheapskate architecture," which transforms such things as chain-link fence to architectural advantage, Koolhaas adopts an approach that has been called, variously, Dirty Realism, The New Sobriety, or Calcutta minimalism:

It has to do with a sort of minimal use of means. As far as that goes there are indeed two sorts of minimalism: a Calcutta minimalism and a detailed, even fussy minimalism. I feel more affinity with Calcutta. It absolutely doesn't mean that we only make cheap things, but I think that the research into how you can carry out as many programmes as possible with as little money as possible is incredibly interesting. I think a building such as Lille

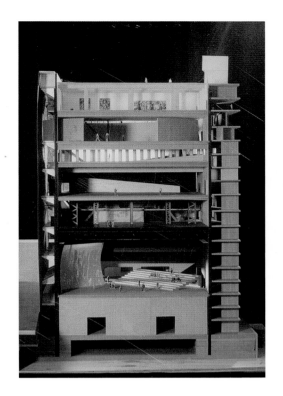

Grand Palais that was built with budgets that would also be valid in Calcutta was an interesting project because it proved that you can discard all those fetishes you might use to seduce people and that you can bring about desirable conditions in a specific context purely on the basis of a real commitment (296).[98]

Koolhaas goes on to say that the sensual and aesthetically driven architecture of today has lost its credibility because it does not address "the great problems of our time," and by these he means Bigness, shopping, and the explosive growth of cities. These are the issues he takes on with research projects, funded by his office and Harvard Graduate School of Design, into the Pearl River Delta of China and the sprawling and impoverished metropolis of Lagos. Giant books like *S,M,L,XL,* co-authored with students, result from these investigations, and their style and content replicate that of Koolhaas. Indeed, part of his brilliance is to have produced a school of thought and practice, as did Le Corbusier; to have cloned himself.

Several of his unbuilt projects, in addition to Parc de la Villette, became models for architects and they all have a characteristic differentiation subsumed within a minimalist grid or simple geometry. The ZKM, Zentrum fur Kunst und Medietechnologie in Karlsruhe, shows this typical mixture (297–8). Won as a competition in 1989, it is a minimum box, with four different façades that superimposes seven different layers of activity in giant open floors. In effect, the delirious skyscraper of New York is placed in an old Baroque West German city that prides itself on townscape, but now this utilitarian cube proclaims some of its difference, the envelope shouts out its interiors. The south façade, facing the autobahn, reveals behind its blurred polyester sheeting a

299 REM KOOLHAAS, *Bibliothèques Jussieu*, Paris, competition, 1993. The warped interior boulevard connects all floors in a single route, the artificial ground not only ramps up and down through the forest of columns, but occasionally it breaks through the floor and ceiling creating a bigger event. Again Koolhaas refines an influential idea, the tilted usable surface peppered randomly with different functions, that is taken up by others, notably MVRDV (see 304).

"robot" running up and down the entire inside space zipping stage sets and electronic equipment to each floor. This is the classic Piranesian cavity with escalators and structures zooming overhead in complex and contradictory ways, especially at odds with customary perspective. The east façade facing the train station is a large projection screen of perforated metal, the west is clad in giant glazed bricks that cover the offices and plant rooms, and the north is another glass filter. Huge walls of black concrete hold massive vierendeel trusses within which activities can occur. Like the Pompidou Center, on which it is partly based, these trays of open space are conceived as flexible fields, a series of Parcs de la Villette stacked on each other.

The corrugated polyester walls, perforated metal and black concrete emphasize the Calcutta minimalism, but what makes it come alive with excitement are the juxtaposition of functions. As Koolhaas says, the entire program of different activities is crammed into a single container to "exploit proximity, provoke tension, maximize friction, organize in-betweens, promote filtering, sponsor identity and stimulate blurring."[99] This "Electronic Bauhaus," as he also calls it, is "a Darwinian arena where classical and electronic media can compete with and influence each other."

301, 302, REM KOOLHAAS, *Grand Palais*, Congrexpo, Lille, 1993–94. The superposition of very large urban functions: Z = Hall for 5,500; C= three halls of 1,500, 350 and 500; E= exposition area of 18,000 square meters. The materials and structures are simply conjoined, there is no attempt to relate the distinct grammars or activities. As with Le Corbusier and Frank Gehry, it is the poetry of industrial materials presented in brutal opposition. Note the fractal organization of the windows, mirrored surfaces on the grand stairway and metallic acoustic reflectors. (Christian Richters, Charles Jencks).

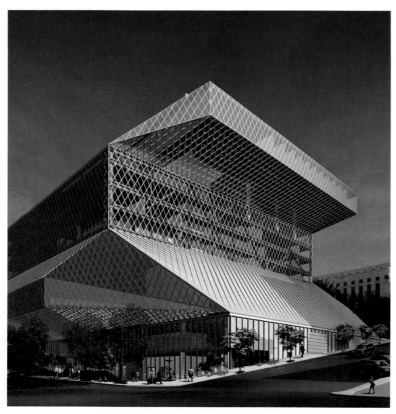

300 REM KOOLHAAS, *Seattle Public Library*, Seattle, 2000–3. The new library conceived as media in competition: the book versus all the other information sources. Since most libraries are a muddle of one department expanding over another, here flexibility in the form of open platforms and slopped in-between floors copes with change and gives a strong visual identity. The angular sculpture is meant to complement Gehry's folded sculpture at the EMP (383) and construct Seattle's new image. As usual with Dutch architects, the functions were originally laid out as a series of stacked diagrams (five platforms – parking, library space, auditorium, administration and meeting rooms). Then in-between space on the angles provides extra light, and room for offices, play space for children, software zone, reading rooms and roof terrace. The diagrams are unified under a single skin (reflective, perforated and transparent). (OMA).

Another project, also unbuilt but equally influential, was the Jussieu University Library designed for Paris in 1993. Here again floors of different activities are conceived as fields of statistically conceived functions spread out without hierarchy. The innovation, that was immediately taken up by other Dutch architects, was the folded and warped floor that turned the entire building into a ramp of continuous movement (299). Folding, as we will see, became *the* approved method for handling difference that year, but what made Koolhaas' scheme different from the American versions of this idea was that the folds were skewered by an endless grid of columns and contained in an unconventional box. These ideas from the ZKM and Jussieu projects finally found fulfillment in his Educatorium building for Utrecht University, 1997, and the library and media center which he is building for one of the founders of Microsoft, in Seattle (300).

As architecture Koolhaas' work spurns refinement and takes pleasure in straightforward juxtapositions of large-scale elements conceived statistically. The Congrexpo Grand Palais in Lille is typical, even in its hybrid name. It is a compilation of congress hall, exposition space, and huge auditorium for 5,500 people (301, 302). A leaning polyester wall sits on a giant base of treacly black stone holding the parking and confronts a glazed wall of "broken" fractal windows. Again it is the Calcutta rather than Miesian minimalism. God is not in these details, but rather the zeitgeist of late Capitalism and bricolage. Certain moments, such as the fractured, mirrored grand stairway, become celebrations of mass culture. They ripple with life during an urban festival when 5,500 fans stream into a pop concert, or automobile salesman stream out of a lecture and into the adjacent hall to examine their 23 types of Toyota. Difference reigns in the products. But Bigness is in charge of the structure, statistical architecture is turned into a tough urban poetry, and one with no overriding theme or message beyond juxtaposition. In this Koolhaas' method might be compared with that of Venturi, Stirling and Hollein. Where they have a commitment to the difficult whole and morphing parts together, he lets the different parts express themselves within a neutral matrix, and collide.

The contradictions between the generic and the differentiated become acute and are reflected in Koolhaas' manifesto *S,M,L,XL*, produced with the graphic designer Bruce Mau (303). Partly this extra-large tome was a classic Post-Modern hypertext mixing genres as the ultimate hybrid book. As the authors write on the jacket, not only is it a "novel," and extended personal confession of Koolhaas' life, but it "combines essays, manifestoes, diaries, fairy tales, travelogues, a cycle of meditations on the contemporary city, with work produced by Koolhaas's office . . . .." The piling on of images over 1345 pages, its occasional pornographic spreads and comic strips, guaranteed it was a popular success, especially among the MTV generation and architects persuaded of its message. If the form was PM, the content was often resolutely ultra-modern. Describing the *tabula rasa* of Singapore and (exulting in) such Modernist developments as the huge, soulless Bijlmermeer housing development in Holland, what Koolhaas describes acidly as the "Las Vegas of the Welfare State," he comes to terms with the forces that are destroying "what we used to call the city."

The essay on Bigness is part description and part aphoristic manifesto for the new mutation in city proliferation. Its argument by telegraphic assertion is again reminiscent of Le Corbusier, and even more apocalyptic in tone:

> Bigness is ultimate architecture...Such [a big] mass can no longer be controlled by a single architectural gesture...Issues of composition, scale, proportion, detail are now moot....The humanist expectation of "honesty" is doomed: interior and exterior architectures become separate projects...Bigness is no longer part of any urban tissue. It exists; at most, it coexists. Its subtext is *fuck* context...Only Bigness can sustain a promiscuous proliferation of events in a single container...Although Bigness is a blueprint for perpetual intensity, it also offers degrees of serenity and even blandness. It is simply impossible to animate its entire mass with intention...Bigness is impersonal: the architect is no longer condemned to stardom...Beyond signature, Bigness means surrender to technologies: to engineers, contractors, manufacturers; to politics; to others...Bigness, through its very independence of context, is the one architecture that can survive, even exploit, the now-global condition of *tabula rasa*...Bigness surrenders the field to after-architecture'.[100]

As a description of the urban condition, Bigness has some obvious truths. In many respects the city is out of control,

303 REM KOOLHAAS & BRUCE MAU, *S,M,L,XL*. The most influential book of the 1990s in architecture mixes manifestoes, fairy tales, comic strips, amusing travelogues, the encyclopedia of a mad architect, beautiful photographs, pornographic asides, silly wallpaper buildings, brilliant aperçus, the architecture of OMA, dramatic commentary ("Alas!"), unreadable type, too-readable big type, secret autobiography and much else besides. Monty Python introduced to Le Corbusier by Salvador Dali. No comment.

and has nothing whatever to do with architectural merit or value. It is "after-architecture," and mega-development as he puts it brutally, does *fuck* context. One might also say that it does the same to quality and any distinctions that get in its way, an issue Koolhaas avoids. Although he often claims to be describing an inevitable trend, as supposedly neutral research, his counsel often looks like surrender, not criticism. Another weakness of the argument is that, counter to what the book jacket claims, the issues of economics and politics are not engaged. These are, of course, the real engines behind what Koolhaas describes: the Group of Seven that steers the world economy; the 380 corporations that control 75% of world trade production. Or, what leads to fast over-development, the concentration of land ownership and development capital in the hands of the few and its sudden descent onto the urban periphery.

The city, it is true, has always been driven by economic forces and in this sense has always been out of control — whatever Alan Greenspan and his apologists may hope. As for architects, they have never built more than 5% of a nation's buildings, and usually less than 1%. What Koolhaas brings to attention is not some new condition, but the exaggeration of previous ones. And whereas, for instance, Venturi also identifies the split between inside and outside, and contradictory forces, Venturi also writes of the "obligation toward the difficult whole" — the context, and architecture.

Rem Koolhaas' great contribution, however, is to enter areas of fast production — such as the Atlanta suburbs, or the Pearl River Delta — and find the opportunities for statistical superposition — quantitative architecture. In writing and filming his experiences in Singapore, he instantly becomes a Walt Whitman of that corporation: both a very funny witness-poet and an amateur sociologist. The comparison with Le Corbusier visiting America, "the land of the timid" as he chided it, might be sustained. Koolhaas as itinerant visionary, spending 550 nights in hotels over 13 years, flying 650,000 kilometres, as one of his mad-statistical maps reveals, is a global-airplane-urbanist.[101] He makes pithy generalizations about a world city after only one week's acquaintance and, like a good journalist, may go right to the heart of a problem. His projects, because they are radical mixtures of urban functions, are even Post-Modern when they exploit metaphor, symbolism and the radical diversity of function. But his intentions remain ironic and descriptive about amnesia and the tabula rasa; as an ultra-Modernist he looks to exploit, not counter, these forces. Most ironic of all, it is another Modernist, Richard Rogers, who has risen to this challenge and provided a more developed urban theory. At the level of planning his work carries forward the ideas of complexity theory, Jane Jacobs, Leon Krier and many contextualists who seek to stitch the city together.[102]

THE SUPERDUTCH AND "DEMOCRATIC" STATISTICAL ARCHITECTURE

Many of the leading Dutch architects worked in Rem Koolhaas' office, collaborated with him or were greatly influenced by him. Among these are Kees Christiaanse, Dobblelaar, De Kovel/De Vroom (DKV), Willem Jan Neutelings, Will Arets, UN Studio (Van Berkel and Bos), Erik van Egeraat, West 8 (Adriaan Geuze), NOX (Lars Spuybroek), members of Droog Design and above all, Winy Maas and Jacob van Rijs – the group called MVRDV.[103] The list is impressive and worthy of being called a School – like The School of Foster in Britain. But it raises several contentious points that came into focus at a seminar at the Architectural Association in May 1998, called by Ole Bouman and others of his Dutch magazine *Archis*. The subject was "Is there a Dutchness in the state of Architecture?" This sounds like a silly and chauvinist idea, especially in the age of globalization when every tiny trend has many international followers. How can there be a national architecture; should one brazenly promote it; is this not Texas hubris writ large? If Dutchness did not really exist, except as branding, it was clear that "Remness" very much did. Countless architects from the Netherlands and elsewhere were now designing urban fields based on statistical research and warping their floor into continuous ramps, notably the groups called Mecanoo and MVRDV.

But after the appearance of Lootsma's *Superdutch* the nationalist argument becomes more complex. There *is* a discernible coloration to all these architects that owes as much to a Calvinist and pragmatic attitude as it does to Koolhaas. Just as the High-Tech trend was quintessentially British, from the 1970s to 1990s, the Cool-Quantitative trend is typically Dutch. The difference is that British architects would certainly refuse a parallel label of *Superbrits*, whereas those in Holland are prepared to go along with the branding. English reticence and understatement versus pragmatism; social propriety versus the market? Or hypocrisy, Gore Vidal might say, versus cynicism? Whatever the truth, Dutch architects roared onto the scene in the late 1990s the way Japanese designers did in the 1960s, and in both cases national marketing played a role. This story is well told by Bart Lootsma and I will not repeat it.[104]

What is also apparent from his account is that Holland is the country where planning and social control have gone furthest. Since a large proportion of the land is reclaimed sea, since the Dutch have had to control as well as build this second nature, their country is more artificial, synthetic, socialized and corporate than anywhere else in the world, with the possible exception of Singapore and Hongkong. However, unlike those two areas, the Netherlands has a deep counter current. With a fitful history of democracy and individualism going back eight hundred years, the Dutch have institutionalized a high degree of nonconformity. Amsterdam and its counter culture of the 1960s is a good example of this current, and the anarchist designers, Droog Design, typify the sensibility today. The result of these two contradictory traditions – welfare-state regulation plus free market individualism – creates a *different* form of democratic architecture. It means that there is a national debate on architecture and planning, supported by such enlightened bodies as the Berlage Institute and NAI (National Architectural Institute), and a host of socially progressive rules and programs for cities and housing. These are rare qualities to have all at once, perhaps only finding a parallel in Finland. They are certainly not found together in America, Britain, and other countries where the free market dominates. Positively it means that the Dutch government is realistic about the contradictions it faces: an expanding population, growth in single story houses for single parent families, the resultant sprawl – but also the desire to keep the countryside.[105] Negatively it means the Dutch feel overmanaged, domesticated, penned in and farmed as if they were so many human animals. The contradictions also mean that Dutch architects, like Rem Koolhaas, West 8 and MVRDV, have developed a pragmatic irony that presents the social and democratic alternatives facing Holland with an amusing straightforwardness. It is this style of thought that has to be respected, that gives the soubriquet "Dutchness" some credibility. An upside-down nationalism.

MVRDV, for instance, construct datascapes (diagrams and computerized maps of the planning rules and sociological trends) that bring out both democratic choice and the crazy anomalies that sometimes result from the rules of development. While the rest of the world suffers its planning contradictions in quiescent rage, while architects tear their hair out and try to forget the sillier constraints – some of which are literally medieval – MVRDV exults in turning them into automatic architecture, expressive structures, wildly logical diagrams of sometimes illogical laws. For example, to circumvent yet carry out rules entailed by Cor van Eesteren's master plan for Amsterdam, they have designed some housing units as thirty-foot flying cantilevers and actually had them built (304). Five timber boxes shoot out over open space away from their pragmatic, prison-like social housing (with real gridded metal bars) as if they were escapees from the welfare-machine. The wooden siding on all sides and the bottom of these flying wedges make the escape all the more amusing and symbolic ("back to nature?," "wood hiding the real steel cantilever?").

Why do these five blocks jut out? The argument seems to emerge inevitably from the social assumptions and rules of planning.[106] Needed: one hundred dwellings for the elderly, those senior citizens over fifty-five. Site restrictions: determine the slab plan, height of nine storeys, view corridors and exterior, communal space. Result: no space for thirteen houses. Solution? Five cantilevers holding the missing thirteen dwellings. Articulation? Social housing should be humanized, hence wood on both façades. By law citizens are given one aesthetic choice, hence the various balcony colors – orange, yellow, purple, green or steel mesh. So far, so pragmatic and highly amusing. Requirements ruthlessly followed inevitably produce diversity and differentiation. This is indeed the argument of MVRDV, challenging the supposition of their teacher Koolhaas, that the modern condition must produce the generic.[107] Of course one can spot the fallacy on both sides of the debate, since initial assumptions and planning rules can be questioned, and there is always more than one solution to the same set of regulations. Indeed, this questioning of statistical determinants is precisely how one group of designers challenges the next, producing their supposedly scientific response to an architectural brief. Dutch design evolves within this style of thought, giving it identity and rigor.

This is a liberating view of constraints and contradictions, for who does not want *some* social housing, planning rules and mass production? MVRDV takes the sting out of Modernist repetition by combining it with other tactics: diversity, exceptions to the rule that prove the rule, and ironic hybridization. These tactics place it directly in the bloodline of Post-Modernism stemming from Lucien Kroll and other participatory designers of the late 1960s. The difference is that MVRDV lets the opposite forces of democracy do the designing rather than the individuals. At a certain level of abstraction societies are democratic because of laws, not people, regulations that entail civility, ecological sus-

tainability, and public commonwealth. It is as hard to fall in love with a planning law as it is for an architect to get excited about plumbing diagrams, yet in an important sense that Dutch architects have discovered such regulations constitute the by-product of sensible social experience. In Holland, by law, many competing groups have to be consulted before a design is passed and so most architecture is created by a Darwinian process of planning selection, where planning is seen as an inclusive conjunction of all these laws and participatory processes. There appears to be little room for autonomous architecture here – the sculptural gesture of Gehry, the intellectual play of Eisenman. Yet these gestures begin to emerge, however tentatively, as the result of exploiting contradictions within the determinants themselves.

Another case in point is the public broadcasting company collective designed by MVRDV in Hilversum, called VPRO. Merely to write these acronyms one after the other calls up sinister overtones, the many initials of the Soviet secret police, as they rotated their brands in the early 1920s (NKVD etc.) and, given the hip sophistication of the designers and media, one cannot rule out an intended irony here. We are again close to that creation of Pop theorists of the 1960s, "the knowing consumer." The Dutch architects and these independent broadcasters obviously know their Le Corbusier and several of his schemes. These include the Domino block and they postulate an artificial ground of concrete slabs held on columns into which are slotted different kinds of villas. In this case thirteen stations, and villas, that had been scattered around the city are brought together (305 databurst). Le Corbusier wanted to save the countryside and contrast with it. This is the goal of these designers, who have intruded as little as possible on the adjacent woodland and heath, and even added a green garden on the rooftop. Rem Koolhaas' idea of the building as a continuous, open, folded landscape is also appropriated, knowingly. The different offices are linked by giant ramps and "superstairs" – or, depending on one's view, "mini-amphitheaters." The entrance and executive car park, half-way up the building, is indicated by the giant fold in concrete projected on the surface. As Le Corbusier demanded, "the section *is* the elevation." The concrete frame and glass infill are handled with that cool straightforwardness marking it Calvinist, or at least Superdutch. No expressive gestures are allowed, no spatial hierarchy, no axiality, no orientation, no façade design, no composition. The "no"s suggest it is architecture in denial. But this is Holland where Mondrian's "no"s established an extra emphasis on the few "yes"s that were left: the grid, primary colors and dynamic and subtle balances between them. MVRDV appears to let the statistical analysis and functions determine the composition.

The variety and differentiation come from the requirements considered abstractly. A series of courtyards, or excavations of the frame, penetrate the volume. The optimum percentages of daylight and heat emission are endlessly cal-

304 MVRDV, *WoZoCo*, Sheltered Housing for 100 dwellings, Amsterdam, 1994–97. Five cantilevers shoot out eleven meters on the street side, and their multicoloured balconies protrude even further – covered in "humanist" wood, the PM ironies on the ultimate modern form are a bit heavy. Life is a bit springy in these apartments, but they are a logical solution to the contradictory constraints – site lines, open space, height restrictions, room for 100 units of social housing. The backside has an equal opposition between the individualized and generic. (Hans Werlemann).

culated. These data, and the context, determine whether the glass is green and insulated, or blue and mirrored, or clear. The heterogeneity is further accentuated by allowing the broadcasters to choose their furniture and fittings. An interesting mixture results where a Baroque chandelier and Turkish rug confront a particularly Spartan concrete. Is this Embarrassment of Riches, or rather let the Consumers and Calvinists confront each other? On one level it is the old radical eclecticism, recalling Gehry's wry collisions, but now carried through with a Dutch matter-of-factness. Deadpan incongruity, the automatic juxtaposition of difference without comment.

In effect it is a new kind of Dutch Still Life, striking because of its very understatement. It is an art form MVRDV pull out of the electronic air through their datascapes, as if democratic society were responsible for the resultant incongruities not the designers. The supreme examples of this are their "Metacity/Datatown" of 1999 and the Dutch Pavilion for EXPO 2000 in Hannover (306,307). Their Datatowns are virtual cities based on different statistical assumptions. Suppose a city 400 km² with a population four times that of the Netherlands: Koolhaas' densification densified. Imagine if it were a self-supporting area and that everyone was a vegetarian — how much space would be needed for the different functions? Or vary the assumptions and imagine the waste not being recycled, then how much land would be needed? These statistical assumptions, easily manipulated by the computer as datascapes,

305, 306 MVRDV, *Villa VPRO*, Hilversum, 1993–97. The artificial ground is warped and excavated for a public broadcasting company, a collective of thirteen villas. Setbacks and courtyards picked out in various kinds of glass give identity to the different studios, while on the inside a continuously changing open space is taken over and personalized by each group. The notion of providing a generic structure that appropriated differently has many roots, including Le Corbusier, Habrakan and Hertzberger, and the incongruities that result — Turkish carpets and chandeliers — are positively celebrated by the architects. Of equal interest are the small amphitheaters of space that result from the steps and warps in section. (Hans Werlemann).

307 MVRDV, *Dutch Pavilion*, EXPO 2000, Hannover. A stack of synthetic ecologies and artificial grounds determined as a statistical representation of the future Dutch landscape. From the top down can be found 1) windmills, and water on the artificial lake that flows into 2) sheets of water in an exhibition space and then to 3) a forest grown with high-powered lights. Next level down 4) is an auditorium with projection space, to 5) an agricultural section of smaller plants again artificially lit, to reach 6) a ground floor and grotto of houses and shops. Views and movement are celebrated by the exterior staircase. The Danish oak trees seem to like their artificial suns. When the Sun King Louis XIV said "*forcer la nature*" he never had this in mind. The sustainability of the closed cycle makes sense, the juxtaposition of gardens and moods a delight, the remorseless logic humorous, but the question is raised: "will all of life be managed and pharmed?" No wonder a vocal group in Holland want more wilderness. (MVRDV).

result in the stacking of artificial landscapes. Stark choices, those that face the Dutch population, in a less extreme form. The solutions entail different sorts of planted skyscrapers, an idea envisioned by the group SITE in America, twenty years previously, but unbuilt. MVRDV, empowered by the Dutch situation and the computer, construct these hybrid towers and like SITE exploit the logic for its pleasure and humor.

Their Hannover tower, for instance, alternates floors of open greenery and enclosed work-space, then surmounts them with wind turbines and a roof garden. At the top a pond collects rainwater and it is circulated throughout, forming an efficient cycle along with the heat re-circulated from the auditorium below. Ecological motivations alternate with economic efficiencies, nature's cycles intermingle with human activities. One floor is a grid of trees in pots whose bases penetrate the floor below forming an interesting sculptural ceiling. Strange and sometimes appropriate associations are made. Edible plants and flowers occupy floors in repetitive rows, recalling the factory farms of Holland

308, 309 WEST 8, *Schouwburgplein*, Rotterdam, 1992–97. An artificial ground 35 cm and made up of lightweight materials – wood, granite, epoxy concrete, rubber and perforated metal – is raised over a parking garage. It holds different services and equipment for the knowing consumer to appropriate. The architect Adriaan Geuze imagines that the urbanite today is self-assured and fully able to orchestrate the public space for many different activities. Here football, skateboarding, roller-blading, busking, are normal, while concerts and outdoor theater are occasional. Lovers are meant to play with the coin operated spot-lights thoughtfully provided atop hydraulic cranes, angular moving arms that recall those in the Rotterdam harbour. (WEST 8).

which mass-produce a remorselessly standardized nature. An exterior stairway wraps the open and closed volume like coil of black DNA. Semi-transparent screens and varying colors classify the activities like boxes of data on the computer screen. Again the art consists in letting the heterogeneous requirements express their own necessity, in *not* intervening, as for instance Mies van der Rohe might have done with an integrated aesthetic. That would be 1984 handled more heavily. What also rescues this pragmatism from turning into brute exploitation is the implicit critique of the system. Hedonism confronts functionality, playful oddity relieves the utilitarian motives. One can see how such violent contrasts heighten consciousness by comparing them with a subsequent scheme based on the same idea.

Deltapark is a very wide groundscraper of factory farming proposed for Rotterdam by the scientific researcher Jan Broeze.[108] Imagine a rectangle of space one kilometre by 400 metres, stacked six storeys high. It would be a ware-

house of concrete trays the size of fifteen Wal-Marts plus thirty Discount stores. Inside is proposed a floor of 300,000 pigs turning out pork and manure, 1.2 million chickens clucking, 20,000 fish jumping, and a giant vegetable garden churning out tulips and tomatoes. Where it is very dark in these slabs, mushrooms and chicory would supposedly thrive or, at the bottom of the building, nature be slaughtered and packaged for transport. Everything is recycled, everything balances each other, it is all very ecological, organic and efficient. Even the diseases are controlled by the managers (not farmers). *Animal Farm, Brave New World, 1984* and current Dutch utilitarianism are all rolled into one. Something like it is bound to be created, and may indeed be an improvement on current factory farming and unsustainable practice. But the architecture is animal Auschwitz all the way, missing the ironies and juxtapositions of meaning that MVRDV discover in such forces.

Another Dutch group, called West 8, takes a pragmatic approach towards urban realities and then like MVRDV exploits them for their creative potential and ironic conjunctions. Adriaan Geuze, the leader of this collective, criticizes the monoculture of Modernism and proposes instead an urban landscape where the city-dweller is provided a spectrum of activities from which to choose.[109] In effect, this character is assumed to be a sophisticated agent, again the knowing consumer who navigates a complex environment. But he is also something of a caveman and chameleon:

A contemporary citizen with his mobile lifestyle and ever changing addresses and activities should not be pushed to live in a functionalist home with a "view" over Arcadian nature; the

Modernist ideal…Like a caveman, hunting and collecting for weeks in a chaotic and violent nature, finally returning to feed the tribe, to fertilize the women and be hypnotized in ritual dance around the fire, the contemporary city-dweller always returns to the base…The contemporary city-dweller is self-assured and intelligent. He has a capacity to anticipate changes in his environment and adapt like a chameleon.[110]

This view of the active urbanite is a refreshing alternative to other stereotypes of city-man as conformist, victim, or alienated and uprooted migrant, the "mechanized barbarians" of T. S. Eliot, and the types that formerly characterized sociology. Geuze's mobile cavemen may be as equally marginal as these previous characters, but they *do* exist in some number and his urban landscapes are particularly suited to them.

A large public square in Rotterdam, the Schouwburgplein, typifies his pragmatic bricolage (308–309). It is designed for theatrical self-expression, in fact it is called a Theatre Square by Geuze and is surrounded by the kind of activities one finds on 42nd Street – cinemas, cyber-cafes, restaurants, honky-tonk and actual theatres. Here skateboarders show their stuff, musicians and buskers entertain, roller blades skim over the sheen of concrete-epoxy, water spouts from programmed fountains. At night the flat surface is animated by different types of lighting, while as Geuze hopes and shows in photos, "lovers capture each other" in embrace; or, alternatively, they put a guilder in a slot and dial the spot-light atop a 35 metre crane, and aim it at their paramour. Caveman on this stage can also play football, or erect a tent (the equipment and holes in the artificial ground are conveniently supplied). A seventy-metre long bench provides the audience seating. Tough industrial ventilation towers, for the car park underneath, act like monumental dolmens. Five kinds of lightweight flooring – rubber, perforated metal, granite, wood and epoxy – form the urban surface that embeds the services and equipment within its skin. This is landscape as synthetic utility. The architecture, in so far as one can see it, is in performance, both of the cranes and moving people. Like Koolhaas's schemes it is architecture conceived as the animated and dense surface, something to be used as much as possible. A hyperactive landscape not Arcadian retreat.

Geuze like Koolhaas and MVRDV is a trenchant critic whose words combine sarcasm, polemic, poetry and description in equal measure. At the RIBA in early 2001, he mixed a barrage of statistics with acid comment:

Dutch success in architecture? In spite of the government's pretense, a few of us are skeptical. It is often shallow because of the program and requirements. We have had ten years of a booming economy and growing population, now sixteen million. With 100,000 new dwellings a year, a million every ten years, we demonstrated what this would look like as three-storey houses, and the Los Angeles policy of sprawl, eating up the landscape. All the media and Rem appeared. We demonstrated with these mod-

els that the urban policy had no meaning. The seven Dutch suburbs were all similar. No differences; monotonous row living; we flew over Holland and filmed it and sent it to the Venice Biennale. However, these demonstrations didn't influence government policy at all. . . . In Holland there are not so many rich or poor as in Britain or America. Eighty-five per cent of the population are middle class, with an equal share of money and power. . . . Architects get into this cycle, with little fees, and design 80 to 120 houses at a go, at the same density, always a row house. Then, if they are lucky, every ten years they get a museum to design. That's life. The building industry is incredibly industrialized with only ten players controlling the social housing, and that constitutes thirty-five per cent of the total. UK architects are jealous of this, but if you want to make a statement all you can do is make your 120 houses "a yellow statement." The market is monopolized, and the contractors build the statements – how shallow. . . . Please don't take Holland as an example – you have the UK urban renaissance [of Lord Rogers' Urban Task Force].[111]

Actually Rogers and his group had been hard at work studying Dutch housing and recommending it to Blair's government as one alternative, and this little example of the grass is greener on the other side of the Channel is instructive. It reveals the way different nations, with all their faults, may have some important urban lessons for each other.

Of particular relevance is West 8's strategy for developing the docks in the eastern harbour of Amsterdam. Called Borneo Sporenburg after the area, the scheme consists of two peninsulas stretching over the water like two curves of Amsterdam canal housing that have been straightened out and flattened (310–313). The traditional burgher house on a canal has much to recommend it, and Adriaan Geuze is not above illustrating some of its virtues with interior perspectives of Pieter de Hooch and other painters of the Golden Age. Public space is kept to a minimum to allow a greater density of private space with interior gardens, small patios, and roof terraces – voids cut through the private realm and layered with changing light as in a Vermeer. As he says, "There are no dubious semi-public zones, no obstacles and no front gardens," just a tight staccato of water-street-house.[112] In effect we are back in the early 1970s learning the Lessons of Pruitt-Igoe that public open space, not owned and looked after by anyone, is a possible area of crime, or at least vandalism. *Defensible Space*, the polemic written by Oscar Newman in 1972, may have overstated the case against modern housing estates, since there is no such thing as the architectural determinism of life. Still, there are tendencies for public space that is not possessed to become appropriated by the wrong sort of modern cavemen.

This high-density low-rise inevitably resembles the mass of endless row blocks that Geuze showed were a consequence of government policy and a huge middle-class, yet the blocks are much closer and longer than those of the suburbs. Koolhaas densification is at work again, 100 dwellings

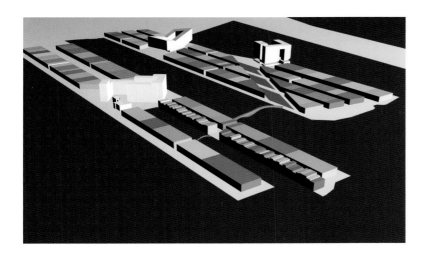

310–313 WEST 8, *Borneo Sporenburg Peninsulas*, Amsterdam, design 1993, construction 1996–2000. A Water City close to the downtown, this development has proven popular also because of the variety of housing types and styles. More than twenty architects designed various patio-types with hollowed out interior spaces – voids Adriaan Geuze calls them – that can either be filled in by the inhabitants or turned into gardens or private patios. Low-rise high density housing at 100 units per hectare creates the kind of urbanity of the traditional city. Public space is minimized to maximize the private realm, an introversion made acceptable by the presence of wide open water. Three monumental housing blocks, in scale with the adjacent warehouses, are skewed from the grid, thus providing orientation and a visual response to each other. Urbane variety within a sensible typology makes this the most recent post-modern standard to surpass. (WEST 8).

to the hectare. But three strategic choices keep the repetition from becoming monotonous. First is the site: the docks, cranes, boats and water life that make what Geuze calls Water City full of interesting animation. Second are the three large apartment volumes twisted off the grid, monumental incidents, in scale with the harbour warehouses. These large-scale sculptures inflect towards each other forming a three-sided trialogue, an urban discourse across the water. One of them, a heavy block called The Whale, social housing clad in zinc, became sought after and oversubscribed by six times. Living close to downtown Amsterdam is obviously an attractive proposition if the conditions offer architectural interest, a motive that the developer New Deal sought to exploit.

This led to the third quality giving variety, the choice of over twenty architects to design different patio-types. Famous architects were set against each other – Steven Holl versus Aldo Rossi, Rem Koolhaas versus MVRDV, Enric Miralles versus Ben van Berkel – and a host of Dutch architects were also led to compete with ideas for varying the typology within a larger series. The result is that the 2,500 dwellings have a diversity of color, style and layout comparable to the historic city. Indeed it is reminiscent of a development in Antwerp, at the turn of 1900, where within a common morphology every house is different (314). To fur-

ther this difference Geuze has designed sculptural bridges connecting the artificial peninsulas. Each has figural symbols built into the structure and lighting, seagulls and hawks, and the bridges themselves seem to leap and dip as if they too were animated.

These strategies make the Water City an exemplary model of the heteropolis for Holland. Along with the IBA program in Berlin and the development of Barcelona over twenty years, they become standards for the Post-Modern paradigm to meet or surpass. It is interesting to recall the zigzag route traveled by this tradition as it sought to deal with the failures of mass-housing and the erosion of the city. With housing, the few self-build structures of the 1960s were followed by the participatory architecture of the 1970s, and the community architecture of the 1980s – the methods of Kroll, Erskine and Moore among many others. Social diversity was signified by so much radical eclecticism, particularly that of Robert Venturi and Frank Gehry who consulted closely with their clients and honored their cultural and aesthetic values. The second main direction concerned the typological models of Rossi, the Krier brothers and Ungers, and then the juxtaposition of these types proposed as collage city by Colin Rowe. This strategy of piecemeal utopian planning reached realization in Barcelona and Berlin where different architects were asked

314 Housing, *Cogels-Osylei*, Antwerp, 1889–1910. Rows of burger housing at the turn of the last century encouraged individuality within a basic structure of regulations. Oppositions of style, typology and history occur one after the other varying from Neo-Medieval to Renaissance, Venetian, Stick Style and, far right, Art Nouveau.

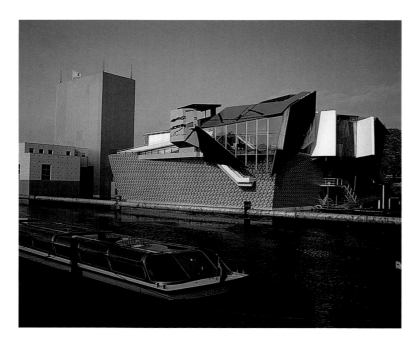

315 ALESSANDRO MENDINI *et al*, *Groninger Museum*, Groningen, Holland, 1990–94. A collage of different pavilions, designed by different architects, is placed as a bridge-building in a canal. This accentuated difference defines the various aspects of the collection. The brick cylinder holds the traditional art, the aluminum contains the Applied Arts, the gold rectangle carries the treasure and marks the entrance, light green and pink pavilions contain offices and café, the speckle volume houses the new art and the explosion of steel and glass, by Coop Himmelblau, was the receptacle for the old visual arts. Legibility through opposition and the Exquisite Corpse dreamed up by the Surrealists become methods for articulating heterogeneity. Michele de Lucchi and Philippe Starck also contributed their efforts to this collage.

to fill in parts of the collage. With recent Dutch architecture, and particularly the Water City of Borneo Sporenburg, there is a partial synthesis of these trends. There is the collage of typologies – city grid, patio house, skewed monument. There is the employment of many different architects producing diverse solutions yet working to a common framework, and there is some participation, with the inhabitants filling in their patios, and making small modifications to their dwellings, piecemeal. This is cumulative progress of a sort, where the paradigm develops through learning and competition.

Dutch architects are more committed to acknowledging diversity on a statistical level than they are interested in resolving the design complexities that arise from it. They are midwives of software programmes that handle information, "data managers" who hope to extract diagrams from forces acting on a site, empiricists constructing datascapes more than visionaries or critical thinkers trying to change society.[113] *Superdutch* has yet to become a high art form, and there seems no real desire to make it one. The bricolage of many requirements and tastes is presented

and represented as an important fact of democratic life. This complexity is how life is in an advanced pluralist society. Do not dress it up; neither glorify nor suppress it. In the Groningen Museum, for instance, Alessando Mendini led a team of different architects who were given their head to each produce a separate part of the building (315). The result is the *corpse exquis* of the Surrealists, with a head by Philippe Starck and Michele de Lucchi, a midriff by Mendini and a tail by Coop Himmelblau. The head, in local Groningen brick, contains some of the historic art of the region and the other sections hold different collections, so there is some expressive logic to the mixture. As a set of juxtapositions the museum enhances the experience of difference, and the interior spaces of Coop Himmelblau create marvelous moments of vertiginous delight, but no one would claim the relationships are controlled or even thought through. This is not Venturi's "obligation towards the difficult whole," but the best Dutch work does engage with a central issue of our time, the irreducible diversity of the heteropolis.

HYPERDIVERSITY AND NATIONAL IDENTITY

How much diversity can a city, and a nation, manage before a culture fragments along ethnic and other lines? The question cannot be answered in the abstract because both a municipal area and a people are historical entities locked into cultural time. The pluralism and tolerance of New York is quite different from Istanbul, Tokyo from Berlin, London from Montreal though they have all become global conglomerates. One model for the heteropolis will not fit all cases and, indeed, goes against the very idea of a paradigm that understands such large institutions in a growing, cultural context.[114]

One of the interesting aspects of globalization, however, is the way that ideas and institutions jump national boundaries. Notions of pluralism and eclecticism, worked out in America in the 1970s, influence the Dutch one way and the Australians another. A case in point is the National Museum of Australia completed in 2001. The NMA was built to celebrate one hundred years of Australian Federation, a pluralist aim by definition, and it was built to house a mixed collection of national treasures, some of them highly charged with contentious political content. Historical grievances are embedded in the artifacts, the roles and rights of the Aborigines, Irish, Italians and Colonials speak directly through the collection.

But the place for this celebration of diversity, Canberra, is itself highly unified in urban form, and integrated within an Anglo-Saxon style of liberal politics. Like Washington DC, on which it is partly based, Canberra is spread out in a leafy, romantic landscape. It is a capital city lacking its city, its main ceremonial axis is neither the Champs Elysée nor an avenue of governmental buildings, but rather a series of

316 ASHTON, RAGGATT, McDOUGALL, (ARM), National Museum of Australia, Canberra, 1998–2001. In the distance is the entry canopy, the Boolean string as a twisted guide and cover for entry, which starts as a Pop loop-di-loop and ends as a walkway facing Uluru, Ayer's Rock, a symbol of Aboriginal homeland. In the foreground is the Garden of Australian Dreams, designed by Richard Weller and Vladimir Sitta as a palimpsest of maps on which one can walk. The basic opposition is the ideal grid of suburban bliss set against the meandering Aboriginal routes of Dreamtime. In the left background can be seen the black concrete forms of the Gallery of First Australians and, to the right, the travelling wave in the form of a balustrade picked out in colors of a national football team.

suburban villas fighting off encroachment like Old Southern Mansions. The official architecture, for the most part, is the kind of Modern-Classical hybrid that typifies corporate politics when it is trying to be polite and powerful. The new National Museum, however, is the reverse of all this integration. It takes the themes of diversity to an extreme and, significantly for my argument, mixes the two methods of dealing with pluralism that are dividing debate, and that separate this chapter from the next: eclectic collage versus folding in difference. Because of this it asks to be read for its various cues in some depth.

The entryway summarizes the different philosophies. One arrives by car or bus to face not a gateway, but a giant red-and-orange question mark leaping overhead like a twisted triumphal arch on a holiday (316). This shoots off one way towards the hills ending in a curled up piece of steel, reminiscent of a skateboarder's delight (or a sculpture by Richard Serra). The other way, acting as a canopy, it leads one into the gallery and main hall of the museum. This exuberant gesture sets the tone for the entire compound and becomes its icon, as distinctive for Canberra as the Opera House shells are for Sydney. It turns out to be a key for deciphering the rambling layout, a kind of Ariadne's Thread that snakes in and out of the building, leading one through what is in effect a labyrinth, a right of passage into Australian identity.

The architects, Ashton, Raggatt and McDougall (ARM), identify some meanings behind the unusual form – a Boolean String, a knot, and a Rainbow Serpent from an Aboriginal Dream-Time story. They list these references matter-of-factly, as if they were perfectly ordinary and known to most Australians. Yet it is the more accessible meanings that come to mind on first encounter – the fairground associations, the loop-di-loop of a roller coaster. These overtones suggest a wild ride of discovery, that tracking through the national psyche will involve sudden reversals in fortune, feelings reinforced by the violent contrasts of the central, sunken garden, around which the compound snakes. Here one finds fragments of an Australian map, a Mercator grid juxtaposing memories in white, red and grey (as Peter Eisenman did for similar reasons in Berlin, to remind one of a suppressed past). The garden, designed by landscape architects Richard Weller and Vladimir Sitta, combines both idyllic images and disturbing signs, a stepping stone map and the sites of massacres. This sets an opposition of themes to which one continually returns. History is seen as a contrast of desire and repression, hope and horror. For instance, a luscious palm hints at a tropical paradise, while a row of Italian alders tilted north at an angle of twenty degrees signify immigrant longings for the European homeland. The meaning of such cues may be missed at first, but after walking through the whole building one realizes that humour and conflict are around every corner and in every exhibit.

While one is contemplating the massacre sites, for

317 ARM, *Main Hall* above the Garden of Australian Dreams. The two Christian vesica-shapes gaze over the travelling wave and supergraphic signature of the Prime Minister who encouraged the federation of Australia. Note the way some volumes are interrupted and overlapped in colour: this is meant to suggest the way Australian identity can be pieced together as a puzzle of sameness and difference.

318 ARM, *Main Hall interior* with faint hints of many buildings and an intended allusion to the windows of the Sydney Opera House. The space is actually generated by a five-sided volume, the Boolean string, that twists the arises thereby cutting sharp edges (see 320 to follow the Boolean string through the site). (ARM/RPvHT).

instance, the eye is drawn to the balustrades surrounding the garden that rise and lower their arms, like a football crowd responding to a "Mexican wave" for the home team. The curving structure is a reference to the popular Melbourne Cricket Ground and, in its garish red, black, white and yellow, the colors of many football teams. The forms are also a comment on the way that national sport re-tribalizes the masses (and what is *more* nationalist than football loyalty?). But then, above this riot of populist cheering is a severe modern façade with a horizontal strip window, some grey dimples (supposed to be braille coding of Aussie phrases) and two vesica-shape windows set on the diagonal (esoteric, sacred forms) (317). These disjoint shapes throw a bit of cold water on the political Disneyland below, a high-minded rebuke to the chauvinism of football. We are engaged in more than a dialogue here, something between a debate in parliament, a shouting match in a pub, and a Sermon on the Mount. The four main blocks that ring around the garden both assert their autonomy and their relationship to the whole and this similarity in difference is meant to puzzle the viewer, indeed pose the question of Australian identity as a puzzle. How do we fit together these blocks, how do the ethnic chunks of Australia relate to each other? This is a complex puzzle that has to be solved anew by every generation.

By contrast the Main Hall is a place of flowing motion and ethereal peace. The white domical shapes recall several things, but their strength is that no single reference is clear (318). Suggestion reigns, words come to the tip of one's tongue and hang there: the Sydney Opera House, the supports of Saarinen's TWA airport, the shell curves of Felix Candela, the Cabinet of Dr. Caligari? It suggests these things without naming them, a quality of the enigmatic signifier. One reason for the ambiguity is that the space is generated from the subtracted shape left by a five-sided Boolean knot, and in this sense without a recognizable origin.

The National Museum of Australia sets the proposition that identity comes from facing difference, from finding it enjoyable as well as distressing. The complex adopts conventional signs of ethnicity in a highly charged, colorful and unusual way. Fragments from the past are blown up in scale and turned into supergraphics. The E and Y from the "Eternity" signature of the Sydney street evangelist Arthur Stace, that have become an Australian cliché of the lonesome wanderer, are amplified and stretched across façades. They are signs of individual loneliness and, for those in the know, cryptic emblems of the fish and Christianity. And this allusiveness plays an important creative and political role. Once the game of hunt the symbol has started — and it is impossible to avoid here — one becomes sensitized to further possible meanings. This provokes both intended and aberrant readings and makes people take a position on difficult questions for themselves. The national identity of the hyphenated-Australian, it suggests, is something of a game to be enjoyed, a stereotype to be challenged and an inheritance to be re-invented.

Another one of these enigmas concerns the question of architectural representation itself. Is it right, or reasonable, in a pluralistic democracy to quote other architecture and, if so, should the quotes be overt, understated or cryptic? One of the problems of Modern architecture was that its pretensions to originality often obscured covert plagiarism. At the National Museum of Australia quotation marks are out in the open, disarming charges of theft. For instance, the zig-zag motif is lifted explicitly from Daniel Libeskind's Jewish

319 ARM *The Not Villa Savoye*, left, is tested against Aldo Rossi's Not Modena Cemetery, off to the right. The windows, wall and arcade are elided. Blackness, XXX's, shadow lines and inversions of the stairway all signal a conscious re-reading of exemplary buildings. (ARM).

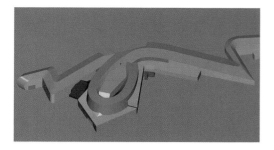

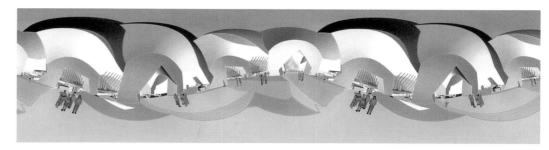

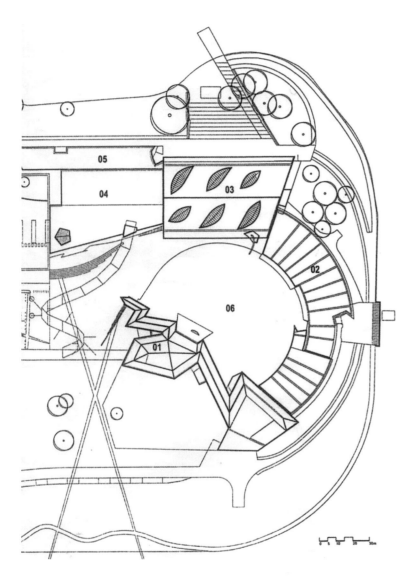

320 *The Site plan and Boolean string.* A linear route, like the Rainbow Serpent of traditional paintings, threads its way on the edge of the peninsula. At some points it penetrates the building, uniting it to the landscape; at other points, such as the Main Hall, it is knotted together; in the Gallery of First Australians it becomes a beginning and end of the zig-zag journey.

Museum in Berlin, and it has several justifications. The most obvious is the parallel of two different genocides. But there is also the way the shape gives a figural direction to the Gallery of the First Australians (as it is also known) and connotes the anger of the lightning-bolt. This is neither a deceitful not gratuitous reference. There is a world of difference, as any scholar and lawyer knows, between honest and open citation and covert copying. Everywhere the architects Ashton Raggatt and MacDougall are citing authorities they find relevant, or functional, or amusing, or instructive.

321 *The Boolean string*, the cosmic focus, points up towards Uluru, Ayer's Rock, and a peeled curve and the hills. Richard Weller and Vladimir Sitta design with ARM.

But national identity includes more than an acknowledgement of subcultures, a compilation of eclectic fragments, and here the architects have developed another strategy. In a key text written by Howard Raggatt in 1992, *Fringe de Cringe*, the architect invents a possible Australian voice located far from all centers, on the fringe, the place of the "ex-centric."[115] As he writes, "So instead of bewailing as Robert Hughes has done the great Australian Cringe and the thousands whose unwanted humility perpetuated the cultural imperialism of the Centre, it is the Cringe itself, which becomes for us a strategy and an operation of design."[116] This peripheral location allows one to exaggerate quotation, to combine and test precedents, and produce *subversive* mongrels. It is important not to miss this negative logic, as have some critics who think that the quotations are simply appropriations. But Raggatt's are a series of anti-canonic canons, and "nots" marked for all to see in very evident black: the "Not Villa Savoye," the "Not Vanna Venturi House," and so forth (319). In Australia, when asked how you feel you answer "not bad." The double negative, according to this theory, locates Australian identity precisely in the Not-Centre. Here in the southern hemisphere where the sun is strong but from the "wrong" angle the Not Villa Savoye is rendered in black, not white, and other changes are made to its shadows and details. Transformation, at once, liberates architects from slavish imitation while allowing them to combine prototypes. On this same building, for Aboriginal Studies, fragments are spliced from Le Corbusier, Aldo Rossi and Romaldo Giurgola. A series of XXX's over the side façade functionally serve as railings but also point up the statement "not, not, not." Still, in the same building, are quotes from the front of the Canberra Parliament, but now in deep red and black, the coloring of the Aboriginal flag. Since one can see this real Parliament House in the distance, the reference makes its political point quite strongly: "that building is not the Aborigine's parliament, nor was their identity acknowledged in this national monument." "Not-ness" is thus asserted not only as an Aboriginal, but also as an Australian essence. If one is willing to follow this negative logic, it is a brilliant turning of life on the fringe into an identity.

The National Museum of Australia faces an architectural problem often avoided, that is, finding relevant new metaphors for the public realm that are not hackneyed. Giurgola's Parliament House contributed to this discourse with its idea of the citizen walking on top of the *res publica*, an idea that Norman Foster followed in Berlin's Reichstag (3–5). But neither of these two political monuments engages the pressing issue of cultural pluralism. This the NMA does and does so completely that it becomes the standard to surpass. As I have suggested its brilliance is in the choice of valid metaphors that go to the heart of contemporary reality, and then beyond them. Its notion of a building generated by tangled axes that become a knot, and then a Boolean string, and then a wandering path through a puzzle has the advantage of being a single architectural idea with several variations (320). It is one that naturally ties together diversity without necessitating a single style, as does the Parliament House. It alludes to the Aboriginal tradition of taking possession of the land by walking it, by dreaming it with vivid images. It alludes to their dot paintings and abstract markings with the black bumps, and braille messages that contain secret well-known phrases: "who is my neighbor"; "Mate God knows"; "Good as Gold"; "Sorry"; "Time will tell"; "Love is blind"; "She'll be right." Voices can be heard in a different pitch, voices of convicts, Europeans, English, Irish, architectural buffs and football enthusiasts. All of these allusions and messages force one to go slow and ponder the enigma of a nation with nations inside it, the conundrum of being a hyphenated-Australian. When the landscape grows around the buildings, when they age and settle in, the brash cacophony will, I believe, become a much more convincing discourse of pluralism.

As it is, the fragmentation and preponderance of inexpensive shed-like volumes have distracted critics from its deeper significance. It *appears* too discordant; it does not use the site to full advantage, bring people up to the roof or over the water, exploiting fully the extraordinary landscape and views. It has the vice of its virtue, that is, embodying conflicting symbols.

Yet the idea that I find convincing in the end, and one that vindicates its hyperdiversity, is that of the Boolean string. This is a new method for creating architecture (321). Derived partly from science and the theory of knots it is a singular form that pulls together difference in a smooth way. Take a five-sided loop on a walk, curl it around the site, knot it up tight in one place, unravel it straight and hurl it at the

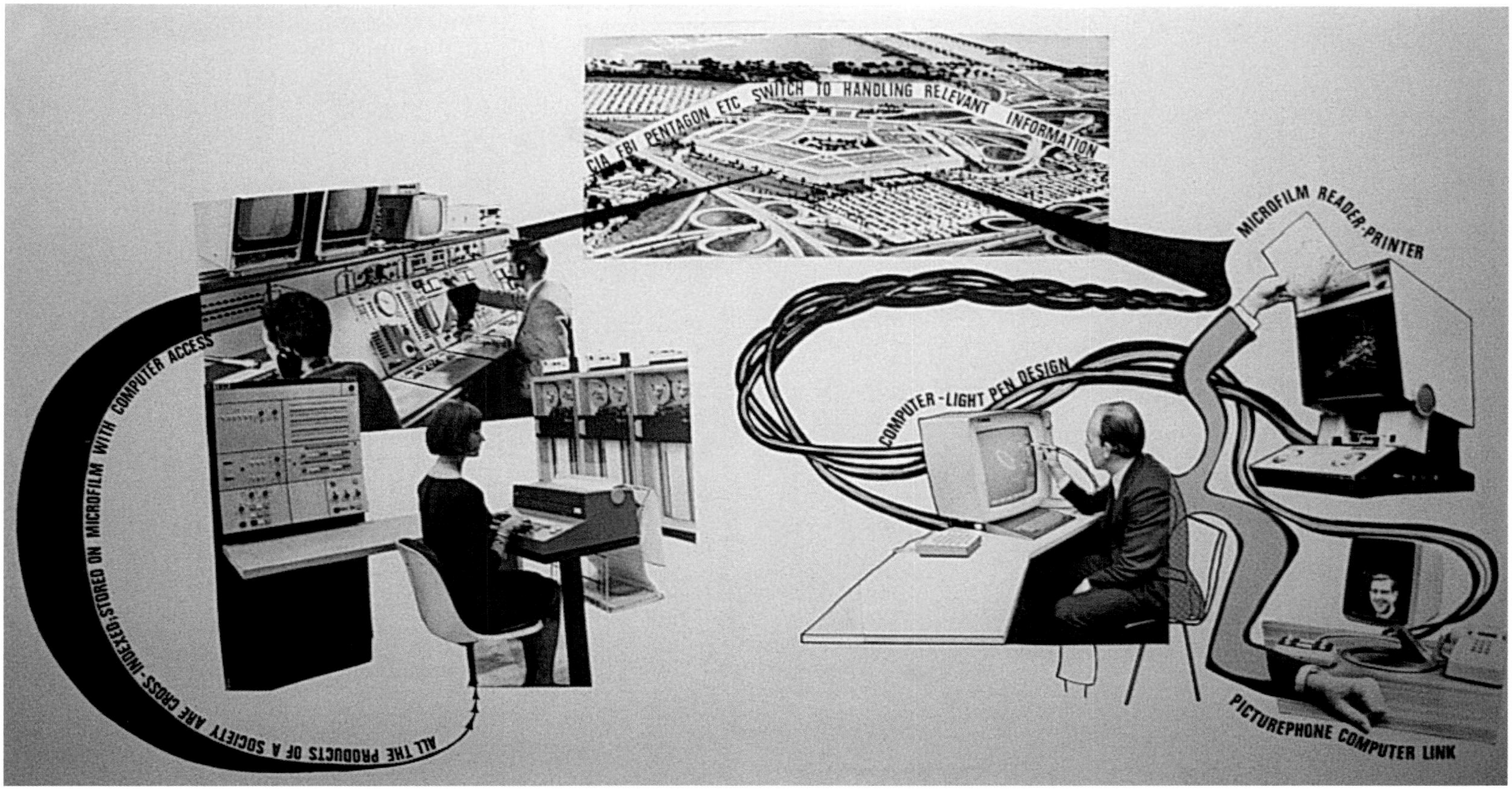
CIA FBI PENTAGON ETC SWITCH TO HANDLING RELEVANT INFORMATION
MICROFILM READER-PRINTER
ALL THE PRODUCTS OF A SOCIETY ARE CROSS-INDEXED-STORED ON MICROFILM WITH COMPUTER ACCESS
COMPUTER-LIGHT PEN DESIGN
PICTUREPHONE COMPUTER LINK

322 CHARLES JENCKS, Prediction of a future "Internet," made for *Architecture 2000* in 1969. The designer sits at a console with a light-pen and calls up all the products of a society that have been programmed by information gatherers down at the Pentagon. This ironic critique of the defense department accidentally stumbled on a truth, and the Pentagon accidentally created the world wide web some years later. In a larger sense, however, the prediction has still to come true since direct consumer shopping has yet to become commercially viable, and truly pluralist.

hills. It does not sound any more propitious for architecture than Utzon's orange peels that generated the Opera House, Gehry's worms that created Bilbao, Libeskind's chaotic spirals of the V&A or Eisenman's blobs for Santiago de Compostela – but like all these strange generating metaphors it has started architecture again, on a new route, and that is what we ask of a new national museum, something to engage the imagination. A form that does not have any familiar reference and thus allows the infinite projection of difference.

VIRTUAL COMMUNITIES IN THE FRACTAL HETEROPOLIS

The National Museum of Australia is reminiscent of late 1970s Post-Modernism in its radical eclecticism and supergraphics and yet a further step beyond that paradigm. As I have suggested so many of the buildings and theories of the late 1990s develop ideas broached in the 1960s, but in a new way. A reason for this continuity amid change is that the technology, and globalization that stem from it, have also developed from a common source. The heteropolis, evident then, has simply grown in size and become more common. The global village and Marshall McLuhan's idea of a world society linked electronically has become more of a reality. The attendant diversity, cultural pluralism, individualism, fragmentation and new communicational networks were all trends experiencing runaway growth. Some negative implications could be foreseen. When these forces were perceived as a threat to the city, particularly with the sprawl of Los Angeles in the 1960s, the urban sociologist Melvin Webber sought to explain why this city he loved was still – in spite of its physical disappearance – a coherent entity, made up of communities.

He formulated the notion of "urban realms" and said that they continued to exist but in ways that were no longer apparent. Communities depend, as their root-word suggests, on communication and since that was increasingly independent of any particular place, then so too would be the community.

> The spatial patterns of American urban settlements are going to be considerably more dispersed, varied and space-consuming than they ever were in the past – whatever metropolitan planners or anyone else may try to do about it.[117]

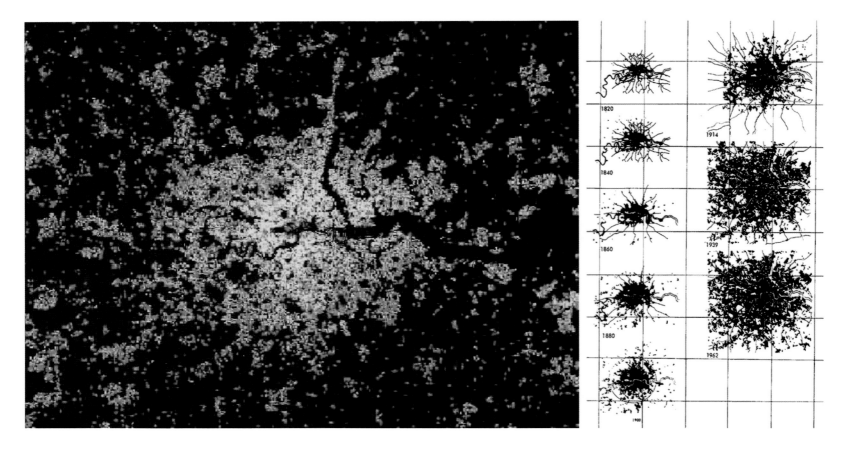

323 MICHAEL BATTY AND PAUL LONGLEY, *The Fractal Metropolis*: London's population density in 1991, an heteropolis with self-similar structure at various scales. At the largest scale, only the void of rivers and protected landscape are identifiable. The fractal growth of London from 1820 to 1962 is seen to the right. Le Corbusier, horrified by such images because he could not see the complex order, dismissed this as "tentacular sprawl." (from Michael Batty and Paul Longley, *Fractal Cities: A Geometry of Form and Function*, Academy Press, San Diego, CA and London, 1994).

Such predictions may have been easy to make in the sixties, but Webber draws a further conclusion that is less obvious and just as important. The place-centered community of the past was giving way, with the increase of communicational means, to the interest-centered realm. Such "interest-communities" could be anything from a dispersed business to a civic society connected by telephone to a set of friends linked by computer today. The significant factor was not architecture or the city, but linkage:

> Spatial distribution is not the crucial determinant of membership in these professional societies, but interaction is . . . we thus find no Euclidean territorial divisions — only continuous variation, spatial discontinuity, persisting disparity, complex pluralism, and dynamic ambiguity.[118]

Webber was writing in the early 1960s, but forty years later his and McLuhan's thoughts have become the staple of those who write about the city in the digital age. For instance, William Mitchell, in *City of Bits*, 1995, and *e-topia: "Urban life, Jim — but not as we know it,"* 1999, foresees these same nonlocal forces further eroding the physical city and the determinants of place.[119] The specific community on the Internet will be globally distributed and created by common interest. One's identity will no longer be limited by where one lives, by house and neighborhood, but extended by fax and web-page. It is a droll and unexpected new world, post-the nature/nurture debate. You are not just your genes plus environment, but all this plus your e-mail, cell-phone number, voice mail and PDA: these give place and identity to your soul, even body. In McLuhan-speak, you inhabit not only a room in a house, but the cyberspace of your doctor's digitised profile.

William Mitchell, like MVRDV and West 8 and contrary to Koolhaas, sees the implications of the electronic village as furthering differentiation, not sameness. Online shopping will empower individual choice, as predicted often in the 1960s, and customized design (322). As McLuhan wrote, with electronic production methods it is as cheap and efficient to manufacture eighty different tailpipes as eighty similar ones. Fordism has given way to Post-Fordism, the economy of decentralized, small-batch production has since the 1980s supplemented Modernist mass-production. And one should emphasize, so as not to fall into the usual either-or thinking, it is addition *not* replacement. The city of bits, or e-topia, just adds another layer of reality to what is already a palimpsest of systems. The future urban realms will simply become more complex.

But the great question for architects and urbanists is: what will it look like? What possible style and organizational principle can underlie the sprawling diversity of the hundred-mile city? At the level of the whole city there will not be walls and boundaries that define it; nor monuments and districts; nor a common geometrical layout like Washington DC; nor even the road grids and superhighways that 1970s urbanists foresaw. All of these previous definers may continue to play some role, at smaller scales, and perhaps a river, seaside or mountain range will define it from afar. But the heteropolis, now defined by one hundred different ethnicities and interest-groups, will have a different kind of order, a fractal organ-ization. As satellite photographs show it will have recurrent patterns that are self-similar not self-same, a tissue of parks, squares, roads, and houses with a recurrent grain and dimension. As Michael Batty and Paul Longley show in their *Fractal Cities* of 1994, a few global giants such as London will only be fully comprehensible as fractals (323).[120] There is a rich, subtle organization here; it is not all chaos and if one is attuned to its inherent qualities, an enjoyable order. But again the lesson is a pluralist one. It is only the global city with several multinational headquarters and the spread of a large population that is going to become a complete heteropolis. The regulations, culture, economy and history of each city will determine whether or not it evolves towards this hyper-diversity.

324 LE CORBUSIER, *Philips Pavilion*, Brussels World's Fair, 1958. A premonition of things to come. Prophesying what he called the second machine age, Le Corbusier designed one of the first multimedia events housed in a biomorphic structure. He even conceived it in body metaphors – "a stomach assimilating 500 listener-spectators, and then evacuating them automatically at the end of the performance, in order to provide room for the next five hundred." Most importantly he chose cosmic images for the perfomance. Body, biomorphism, smooth continuity, emergence, drama of cosmogenesis – it epitomises the new paradigm. (*Dokumentation Le Corbusier*, Stiftung Heidi Weber, Zurich).

The New Paradigm I —
Complexity Architecture

A SWARM OF COMPETING NAMES

As I mentioned in the introduction we are at the beginning of a shift in architecture that stems from a more general change in science and culture. Among Modern architects only Le Corbusier had inklings of the shift underway with his biomorphic structures and endless prophecy of a second machine age about to arrive, an electronic one bringing harmony to mankind (324). In some respects his work is worth comparing to present endeavours, as I shall do in passing, but it is obvious that his hopes for global harmony have hardly materialized.

It is also clear that, aided and abetted by the computer, it is much easier today to grasp the new paradigm, both conceptually and practically. On a philosophical plane it is part of a new cosmology. It conceives the universe as a dynamic, unified process that we are still very much a part of, a single creative unfolding event that includes us in the plot. Furthermore, the dynamism is ubiquitous. It portrays all the elements within the cosmos, from the atom to the embryo to the galaxy, as self-organising systems that are constantly shifting. We inhabit neither a static universe created by an external deity nor a mechanism, as the Modernists conceived it, but rather a cosmogenesis that is continually developing. Words describing this process are inevitably reductive, partly because we do not fully understand its holistic nature and partly because it is so all encompassing. But to capture its essentially dynamic quality, we might emphasize the creativity and surprise of a universe that evolves in phase changes — sudden jumps in organization.[121] These breaks in symmetry are similar to the way that water, losing or gaining heat, can be transformed suddenly into ice or steam. The history of the cosmos over some thirteen billion years — presently its assumed age — can now be conceived as progressing from perfect super-symmetry to more organized and differentiated states. Symmetry *breaking* is itself a new concept of the new paradigm and its importance for a profession founded on symmetry *making* cannot be overemphasised.

Peter Eisenman, one of the most important protagonists of the movement, has debated at length the virtues of several generic labels: chaos, complexity, emergence, morphogenesis, folding, nonlinear and fractal were some of the contenders he considered. In the early 1990s he emphasized a different term:

During the fifty years since the Second World War, a paradigm shift has taken place that should have profoundly affected architecture: this was the shift from the mechanical paradigm to the electronic one.[122]

Electronic or digital architecture, are these appropriate terms? Like many architects he felt that the new technology and media culture, so apparent at the time, were sufficient as definers though he granted that changes in philosophy, society and thought were equally important. This quickly proved true. Younger designers who had worked in his office, Jeff Kipnis and Greg Lynn, put forward a theory of folding based on the philosopher Gilles Deleuze's *Le Pli*, 1988, published in English in 1993 as *The Fold, Leibniz and the Baroque*.[123] *Le Pli* concerned folding that was as much metaphysical as physical — the way the mind was joined to the body in seamless continuity.

Soon many young architects around the world were discussing the implications of folding, both philosophical and practical. Warping the floor, wall and ceiling into a continuous and seamless surface was also an idea of Rem Koolhaas', as we have seen in the previous chapter, and so the academic avant-garde started to wrestle with the complex thoughts of this French intellectual. However, Frank Gehry, the other American protagonist of the movement, likes to appear intuitive and non-theoretical especially when confronted with the cerebration of Eisenman. His architectural folding is presented as a consequence of more immediate origins, sometimes stemming from bending fabric, sometimes from the previous stone undulations of the Late Gothic sculptor Claus Sluter. Formal not philosophical generation.[124] As with any paradigm there are many mixed motives that drive it forward and they cannot be reduced to a single technology, social trend, or formal system.

Nonetheless there are many polemicists who try to capture the essence of a movement knowing that if they do so they might also catch its wave. It is important then to mention some of the contenders and their definitions of the paradigm. A series of small booklets have appeared, edited by Antonino Saggio, that emphasize the importance of the new technology. Typical of these is *Natural Born CAA Designers*, the argument that CAD or Computer-Aided Design has, since its origin at MIT in the 1960s, finally changed a whole generation of the young.[125] They are, as the title has it, nat-

325 Born in Newark New Jersey in 1932, Peter Eisenman was trained at Cornell and Columbia University and then at Cambridge in England where he came under the influence of Colin Rowe, and also Italian Rationalism. Looking for an autonomous formalism, he found it first in geometrical transformations. Impressed by the way Rowe and Rudolf Wittkower abstracted a nine-square grid from Palladio's work, Eisenman decided that diagrams such as these were the intellectual underpinnings of architecture. Techniques such as axonometric projection and wireframe modeling could generate a building just as the deep structure, that Noam Chomsky revealed underlay language, might generate a surface structure. Underlying rules for Eisenman were such things as rotation versus frontality, or decomposition, or later superposition and folding. These operations were to be recorded in architectural form. His early houses, ordered serially House I, II, III...XI like Euclidean propositions, were also accompanied by serially ordered diagrams. In a humorous sense the diagrams *were* the final content of the building. To emphasize the paradox – generation more important than building – Eisenman called the real structures Cardboard Architecture. But, paradox on paradox, the markings on the structure and the generative rigor gave the final result an astonishing presence, even sensuality. Sensing this reversal of a reversal Eisenman adopted the paradox as his method.

His early houses, up to the late

1970s, have an inventive beauty made all the more quixotic because they question functionality, show us that we could love things that do not work. Always an intellectual maverick, he produced "impossible buildings" and densely layered puns, especially through his Deconstructive period of the early 1980s. By the 1990s and with the aid of a computer and the young, he developed a third period of his work. Initially inspired by theories of Folding, derived from Gilles Deleuze's influential book *Le Pli*, this soon became just one more course for his insatiable mental appetite, something he instills in others. He has taught continuously in architectural schools since 1961.

Eisenman feeds off one *nuova scienta* after another using devices drawn from fractals (self-similarity, scaling, superposition), from DNA research (his Bio-Centrum project), from Catastrophe Theory (again the fold), from rhetoric (catechresis), from Boolean algebra (the hypercube) and from psychoanalysis (too many theories to remember). I seem to remember that he told me that he had *two* psychoanalysts, one to refute the other, and there is no doubt psychic agility is part of his armory. At the same time, he has an endearing love of football (both European and American) especially when he contemplates all the possible combinations of plays and players.

His vermiform grammar of the 1990s, though not as accessible as Gehry's, was instrumental in opening the new paradigm. Leading the younger group of theorists such as Jeff Kipnis and Greg Lynn, and working tirelessly with his wife Cynthia Davidson, the critic, editor and creator of *ANY* magazine, his example remains a beacon for American practice. It is always architectural, more humorous and beautiful than at first appears and never uninteresting. Of what other architect is that true? His notion that architectural objects should generate themselves thereby revealing the 'interiority' of the discipline (*inside* architecture) leads to critical and provocative results.

Eisenman's love of game-playing may have deepened when he was a cheerleader for the football team at Cornell in 1953–54. Cheerleading certainly helped develop his later gift for creating teams of architects and overseeing them, a talent he also picked up from his friend Philip Johnson, a godfather who presided over two generations of American architects. Furthermore, Eisenman loves to scrutinize his past, psychoanalyze it to see if it will tell him where to go next. In one happy discovery – given his propensity to find lack of roots in current reality – he found that an anagram of his name almost spelled Amnesia. Further reflection resulted in one of his own serially produced propositions – P1, P2, P3 – and another amusing pun-with-a-point. P3 became the name of a secretly organized world conference on architecture, taking place in Charlottesville Virginia in 1982, at which the major global players rolled up, like Mafia bosses attending a country house retreat. The appellation played on the fact that P2 was the name of a real Secret Lodge, recently exposed in the media, which included insiders from the Mafia and the Vatican. So his trumpeting P3 achieved two results. It put his own name (Peter the Third) on the conference and gave it the edge of paranoia that journalists love, thus guaranteeing notoriety. Eisenman might have become the new Godfather, but his interest was more in creating provocative architecture (and discourse) than in leading the team. Nonetheless, his desire to be at the center of architectural debate has never slackened, from the creation of the Institute for Architecture and Urban Studies and the journal *Oppositions* in the late 1960s to his role in the executive committee of the Anyone project and *ANY* magazine throughout the 1990s.

urally born to virtual design and simulation, able as Jeff Kipnis puts it to deform and inform architectural shape through the digital media. De-formation is the twisting, warping and folding of grids and vectors by the computer; in-formation is obviously all the datascapes that architects can derive from research that might impinge on the form. The results of these manipulations are now evident at every school of architecture in the world – one good reason why the new paradigm *will be* tomorrow's architecture, whatever else we might think about the approach.

Architectural Design, the London magazine always quick to pick up a youth movement, started publishing serial issues on *Cyberspace* and *Hypersurface* labelled I, II, III as if they would breed on forever in the digital highway like a runaway virus.[126] Many articles and books that illustrate parts of the new paradigm carry the cyber and hyper label in their titles, inadvertently warning their readers that the architecture inside the covers will be more virtual than built. This, it has to be said, is a necessary ailment of the electronic age. The hypersurface is usually more hype than surface. As with all new movements, the rush of exploitation produces a rash of silliness and then a crash of expectations, the Dot.Com bubble being the financial counterpart to the architectural. New paradigm in economics? We have heard it many times before, one more reason I stress criticism and irony when approaching the new paradigm in architecture. We are concerned here with results, finished buildings judged as architecture, and although ideas and techniques play the significant, generative role they do not fully justify the work.

The questions of style and form are equally important and, again, there are several competing terms. One of the first comprehensive exhibitions on this aspect of the movement, in Pittsburgh 2001, was called *folds blobs & boxes* reflecting the theories of Greg Lynn.[127] Blobitecture and Blobmeisters became the phrases of choice in New York about 1995 when the group around Eisenman and his wife, Cynthia Davidson, and their magazine *Any* discussed the shift. Equally current were similar formal tags – waves, twists, fluid landforms – or historical parallels, Baroque, Rococo, Art Nouveau and Expressionism. The problem with the latter terms was the specific formal motifs associated with each, and the new paradigm was concerned with a more general shift. A collection of this work in 1999, edited by Peter Zellner, was called *Hybrid Space* and subtitled "New Forms in Digital Architecture".[128] Once again ninety per cent of the material was unbuilt, promise not performance, and the label was problematic. After all, almost every Post-Modern architect since Aldo van Eyck has claimed to be committed to hybrid, inbetween space and the concept develops way beyond this earlier source.

The new paradigm is neither just formally nor technologically led, though a blob grammar generated by the computer is important to it. Peter Eisenman, following French philosophers Foucault and Derrida, believes the change in worldview to be connected to the post-humanist condition where man is displaced from all traditional co-ordinates, and the role of architecture is to further "dislocate the knowing subject".[129] Hence his emphasis on destabilizing form, that unfamiliar interstitial space that can now be designed by computer midway between the figure and ground. While this metaphysics can be questioned – why should architecture necessarily destabilize? – Eisenman's concentration on the significance behind the new paradigm is quite right. It is not just a question of new form and technology but the cultural meaning of the new paradigm, and here he has much to say of relevance, particularly about the importance of the human body and how it affected by unusual space. And if one is reduced to computer metaphors at least let them be sophisticated and connected to biotechnology, the interface between the organic and electronic, where the most interesting implications reside.[130] The body *and* the machine, the cyborg, the 'both-and' of Post-Modernism are challenging concepts for the built environment which is both living *and* artificial.

But in the end the new paradigm concerns the new worldview illuminated by important ideas. These, such as emergence, have been around for fifty years before the computer started to represent this extraordinary quality of self-organizing systems.[131] Moreover, we began to understand an expanding, self-organizing universe in the early 1930s, well before the electronic revolution of the 1960s. Indeed, the life sciences and systems hypothesis had led theorists such as Jane Jacobs and Robert Venturi to privilege complexity twenty years before Complexity Theory caught on as the unifying idea behind contemporary science, in the mid 1980s. The computer may be very important, and media too, but the content of both have been shaped essentially by ideas, history and culture. To believe otherwise is to fall into techno-determinism, that old Modernist trap. It may be venerable but it is as reductive as ever. For all these reasons I believe Complexity Theory is the most suitable label for defining the new paradigm and it well illuminates notions of how the universe evolves, and jumps, towards more complex systems. Hence the title of this chapter, and the following one on fractals, one of the key sciences of complexity that has emerged to explain the geometry of nature.[132]

There are several ways to define the idea in general, and an unexceptional synthesis of them might be the following. Complexity is the theory of how emergent organization may be achieved by interacting components pushed far from equilibrium by an increase in energy, matter or information until it reaches a critical threshold between order and chaos. This important border is where the system often jumps in a new non-linear way and is sustained through feedback and the continuing input of energy. In this process quality emerges spontaneously as self-organization. Meaning, value and a greater degree of freedom are all positively associated with greater complexity.[133] So, I would argue, is multivalent architecture.

SOME ARCHITECTS

The new paradigm is loosely held together, as is obvious, by differing motivation. The consensus does not unite around a single label and movement but, such as it is, exists as the sharing of concerns. These can be conceived as overlapping sets, preoccupations that tie one group to another and then that one to yet one more. Many architects focus on the new digital technology and media, others are concerned with generating new shape grammars and a few are motivated by the underlying ideas of emergence. Enough buildings have been completed in the overall paradigm to get a good idea of its potential. Among the most important are Peter Eisenman's Aronoff Center, Daniel Libeskind's Jewish Museum and Frank Gehry's Bilbao Museum. There are also the less publicized buildings of Rem Koolhaas, Zaha Hadid, Morphosis, Enric Miralles, Coop Himmelblau, Ben van Berkel, Shoei Yoh, FOA, Zvi Hecker, the groups ARM, Oosterhuis and Spuybroek and Ushida Findlay. Beyond this are those on the cusp of the new paradigm, those committed to part of its program: among the most notable are Kisho Kurokawa, Will Alsop, Renzo Piano, Santiago Calatrava, Ken Yeang and Nick Grimshaw. And then there is the important theoretical work of Greg Lynn, Jeff Kipnis, Neil Denari, Reiser and Umemoto as well as research on the new theory of urbanism we have seen, the Fractal City, by those such as Batty, Longley and Graham Shane.

This list, by no means complete, is biased towards the Anglo-Saxon world with which I am familiar, but it is representative. If it is true that one swallow does not make a summer, it is also true that fifty buildings *do* make a significant tendency. Complexity Building, Cosmogenic Design, Cyberspace, Nonlinear Architecture, Blobitecture, Hybrid or Hyperspace – a strength of the trend may be that it has no accepted label, but it is deepening its roots and now has many practitioners. Its indefatigable pilot and thinker is Peter Eisenman (325).

ANIMATED MATTER

Young designers and architectural offices had been using computer-aided design, CAD, to facilitate production throughout the 1980s but it did not become a tool to create radical architecture until the 1990s. By 1987 Frank Gehry had started to use a curved vermiform grammar in his work, warping box-shaped volumes with his Vitra Museum in Germany. Two years later, while designing a fish-shaped pavilion in Barcelona, he used the computer to generate a smooth and economically dimensioned steel structure (2). At the end of 1988 Peter Eisenman conceived the Aronoff Center for Design and Art using a computer to generate a series of tilted forms. These unusual shapes mediated between a pre-existing 1960s building and the landscape be-

coming in his words "interstitial", or in-between the old and new. The blurring thus became a new form of Post-Modern contextualism.

In historical perspective, Gehry's and Eisenman's buildings could be considered the first in the new paradigm because their novel grammar was produced as the interaction between a designer and a digital programme. In both cases it was more than facilitation by machine, that is, a co-creation between designer and software.

In the case of Eisenman's building this interaction results in a grammar midway between the curved and square. Looked at as a series of diagrams, the plans seems to oscillate like vibrating strings, a series of iterations the computer can easily dimension (326,327). Solid masonry and concrete, the ultimate image of dead matter, seem to come alive with movement. And this intention is not only expressed in the diagrams, but also the elevation and details of the building. The tilts and shifts have their own logic, their own autonomy, their own will to exist. Eisenman calls this potency of the diagram the "interiority of architecture", because it is generated from *within the rules* he has set up, and discovered. For him it is the basis of a critical architecture, something that lies only within its being, different from painting, sculpture, environment, etc.[134]

The diagram becomes hyperactive in this Cincinnati building. Its oscillations jiggle into the previous modern structure to its side. It stacks up activities onto the older one, just as one geological formation pushes sediment and rock onto another. The result is part collision – the earthquake of forms so apparent – and part intermeshing of tectonic plates. A fresh kind of hybrid results from these waves of compression: a staccato, clunky, somewhat awkward language that, nevertheless, has its own peculiar grace. This becomes convincing because the idea is carried through at so many scales, with volumes and surfaces that are self-similar. They are mid-scale, often about the size of a person and always subtly changing like a fractal, thus constantly attracting our interest (328). As the architect Henry Cobb has argued, they become a new form of constructed ornament, and one that roots the human body in what would otherwise be a labyrinth of confusion.[135]

These mid-scale forms weave in and out of each other like a tartan, or shake and tilt against each other like shards after an avalanche. The logic behind the Stuttering Cubes – and Eisenman, like Palladio, invites the user to become involved in the high game of architecture – is a color code marking the design process. Light-blues, flesh-pinks and greens relate what chunk belongs to what design idea and why it is shifted or tilted or shimmering. The overall result is a new system that is reminiscent of the Rococo, or the pastel delicacies of Robert Adam. Rococo also shimmers in fractured planes of light and Adamesque architecture has a similar color-tone, but their ornament is a figural shape placed against a ground. Eisenman's new ornament consists of fig-

TILTED CURVE TRACE

TILTED CURVE TRACE 600

TILTED CHEVRON TRACE

326 EISENMAN ARCHITECTS (with Lorenz and Williams), Aronoff Center for Design and Art, University of Cincinnati, 1989–96, staccato segments wrap into existing zig-zags – a new urban grammar of contextualism generated by overlaps, torques, chevrons and oscillating waves. These mediate between the landscape and the pre-existing building. The oscillations appear like the strange attractors that animate so much inanimate matter.

327, 328 *Aronoff Center for Design and Art*, drawing of atrium with self-similar windows, lighting elements, bridges, columns and wall segments.

ures placed on figures and, of course, the prettiness of Rococo and Adam could not have been further from his mind.

He seeks to provoke and shock, to decenter perspective, deprivilege any one point of view, cross boundaries, blur categories (especially the boundary between the old stepped building and his new segmental attachment). "There is no preferred place for the viewer to understand", Eisenman says, invoking the contradictory perspectival space of Piranesi.[136] To achieve these multiple readings he has adopted several different methods which, characteristically, are diagrammed clearly, so that aficionados can follow the moves. Chevrons are tilted back and forth off the existing building; they set up one system against which a segmental line – mostly of studio space – is played. This line is "torqued", "overlapped", and "stepped" both as a solid and void. Other moves are made, which are hard to understand, but the result is a relatively new way of generating a sensual architecture. On a positive level, Eisenman has created a new fabric that is always changing subtly, one in which the architectural drama consists in traces of the design methods pushing through each other. Basically, a set of seesawing, blue chevrons marks the old grid while the pink and green segments mark the new formal methods; a tilt to one side, an earthquake to another and the trapezoidal crush of windows and floors between.

On a functional level this grammar has created a series of in-between spaces that work very well. The old and new buildings meld together, connected by overlapping hallways

329 *Aronoff Center for Design and Art*, promenade architecturale, atrium looking west, a space that is intermediary or inbetween the atrium and classrooms. This "interstitial space" is actually a popular meeting area and place for semi-public juries.

and stairways. Some of this transitional space is large enough to become a place of informal meetings, an area where the ritual of design juries can be observed from afar (329). Students of different years and disciplines can thus interact and learn from each other, a primary form of education in the arts.

It *is* a novel visual language of staccato landforms and straight segments. Whereas Greg Lynn and the younger designers using the computer propose a more supple, continuous forms, a single roof that slides over different areas and only inflects a bit to accommodate a function, Eisenman's grammar is more charged. As Sanford Kwinter has argued, structures that interest recent scientists are often concerned with "matter in the throes of creation"; that is, matter pushed far from equilibrium so that it self-organizes.[137] This kind of matter is not inert and dead, but like liquid crystal an in-between material.

Here we touch on a key insight of the new paradigm in science. The Nobel laureate Ilya Prigogine, who has done more to interpret the issues at stake than others, speaks in metaphorical terms about the way that "blind matter" – pushed far from equilibrium – can suddenly "see". Per Bak's self-organizing criticality, the theory of how sandpiles self-organize when they reach a critical state, is one example.[138] Each piece of sand, when the pile reaches the critical angle, is in touch with every other one, can "see every other one", and this sudden holistic organization brings the system to life; or, rather, to lifelike dynamic behavior. The same is true of tectonic plates pushed to critical compression, or any material system pushed to the threshold between order and chaos. Examples of such self-organization can be found on all scales of nature, from the simple sandpile to the turbulent red spot of Jupiter. To present, and represent some of these forces, especially the trapped twist and a strange attractor, I have developed a series of landforms (330,331). Earth self-organizes as it is pushed by plows into self-similar forms, and these become the ordering principles for paths as well as the water that sets them off.

All matter in a state of criticality, balanced at the border between order and chaos, becomes subject to sudden phase change, to symmetry breaking. Because this state of self-transformation resembles that of a living organism it can be seen as animated matter, parallel to a superorganism. The entire earth as an interacting system has been recently christened Gaia for this reason, and contrasted with the modern notion of matter as essentially inert and passive. Following the arguments of James Lovelock and those that developed Gaia Theory, and the scientists working at the Santa Fe Institute, one can now understand the potential for all dead matter to act, at the threshold of chaos, in a spontaneous, interactive way – as if it were free.[139] It behaves as if it had a mind of its own, although of course it does not really think or feel. Rather, as the first Post-Modern philosopher Alfred North Whitehead understood, even in 1925, matter

330 CHARLES JENCKS, *Landform twist*, Scotland, 1994. Wave-forms in the landscape twist to views in two different directions, first to the lakes and then to the landscape. Paths are folded into a unity and unfold in these two opposite directions. The forms are a result of earth-moving equipment, the self-organizing properties of sand and gravel and a new landscape language of twists based on the soliton wave. Deformed Henon attractor inscribed shows similar self-organizing shapes.

331 CHARLES JENCKS (With Farrell Partners, Ian White Associates) *Landform Ueda* at The Gallery of Modern Art, Edinburgh, 2001, with the strange attractor called the Ueda deformed and inscribed. Viscous matter such as hot wax, oil, sand and gravel flow into attractor curves that are fractal and self-similar to each other. Turbulent knots of resistance emerge, such as the one where the causeway hits the landform. Here nature is used to present a related form of natural self-organization.

given organization displays emergence.[140] Post-Modern science has turned the worldview of Modernism on its head. Instead of concentrating on the way we can act like machines, it privileges the way matter can act like us. Elevationism versus reductivism. Both paradigms of course have their truth.

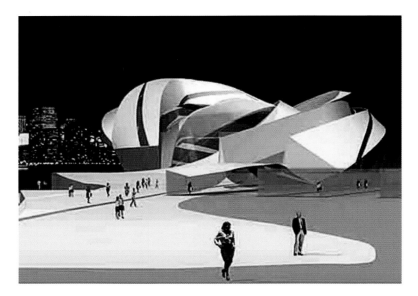

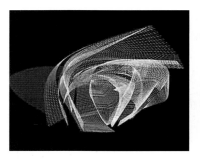

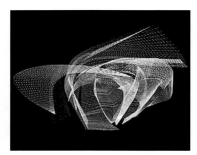

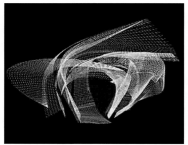

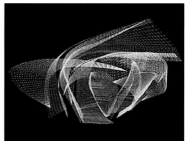

332 a,b PETER EISENMAN, *Staten Island Institute for Arts and Sciences,* 1997. Computer renderings of night-time view and interior. Fluid fractals.

333 *Staten Island Institute. Diagrams of site plan* and overlays of computer drawings, showing various transportation methods and horizontal cuts through the site – one-third and two-thirds of the way up the building.

In diagrams that help generate buildings Eisenman explores the territory between these two complementary views. One set concerns the liquid crystal, an in-between material that undergoes a phase transition as it oscillates between liquidity and hard crystal depending on the electric field and the way this effects molecules. Another set of Eisenmanian diagrams for a library project concerns the way cerebral activities, mapped as a landscape, can deform the building site, and interpenetrate with it. In this example brain-patterns partly generate landforms. Again one should emphasize the in-between, the hybrid state, part representation of brain-waves and material conditions, and it is the computer that allows these patterns to be folded seamlessly into each other.

For a museum and ferry terminal on Staten Island in New York, Eisenman mixes movement patterns into a landform building (332). White spirals of translucent glass and steel flow over a dense traffic intersection of boats, pedestrians, and buses. The movement of traffic becomes one generator of the forms, while wind and water also play a role. Diagrams of

laminar flow used to test airplanes and boats create a swirling grammar of what he calls "warped striations and deep V-shaped sections" (333). It rises and curves in tangents, like an ice-flow bent around a rock. Eisenman contrasts this museum with the Guggenheim museums of Frank Lloyd Wright and Frank Gehry because it is not centroidal and complete. "The spatial experience" is different because it "becomes an incomplete narrative, a destination without an end"[141] Again his desire is to destabilize perception, blur categories, challenge "the existing space-time regime".

Perhaps he overstates the opposition with the two Guggenheims, but the result, if built as seems possible, will be sensuously beautiful, tactile and related to the body. As Eisenman says these affective properties are related to Delueze's idea of folding:

> Folding changes the traditional space of vision. That is, it can be considered to be effective; it functions, it shelters, it is meaningful; it frames, it is aesthetic. Folding also constitutes a move from *e*ffective to *a*ffective space. Folding is not another subject [like] expressionism, a promiscuity, but rather unfolds in space alongside of its functioning and its meaning in space – it has what might be called an excessive condition or *a*ffect.[142]

In these drawings and designs we are again close to the enigmatic signifier of Ronchamp, and it is interesting that Eisenman acknowledges at least some associations such as

334 PETER EISENMAN, *City of Culture*, Santiago de Compostela, 1999
–2004. A landform comprising six buildings conceived in three pairs: The
Museum of Galician History and the New Technology Center are one
pair; the Music Theater and Central Administration building are a second; and the Galician Library and Periodicals Archive are a third. The
pairs are intermixed to "further complicate and enrich one's experience...a rare opportunity to develop the interstitial space of the site."

335 *Diagrams of old Santiago, the coquille shell, and the site intermixed* to
produce interstitial space.

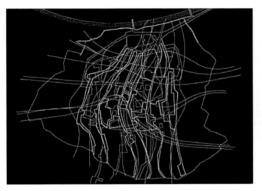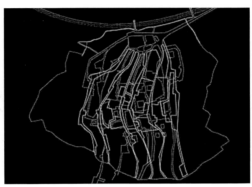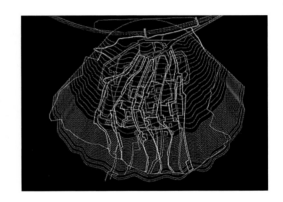

Robert Morris' *Hanging Felt Pieces*. These are blobs of dark
felt that droop from wall to floor and back again. It is possible to see other images, such as curving freeway ramps and
magnetic explosions on the sun, the swirling of gas clouds.

The irony is that Eisenman both intends *and* denies such
meaning. For instance, in the landform for a culture center in
Santiago de Compostela, he argues that we have reached a
"post-semiotic sensibility" of touch, a "haptic and mobile
culture of affect". But then he goes right on to generate plans
with the highly loaded semiotic sign of the coquille shell, the
symbol of old Santiago, and its ancient city plan (334–6). We
can applaud the confusion in this case because it means that
several types of diagram are intermixed, not just syntactic
ones. The radiating undulations of the coquille shell ripple
through the landform generating alleyways between rolling
inhabitable hills. The old town center of Santiago is also used
as a generative diagram, but now deformed as a grid and set
of streets. Eisenman insists, several times, that he has gone
beyond "obsolete explosive models' of figure and ground" to
produce a novel "new figure/figure":

> Contraction and implosion are intermeshed into the folded and
> warped surface of the coquille shell (producing neither figure nor
> ground but both at once), which reactivates the town plan and
> creates a new kind of center.[143]

Well, yes and no; the landform rippling up and down
recalls medieval hill towns and Native American earth-
works. But at the same time its interior space will be a novel
rendition of the overlapping V-shapes of his new grammar.
Under construction, and chosen as a result of what
Eisenman calls "the Bilbao Effect", it promises to challenge
Gehry's Bilbao as a harbinger of the new paradigm.

Because of his deep commitment to architecture and its
autonomy, its "interiority", and because of his equal concern to develop new shape grammars with the computer,
Eisenman is an undoubted leader of the new paradigm. His
obsession with the syntactic generation of form may be limited, but it is often, as at Santiago, covertly mixed with
semantic dimensions and it is the crossing of several grammars that give his work greater integrity and interest. At a
time when other architects have lost faith in the autonomy
of their art, Eisenman's example is right to the point, even
in some ways heroic. Though not an artist like Le Corbusier,
who he resembles in some ways, Eisenman also stands up
against the reigning indifference to deep creative thought.
Churning out texts and diagrams year after year he soldiers
on in a world more or less oblivious to his message. Not surprisingly he has created a band of followers, acolytes and
academics who try to fathom his gnomic writings and bril-

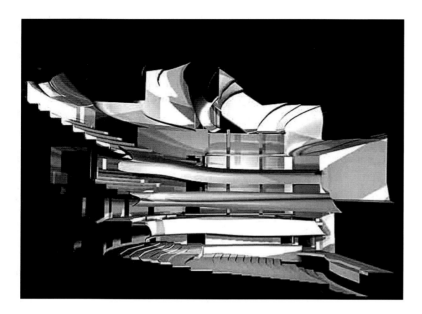

336 a,b *Santiago. Interior linear atrium* with its movement systems and overlapping functions.

liant insights. Perhaps all his efforts will produce, as Le Corbusier's did, a new academy, a system of thought and analysis for design. Like Palladio and the prophet of *L'Esprit Nouveau* there is the intention to provide a teaching method, to *faire école*. We will examine that school next, but for me the lasting value of Eisenman's work is the way it has reanimated matter, used the computer to reveal common ground between realms of the living and the non-living, and reasserted the art of architecture.

NEW COMPLEXITY AND THE BLOBMEISTERS

Eisenman runs his office as a network, a democratic school where young designers can interact and learn from each other, and he also directs it autocratically, like the atelier of a nineteenth-century master. If you wander into his open-plan studio on 25th Street in New York, as I have done over the years, you may hear him barking out orders, or speaking very openly and loudly with some eminence on the telephone. The atmosphere is both tense and friendly, like the workshop of an extended family. In the late 1980s four Young Turks were working in this office, all of whom were to have an influence on the complexity paradigm: Mark Wigley, Sanford Kwinter, Jeff Kipnis and Greg Lynn. It is important to stress this context partly because it differs from other offices and it results in the exchange of ideas that have a collective authorship. Here, however, I will concentrate on the ideas of Greg Lynn because of all the theorists his writings are the most developed and published.[144] His work may have an impact on architecture comparable to Colin Rowe, with whom he is in constant virtual argument. Indeed, one of his objectives is to define a new paradigm of complexity that will supercede Rowe's *Collage City* and the Post-Modern notion of radical eclecticism.

Like many young designers Lynn accepts the PM critique, the charge that Modernists imposed an oversimplified design method on an heterogeneous society, but he seeks new ways of dealing with heterogeneity that are not based on contradiction, juxtaposition and a collision of ideal grammars. This position was put first, along with Jeff Kipnis, in the *Architectural Design* of 1993 devoted to folding, a manifesto of the new movement. For Rowe's method of composing with different ideal types that are "fixed, exact, striated, identical and static", he proffers those topological grammars that are "dynamic, anexact, smooth, differentiated and stable". He summarizes the "post-contradictory work" as:

> topological geometry, morphology, morphogenesis, catastrophe theory or the computer technology of both the defense and Hollywood film industry — [which] are characteristics of smooth transformation involving the intensive integration of differences within a continuous yet heterogeneous system. Smooth mixtures are made up of disparate elements, which maintain their integrity while being blended within a continuous field of other free elements.[145]

The essence of his argument is that, with new computer software, it is possible to blend and mix heterogeneous elements in a smooth continuity using such synthetic methods as morphing, folding and blurring. The ultimate tool of reconciliation is the topological types that are called isomorphic polysurfaces or – in the animation argot of Hollywood – those methods known by the Donald Duck names, "meta-clay", "meta-ball" or simply "blob". Blobitecture, according to this argument, will inherit the earth, because it is a more pliant and general system of design than, for instance, the simple compositional types based on sphere, cone, and rectangle etc.

Lynn senses the latent humour, and terror, of this situation when while shopping for a toothbrush he finds that AutoCAD has designed all the available options.

> Then I found a toothbrush that looked like it was designed in Alias, a program that I liked to use at the time – and I bought the one designed in Alias. If you look at cars, or follow industrial design culture, you can readily identify these programs' impact on product design, as now in architecture you can tell if someone is designing with FormZ, 3-D Studio or CATIA because it is all in the mathematics. You can really see the influence of the software package on the design.[146]

Form follows software? Software may influence style and the manipulation of parameters but, as Lynn points out in this interview, it does not have any particular ideology or politics built into it. The important thing is that computer software can handle multiplicity and realize that goal of Post-Modernism where mass-housing can be personalized, with differences in shape, color and material that were not possible before. His project, the Embryologic House, foresees a factory made production line resembling that of cars and clothes where a great variety of choice is available (337). Signifi-cantly, and perhaps predictably, this system is within the curved, blob grammar. Whether or not a major automobile company will take up his challenge remains to be seen. None heeded the call of Le Corbusier, in over forty years, for a standardized housing model; but then perhaps the market will finally open up with the new possibilities of individuation.

The blob grammar is contrasted with both Classical design and Post-Modern collage as being more flexible, amorphous, supple, fluid, incomplete, non-ideal and pliable. It also is closer to organic shapes and the body than machine-age architecture. Furthermore, like the fold, it is smooth and continuous not disjointed and disjunctive. No doubt its extreme versatility operates at the formal level, and not on the semiotic or cultural plane. Blobs, after all, are associated with viscera and other unmentionables – indeed, there was even a short-lived movement in British architecture, in 1959, of very similar form, known as Bowelism, and this had no output. Associations, similarities, analogies and labels obviously matter as much as physical results, and

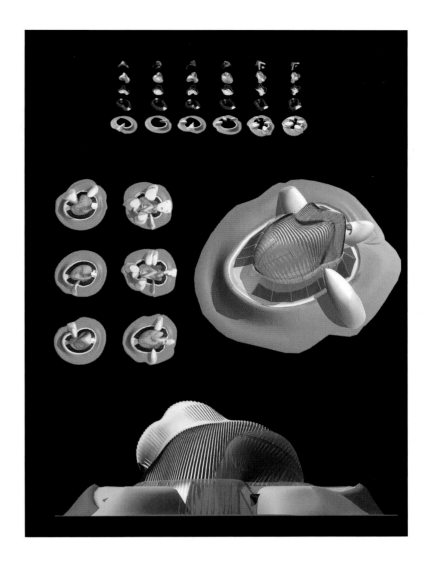

337 GREG LYNN, *Embryologic House*, 1998. Different models are enclosed with a surface of 2048 panels, all of which are unique in shape and size. The panels are networked so that a change in any one is coordinated with every other one in the set. The volume is defined as a flexible set of curves rather than a fixed set of rigid points. Openings and windows are seamlessly incorporated into the surface made from wood, polymers and steel, all fabricated by robotic controlled milling and water-jet cutting machinery. At the base, a bermed garden in pink with white blob rooms; then a canted greenhouse skirt; then a monocoque structure of steel girders covered by an aluminium skin with photovoltaic shading.

"blobs", as the market researchers say, obviously have an image problem, among others.

Nevertheless, Lynn and the other young computer designers are fundamentally right: the blob grammar is more general and flexible than others, and it will probably continue to gain adherence. Its power is the ability to gather a set of differential forces, give them weightings and then combine them as a series of smooth spline surfaces. At its simplest this can be seen in two diagrams showing simple polyhedral shapes becoming fused into a single spline surface. To see how this blob grammar is more supple and complex than others one must follow Lynn's argument at some length:

> the weights of one spline surface can effect those of another spline surface (338). These resulting structures are called blobs for their ability to mutually inflect one another and form composite assemblages. The blob is an alternative example of a topological surface exhibiting landscape characteristics although it does not look like a topography.

The connection with landscape and landforms, we have seen, is an important consequence, but so too is the way the blob grammar challenges both classical holism *and* collage:

> These blob assemblages are neither multiple nor single, neither internally contradictory nor unified. Their complexity involves the fusion of multiple elements into an assemblage that behaves as a singularity while remaining irreducible to any single simple organization.

Lynn, following the recent insights of the biologist Lynne Margulis, understands higher organisms as fused assemblages of micro-organisms acting symbiotically. The new paradigm emphasizes the holism of our bodies as made up of an ecology of simpler organisms acting through feedback to achieve a singular stability. It is the number and quality of interactions that matter, that distinguish a simpler from a more complex organism, or design. Thus he argues that the blob is a more complex and developed form than, for instance, the primary forms of Classical and Modern architecture:

> The difference between simple and complex systems is relative to the number of interactions between components. In this schema, there is no essential difference between a more or less spherical formation and a blob. The sphere and its provisional symmetries are merely the index of a rather low level of interactions, while the blob is an index of a high degree of information, where information is equated with difference. Thus, even what seems to be a sphere is actually a blob without influence: an inexact form that merely masquerades as an exact form because it is isolated from adjacent forces.[147]

In the past architecture has always sought simpler symmetrical forms, those that Vitruvius and Le Corbusier recommended such as the sphere, cone and cylinder. However with the new cosmology that emphasizes symmetry breaking, the evolution of the universe towards more organized states with higher information content, we can now appreciate the fundamental, if bizarre, inversion. Vitruvius and the Greeks were right to look to the body as "the measure of all things", and make it the standard for architecture, but they reduced it to simple harmonies and shapes rather than expanded architecture to the real complexity of life. The blob is a complex sphere and our bodies are evolved blobs. QED complexity architecture, high in information, will be blobitecture.

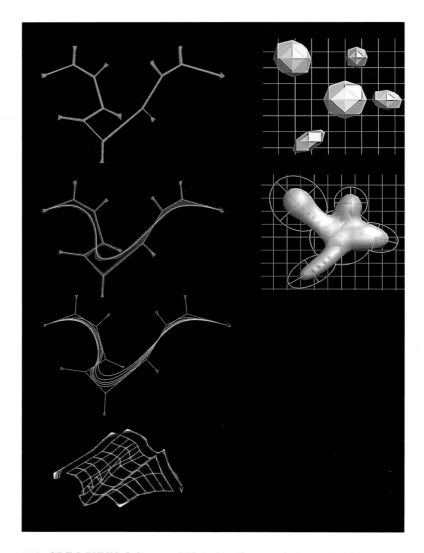

338 GREG LYNN, Splines and blobs handle more information than symmetrical forms, 1999. The spline can integrate many variables into a continuous form. Reading down from top left: a simple two-degree spline, or polyline; a seven-degree spline, where the more continuous curvature is determined by seven adjacent points and weightings; a superimposed series of splines sharing the same control vertices with different degrees of influence; a spline surface, or mesh, constructed from groups of splines connected across one another, in u and v directions.

From top right: the symmetrical figure versus the combined blob. The disconnected symmetrical figures are, below, fused into a polysurface. Combination and symmetry breaking can handle a higher degree of information; an organism and building is the singular symbiosis of many such parts. Symmetry breaking, up to a certain point, increases effective complexity (see text).

339 A brief history of biomorphic buildings.

Well, I simplify to make the point. And besides, there is a lot more to architecture than can be captured with formal systems on the computer. There is history, cultural meaning, semantics, and performance among other things. But one can understand Lynn's general insight. Computer design allows us to incorporate a greater complexity than before, to

Frederick Kiesler, *Endless House* 1936-1959

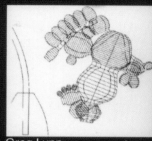

Greg Lynn
Cardiff Bay Opera House 1995

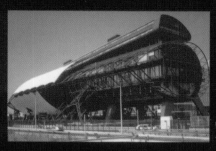

Will Alsop, *Hotel du Departement*
Marseille 1993-1995

Will Alsop, *Peckham Library*
1999-2000

Will Alsop, *Rotterdam Project* 2001

Frank Gehry, *Horse's Head* for Peter
Lewis 1993 & Berlin Bank 1997

Frank Gehry, *Experience Music* Project
Seattle 1995-2000

Balkrinshna Doshi, *Hussain-Doshi Gufa*,
Ahmedabad 1995

Ushida Findlay, *Truss Wall House*
Tokyo 1990-1991

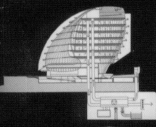

Norman Foster

Greater London Authority
1999-2000

and

The Music Centre
Gateshead 1999-2002

Lars Spuybroek, *Toilet Block*
Zeeland 1997

he chose the oval form as a unit, based on the existing oval of the harbour. In effect, a higher order of complexity is achieved here than in Kiesler's structure, because symmetry is mixed with the proliferation of assembled parts.

Will Alsop, the British Blobmeister, in his Marseille building of 1993 extrudes a pinched oval-shape in a line. Like Gehry's work at Bilbao the ovoid is given a sharp edge and axial direction, again the mixture of symmetry and broken symmetry he uses in other schemes. In contrast, Gehry's "Horse's Head" and his Music Project Building in Seattle are, like Kiesler's Endless House, more radically sculptural and amorphous. They ripple and shake to no apparent tune, structural or otherwise. Balkrinshna Doshi's domes with ribs and skylights and Ushida Findlay's Truss Wall House are both deformed regular shapes with complex attachments. Norman Foster's recent curved shapes are much the most regular of this set, being distorted eggs and globular clusters: order, simplicity and symmetry dominate. Finally, Lars Spuybroek's Toilet Block has the linear blob-shape of a boat's hull with the deformations of its ribs following a smooth transition. Its use, natural wind tunnel effect, semantics and form all underscore each other with considerable wit (women to the left, behind the exhaust pipe, men to the right behind the grille). Formally the structure shows both a high degree of variation *and* symmetry about an axis.

These projects clarify an issue behind Lynn's concepts. Although increasing information often increases complexity, the degree of organization, is *not* just a measure of increasing information. An encyclopedia has more information than a novel, some lesser developed species a longer sequence of DNA than the human. It is true increasing information increases complexity, but only up to a certain point, after which it becomes complication and the system actually becomes simpler. This general point is made by the Nobel laureate Murray Gell-Mann in his *The Quark and the Jaguar*, *Adventures in the Simple and Complex*. What he calls 'effective complexity' occupies an intermediate area on a continuum between increasing order and increasing disorder, the completely regular and completely random.[148] The point is suggestive and helps illuminate why some combination of symmetry and randomness would have a more "effective complexity" than either the amorphous or the regular blob. It is a rough measure of value, what I have defined as organized complexity in *The Architecture of the Jumping Universe*.[149] And this phrase, organized complexity, takes us right back to the beginnings of Post-Modernism and the writings of Jane Jacobs. As she pointed out in 1961, using the life sciences as her model, a city is a problem of

weight and deform these variables in a smooth coherence, to fabricate the results cheaply, and to produce forms that are closer to nature and to our bodies. A brief overview of biomorphic architecture underscores these points, and again shows that we are at the beginning of the journey rather than very far along the route, and reveals a lacuna in the argument so far (339).

The discussion begins at the top left of the diagram. Frederick Kiesler's Endless House, designed over a period of thirty years from the mid-1920s to 1959, is the canonic beginning of recent biomorphic history. Four ovoid shapes with irregular curves are joined up to sit above rough slabs. Exterior apertures, like eyes or petals, open to the view and sun. The topological surface is continuous, the inside space is "endless" folding together walls, ceiling, floor and furniture. The blob grammar is mostly amorphous, scaleless, primitive, and crude – intentionally so, an example of "weak form" and the Arte Povera current in the 1950s. By contrast, Greg Lynn's design for the Cardiff Bay Opera House, 1995, simplifies and structures this blob grammar. It achieves orientation and scale partly because the competition brief specified a symmetrical opera plan, and because three different types. The first is simple orders and basic geometry, such as highways and squares. The city is also a more complex problem of statistical probabilities or disorganized complexity; but above all it is one of organized complexity, that is high information structured into complex organs such as a neighborhood street.[150]

With effective or organized complexity in mind let us look at two recent examples of this architecture. In the late 1990s Christian de Portzamparc designed a mini-skyscraper of twenty-four storeys for the Paris fashion conglomerate LVMH on New York's stylish 57th street. The shopping wars demanded a certain expressive license, the not-so-hidden agenda to be sexier than thou. So, Louis Vuitton luggage, Moët & Chandon champagne, Guerlain perfume and Christian Dior, among other brands gathered into the flagship, took on the block. The Chanel tower (and empire) is to the left, the old Classical Chemical Bank to the right, and the icy-grey IBM across the street. In terms of finesse and subtlety Portzamparc easily wins.

His tower turns and fractures its shape to relate to neighbors at different scales, while also breaking up the mass (340). These fractures are also a clever response to zoning codes and setback laws. The fold is used effectively to create six façades on the front and avoid reflecting the monolithic IBM, his avowed purpose. The fold, really more of a prismatic pleat, also turns the side façade into the front, and brings pedestrians into the entrance. Sandblasted windows of four different types further refine the exterior fractures, and interior lighting, suggesting a fractured geode exposing its crystals. A green glowing halo of multifaceted planes thus steps up the front to reach the big room at the top where receptions are held. This is surmounted by a switchback of the basic grammar which becomes a sunshade and a cap. Vertical unities are thus played against horizontal window bands that are given a diagonal accent. On the inside nothing of comparable interest occurs; other architects were involved. But in terms of the exterior skin, the effective complexity is much higher than either the normal Classical building to the right, or the heavy IBM across the Street.

In sharp contrast to this urbane sophisticate is Lars Spuybroek's Fresh Water Pavilion located in a flat Dutch artificial landscape of saltwater marsh. Here is the first truly interactive blob building, and a built version of Kiesler's Endless House where no surfaces are completely horizontal and wall, floor and roof undulate into each other (341). Now it is the content of body experience that has determined the form, something that can be compared to a prosthesis such as an artificial arm or leg, or the extension of the body such as a moving automobile. Whereas the New York office interior has an inert background for business meetings, this pavilion has an active set of sensors that respond to one's every move. Only the Dutch government would have commissioned such a water-body-machine as a high-art playground. The image looks midway between a whale that swallows children and a high-gloss worm, but Spuybroek compares it to a Maserati. Because it is located on a salty island and threatens to go brown, its shining stainless steel surfaces will continue to inspire users to polish it back into mint condition. Its special alloy calls for this.

There is no question that the building engages the body, both visually and kinesthetically. In the usual interaction with machines, such as driving a car or bicycle, one's body responds unconsciously to weight, direction, flow and continuous information. This second nature is itself so common and integrated into culture that we fail to appreciate we are already cyborgs, cybernated organisms, a truth this pavilion wants to extend. Now the prosthesis surrounds the whole body and as one walks, jumps or skateboards through the building, it gives out pulses of blue light in response, sets off electronic music, or releases small water waves. A bigger jump produces bigger ripples, or perhaps puffs of mist, chunks of ice, or a well into which one can drop sand. The total experience, the *gesamtkunstwerk*, is meant to induce a political debate about water in a country under attack by water. Or at least entertain the Dutch with this life-giving element. So an electronic, haptic architecture – a desire of both Eisenman and the Blobmeisters for many years – has finally reached its first stage, of birth.

What about the architectural shell? The interior structure, like the hull of a Dutch schooner, consists of elliptical frames of changing dimensions: fourteen pulsate up and down connected by a braid of splines that fan this way and that. Perhaps the exterior is not meant to be looked at, even if it is a Maserati, because the shape is amorphous, weak form again, a beached slug lying limp on the sand. It *is* interesting, even provocative and enigmatic, but aesthetically speaking evasive and without gesture, beginning or end. All middle, one might conceive it as Jonah's large intestine in which the real experience goes on inside. There the building and the participant interact, learn how to play with each other, a wrap-around bicycle, a responsive tummy.

Needless to say, in terms of "effective complexity", this building is more developed than the New York office. Its failings are typically those of biomorphic architecture in its first stage: lack of scaling, strong form, and semantic sophistication. Like so much failed Modernism it is the unintended metaphors and overtones that decrease its complexity, turn it into the wrong kind of one-liner, a slug. But, comparing it to the countless other blob buildings, as interactive, body architecture it has yet to be surpassed.

Other Dutch architects, especially Kas Oosterhuis and Ben van Berkel, have used the computer to explore the same territory between the body and architecture, the living and non-living, though the results are not necessarily curved and biomorphic. The Möbius House of van Berkel is an abstraction of the well-known Möbius strip, but it is carried out in angular concrete and glass forms – not literal curves of the famous loop (342).

341 LARS SPUYBROEK & NOX, *FreshH2O eXPO*. Water pavilion and interactive installation, Neeltje Jans Island, Holland, 1997–98. An undulating blob made from fourteen elliptical frames that vary in dimension over which splines of stainless steel braid. The endless interior has sensors that respond to movement and jumping, sending out pulses of blue light and waves of various size. Other interactive elements celebrate the place and danger of water. (NOX).

342 BAN VAN BERKEL, UN STUDIO, *Möbius House*, het Gooi, Holland, 1993–98. The separate and intertwined lives of a couple are conceived as an endless Möbius strip. Their various activities in a continuous space generate flowing forms that curve endlessly back on themselves. In construction, however, these are translated into the angular shapes of glass and steel and reconceived as a walk in the woods.

working
living
sleeping
living
working
sleeping

343, 344 AVIGNON, CLOUET, CORTELLA, *The Fungal Garden*, Chaumont Garden Festival, Chaumont-sur-Loire, 2001. A white gauze stretched over a dark frame that holds an interior tunnel of white foam. Against the charred trees this becomes a chrysalis, or flower, or spider-web of life. On the inside petri dishes hold over 250 species of colorful moulds, pinioned like flowers on a branch, or butterflies on display. The wit of having the splines hold both the foam and the petri dishes, in a very relaxed way, and the transitions between gauze and growth are masterful. A tiny aviary of butterflies culminates the route, the metaphor of transformation complete.

345 JAMES WINES & SITE, *Covered Walkway*, EXPO 92, Seville 1992. Note the way the water-wall creates a terrarium in section by the brook. The four elements, earth, air, water and sun, are dramatized in this mixture of planting and technology.

NEW METAPHORS OF NATURE

The landform, blob and topological surface are methods of dealing with complexity, but they are also latent metaphors close to those of nature. A computer is not a brain, an ecology is not a body, but these are all analogies of each other. Metaphors are a "carrying over" from one area of experience to another and an important aspect of the new paradigm is to reveal our continuity with nature. The ecological movement is clearly the locus for this carrying over. Since it is ubiquitous in all areas of architecture, and has become a justification for every act of building whether practically justified or not, I will concentrate here on the expressive and conceptual aspects of green architecture. These challenge previous paradigms as much as does computer design and in a similar way: they blur categories of the living and dead, self-organizing nature and self-organizing matter.

Striking examples of this blurring are presented at the annual Chaumont Garden Festival in the Loire Valley. One might expect gardens with buildings to mix the primary distinctions and a particularly convincing example was the one designed by Benjamin Avignon, Saweta Clouet and Jean-Luc Cortella from France. These designers, like those of the Freshwater Pavilion, adopt the blob grammar, but they give it added strength by juxtaposition with charred black trees and strips planted with different grasses (343,344). A white gauze of transparent fabric bumps and undulates through the black trees, metaphor of a chrysalis, and this lacy skin shields an interior tunnel of white

polyurethane folds. A pathway of beaten lead provides a strong physical anchor to one's body – this is not the usual disorienting walk – and here the metal splines weave in and out of the walls to hold petri dishes. The effects are brilliantly appropriate to the display and message. It is a fungal garden, a garden of different moulds displayed sensitively as both "flowers" *and* plastic experiments in self-organization. The melodrama of black death versus delicate life is acceptable in a popular festival, and it makes the didactic message – the continuum of life and plastic – acceptably tongue in cheek. The lowly fungus is here elevated to a proper place high in the rank of culture. After all, it is one of the five main phyla of life, along with animals and plants. The largest living body in the world is a superorganism of fungi, and the most extraordinary examples of self-organization are evident in the slime mould. In its varied life cycle this amazing mould will coagulate as a colony, disperse, grow up a pole of itself, jump and fly off to a new territory. How many animals or plants can do this – and it cannot even think! To celebrate its esteemed place in the new paradigm, in 1996 I gave a jar of bottled New Orleans swamp slime, properly relabeled as slime mould, as a present to Peter Eisenman.

The group SITE, led by James Wines, has for twenty years made an art out of the ecological imperative and it is this that sets their work above the utilitarian mainstream. For instance, their highly functional walkway at EXPO 92 in Seville provides shelter from the sun, and cool misty air but, like the French gardens of Chaumont, also makes very

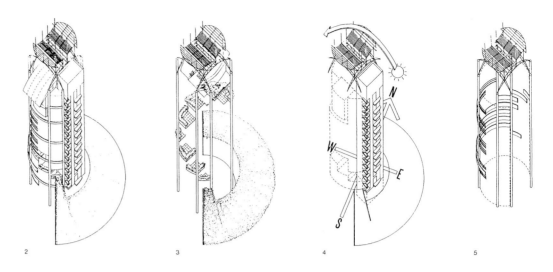

346, 347 KEN YEANG, Menara Mesiniaga, Kuala Lumpur, 1991–93. What Yeang calls "the bioclimatic skyscraper" is a new green tower responding to the environmental conditions of the site, the sun, the view and wind – here in a spiral of green skycourts.

adroit connections between the artificial and the natural (345). A water-wall snakes through the glare and heat equating glass and liquid. Plants and trees grow on a roof, over which the monorail runs, more plants hang from the ceiling, and a small brook meanders at the base of the glass wall calling attention to the cut through the earth at one's feet. Here in cross section was displayed the natural beauty of the earth's living cycle: rocks, gravel, top soil, living and dying plants. The real elements and their interaction, as in one of John Ruskin's geological drawings, become the ornament. So an ecology lesson and air-conditioning are turned directly into an art-form. When Le Corbusier said the techniques of life were themselves the instruments of poetry he had such transformations in mind.

High-Tech architects now routinely incorporate growing plants in their structures, and for this reason and other green concerns they have been re-christened as Eco-Tech.[151] Norman Foster, Richard Rogers, Renzo Piano, Dominique Perrault and Jean Nouvel feature the sprouting atrium as a green badge of honour. To proclaim their commitments, Christian de Portzamparc, Mario Botta, Antoine Grumbach and Emilio Ambasz grow trees all over their buildings, especially on the roof. Beyond the symbolism and pleasant ambience created by greenery, countless techniques of energy-saving have been invented by these architects, most of them worthy. But they have not necessarily made an art of the new view of nature. And few have gone as far as Ken Yeang in trying to theorize, and then actually measure, the ecological implications of their tall, mass-produced buildings.[152]

The contradictions are obvious, most of all to Yeang himself, because the technologies, materials and ways of life that go on in the skyscraper are inherently unsustainable.

Nonetheless, since the world will not shrink from building such leviathans, even after 11 September, 2001 it is important to lessen their impact – the argument of Ken Yeang's "bioclimatic skscraper". Its most striking embodiment is the tower near the Kuala Lumpur Airport (346, 347). This interpretation of the corporate landmark, called Menara Mesiniaga, explores a new direction for IBM and the ultimate symbol of capital, the skyscraper. Instead of being the usual introverted and smug statement of power, the IBM tower in Kuala Lumpur is a picturesque expression of an emerging technology. Its fifteen-storey circular shape sits on a sloping landscaped base. The top is a irregular tube structure, a sun shade and support for future solar panels. External louvers and voids cut up the cylinder visually, providing external orientation and internal views. Most visible of the energy saving devices are the two spirals, the green sky-courts that twist up the building and provide shade and visual contrast with the steel and aluminium surfaces. The reinforced concrete frame is further punctuated by two types of sun-screens and a glass-and-steel curtain wall, which, along with the sloping base and metal crown, make this essentially High-Tech image more organic. This could be called "organitech", a synthesis of opposites.

Ken Yeang, like Le Corbusier before him, bases a new architecture on five points. First, and derived from the past, are what he calls "valves", the movable parts that respond to fast-changing climatic conditions. Progress today consists in returning to windows that can actually open! Second are "filters", again including new versions of such traditional elements as exterior louvers. Third is the design decision to locate the elevator and service cores on the sides where it is hot, thus reducing the heat gain. Fourth are the sky courts and growing plants used to cool the building, its most obviously green feature. These courts and vegetation, if generally applied to most buildings, could lower the temperature of cities. The "heat domes" that have recently been discovered by satellites to be raising the temperature by as much as five degrees, over such cities as Atlanta, could be completely cleared if such measures became widespread. The fifth point is the contrast between sunshades and clear glass (where the view is good and the sun does not penetrate). All of these measures, and other methods of recycling energy, lead Yeang to the articulate and dynamic skyscraper.

Norman Foster has designed several green skyscrapers, and even one with spiral sky courts, but because this is in London the courts are enclosed and connected on the diagonal for air circulation (348,349). As simulations show, the swelling of the volume half-way up means that the bottom and top are lightened in visual weight. For similar reasons the swelling Egyptian lotus column is lightened and seems to spring skywards. The double curved elevation not only makes the building less bulky than an equivalent rectilinear block, but also much more dynamic in its spiral rush to the top. The aerodynamic shape is further justified because it minimises the reflection of wind at the base, something that plagues the rectilinear skyscraper.

Although it looks like a missile and has the outline of a bullet, there are organic metaphors behind the design. Since the building evolved from an egg-shape into a stretched pointed egg, it shares affinities with other natural growths, not just the gherkin, as the press has dubbed it. Because of its diagonal structural frame it resembles a stretched pineapple, or more accurately, an elongated pinecone. These last two plants show the interesting growth pattern called the Fibonacci series (1,2,3,5,8,13,21,34,etc.). This sequence of numbers, appreciated since the time of Pythagoras, has only recently been understood for its full structural beauty, an insight of the new paradigm.[153] Why does nature use such beautiful spirals of growth? It turns out that the pattern is a form of robust self-organization, the most probable way the units can occupy space given the rate at which they grow. One pinsecale of the pinecone grows after the next at the key angle of 137.5 degrees because this is the angle best suited for occupying space over the growing time of the plant. The structural elements of a pinecone, daisy, pineapple and so many other spiraling plants can support each other most efficiently this way. They can fill in the available space most simply, pack together for mutual support most economically, without either waste space or getting in each other's way.

Examined more closely, it turns out that Swiss Re is *not* a true Fibonacci spiral but what Foster calls a "diagrid structure". But its relevance in terms of how one sees the building is that it *looks* like the growing pattern of the Fibonacci series and this appearance highlights the natural as opposed to the military associations. So, what on first glance may be seen as a projectile, or perhaps a cigar is, on second look, something more like a plant form, indeed nearly *the* archetypal ur-form (since Fibonacci growth underlies most plants). The importance of this deeper reading cannot be overemphasized because it keys into the other visible metaphors of nature, above all the six garden spirals that wind up the outside. These enclosed sky courts, or atria that go up diagonally six storeys, also serve to create natural upward ventilation throughout the building. Because of such a green emphasis the building may become a giant, glowing beacon of natural forces, a cosmic skyscraper. In any case, it is one perfected solution to an architectural proposition: the round, centrally planned skyscraper with top and bottom curves, and satisfying proportions.

Metaphors based on nature underlay the work of Frank Lloyd Wright and the few Modern architects who worked under the label, and philosophy, of organic architecture. This approach, especially where it adopts ecological thinking as in the work of Foster and the organitech designers, is a kind of halfway house in the new paradigm. It acknowledges a basic problem of Modernism and modernization — that a progressive economy usually results in a regressive ecology — and seeks to ameliorate the situation with new

348, 349 NORMAN FOSTER, *Swiss Re Headquarters*, London 1996–2002. Enclosed skycourts spiral to the top, green atria drawing up air. The diagonal grid, or diagrid, is overlaid on a stretched ovoid or egg shape. Natural metaphors of growth and a comparison to plants – pinecone, pineapple, gherkin. Although it appears to, the actual structure does not follow the Fibonacci series of harmonic growth. Nonetheless, this skyscraper is a beautiful and perfected solution to the centralized tall building, a form of propositional beauty.

technologies and solutions. But often it simply translates a previous form and metaphor into green architecture. Nicholas Grimshaw's exemplary geodesic bubbles for the Eden Project are typical in this respect. They create an impressive "cathedral to plants" in an old quarry; they create different biomes including a rainforest; they use a new Teflon product, ETFE, one-tenth the cost of glass; they should be applauded. But as new metaphors for the new understanding of nature, they are old Buckminster Fuller domes clumped together. Nothing is made of their fortuitous resemblance to the eyes of a fly, or the globular clusters of minerals.

More expressive and interesting is Grimshaw's transformation of Waterloo Station in London. Here, with the aid of a computer, he has created a reptilian structure of glass panes and stabilizing fins that ripples its surface like the shock wave of the incoming high speed train as it stops (350). The shimmering patterns, fractal in nature, are like the scales of a snake or the hide of an armadillo, units that vary slightly depending on their place in the structure. This subtle variation is an important index of the new paradigm: understanding the fractal, why it is so prevalent in nature, and why the computer can now bring them to architecture, economically.

The most spectacular examples of organitech have been created by Santiago Calatrava, a Spanish architect from Valencia who works in many countries. Trained as an engineer and architect and following the example of Antonio Gaudi, his works combine the different disciplines of his background within a strongly sculptural framework. Because of such synthetic power, Alexander Tzonis sees Calatrava as establishing "a new paradigm for practice", a claim that has some validity.[154] His structures represent the dynamics of movement and sometimes literally fold open and closed. Their staccato rhythms of light and shadow capture the feeling of motion like a time-lapse film of a horse trotting. The structures push and flex against each other like a straining athlete. Indeed, as Calatrava's drawings reveal, their genesis may be the muscles and bones of the body or, a favorite image, the opening of an eye. Other often repeated forms are the tilted Y-shape, and the zigzag cantilever both given structural and visual sense by his method of profiling, that is, varying the profile of the section to give it maximum strength. Like Gaudi's use of the parabola and other favored solutions, Calatrava continues to develop a personal grammar until it reaches a point of refinement. Most of these elements are brought together in the ultimate

350 NICHOLAS GRIMSHAW AND PARTNERS, *Waterloo Channel Tunnel Terminal*, London 1990–93. The biomorphic expression of a shock wave and undulation. 1,728 panels, many of them slightly different, ripple as the train stops and the energy wave continues, a fractal pattern like those in nature, now possible with computer design.

351–354 SANTIAGO CALATRAVA, *City of Arts and Sciences*, Valencia, 1991–2002. A spectacular urban landscape sunk in the old Turia River, that had been diverted, is open to the public night and day, a white jewel against a blue sky and green blue pool. The parking garage, across from the largest structure, the science museum, is surmounted by a sculpture garden and parabolic filigree. The heart of the scheme, a half-ovoid, becomes a whole blinking eye when reflected in the pool and the canopy rises and lowers. It holds an IMAX theatre and planetarium. External walkways and leaning buttresses pulsate to filter the light. The white concrete structure is everywhere sculpted with curves that profile the play of forces, and it is constructed without blemish, an extraordinary tour de force.

project of the millennium, the £2 billion City of Arts and Sciences in Valencia (351–4).

This is an extraordinary *tour de force*. The tapering and modulated forms of white concrete are impeccably made. The continuous and smooth finish is a consequence not only of Calatrava's design but the patience and skill of the local industrial workers who spend much time polishing the interior of the formwork. The virtuosity also recalls the concrete work of Ricardo Bofill, to which it is superior in finesse and invention.

Seen against the clear blue sky of the dry climate of Valencia the white city comes alive as a shimmering filigree of bones and thin tendons. Reflected in the shallow pools and cut across by walkways and floating tubs of cypress trees, Calatrava has created a water garden inspired by the great Mughal works of the past. Urban theatre is put to public use both day and night since much of the site remains open, and dramatically lit. One can traverse it several ways, like the city-garden of Fatehpur Sikri, and not even have to pay for the pleasure.

At its heart is the planetarium, "the eye of wisdom", that blinks its eyelid on electronic command. Reflected in the still water, the oval and retina become complete, and when the canopy is half closed the planetarium seems to squint and stare. The metaphor may be a bit corny, but at the same time it is convincingly carried through and appropriate for the role of cosmology today: the universe looks back at the eye it has created looking at it. Some critics see this work as epitomizing the biotechnical aspect of the new paradigm.[155]

The largest structure, at forty meters, is the science museum, like the Natural History Museum in London a hundred years before, it is a cathedral to emergent knowledge. A new type of flying buttress leans into this spikey form and it results in a strange metaphor that probably was intended but is no less surreal for that. At night, thirty rigid eyes pop open as light shines out from between triangular eyelids. By day thirty rigid beaks snap out against the blue sky. These forms and associations stem from Gaudi's windows at the Colonia Guell, a building well known to Calatrava. Every view in this airy cathedral becomes a dazzling optical illusion of filtered light. Indeed the strength of Calatrava's work, here is the way it modulates light, breaks down the glare and cuts it up like an Op Art trellis. Nowhere are these illusions more persuasive and gentle than in the sculpture gardens that surmount the parking garage. The louver and light filter reach the level that Tzonis commends as "the poetics of movement".

Considered as a popular millennium project celebrating Valencia and science these crystal palaces are an undoubted success, but in terms of the new paradigm they are, as so much organitech, only partly developed. Although the main structures differ from each other, within a single building the forms repeat endlessly, as in Renzo Piano's work. In effect, the forms are self-same not, as with the fractal, self-similar. They make use of organic metaphors and occasionally stretch them in expressively new ways, but conceptually they remain tied to the rationalist tradition of engineering, the work for instance of Pier Luigi Nervi. This can be seen by comparison with Gaudi's structures, especially Colonia Guell, where the splines and vectors of force are set against each other in a dynamic way. It is one thing to repeat the isostatic lines of force and make them poetic, as Calatrava does so well, but it is another to make them flex and push against each other in a continuously changing way. Fractals and dynamic expression are two signs of cosmogenic process so important to the new world view and its architecture. In the first edition of this book, 1977, I ended with Antonio Gaudi as the exemplar of the new direction, even though he had been dead for fifty years, and it curious that his work still sets a standard on the levels of symbolism, structural expression and the issue to which we now turn, fractal design.

Fractal Architecture

THE FRACTAL LANDFORM AND
CINEMATIC SECTION

Antonio Gaudi was also an inspiration for Enric Miralles, the Barcelona architect who died unexpectedly, at the height of his career, in 2000. Miralles developed notation systems for conceptualizing variable structures, and he employed them on several landform buildings. One method is to depict the sprawling context of his buildings with a Hockneyesque method of photo-collage. That is, he splices together a continuous image of changing perspectives as he moves through and around a building. This form of photo-Cubism reveals the fractal identity of a work, the way forms are self-similar but not self-same. (Fractal geometry derived from Benoit Mandelbrot's theories is illustrated below) Secondly, Miralles devised a method of what could be called "cinematic sectioning": the analysis of a large land-mass by making many cuts through it. The resulting sections reveal a sequence of varying topography, as if one took cinema stills and flipped through them to animate movement across the land. Cinematic sectioning has been used to depict the complex site of the Eurhythmics Center in Alicante, Spain (355, 356). Through the notation one follows the rise and fall of land waves as they move under ramps, and the method also choreographs the movement of people on the ramps. From these and other large-scale movements the building is generated. Indeed, the overall undulation of the Center is another fractal, this time one, which mimics the surrounding mountains. So the landform building not only sprawls like a geological formation but is actually a microcosmic representation; an idea not far from how a Chinese garden miniaturizes and "borrows the landscape."

Cinematic sectioning is a method of controlling the design of very large structures and it was used by several groups who entered the Yokohama Port Terminal Competition in 1995. This was an important event for the new paradigm with Greg Lynn, Reiser + Umemoto and the winners, Foreign Office Architects (FOA), all producing interesting architecture that emerged through nonlinear processes of design. The young team of FOA (Farshid Moussavi and Alejandro Zaero-Polo) worked previously for both Rem Koolhaas and Zaha Hadid and are connected to the Architectural Association in London, with all the apostolic

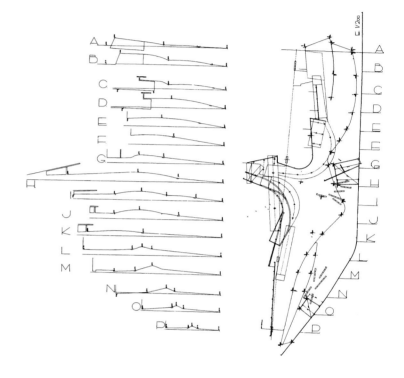

355 ENRIC MIRALLES, *Eurhythmics Center*, Alicante, Spain, 1993–94. The rise and spread of wave forms from A to G and H to P can be seen in this cinematic section.

356 *Eurhythmics Center*, the rise and fall, as Miralles said, "borrows the mountainscape" and its fractal forms.

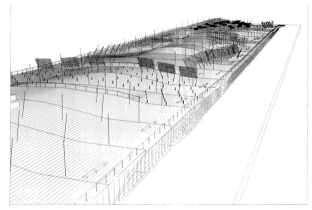

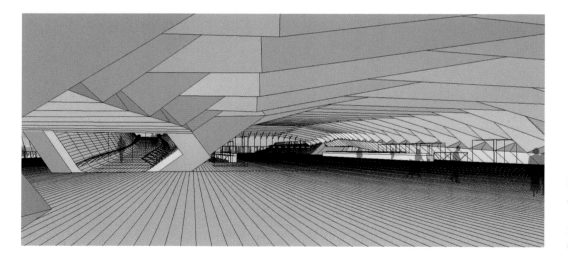

357 FOA, *Yokohama International Port Terminal*, model, 1995. The landform as usable building.

succession this implies. It is no surprise that their entry pushes several ideas of Complexity Architecture – folding, superposition and bifurcation – a step beyond their teachers.

Their landscape-building for Japan is a long, low horizontal-folded plate of steel that undulates across the water (357,358). Its structural strength is provided by the self-similar folds and the gentle undulations of the plates – flowing forms that are obvious metaphors of the sea. Paradoxically, the hard surface resembles a dry desert. It could be a moonscape pockmarked by activities strewn about in a carefully careless way, chaotic compositional tactics that Koolhaas termed "confetti" when he deployed them at the Parc de la Villette.

The multi-layered topography for Yokohama achieves diversity and unity, disjunction and continuity. The architects are looking for a seamless structure, like Lynn and Kipnis an alternative to collage and radical eclecticism, with which to deal with difference; a system they describe as "continuous but not uniform." They achieve this, once again, by folding various functions into a continuous surface full of feedback loops of circulation. When it is finished in 2003, the rich mixture of different uses may be hard to administer because the usual visual borders do not orient and divide different kinds of passengers. One can imagine international and local travelers arriving late for a ship and becoming mixed up together as they head for one of those eye-shaped folds that peer from one level to the next. These "bifurcations," as the architects call them following the complexity paradigm, unite different levels. Importantly they do so with a smooth continuity, rather like the way origami folds unite a complex pattern into a single sheet of paper.

In contrast to Eisenman's staccato grammar at the Aronoff Center, the grid, the fold and undulation are employed in a soft way that blurs distinctions. One floor warps a bit of itself into another, producing a characteristic "floor/door/window" and a sloping "floor/ramp." The question, as with Frank Lloyd Wright's Guggenheim Museum, is how usable this hybrid system will turn out to be. As the model and sections indicate, this ferry terminal is a very abstract system, a landscape of otherness, a surprising flatscape without the usual orientation points; it does not look like a building at all. The generic nature of the scheme, the architects claim following Koolhaas, is well suited to our stage of globalized late-Capitalism. Just as Mies van der Rohe designed the perfect isotropic space, everywhere the same to infinity, they turn their universal system into a kind of transcendental space: a sacred space without a religion. Artificial land, second nature, has reached a strange, functional apotheosis beyond even that of the Superdutch.

By contrast, the Israeli architect, Zvi Hecker, incorporates

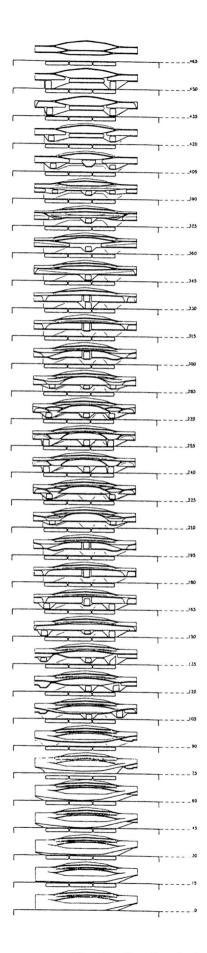

358 The cinematic sectioning shows a folded plate in steel – a self-stiffening structure.

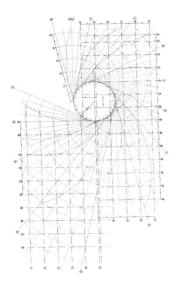  

359 ZVI HECKER, *Heinz-Galinski School*, Berlin, 1993–95. Spiral sunflower geometry (anti-clockwise) plus concentric curves, grid generated complex landforms and self-similar curves and fish-shapes.

representational signs into his fractal buildings, both the spiral and other conventional forms, but these are veiled and only apparent on second glance. The Heinz-Galinski School in Berlin creates an extended landform out of latent metaphors (359–361). Snake corridors, mountain stairways and fish-shaped rooms are pulled together with an overall sunflower geometry. It sounds constricting, but on the contrary these shapes flow together, as the plan reveals. The sunflower, with its spiral of movement towards a center, generates a general order, especially, when tied to two other geometries – the grid and concentric circles. The three systems make every room slightly different and the sunflower spiral results in a very strong pull to the heart of the school (the architect, when he saw it from a helicopter, said it looked like a friendly meeting of whales). Some may find this centrality obvious, the imagery insistent, but actually it is absorbed by the abstraction of the grammar.

This small institution for 420 pupils is the first Jewish school to be constructed in Germany for sixty years. Built in the leafy suburbs of Charlottenberg, it literally keeps a low profile – two to three storeys – and threads its sunflower geometry amid the existing trees. The most satisfying aspect is its urbanity. It creates tight curving streets, or walkways, which give a sense of mystery not unlike an historic town, where contingency has created the odd shapes and spaces. Here a restricted palette of gray concrete, silver corrugated metal and white stucco is interwoven with trees. Each of the three colors corresponds to a different geometric system. This allowed the contractors to understand and build the complex woven structure and, subsequently, allows students and visitors to interpret the complexity of the design.

Several discreet signs, such as a Jewish star, are placed in

360 *Heinz-Galinski School*, entrance, with its Jewish star veiled behind the pillar.

361 *Heinz-Galinski School*, The central, communal space around which the six forms spin. Gray, white and silver materials mark the three generative systems. Note the sign of the plan, upper right, punched out as a spiral void.

the background and their presence is felt at the same level as the architectural symbolism; for instance, the plan of the six petals, which is also punched into the concrete. The latter becomes a decorative logo and explanatory map for visitors. It also suggests the wider intentions of Hecker, which are to produce a cosmic order based on the omnipresent spiral form, and in particular, the solar dynamic of the sunflower. He has underlined the paradox of "a wild project" that has very precise mathematical construction. "Above all," he notes, "is its cosmic relationship of spiral orbits, intersecting one another along precise mathematical trajectories."[156] Here is a case where an architect explicitly engages iconographic aspects of the new paradigm, and the new sciences of complexity. Moreover, these signs and an abstract geometry are finely woven together.

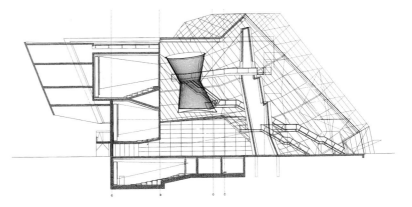

362 COOP HIMMELBLAU, *Cinema Center*, Dresden, 1993–98. Best seen at twilight when the silver-blue and gray forms dissolve into the urban landscape and fracture as a crystal glowing from within. The media center literally projects itself on exterior monitors as well as an explosion of uplighting.

363 The cross section reveals the self-similar angles, and the way movement systems of stair and elevator core are also inflected. Note the hanging "skybar," a double-cone designed with the artist Kiki Smith.

Often the fractal landform emerges as a consequence of urban forces, the large scale of a building program, the project for an infrastructure, or the contradiction between requirements. The intention is not so much to create fractals *per se* as to respond to these forces, and give them dynamic expression. A case in point is the media center designed by Coop Himmelblau in Dresden. Here the conjunction of eight cinemas and a large public space are the catalyst for angular fractals that lean and jut-out onto a public square (362–4). Wolf Prix, one of the designers, is inspired by the idea of creating the public realm, open and free for citizens, and cantilevered out to celebrate its presence. It is, he says, "liberated space carved out of the air" as if it were free as the air we breathe. Coop Himmelblau, has since the 1960s, carried forward the metaphor of their name, a cooperative of blue sky floating in the clouds, an idealistic and provocative metaphor intended to dissolve architecture.

Prix talks about a new space not defined by axes and monuments, as in Classical and Modern architecture, but, following the usual software nomenclature, one determined by tangents, vectors and diagonals. Contrast this with the more fluid method of folding. In the case of the biomorphic designers splines and different vectorial weights mould a more supple blob grammar; but here the vectors pull space apart in large, sharp facets. Seen from the exterior, the crystalline walls lean out precariously following different mullion grids, at different scales. It has fractals of rectangles, forty-five and sixty degrees; it conveys the order of a collapsing ice-floe, or a growing crystal on the glazed side. Around the other side the concrete tilts of the auditoria rake up and loom out in an equally ominous cantilever. It is a

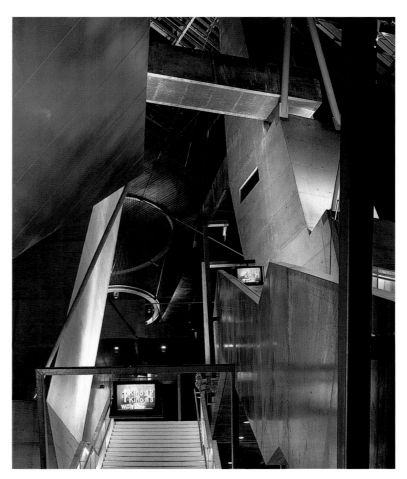

364 The fractal grammar carries through into the interior dramatizing entry up long stairs into a mysterious, dark Piranesian space and thence to the flickering electronic environment, architecture as frozen cinema.

365 ASHTON RAGGATT McDOUGALL, *Storey Hall*, Melbourne, 1993–96. Fractal forms based on the aperiodic tiling of Roger Penrose create larger patterns that never repeat exactly and yet are always self-similar.

threatening frenzy meant, as in some of Eisenman's work, to destabilize the viewer and, at the same time, excite and stimulate. This is haptic architecture of a dizzying kind, the kind of ecstatic architecture that emerged in the 1990s.[157]

Storey Hall in Melbourne is another exuberant fractal, and much more colorful (365–7). ARM, designers of the National Museum of Australia, were asked to remodel one unit along a main street in Melbourne, part of a university in a highly urbanized area. One intention was to hybridize a zone between two Classical buildings, a robust and academic one to the left and a commercial pastiche to the right. Their explosion of green and purple fractals is, however, more of a contrast with, than a blur of, its neighbors. At the same time, like Gaudi's Casa Batlo with which it is comparable, it acknowledges adjacent structures. The cornice line,

window scale and basic tripartition are all comparable.

At street level, Storey Hall presents a large green-and-purple doorway with the green folded plates of concrete blurring into purple folds (blurring, as with FOA, is a favorite term of the architects, here likened to smeared lipstick). As one justification Howard Raggatt cites the fact that green and purple were the heraldic colors of the previous inhabitants, Irish and feminist groups, as another he mentions this and the interior as like an amethyst. In this and other ways, the building takes its cues from history and nature, the typical Post-Modern method of building in time and historical depth.

An important contribution of the building is the development of the Penrose tiling pattern into an order that connects façade, floor, walls and ceiling into a single ornamen-

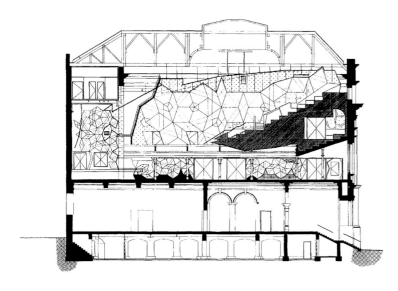

366 The Foyer transforms the color code and fractals into larger folded plates that compress into the space.

367a, b Fractal forms on the interior auditorium become acoustic tiles and a lighting system that, every so often, turn into a superordinate pattern of pentagons.

tal system. Roger Penrose, an Oxford mathematician, inventor and author, discovered a tiling pattern with five-fold symmetry that was previously thought to be impossible. Using a fat and thin rhombus, he created an aperiodic tiling system which, however far it is extended, never results in a cyclical, superordinate pattern larger than a pentagon (other tiling systems repeat at larger scales). This unusual, self-organizing order was later in 1984 discovered to exist in nature. It was termed a quasi-crystal, because it had an orientational but not translational order, whereas a crystal has both. Like a crystal it has a holistic order, but it also has a higher degree of complexity, since the pattern is everywhere slightly different. Quasi-crystals, with this fractal self-similarity, are potentially more suited to architecture than the repetitive use of elements.

Storey Hall suggests a new urbanism different from those of the past, neither the Classical ordonnance, nor the repetition of the curtain wall. It poses an interesting question. What if a whole street were ordered this way, what if a new complexity grammar replaced the monotony of, say, midtown 6th Avenue in New York? What if the city grew like a quasi-crystal, and an ever-changing order emerged which was never quite repeated? As the work of Batty and Longley on Fractal Cities has shown, there is an emergent order at the level of the region and megalopolis (324). The question this building raises without answering is whether the new paradigm can generate a coherent and continuous grammar as articulate and pleasing as its predecessors.

Most of nature's forms are continuously changing as they develop, making small modifications on a reiterated program. Benoit Mandelbrot explained these incrementally growing patterns in *The Fractal Geometry of Nature*, 1977, and contrasted them with the reigning Platonic and Euclidean assumptions. As he writes at the beginning of his manifesto, "Clouds are not spheres, mountains are not cones, coastlines are not circles, and bark is not smooth, nor does lightning travel in a straight line."[158] Rather, most of nature is irregular, fragmented, broken — or related to his neologism coming from the Latin *fractus*. Nature does not, except in the relatively rare instances of such things as planets and snowflakes, adopt a Euclidean form and even these can be carried out with fractal programs. Yet, as Mandelbrot shows, western metaphysicians and architects have disdained non-Euclidean forms as "amorphous" and "pathological." Modern scientists at the turn of the century and after damned them, as the supreme mathematician Henri Poincaré pointed out, as a "Gallery of Monsters."

Today, of course, they have been accepted in the scientific community and in the popular imagination through such things as the Mandlebrot Set and Chaos Theory. Strange attractors with a fractal dimension generate trees and mountain ranges and are shown to underlie the activity of the human brain and heart. Architects such as Daniel Libeskind and Thom Mayne, as well as those I have men-

368 *Primitive fractals*, the beginning stages of complexity (reading down from top left). Random Peano curve, Benoit Mandelbrot. The following generator, acting on the initiator (0,1) yields a way of sweeping a triangle: $N=4, R=1/2, D=2$.

Charles Jencks, *Fractal Table*, Scotland, 1995, with four sets of three self-similar drawers and four tops that pivot at different angles.

Daniel Libeskind, with the engineer Cecil Balmond, *The Spiral*, Victoria and Albert Museum extension, 1995–2003? Generated from a chaotic attractor that rises about a spiral, the exterior "spiral" has straight edges, and planes that rest on each floor below. Aperiodic tiles, "fractiles" in white ceramic underscore the larger fractal shapes, making it glisten like an ice-floe or crystal. This surface has greater complexity than Libeskind's Summer Pavilion for the Serpentine Gallery, 2001, which is conceptually another spiral of planes worked out with Cecil Balmond. Like origami paper architecture, it is a fold of flat aluminium sheets that interlock for support. However, the glistening bolts and seams on self-similar diagonals, as well as the interior exposed structure, do provide an elegant grammar that both follows and contrasts with the larger fractal planes. These tilt and cantilever in the green context as a glowing mineral, a silver pyrite.

Thom Mayne and Morphosis have designed the *Diamond Ranch School* in Pomona, 1998–2001, as a topographical abstraction of the steeply sloping site that is subject to landslides. Manipulating the requirements, including parking for 770 cars and large playing fields, the architects have created a set of simple fractal shapes that reflect the site as well as distant mountains. The main student activities are ingeniously folded into the slope in a central public space that zig-zags in syncopation with the tilted classrooms. Thus continuous landforms of gray concrete and corrugated metal either side provide a linear place of surprise and shade. In effect the meandering spine is a canyon and the adjacent folds are rock-faces and contours, an understated natural metaphor. Cuts at various point reveal planted space and rectilinear forms cantilevered over nature, Euclidean geometry versus an intense fractal geometry on the spine. The overall complexity of this mixture, and the site plan, is of a high order. (Tim Hursley).

tioned, explicitly make use of these attractors and invent such things as "fractiles," that is, aperiodic tiling shapes that never repeat at a superordinate level, just as the Penrose pattern continues to vary (368). These buildings again take up the landscape, both literally and metaphorically, and fold it for the most part with straightened fractal forms. Their shapes are like origami folds, pleats that are easier and cheaper to build than complex curves. The results are a primitive crystalline architecture on the way to becoming more articulate.

Without doubt the most convincing fractal building finished so far is Daniel Libeskind's Jewish Museum in Berlin, in a sense less a building than another usable landform. This won a design competition in 1989, opened in 1998 and finally was fitted out with Jewish memorabilia and artifacts in 2001. Attached to the older museum of Berlin History, it is entered underground from the German building to make the point that both cultures are related and continuous even if darkly so, in a subterranean sense. The history of the Berlin Jews, 240,000 of whom were deported, is integral to German history and Libeskind makes an architecture out of presenting the countless links as broken fragments *and* lines of connection (370–373).

Thus the zigzags are partly generated by lines connecting the points in Berlin where famous Jews and gentiles lived. Some of these references, and lines generating the scheme, are esoteric: those referring, as in previous work, to Mies van der Rohe, Walter Benjamin and Paul Celan, or Modernists who like the Jews were suppressed by the Nazis. But these arcane signs are also set against more accessible ones such as the six-pointed yellow Star of David that the Germans forced the Jews to wear. The same mixture of the esoteric and popular underlies another metaphor, that of Arnold Schoenberg's last opera, the unfinished *Moses and Aaron* which inspired Libeskind. Schoenberg was a quintessential modern twelve-tone composer and the opera breaks off at the point where Moses and Aaron are unable to complete their mission with the people of Israel: "Oh word, thou word that I lack!" – Moses laments his inability to lead the people to the promised land. The building's void expresses this inability to speak the word, whereas the zigzags show Aaron's determination to go forward, nevertheless.

This irregular path is another symbol that has many overtones – lightning bolt, Waffen SS, the dialectical zigzag of history. Libeskind speaks of "the unfathomable nature of the twentieth century," and looking at these bent forms in plan, elevation and detail one can see the architectural equivalent to chaotic Brownian motion, or at least some randomness. This is a route without a clear destination, the wandering search known in science as "the drunkard's walk." The tilts and jagged cuts in the façade are natural metaphors of not knowing precisely where you are going, and a form to be played off against the straight line, the void. Le Corbusier, in his Modernist phase, made the slightly preposterous claim that "civilisation is a right-angled state of mind" and, further, that "man travels in a straight line because he has an end in mind, while the zigzag is the pack donkey's way." This building questions both notions. History, as many have observed, is actually a complex mixture of linear and circular time, but it is Libeskind's point not to reconcile the two. They confront and interlace through each other like Jewish and German history, they do not come to some grand reconciliation.

Most symbolic and powerful is the concrete line, or what Libeskind calls "the voided void," that runs across the crooked forms, to make his basic metaphor: this became a book title, *Between the Lines*. The two lines interact in paradoxical ways. One travels along the zigzag through the galleries always returning to the void down the middle, but this organizational spine cannot be entered, but only traversed. The psychological reason is that the void is a mystery, the presence of an absence, the memory of those who were deported leaving very little, except their names and dates of birth carefully inscribed in two volumes that the Nazis noted down. Because there are few artifacts of their lives the museum has a problem of what to show, and the hollows make this vividly present, caverns to nothingness. At one

369 Daniel Libeskind was born just after the war in Lodz, Poland, in 1946. Most of his extended family had been murdered in the Holocaust, but his father and mother managed to survive. Libeskind was close to his father, Nachman, who lived well into his nineties, a man who kept his sense of humour and enjoyment of life amidst the suffering. Daniel, like his father, smiles a lot and shows the same indomitable optimism. At eleven he left Poland to live on an Israeli Kibbutz and in Tel Aviv where he concentrated on his musical education. Three years later he emigrated to New York and soon changed to architecture and, at the Cooper Union in New York, came under the influence of the architect and teacher John Hejduk. At the age of nineteen he became an American citizen, a status he has kept in spite of his zigzag life alternating between USA and Europe. After this a stint at Essex University, studying with Joseph Rykwert, deepened his historical background. Further travel and teaching took him to the Cranbrook Academy, then Milan, then a host of American institutions and finally Berlin, where he won a competition for a housing block for IBA. Although a professor at several universities he settled in Germany, if constant air travel to all parts of the globe can be called settling.

His early avant-garde projects influenced architects in the 1980s, their mixture of cabalistic and innovative spatial qualities took ambiguity and contradiction as far as they could go. The first real break was winning the competi-

tion for the Jewish Museum, Berlin, in 1989, an extraordinary work of architecture and a commission Libeskind, in effect, had been preparing for during most of his life. Its actual realization was equally remarkable, again a triumph of optimism over reality, and particularly the result of his wife, Nina's, untiring efforts. She organized political consent and support from many parts of the globe, not least Israel. Among other things, Daniel Libeskind is a prophet who energizes the young with his vision and spirit. At the beginning, the Libeskind Studio thrived more on creative student vigor than high pay, and the collegial ambience that Nina created around them.

Some of his early work was built on the themes of war, the tragedies of modernism and the conflict in society. These issues are faced directly and often result in a fractal, mysterious space that translates the content into the architecture. The Felix Nussbaum Haus in Osnabrück is typical. Opened in 1998, it holds the collection of a Jewish artist who survived during the 1930s and early 1940s by hiding in various houses before being captured. Nussbaum painted the horrors of the Jewish diaspora. Libeskind's building presents different parts of the artist's life with changes in the architecture, with cuts and stark shifts in material. A minimalist narrative clearly conveys feelings of anger, claustrophobia, fear – yet dynamism and resilient life.

By November 2001, Daniel Libeskind had won seventeen competitions, lost eight, and rec-

eived six private commissions. In a profession where success can deaden one's sensibility, as much as the more usual failure and loss of commissions, his optimistic energy and infectious good humor are perhaps the most notable qualities. This may be due to the fact that he practices architecture as an avocation of choice, and has not let the professional drudge and occasional defeats get the better of him. For this and much else he acknowledges a debt to his wife, Nina. He reads poetry, draws, and continues to be inspired by musical themes. Indeed his architecture can be read as a kind of musical score, just as his treatment of materials reflects a kind of resonant sound. But he has underscored the difference of disciplines remarking that, while you can compose sad music and write about depression in literature, architecture is naturally an optimistic profession because it builds the future.

370–72 DANIEL LIBESKIND, Jewish Museum, Berlin 1989–2001. Self-similar forms, angles, slashes and lines – a fractal grammar put to symbolic use. A matrix of lines predominate on the faces of the building, connecting places where Berlin Jews lived. "These are the lines across which one could send a message, a letter, an imaginary thought, an intention towards someone, somewhere." Libeskind's work, while highly abstract, has a symbolic core.

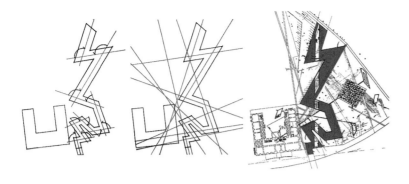

373 *Jewish Museum*, plans showing the void running through the zig-zag, or random walk that turns back on itself. The turns are self-similar, less and more than ninety degrees, and there is no single convergence of lines, though there is a rough direction. (C. J. analysis with Hong Kong students)

374 DANIEL LIBESKIND, *Imperial War Museum – North*, Trafford, Manchester, 1998–2002. The globe shattered through conflict and reassembled as three curved shards: the tall Air Shard marks the entrance, and holds flying instruments of war in its open structure; the Earth Shard is a huge exhibition area with even the floor curving gently, the Water Shard curves down towards the adjacent canal and minesweeper moored there. The aluminium structure achieves both a smooth continuity and, on the Air Shard, a glowing permeability. This huge expressive structure is both a giant advertisement, in the sense of Venturi's Duck Building, and an enigmatic signifier of conflict and its resolutions.

point, where it explicitly becomes the Holocaust Tower, it can be entered. One looks up to find an aura of gray light spilling down the concrete walls, from no apparent source because the roof is capped. This is the termination of the building, and "the dead end of all values."[159] Hollow spaces reverberate with emptiness; heavy blankness seems to squeeze in compression.

Facing the content of this building is similar to visiting a Holocaust Museum, though it is not specifically one of them. Several were constructed in the 1980s, and then many more by the time Libeskind was designing this building. By then writing on the Holocaust had reached voluminous proportions and had led to philosophical disagreements. Jean-François Lyotard, the French philosopher, claimed that Auschwitz was a crime ushering in post-modernity. Zygmunt Bauman's disturbing book, *Modernity and the Holocaust*, 1989, showed some truth behind this. Bauman, like Libeskind, is a Polish Jew who survived the Holocaust and lived for awhile in Israel before emigrating to Britain. He makes the point that modernity is indirectly but importantly connected to the Final Solution. Its emphasis on instrumental reason, cost-benefit analysis, the placement of rational economic calculation above other concerns; its methods of mass-production applied to killing – all these tendencies of modernity which are still present – played into a Holocaust. They have done so again and again with such things as the mass-bombing of Cambodia. Modernity has this dark side,

something that Libeskind confronts and turns into a building art, and this explains its strange ambivalence.

The catacombs of Rome, the underground pylons of Constantinople, the prisons of Piranesi have some of this feeling. But in the Berlin museum this sublime gravitas is momentarily switched into its opposite, and tempered by the white galleries and their shafts of light. These windows are again zigzag fractals or rectangular cuts that punctuate the walk with views of the city and greenery. The most intense moment comes as one climbs the long stairway, bisected by flying beams and window crosses reminiscent of El Lissitsky. These add to the sense of tension. Everywhere light is used to give violent pulses of energy and exterior

375 IWM-N Libeskind asked me to help design the twenty-four fractal gardens, the time zones of the earth, and they are divided up into the main types of warfare. The ground war garden (left) is to the north, the fire war garden is the parking area (right). Earth strata and time are represented by fossils and layers of weaponry. Further gardens (sea and air war) are connected by a fractal water path.

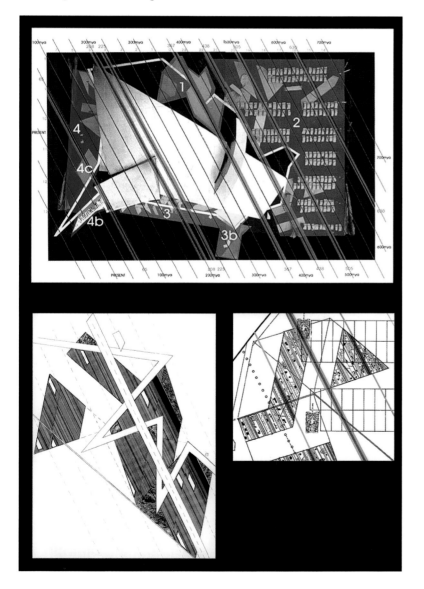

views of the sky. Perhaps the greatest surprise, given its subject and pervasive gray tonality, is the feeling of exhilaration. It is one of the most hopeful buildings in Europe, the harbinger of a new culture, one that can acknowledge its past and make an architecture from it.

Daniel Libeskind, unlike many of the architects discussed here, is not particularly attached to computer design. His projects are shaped more through countless drawings and cardboard models. He works as a sculptor of space, like Gehry, except that he is more concerned with the symbolic and esoteric meaning of his forms, designs that will often have a narrative behind them. A case in point is the Imperial War Museum, North, located in the Trafford area of Greater Manchester (374). This is made from shards of the earth, fragments of the globe, curved sections that symbolize a world in conflict yet one always trying to be reassembled. The earth as a shattered set of shards that must be put back together again has a fourteenth-century precedent in the Kabbalah of Rabbi Isaac Luria, and it obviously has a relevance to the present.

Libeskind sets off three curved shards – the largest "earth segment" is the main exhibition space, the highflying entrance shard is the "air segment" (to hold planes and missiles), the smallest falling towards the canal is the "water shard." "Fire," the fourth Greek element, is what war produces and is evident in the displays. These shards of the earth are then tilted slightly and have oblique windows or voids punched into them; thus the sense of movement and conflict is furthered. On the interior a light-and-sound show animates the surfaces with scenes of war and its consequences, but these simulations are contrasted with real artifacts.

The idea behind the museum is to focus not so much on war and its technologies, but on peoples' experience of conflict. There is a strong social intention behind the Imperial War Museum, North, and a stated desire to reach out to the twenty million people that inhabit this region. Hence the symbolic emphasis on the *north* part of the globe, represented on the site, and the way its Manchester location, also empasized, generates the fractured garden shards (375). These, representing the twenty-four time zones of the earth, are based on Buckminster Fuller's geodesic of the globe, and so they are angular fractals. But the large shapes are curves as well, ones whose bends are so gentle and at such a huge scale as to give the impression that a giant box has suffered melt-down. This uncanny, almost anamorphic quality, is enhanced by the smoothness of the profile and the fact that the Air Shard is constructed of permeable struts so it seems to glow. Libeskind proposes that it becomes a giant screen so that news flashes of war from around the world – CNN, Russiantv, China, the Middle East, Africa, and elsewhere – keep us aware of Churchill's view: that war is a permanent condition of the globe. This depressing idea is conveyed in a straightforward way, with neither sentimentality nor celebration. The fact that it can result in a striking monument

376 FRANK GEHRY, *Fish Lamp*, 1984, and the surfaces of complexity. How to develop a continuously curving grammar? Nature has shown one way in varying the scales, or feathers, with the increase in curvature of the surface. Ironically, although Gehry grasped the point with his early fish and snake lamps, he did not exploit the grammar in his first large buildings with shingles, the Vitra Headquarters, 1989–92, and Bilbao museum, 1992–97. These buildings repeat the same shingle endlessly whereas the bird, armadillo, fish and snake vary the dimension of the unit as the curve changes. Nature produces true fluid fractals, whereas architecture has yet to reach this point. With computer production it cannot be long before it happens, and the new paradigm reaches complete expression.

is all the odder, but Libeskind's best work is inspired by basic symbolic concepts carried through with complete clarity.

FLUID FRACTALS AND FRANK GEHRY

The undoubted master of the fluid fractal is Frank Gehry who, since 1990, has made them the staple of his building grammar. But his interest in the form goes way back and it is important to follow this slow and patient development to understand how he could bring it to fruition in Bilbao. It starts in the late 1960s when he developed the series known as Easy Edges Cardboard Furniture, ideas that were extended crucially in the middle 1980s in a number of fish and snake lamps that used scales to go around tight corners. From these "small scaled" experiments (pun intended by Gehry) he realized two important points: that a curved geometry of light and shadow would emerge naturally from shingled elements, and that it could be economically con-

structed. Further experiments on a small conference room for Chiat Day and an exhibition of his own work in Minneapolis, 1986, abstracted the fish shape into a whole room. Now it leaned to one side, as a broken parabola or segments of a curve, and had a pointed arch that ran down the spine. Already then, by the mid-1980s, he had developed the basic petal shape of Bilbao that was to be varied in so many ways. An actual Fish Restaurant in Japan in the shape of a jumping carp, at the same time, translated the petal-shape section into a rotated curve (376).

Much has been made of Gehry's love for the fish form. As a youth he was taunted by antisemitic locals for being a fish-eater; his grandmother kept carp in the bathtub until it could be used to make gefilte fish for Friday evening's Sabbath meal; it is the sign of Pisces, as well as a Christian sign and, to Freudians, a phallic symbol. When Post-Modernists started using ironic quotations from Classicism in 1980, Gehry responded, 'why not fish?' There are enough reasons, formal and strategic, for him to adopt the shape as a personal talisman, but as far as architectural history is concerned it has two pertinent qualities. Its gentle curve and fat volume can form usable space and, symbolically, it relates building very generally to nature. For this last reason, especially when given a sharp edge, it might be called a petal-shape, and nowhere more than at its apotheosis, the new Guggenheim Museum in Bilbao.

This near masterpiece summarized possibilities of the new paradigm and, as far as a single building can, changed the direction of architecture. When completed in October 1997 the profession and the public realized architecture had curved off on a new tack, and they both celebrated the fact. It was selected over other designs by the entrepeneur/director of the Guggenheim Museum, Thomas Krens. Realizing that the Guggenheim collection, like that of many other museums, was consigned mostly to storage, Krens developed a form of lend lease program for art, imagining the global potential of having outposts in Venice, Berlin, St. Petersburg, Las Vegas and elsewhere. His gamble was that Gehry's unorthodox design would be the booster for the second stage of his risky program. It was, and for the city of Bilbao as well. It changed the fortunes both of this rust-belt metropolis and the fledgling art empire. It even lent weight to that 1980s cliché, the museum as cathedral, art as the new religion.

Considered in the bloodline of Post-Modernism "Bilbao," as it was called simply by architects, was another enigmatic signifier following on from Ronchamp and the Sydney Opera House. It linked together opposite functions and meanings into a multivalent blend and, in particular, its provocative shapes called forth a series of metaphors. Critics spontaneously termed it, among other things, an explosion of light, a ship hitting the rocks or a collision in a harbour, a starburst of energy, unstoppable white lava, overlapping waves, fish thrashing, a Construc-tivist artichoke and a shiny sequinned swimmer about to burst out of her bathing suit (377,378). Metaphors are 'a carrying over' from one idea to another, a metamorphosis of categories and it is this ability to be both suggestive and elusive that, I have argued above, makes the enigmatic signifier so powerful (53). From the entrance the building looks like an eruption of metallic flowers emerging from a white limestone base; it has the presence of a robust, urban plant.

It is the interaction with the city that makes the building convincing. It takes on the colors of the Nervion River to one side, the metallic glint of the cars and trains that run over and beside it, the limestone of the old nineteenth-century buildings. Some of the gallery spaces are rectilinear — an effective contrast to what happens above — and one of them stretches under the high-speed motorway and bridge to reach up on the other side. This petal serves as another entrance. It also becomes another landform that ties the building into large-scale technology and the sprawl of the city, urban realities that are accepted not denied by this inclusive work.

Considered abstractly as a fractal, the building has approximately twenty-six varying petals. They reach in different directions and then come to a point that extends as a vertical line (379,380). Just as the flutes of a Doric column sculpt light and shade, so the pinched petals create a shadow line. The arris or fillet defines each volume in a supple way,

also giving orientation lacking in most blob architecture. Compared to Gehry's later work in Seattle, for instance, the shapes have definition and are less amorphous. In Bilbao the rooms are like leaves on a branch, part of a family of forms. Since they are also non-Euclidean, the contractors initially found them hard to fathom and remember, so each petal was given a name — Cobra, Fish, Boot, Potemkin, Zorro — as a mnemonic device. A consequence of enigmatic architecture is that it has to be named before it can be pinned down, and built. In the square world of New York, or Mies, one can navigate or construct almost without thinking.

The contrasts with Modern architecture are obvious but worth stating. Whereas mass-produced units are endlessly repeated, these differing shapes are easily fabricated by computer. Their slight changes also provoke a response. Here they were systematized in three dimensions by a French software, CATIA, which had been developed to rationalize the complex curves of the Mirage jet fighter. This program allowed the interior steel and exterior limestone to be cut with a minimum wastage, it allowed changes in a design to be immediately understood and costed by all the separate contractors. According to local architects who built the New Guggenheim, the curves added only about ten or fifteen per cent to the basic costs.[160] Before the advent of computer design and fabrication the varying curves would have tripled the price of such a project. The building cost about $100 million and, to drive in the significance of this figure, it turns out to be just half the cost of a comparable museum landmark, London's remodel of the Tate Modern. Thus, through computer production, a fractal building is competitive with a repetitive one. This is one of the deep lessons of Bilbao. It shows we have entered a new paradigm because it is credible at both the sensual *and* economic levels.

The interior is equally convincing, and especially so in the age of the white cube, the period when so much art is decontextualized and treated as an abstract object against a clinical background.[161] It is true most of the galleries here are white, but some are colored, and there is great variation in lighting and shape: nothing so remorseless and deadening to experience as the repetition of eighty-two white cubes at the Tate Modern. There is a very long and large 'fish' gallery with Richard Serra's curved arc at its center piece, and what Gehry calls the Classical galleries with top light spilling down through the center of a square plan, and also small-scaled rooms for prints (381). Some are curved and painted, others are turned into art specific sites for regional work, or commissioned paintings by Francesco Clemente.

The central atrium that provides orientation for all the complexity is the most dynamic space (382). Here all the surfaces come together, pulling in the outside titanium and views of the river and mountains — spinning them together into an ecstatic whirl. There is no other twentieth-century space as rhetorically energetic as this. The result is a new kind of ambiguous architecture, more folded on to itself

377, 378 FRANK GEHRY, *New Guggenheim*, Bilbao, 1992–97. The building is extremely sensitive to changes in the Nervion River and the weather. Metaphors of the New Guggengeim drawn by Madelon Vriesendorp bring out the suggestive overtones of this building – Constructivist artichoke [lower right], fish, mermaid and boat – it is the capacity to mean many more things that makes the enigmatic signifier a multivalent symbol. Compare with Ronchamp (54–59).

380 *Long Gallery, glass walls and titanium* in self-similar curves. Gehry models his buildings at many scales, inside and out. Then the CATIA software (right) works out the volumes following a wooden model and calculates exact dimensions as seen from any point, or any cut through a complex curve. These dimensions are then translated onto the bent steel under-sheets and then onto the pre-bent titanium cladding allowing most of the tolerances to be worked out ahead of time in the factory. Modernist critics, such as Martin Pawley, had attacked this kind of surface because of its dents and imperfections. Conservative critics, such as Vincent Scully, faulted the insubstantiality of the skin, while others remarked on the stains (not Gehry's fault and soon to be cleaned up). But shingled titanium, and the way it reflects light on its own curves, and pillows slightly, has special qualities that have created a new aesthetic.

CATIA

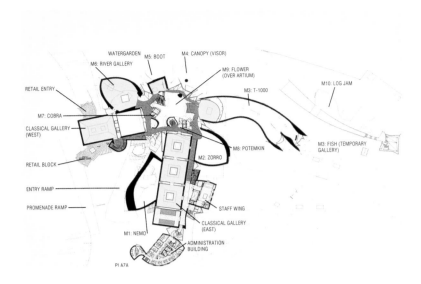

379 *Guggenheim Plan*. The curved petal forms were given names – "Cobra, Boot, Potemkin, Zorro" etc., – so that contractors could orient themselves. Visitors are always returned to the centrally placed atrium, and its views out over the river and mountains. The longest gallery extends under the highway and emerges as a side entrance, a Venturian Highflyer in scale with the high-speed traffic.

than the glass box that introduced Modernist notions of transparency. Here are reflections of reflections, the handling of glass facets and their intersections that cause a virtual image to splinter into a thousand fragments. Views are partly veiled by walls of light that lead the eye up to the public ramps and roof terraces, which in turn give onto the urban landscape – making the museum a true celebrant of the city. Indeed, from the very early box-like shapes of the first scheme to the final realization, Gehry has captured the idea of a miniaturizing Bilbao, a mini version of plural urban fabric. With all this it even manages to reflect nature and the idea of cosmic change as well.

The building is justly celebrated as a great work of architecture, and a hard act to follow, both for Gehry and other architects. Yet for that very reason, because it has become the standard for the new paradigm to surpass, it is worth stressing a shortcoming, and acknowledge some criticism of his approach. The most repeated criticism is that the building upstages the art, overpowers it through sheer bravado. Having visited Bilbao on many occasions I do not find this to be the case. The galleries are understated backgrounds, slightly var-

381 The long gallery curves slightly and creates interesting contrasts with its structure and top-light scoops that twist towards the overpass. The heavy Richard Serra has a perfectly lightweight foil.

382 The atrium has curved glass walls that compress into the space and layer it again with the pinched arris, so that reflections and transparencies are made even more ambiguous. There are so many curves and contrasts that one's eye keeps shifting restlessly, the rhetoric of the moving city.

ied in shape and lighting but never in competition with the art within. The architectural rhetoric, such as it is on the interior, simply heightens one experience, whets one's appetite for seeing, keeps one alert and excited. The problem, as far as the new paradigm is concerned, is a conceptual one, the relation between the details and the whole building.

In a perfected work of architecture, and the New Guggenheim aims in this direction, the underlying philosophy is carried through in the ornament and structure. The Miesian corner I-beam, however much it became a fetish, expressed the Modernist notion of an inner structural truth; the refinements of the Greek temple, Gothic cathedral, and Renaissance church were consistent with the philosophy of the whole building. The failing of this museum is that the fractal nature of the plan, structure and petals is not carried through into the skin. This consists of millions of titanium shingles of the same rectangular dimension. As they go around different curves, unlike the scales of the snake, they are all the same size, not self-similar (375). They have neither the visual nor the logical dynamism that would result had they been dimensioned and cut by computer, as the rest of the building has been shaped. Gehry has admitted this shortcoming, it may be due to the added cost of variations, and he seeks to overcome it in the future.[162] This problem may not concern the first-time visitor impressed by the extraordinary shapes, but on second and third visit, it makes the endless repetition of the shingle seem a bit like wallpaper – and inconsistent with the whole.

The most serious critique of Gehry's recent work is that it is "a computer-driven version of a Potemkin [false-fronted] architecture of conjured surfaces," as Hal Foster puts it.[163] Foster, usually an acerbic art critic, writes that Venturi's distinction between the decorated shed and duck are collapsed into Gehry's "decorated ducks." The Experience Music Project in Seattle is typical of these pop hybrids, and they have the faults of both Modernism and Post-Modernism, the willful monumentality of the one and faux populism of the other. They deny the relationship between interior space and exterior expression, as well as surface and structure, so they are not even good sculpture, but rather "regressive" and "academic," contemporary versions of the Statue of Liberty. There is a *little* truth to these strictures, especially as in Seattle where the rolled I-beams are tortured into double reverse curves (383). The computer-driven robots may have dimensioned and cut the thousands of all-different flanges and stiffeners – and that may have saved money – but as Gehry himself admits the whole $250 million project is excessive: "It's one-of-a-kind. Nobody is going to build anything like it again: it's too expensive – I can give you a flat piece of metal for one dollar; a single curve, like a cylinder for two dollars, but when you smoosh [American for 'scrunch'] it about, it's ten times more."[164] The "smoosh" quoted here for an English audience might have referred to the Nike "swoosh," or "swoopy" image that the client, the

Microsoft mogul Paul Allen, asked for; or perhaps the 1950s America blob, the Schmoo. Whatever gesture or infantile character may have been intended, there is a populist Frank that every now and then hijacks the brain of the deeper Gehry, especially when the building commission is *meant* to express something pop. In this building the musical tradition epitomized by Jimi Hendrix breaking his guitar (which is depicted on the roof).

That is to say, Gehry has a weakness for the naff gesture. He also occasionally falls into the trap of the signature architect, using his brand tune on a building type where it is inappropriate. For instance, the metal cascade solution, fitting for the Samsung Museum of Modern Art where it was first attempted in 1995, is then wrapped all over a Cleveland business school. "Let them eat titanium," "managers are the new artists," such malapropisms seem to imply, and the clients may happily mistake this artistic license for flattery. Semantic meltdown is, as this book sadly reveals, a common failure of the age.

Yet taken as a whole, which is the only way to take an architect's work, Gehry's indiscretions are rare and they come both from his willingness to take risks and his mixed self-assessment. He said on the BBC: "I'm not the great architect for the ages. I am nothing – I'm just an architect, I go to work everyday, I listen to the clients and I try to do my best work."[165] Some of this may be false modesty but, at the same time as he seeks to be the number one architect and get the best jobs, he steps back hesitantly in self-doubt, and seems to say, "I'm not an intellectual, nor a leader, nor a perfectionist, nor any of that. I'm simpler than you think, I'm a *bricoleur*, a backwoodsman, just call me Daniel Boone." These, or words like them, are what he has said to me, as he shrugs off the mantle of a Le Corbusier I put on his back. Perhaps, in his reluctance to be more than a good creative architect, he resembles Alvar Aalto the most (384).

At any rate, like it or not, he has backed into the role of the world's No. 1, leading the new paradigm and getting its plum commissions. Some of this, like the upscale work for Condé Nast, is experimental froth, lucrative jobs that allow him to push architectural ideas as far as money allows (385). In this case, in a cafeteria for those who work at *Vogue* and *Vanity Fair* among other magazines, it means laminated glass that swirls in triple curves, no less. At the centre are a series of goldfish bowls where the prime denizens of the deep go to "see and be seen," where a power lunch is carefully orchestrated theatre of about ten people per table, set up on a stage. There the chosen few carefully calibrate changing social relations through what must be the ultimate glass curtain wall – frozen in the shape of a billowing curtain – not only to spy the other dazzling luminaries, but to see further billows of blue titanium. This is pure visual pleasure. The fractal grammar of the cafeteria pushes the Bilbao fillet one swirl further, to a gentle double-S, a minor innovation but an effective visual trick. It creates ambigui-

383 FRANK GEHRY, *Experience Music Project*, Seattle, 1995–2000. The structure has 280 undulating, different, heavy ribs with reverse curves. These were rolled by a robotic machine especially made for the job, and the curtain walling was also dimensioned and cut in thousands of different pieces by a computer. The resultant blob grammar can be glimpsed above, 339, but the clunky and expensive structure is revealing enough. Too heavy a price was paid to torture I-beams into reverse curves: nature does not bend against itself this way. Ironically, as Gehry points out, a building often looks better before it is finished, when all the layers of construction (and reality) can be seen in contrast, and understood. (FOG/A).

ties between foreground and background, glass and titanium, transparency and reflection.

In other cases his success means he can often pick the most prestigious job going, such as the project for the New Guggenheim in New York. This, if built, will be either a spectacular success, or cataclysmic failure, the ultimate risk-taking in a new society of high risk.[166] Pitched at about $1 billion, it is the ultimate gamble in an art world that has inflated along with the 1990s stock market. The problem for museums, as investors on a roll, is how to ride the wave without being crushed. Not to get into the market and build an eye-catching monument, and expand, is to miss an opportunity and lose out to competitors. The cost of a spectacular museum such as Bilbao may be as low as $100 million or higher than the Tate Modern's $200 million and, if successful like them can be a money spinner. Studies of the New Guggenheim in Bilbao showed it brought in 1.3 million visitors in 1998, 1.1 million in 1999, and by 2000 a total of 3 million. Visitors were mostly from outside the Basque Country, 87%, and they directly increased the tourist spending by over $400 million in two years. The additional tax revenue for the city amounted to more than $70 million, and the museum attracted 137 corporate members, with all that implies for the fortune of the region.[167] The implications of the Bilbao Effect were obvious. If a city can get the right architect, at the creative moment in his or her career,

and take the economic and cultural risk, it can make double the initial investment in about three years. It can also change the fortunes of a declining industrial region. To put it crudely, the tertiary economy of the culture industry is a way out of modernist decline: post-modernize, or sink.

Hence the countless demands for little or big Bilbaos elsewhere: Daniel Libeskind's V&A in Britain; Koolhaas' work for the Guggenheim/Hermitage alliance in Las Vegas; Calatrava's City of Arts and Sciences in Valencia; Eisenman's design for Santiago; and Coop Himmelblau's winning project for Lyon (386). These are just the most worthy designs in the new paradigm that flow from the Bilbao Effect, and there are even more in other paradigms that result from the same pressures. Like the outburst of cathedrals in the first millennium, this second flowering has social, cultural and spiritual origins. But the museum as cathedral poses great economic and philosophical risks.

385 FRANK GEHRY, *Condé Nast Cafeteria*, New York, 1996–2000. Laminated glass panels with a twist and S-curve are self-similar fractals related to those in the background in blue titanium. The fillet or pleat of Bilbao reaches maximum complexity. Gehry characteristically pushes ideas on small-scale, high-cost commissions. (Condé Nast).

Artists are not saints, curators make bad priests, museum directors may not understand big business, the art market may crash, and as Matthew Arnold long ago observed, art is no substitute for religion. None of these truths, however, stop the runaway growth, nor the displacement of the church, as the central actor in the city, by the gallery. Nor guarantee the money will continue to flow to support the leviathans once they are built.[168] High risk indeed.

The Guggenheim for Lower Manhattan was secretly under design in 1998, and finally unveiled in a series of campaigns, starting in early 2000 and continuing with the extraor-dinary touring exhibition of Gehry's work, in 2001–2. Herbert Muschamp and *The New York Times* were ardent supporters of the proposal, and by November 2000, after Krens had raised a lot of money and Mayor Rudolph Giuliani and the City got behind it, with a pledge of $32.8 million, it looked a distinct possibility. The arguments gained credibility after a study by financial specialists, McKinsey & Co. They showed the potential benefits, presumably based on the Bilbao Effect: an annual museum attendance of 2.5–3.5 million visitors; an annual economic impact of $570–710 million; 4,300 to 6,700 new jobs created, and an annual increase in city and state tax revenues of from $50 to $70 million.[169] If the gamble worked New York would have a new focus over the East River, exploiting the beautiful edges of a city that has always sold them off for highways and warehouses. Finally Manhattan, invariably nervous of high culture and great architecture, might take the plunge. The river site could become the new Venice.

Gehry's proposal, like all of his schemes at the halfway stage of development, looks exuberant, dangerous, imprecise and possibly brilliant. At this point it consists of a forty-storey glass-and-masonry tower, that unfurls, and a lower set of metallic curls that billow above five massive pylons and a covered public park (387,388). The metallic curls are in scale with the urban backdrop, and this means they are massive ribbons of about ten storeys each! The metaphors of travelling clouds and cascading waves lie behind their generation, and it is obviously a gamble whether their huge size will make them empty gestures or heroically floating images of nature. Equally ambiguous at this stage are the public water gardens. They might become either damp, dirty, windswept plazas, or a convivial place for those thousands who work near Wall Street; a set of rounded piers with sculpture, where one might shelter and explore while the ships pass nearby, or perhaps go to a public meeting. The proposal is curved in plan and opens out above to let in enough light and air. Given the architect's record of developing a scheme well beyond this notional stage, I would say that he might well give the giant clouds substance and real materiality and scale. But it is too early to say, and there are the questions of his age, early seventies, and above all the uncertainties caused by September 11, 2001. As he said in an interview that November:

Priorities are going to change. Architecture might become marginalized because safety will become paramoun. – We've enjoyed a period of euphoria in the last thirty years in the US and in Europe for the last ten. We were happy, we enjoyed ourselves – That period has perhaps ended. Now we must think more about safety – I don't think [the New York Guggenheim] will ever be built. It was just a dream.[170]

But equally, after a period of recovery and reflection, it is possible that the building could become a symbol of New York's regeneration and hope. It has the potential to become something more than a museum, a true public building if the programme expands as it might. The risk Gehry and the Guggenheim have taken so far, must be equaled by the politicians and businessmen. A museum with an ice-skating rink at its heart is not enough to sustain the rhetoric and cost of the form. As for the new institution "museum as cathedral," by November 2001, as sceptics predicted, it was going bust. Admissions at the Guggenheim were down by almost

386 COOP HIMMELBLAU, *Musée des Confluences*, competition wining entry, January 2001. Situated at the confluence of the rivers Rhône and Saône, and also next to trains and bridges as at Bilbao, this science museum is seen by the architects as a "crystal cloud of knowledge/a hybrid." The crystal part is a monumental urban anteroom, while the cloud is the black box of an interactive museum. A double cone connects the two. This typology and some of the forms are similar to the architects' work in Dresden (361) although here the blob grammar replaces the angular. Like Gehry's cloud metaphor for New York, the huge billowing structure floats above public space on giant pylons of services and freight elevators.

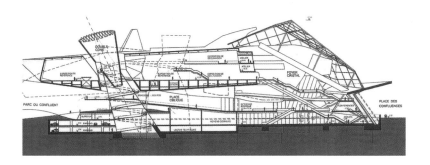

Born in Toronto in 1929, Frank O. Gehry studied architecture at USC in Los Angeles and then urbanism at Harvard. Working in the early 1960s with pragmatic Modernists such as Victor Gruen and William Pereira, he developed a skill at commercial realism, something that was further transformed by contact with artists, in particular Rauschenberg, Johns and those in LA. From them he learned that throw-away objects could be beautiful, or at least interesting and evocative. Using detritus and the disregarded as his material, he fashioned an *ad hoc* aesthetic in his own house in Santa Monica, of 1978–79. For the next ten years he produced one inventive bricolage after another, from cheap materials such as chain-link fence, and turned Dirty Realism into Clean Poetry. Perhaps he learned this aesthetic from working part-time in his grandfather's hardware store between the ages of ten and seventeen. In any case, the funk aesthetic of the artists, and wood-butcher architects of the West Coast was taken to new levels of heterogeneity. The variety of materials and styles reflect by analogy the heterogeneity of Los Angeles life, and for this reason Gehry led the LA School of Morphosis, Eric Moss, Frank Israel, Craig Hodgetts and Ming Fung. Sometimes also called the Gehryschule, this is an institution for which he does not seek credit. Not only is he an autodidact, but also something of a loner, a reason he prefers the label of "Daniel Boone" before others.

A regret of his life was chang-ing his name from Goldberg to the "less Jewish" Gehry, something he did a few years after he left Canada at eighteen. His admitted paranoia when he first started practice stemmed not only from his background, but his taste for the disregarded and the fact that he was something of an outcast among West Coast architects. The frontispiece to his 1984 monograph features his words "Being accepted isn't everything," and he has been in analysis for years by his good friend, Milton Wexler. As in Eisenman's case, this has made him very self-aware and sensitive to others, particularly clients with whom he has formed close relationships. It has also meant he adopts several persona, has appeared in several roles including that of "Frankie P. Toronto" in *Il Corso del Coltello*, a performance in collaboration with artists. He was also photographed as a Toronto Maple Leaf Goalie (he actually plays hockey, with his office team). While for many years on the fringe in LA, with his competition winning entry for the Walt Disney Concert Hall, in 1988, he finally made it right into the heart of the city. But even this victory was delayed, and building had to await The Bilbao Effect before the local power structure was shamed into funding the design.

If his first period was a kind of Modernist minimalism carried out with cheap materials, then after 1975 he developed a post-modern spatial complexity with layered structure, exposed studs, and interpenetrating services. The juxtaposition of different materi-als and objects combined with pavilion planning led to the next step. At a poetic level this consisted in a method akin to Surrealism and the Still Lifes of Giorgio Morandi. The Winton Guest House of 1983–87 best illustrates this compositional technique of placing one abstract volume and material against another. The last period starts with the work for the Vitra furniture company in 1987, his first European commission. Here Gehry goes on to explore the vermiform grammar that Eisenman was also developing. Growing out of his fish and snake lamps, these curved forms were at first chunky and warped, created by taking cheap boxes of space and distorting them slightly. The pragmatic realism of this approach was deepened by the use of computer software, the French CATIA system, which could rationalize the shaping of stone and steel, cutting out waste, using all the leftovers. Thus, by 1991, after going through four stages of patient develop-ment, Gehry turns the commercial realism of the early years into the uncanny lyricism of Bilbao, and when this is finished in 1997 his efforts are finally acknowledged on the world stage.

Essential to this story is the support of his family, particularly that of his wife the Panamanian-born Berta Isabel Aguilera. She not only handles the office finances but provides the ironic humor, and perspective, when Gehry dines with power brokers and Presidents. Gehry is not pompous, and a key to his success is that he actually likes his clients, a rarity among architects.

388 FRANK GEHRY, *New Guggenheim Museum*, New York, 1998–. The model shows the East River context of piers and sixty-storey skyscrapers. Historically the city has not exploited its two great rivers beyond their utilitarian roles and this building could set a precedent for looking outwards. The fractal landform has here risen to forty storeys, in the tower, and consists of twenty storey billowing clouds – a fantastic gamble.

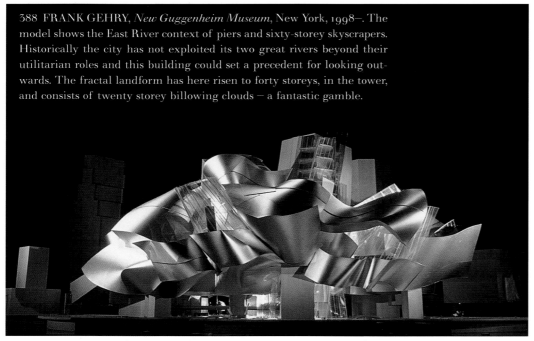

387 Above: LAB with Bates Smart, *Federation Square*, Melbourne, 1997–2002. Containing a museum of Australian art, cinemas, a glazed atrium for public meetings and an outdoor amphitheater for political events of the city, this fractal landform summarizes so much of the new paradigm. Its enigmatic shards suggest a new contextualism: the glass, metal and sandstone of surrounding buildings is here splintered and reassembled in a dynamic way. Spatial themes fold their way throughout the plan and section, uniting difference in a seamless continuity. The building dissolves the city grid to the north into the parkland to the south using fractal geometries at several scales to do so. Like Eisenman's Santiago landform the result is a form of neo-medieval urbanism, the city fabric as the new icon.

60 per cent, revenue was running at half its estimate, staff cuts were headed towards 40 per cent, the two new Guggenheims in Las Vegas (by Koolhaas) achieved only 40 per cent of their attendance targets, and Krens was in "prudent retreat."[171] The architecture may be an energetic symbol of rebirth, but the city and institutions have yet to show equal courage and imagination.

AFTER SEPTEMBER 11TH — THE NEW PARADIGM AND RISK SOCIETY

Daniel Libeskind, when he speaks about it, is optimistic about the future in spite of September 11th and the subsequent war. Gehry is somewhat pessimistic, and characteristically self-doubting ("we enjoyed ourselves"). Like Allan Greenspan speaking at the height of the boom about "irrational exuberance," there is a sense of guilt in America as if the country had the good times for too long and now has to pay extra for it. Peter Eisenman's response to Gehry was defiant: "We can't hide behind anonymous buildings. Urban living is about density and we're still going to need skyscrapers. We have to live our life, and carry on building symbols that are worth attacking. And if Frank stops building Gehry buildings, I quit."

Given the pessimism, some obvious truths might be reiterated. The new paradigm is at its primitive beginning, not its high point, and it will be led not by the older generation, but the young — the fifty or so I have mentioned above, or those to be found in such avant-garde anthologies as *Archilab*.[172] Architectural culture and most schools of architecture are irreversibly committed to developing its implications. At the same time, it is true that safety measures of all kinds will be introduced, as well as further ecological regulations. Maybe in response to excess, what Rem Koolhaas called "the new sobriety" will prevail for a time. It would not be a surprise. Pared down, understated building with no pretension has been the reigning mode of late capitalist production since the 1950s; so it is hardly "new," even if perhaps too sobering.

An incredible irony of this book is that the Post-Modernism it describes was started in the early 1970s, when Minoru Yamasaki's housing in St. Louis was dynamited by the authorities, and it comes to an end after his twin towers were blown up by terrorists. One act of social change cannot be compared to another act of war, nor the critique of Modern Architecture with a tragic mass killing. They have nothing to do with each other, except an architect in common and the fact that they both illustrate aspects of contemporary life. As for the architecture of the World Trade Center, Yamasaki's towers were rather smug symbols of late capitalist power. As Paul Goldberger wrote at the time of completion, in 1973, "[they are] boring, so utterly banal as to

be unworthy of the headquarters of a bank in Omaha — they are pretentious and arrogant; it is hard not to be insulted by Minoru Yamasaki's belief that a few cute allusions to gothic tracery at the bottom and top could make a 110-storey tower humane."[173] Now that they have ceased to exist, they have come to symbolize other things including tragic loss of life, America's lost power, the despair and trauma of New Yorkers and all the terrible suffering that implies. It seems to be obscene to talk about them in any other context, so fixed they have become in our eyes and mind with that moment of horror. Yet coming to terms with their other meanings is part of reconsidering September 11th and so too is facing up to their architectural symbolism. Obviously they were *the* target, partly because of this and their height, and in 1993 also, when a previous attempt was made to bring them down.

The problem of architectural symbolism still remains the one I pointed out above, of univalent content. What can an architect symbolize in a commercial era that devotes its extra money not to publicly credible functions but to monopolies, big business, world fairs, great engineering feats, and shopping? Some major changes have occurred in the west since that question was asked in 1977. Ecological issues have become more pressing, the global market has deregulated somewhat, shopping has become in Koolhaas' phrase "the terminal condition of man," and the museum has emerged as *the* public building type of the time. Art, science and cultural centers are far preferable as civic expressions of pride and democracy than the corporate monument to the global market. The twin towers of the World Trade Center were not only arrogant, as Goldberger wrote, but confused as symbols. Their aetiolated Gothic neither had the confidence of the Woolworth skyscraper, the Cathedral to Commerce of 1914, nor the strength of a Modern purist tower, such as Saarinen's CBS of 1961. Its confusion partly stemmed from the very ambivalence of its content. How can a skyscraper express world trade without becoming a triumphalist assertion of American dominance? Yamasaki did not face the ambiguities and complexities of this task, a supremely architectural one.

The other contemporary issue that September 11th throws into high relief, in the context of Post-Modernism, is living with the problems that Modernism has caused and is causing. This has given birth to the notion of the Risk Society as defined by the sociologists Ulrich Beck and Anthony Giddens.[174] A host of uncontrollable forces are released by modern development such as global warming and the hole in the ozone layer. Everyone in a risk society becomes conscious that such things as the Thalidomide tragedy, or the outbreak of mad cow disease (BSE in Britain) are inevitable if unintended consequences of progress. A sense of insecurity starts to become widespread in a risk society, the anthrax attacks and bio-terrorism being only the most extreme example of this pervasive anxiety and not a very good one since it was intended to cause panic.

More insidious are those mistakes, failures and unintended consequences of modernization. Each one made people doubt the experts, question the politicians, become aware that culture and nature were becoming inextricably linked in unpredictable ways through feedback. Some of these milestones were failures of professional responsibility: the ecological damage caused by the sinking of the Torrey Canyon, Exxon Valdez and other oil spoils. The supreme example of experts losing control was the nuclear meltdown in Chernobyl, 1987. But the rise of superbugs and strains of tuberculosis resistant to penicillin further eroded confidence in scientists and their regulators. The BSE crisis in Britain and Europe – "beefgate" – was a supreme example of the politicians misleading the public, and going into denial as they did so. They did not know the real consequences of mass-produced beefburgers, but they had to pretend that they did and quite publicly make their own children eat their first words. And there have been social and political upheavals striking at the heart of the modernist settlement: the May Events of 1968, the collapse of Communism; the anti-globalization movement, deregulation. One cannot say the welfare state has withered away because of such events, and shifts in power, but they have certainly underscored the presence of risk in all areas. The hole in the ozone layer, the possibility of earth being hit by an asteroid – such threats are now an essential part of the daily newspaper, if not daily life.

The two sociologists who coined the concept of the risk society point out that it means living "after nature and after tradition." Nature is no longer independent from the economy and scientific manipulation, and tradition can no longer cope with the way individuals live in a deregulated, global society. The results of these two shifts they call "reflexive modernization" because the new society has to reflect back on a first modernization, and its unpredictable consequences. It is conscious of the feedback of all processes – hence the pervasive feelings of insecurity – and it must debate the implications. This is non-linearity again. The key questions usually have complex answers. No one is in control, however much politicians or lawyers or experts pretend, and most people now realize this. Post-Modernism in architecture has been the response to the failure urban planning, of Pruitt-Igoe, and other misconceived social housing of the fifties and sixties. If one reflects on the list of crises above, one can find Post-Modern responses, but none of these have cleared up the problems. They are chronic to modernization itself, endemic to advanced economies. The conclusion follows that as long as the modern world continues to grow and cause new problems, there will be a Post-Modern critique and a set of alternatives for debate. No easy answers, just hybrid ones, reflexive ones, more choices and a few propitious inventions.

Such notions are consistent with the new paradigm and its emphasis on self-organizing systems and feedback. The notion of an external deity in charge of the world was replaced by the modern belief that the world was a predictable machine. This concept has itself been replaced by the idea of cosmogenesis, the picture of the universe as a dynamic process that often jumps to new levels of organization. This is not a contemporary form of animism, the belief that a life-force exists in all things, but rather the concept that when matter is pushed far from equilibrium it will self-organize and become animated like life. This is a world more chaotic and full of risk and choice than the mechanistic paradigm it is superceding, because it shows we are more and more part of the problem *and* its solution. But, positively, it also shows we are fundamentally built into the laws of the universe, and these laws are finely balanced to an extraordinary degree. For instance, cosmogenesis is poised delicately between expansion and contraction, and it has been so balanced for thirteen billion years. The tuning of the kinetic force and gravity was just right, as exact as one over ten to the 59th power, that is, with an accuracy of more than one part in a billion billion. A series of other coincidences concerning the constants and forces of nature are equally surprising. The universe has just the right properties to allow intelligent life to arise. The strengths of nuclear and electrical forces have to be very close to what they are or else planetary systems and life could not have started. Miracles sound more plausible than such fine-tuning – which is why some scientists say "the universe looks like a put-up job" – as if it were designed by a very accurate Swiss watchmaker. And this extraordinary balancing act continues for nine billion years, on and on and *before* Richard Dawkins' Blind Watchmaker, that is Darwinian evolution, even starts to work!

Such insights, occasionally discussed as the Anthropic Principle, do not mean the universe was created for our purpose, or is altogether benign. But they do suggest the modern world-view is misconceived. That paradigm argued we are the great exception to a mechanistic nature, or that the universe is pointless, or that we are alienated from it. Previously, the Greek and Renaissance philosophers held that man was the measure of all things and the center of the universe, and they built architecture around such anthropocentric beliefs. But actually the universe itself is the measure of all things, and its extraordinary laws and different harmonies are the ultimate referents at each level of organization. The point is to find scaling all the way up and down the cosmic hierarchy, and relate to all forms of self-organization, all of nature. The fact that we can comprehend and celebrate the positive aspects of cosmogenesis forms the basis for architecture. I believe this is, in part, an optimistic worldview and it is giving birth to an exciting new architecture and iconography. We are at the beginning of the new paradigm, and it is far more interesting and full of promise than the modern world we are slowly leaving behind.

Notes

1 Some of the key texts on complexity theory were the following: Ilya Prigogine and Isabelle Stengers, *Order Out of Chaos, Man's New Dialogue with Nature*, Bantam Books, New York, 1984; John Briggs and F. David Peat, *Turbulent Mirror*, Harper and Row, New York, 1989; Ian Stewart, *Does God Play Dice: The Mathematics of Chaos*, Basil Blackwood, Oxford, 1989; M. Mitchell Waldrop, *Complexity, The Emerging Science at the Edge of Order and Chaos*, Simon and Schuster, New York, 1992; Roger Lewin, *Complexity, Life on the Edge of Chaos*, J. M. Dent, London, 1993.

2 John Watkins Chapman first used the phrase post-modern in the 1870s, and like all the early usages only briefly and in an article. The only word to have any effect before the 1960s was post-industrial, its first cousin. In 1959 Irving Howe wrote an article on post-modern fiction as modern fiction in decline; in 1971 and 1975 Ihab Hassan used the term in essays to cover the literature of silence and ultra-modern tendencies. There were also myriad "posts" in magazine articles (post-civilization, Post-Christian, post-tribal etc.) but the post-modern movement did not catch on until after the architectural shift in the middle seventies. I have traced the seventy or so "posts" in *What is Post-Modernism?*, Fourth Edition, Academy Editions, London, John Wiley, New York, 1996, pp. 14–15.

3 Charles Jencks, *Critical Modernism*, RIBA Annual Discourse, September 2000; "Canons in Crossfire," *Harvard Design Magazine*, Summer 2001, no. 14, pp. 42–9; and lectures and publications in Vienna 2001.

4 See Mies van der Rohe, *Industrialized Building*, originally printed in the magazine *G Berlin*, 1924, and reprinted in Ulrich Conrad's *Programmes and Manifestos on 20th-Century Architecture*, London, 1970, p. 81.

5 Peter and Alison Smithson, *Architectural Design*, October 1969, p. 560.

6 P. Smithson, *AD*, May 1975, p. 272

7 A. and P. Smithson, "Gentle Cultural Accommodation," *L'Architecture d'Aujourd'hui*, Janvier/ Fevrier 1975, pp. 4–13, quote from p. 9. The Smithsons contend that they didn't write this, although it is typical of their ideas. See *Architectural Design 7*, 1977 and my answer.

8 See Tom Wolfe, *The New Journalism*, Picador, London, 1975, pp. 54–56, and my article "The Rise of Post-Modern Architecture," *Architectural Association Quarterly*, London, Summer 1976, pp. 7–14.

9 For the call to morality see Sigfried Giedion, *Space, Time and Architecture*, Cambridge, Mass., 1971, pp. 214, 291–308, For the "Heroic Period," see Peter and Alison Smithson, *Architectural Design*, December 1965.

10 Sant'Elia's "Manifesto," 11 July, 1914, is quoted from *Futurismo 1909–1919*, exhibition of Italian Futurism organised by Northern Arts and the Scottish Arts Council, catalogue, 1972, p. 49.

11 A more rigorous comparison of architecture to language is made by architectural semioticians who substitute technical terms for these imprecise analogies. For our general purpose however, the analogies will suffice, as long as we don't take them too literally.

12 A point made by Umberto Eco in "Function and Sign: Semiotics and Architecture," published in *Structures Implicit and Explicit*, Graduate School of Fine Arts, University of Pennsylvania, vol. 2, 1973. Republished in our anthology edited by Geoffrey Broadbent, Dick Bunt and myself, *Signs, Symbols and Architecture*, Wiley, 1980.

13 See Umberto Eco, "A Componential Analysis of the Architectural Sign/Column," in *Semiotica 5*, no. 2, 1972, Mouton, The Hague, pp 97–117.

14 See for instance Herbert Gans' description of the five major "taste cultures" in his *Popular Culture and High Culture*, Basic Books, New York, 1974, pp 69–103.

15 See G. L. Hersey, "J. C. Loudon and Architectural Associationism," *The Architectural Review*, August, 1968, pp. 89–92.

16 E. H. Gombrich, *Art and Illusion*, London, 1960, pp. 3, 16–3, 17.

17 Nikolaus Pevsner, *An Outline of European Architecture*, Harmondsworth, 1964, p. 374.

18 I've discussed these debates in *Modern Movements in Architecture*, Harmondsworth, New York, 1973, pp. 3, 18–28, and footnotes for references, The Italian press took up the controversy and applied the metaphors of "refrigeration" in English criticism (if my memory serves me).

19 Philip Johnson, "The Seven Crutches of Modern Architecture," *Perspecta III*, New Haven, 1955; "Whence and Whither, The Processional Element in Architecture," *Perspecta* 9/10, New Haven, 1965.

20 See John Jacobus, *Philip Johnson*, George Braziller, New York, 1962.

21 Letter to Jurgen Joedicke, 6 December 1961 reprinted in Jacobus, op. cit.

22 See Robin Boyd, *New Directions in Japanese Architecture*, New York and London, 1968, p. 102.

23 See *CIAM '59 in Otterlo*, edited by

Jurgen Joedicke, London, 1961, p.182.

24 See *Learning from Las Vegas*, op. cit., pp. 130 and 149.

25 A fairly complete bibliography of these writings and comment on the Venturi Team can be seen in *Learning from Las Vegas*, revised edition by Robert Venturi, Denise Scott Brown and Steven Izenour, Cambridge, 1977. For criticism see my review, "Venturi *et al* are Almost All Right," in *Architectural Design*, 7, 1977.

26 See *A+U*, 74:11 devoted to their work from 1970–74, p. 43.

27 See my "MBM and the Barcelona School," *The Architectural Review*, March 1977, pp. 159–65, and *Arquitectura* Bis, 13 and 14, Barcelona, May–June, 1976.

28 Conrad Jameson's writings have mostly been published in England, in various journals. Among the sources are: "Social Research in Architecture," *The Architect's Journal*, 27 October 1971, and following controversy; "Architect's Error," *New Society*, 8 May 1975, and following controversy; "Enter Pattern Books, Exit Public Housing Architects: a friendly sermon," *The Architect's Journal*, 11 February 1976, and following controversy; "British Architecture: Thirty Wasted Years," *The Sunday Times*, February, 1977, and following controversy. Jameson, unlike other polemicists, really knows how to fire the nerve-ends of Modern architects. His book, *Notes for a Revolution in Urban Planning*, was published by Penguin and Harper and Row, 1978.

29 Maurice Culot, one leader of ARAU in Brussels, spent ten days at Port Grimaud discussing its implications with the architect François Spoerry. In conversation, June 1977, he told me he was convinced this was the type of housing for the people, but that his local Communist leaders, some attuned to 1930s models, might not accept this.

30 David Gebhardt, "Getty's Museum," *Architecture Plus*, Sept/Oct., 1974, pp. 57–60, 122. See also Reyner Banham, "The Lair of the Looter," *New Society*, 5 May 1977, p. 238; *Building Design*, September 13 1974; in England, *The Observer* and *The*

Times ran articles on the building.

31 Colin Amery and Lance Wright, "Lifting the Witches' Curse," *The Architecture of Darbourne and Darke*, RIBA Publications, 17 May–29 July 1977, exhibition handbook, pp. 7–8.

32 Andrew Derbyshire, "*Building the Welfare State*," Conference *1976*, RIBA Publications op. cit., p. 29.

33 Ibid., p. 50.

34 Aldo Van Eyck, "In Search of Labyrinthian Clarity," *L'Architecture d'Aujourd'hui*, Jan/Feb., 1975, p. 18.

35 RIBA Conference, op. cit., p. 62.

36 The 1968 Skeffington Report recommended greater public participation in planning, but so far this has led only to increased consultation, or the minimum choice about room layout, location of partitions, etc., as in the PSSHAK project, or to the development of plans, as in the Swinbrook project of North Kensington.

37 See *Architectural Design*, 3, 1977. p. 191, the issue devoted to Culot, Krier and Tafuri.

38 Hannah Arendt has written about the public realm at length in *The Human Condition*, Chicago, 1958, and *On Revolution*, New York. 1963. Her ideas have influenced George Baird, Kenneth Frampton, Conrad Jameson and Nikolaus Habraken among others in the field of architecture.

39 See Graham Shane, "Contextualism," *Architectural Design*, 11, 1976, pp. 676–79, for a discussion and bibliography.

40 Colin Rowe, "Collage City," *The Architectural Review*, August 1975, p. 80.

41 Ibid., pp. 80–81.

42 See Nathan Silver's letter to *The Architectural Review*, September 1975, and following exchanges.

43 Kent C. Bloomer and Charles W. Moore, *Body, Memory and Architecture*, Yale University Press, New Haven and London, 1977, pp. 41–2.

44 Carl G. Jung *et al*, *Man and his Symbols*, Aldus Books, London, 1964, p. 78.

45 See Rudolf Wittkower, *Studies in the Italian Baroque*, London and New York, 1975, p. 63.

46 For the notions of layering see Colin Rowe and Robert Slutsky, "Literal and Phenomenal Transparency," *Perspecta* 8, pp. 13–14; for "compaction composition" see my *Le Corbusier and the Tragic View of Architecture*, London and Cambridge, 1973.

47 Robert Stern has written on Post-Modernism in various journals, among them *Architectural Design*, 4, 1977, and has defined three aspects to it: contextualism, historical allusion and applied ornament. In America the social and participatory aspects of Post-Modernism are considered unimportant as the argument is conducted more on the stylistic and semantic levels. Stern has discussed "inclusivism" in his *New Directions in American Architecture*, New York and London, 1969, re-edited with a postscript on Post-Modernism, 1977.

48 *Architecture d'Aujourd'hui*, ibid., p. 60.

49 See chapter 3, *Late-Modern Architecture, Selected Essays*, Academy Editions, London and Rizzoli, New York 1980.

50 The Chicago Seven were formed in 1976 partly in response to other city groupings. By the time of the Townhouse competition, March 1978, they included eleven architects: Thomas Beeby, Laurence Booth, Stuart Cohen, James Freed, Gerald Horn, Helmut Jahn, James Nagle, Kenneth Schroeder, Stanley Tigerman, Cynthia Weese and Ben Weese.

51 See "Roma Interrotta," *Architectural Design*, vol. 49, no. 3/4, 1979, p. 163.

52 Hiroshi Hara, an Interview with David Stewart, *AAQ*, vol. IC, no. 4, 1978, pp. 8, 10.

53 Umberto Eco, Postscript to *The Name of the Rose*, Harcourt Brace Jovanovitch, New York and London, pp. 67–8.

54 See Stephen Kieran, *VIA II*, "On Ornament," Pennsylvania, 1977; a symposium at the Architectural Association in December 1978 on "The Question of Ornament" (unpublished). Boyd Auger, "A Return to Ornament," *The Architectural Review*, 1976, and subsequent correspondence: an exhibition at the Cooper-Hewitt Museum

organised by Richard Oliver, 1978;
E. H. Gombrich, *The Sense of Order,
A Study in the Psychology of
Decorative Art*, Phaidon, Oxford, 1979.

55 Several of these meanings were pointed out to me by Charles Moore in a
discussion, March 1979; others can be
found in Martin Filler's excellent article on the Piazza in *Progressive
Architecture*, Nov. 1978, pp. 81–87.

56 See pp. 79, 88, 128, 130, 146 and also
note 62.

57 See for instance Peter Davey's issue of
The Architectural Review, September
1983 on "Romantic Pragmatism."

58 For a discussion of the politics behind
the Biennale see my article "Free
Style Classicism," *Architectural
Design*, 1/2, 1982, pp. 4–7.

59 See my "Mario Botta and the New
Tuscanism," in *Architectural Design*,
9/10, 1983, pp. 82–85 and "The New
Abstraction" by O.M. Lingers,
"Abstract Representation,"
Architectural Design, 7/8, 1983,
pp. 23–58.

60 Op. cit., p. 37.

61 Op. cit., note 74.

62 Tom Wolfe, *From Bauhaus to Our
House*, Farrar, Straus and Giroux, New
York, 1981. Wolfe bases large parts of
his satire, without acknowledgement,
on earlier editions of this book. His
amusing invention "fear of the bour-
geoisie" is, however, his own. See my
"Wolf Bites Wolfe Supplement," no. 1,
1982, *AD* News 1–5. Helen Searing,
*Speaking A New Classicism: American
Architecture Now*, with an essay by
Henry Hope Reed, Smith College
Museum of Art, Northampton, Mass.,
1981, 1900. See my *Post-Modernism,
The New Classicism in Art and
Architecture*, Academy Editions,
London, 1987, "Wrestling with Mega-
Build," pp. 228–37, and references
there.

63 Demetri Porphyrios, "Classicism is Not
a Style," *Architectural Design* 5/6,
1982.

64 'The Great Debate: Modernism versus
the Rest" is now available in part in
Transactions III, RIBA Publications,
London, 1983. My own article "Post-
Modern Architecture, the True
Inheritor of Modernism" and Kenneth

Frampton's "Modern Architecture and
Critical Regionalism" are one set of
opposites, but there are others who
join the debate: Will Alsop, Peter
Hodgkinson, Richard McCormac and
Jules Lubbock.

65 The term and concept were coined by
me in February 1980 and published as
a profile and as "Post-Modern
Classicism — The New Synthesis,"
Architectural Design, 5/6, 1980.

66 Robert Venturi, "Diversity, Relevance
and Representation in Historicism, or
plus ca change…" *Architectural
Record*, June 1982, p. 116.

67 *Ornamentalism*, by Robert Jensen and
Patricia Conway, Clarkson N. Potter
Inc. New York and Allen Lane,
London, 1982.

68 E. H. Gombrich, *The Sense of Order*,
Phaidon Press, Oxford, 1979.

69 See my *Skyscrapers-Skycities*, Academy
Editions, London, 1980, Rizzoli, New
York, for a discussion of these
metaphors.

70 See *The Architectural Review*, June
1982, largely devoted to the Classicism
of the Taller Bofill: quote from p. 32.

71 The New Classicism is an attractive
name for Post-Modern Classicism: see
the exhibition catalogue by Helen
Searing, *Speaking A New Classicism:
American Architecture Now*, with an
essay by Henry Hope Reed, Smith
College Museum of Art,
Northampton, Mass 1981.

72 Buildings designed six or seven years
before they are completed inevitably
look, in our world village, old-hat
when they are finished; often the
more influential they are the older
they look, because the fast-food architects beat them by many years to publication. This is sad because it takes
the edge off some of the innovations.

73 For this interpretation, see my "The
Museum as Acropolis" in "Abstract
Representation," op. cit., note 74,
pp. 110–119.

74 See my "Symbolic or Signolic
Architecture," *Art and Design*, London,
October 1985, pp. 14–17, 48, and
Symbolic Architecture, Academy
Editions, London, Rizzoli, New York,
1985.

75 John Barth discusses the search for a

wider audience in "The Literature of
Replenishment, Postmodernist
Fiction," *The Atlantic*, January 1980,
pp. 65–71; quote, p. 70.

76 For some of these compromises see
B. M. Lane, *Architecture and Politics in
Germany, 1918–45*, Harvard University
Press, 1968, p. 181; Sibyl Moholy-Nagy.
*Journal of the Society of Architectural
Historians*, March 1965, p. 84; my own
*Le Corbusier and the Tragic View of
Architecture*, Penguin and Harvard,
1974; *Modern Movements in
Architecture*, Penguin,
Harmondsworth, 1973, pp. 45–51, and
much literature on the subject pub-
lished since then.

77 See Patricia Leigh Brown, "Disney
Deco," *The New York Times
Magazine*, 8 April 1990, pp. 18–24,
42–49, 68.

78 Ibid., p. 24.

79 See my *Post-Modernism, The New
Classicism in Art and Architecture*,
Academy Editions, London, 1987,
"Wrestling with Mega-Build,"
pp. 228–37 and references there.

80 See Leon Whiteson, "Disney Design,"
The Los Angeles Times, 25 January
1990, section E1 for "hokey-tecture"
and quotation from Michael Graves.

81 Applied signs are "signolic," multivalent relations between signs, space,
function, etc., are "symbolic"; see my
Architecture Today, chapter entitled
"Symbolic and Signolic Architecture,"
Academy Editions and Abrams, 1988,
pp. 316–22.

82 See reference note 77, p. 49 for James
Stirling quote.

83 "Socitalism," socialised Capitalism
rather than the Eastern European cap-
italised Socialism, is a concept and
phrase I developed in *What is Post-
Modernism*, Fourth Edition, Academy
Editions, London, 1995.

84 See Michael de Courcy Hinds, "Vast
Project Heads for '93 Finish," *The
New York Times*, Section 8, 23 March
1986, pp. 1, 18, ff.

85 Paul Goldberger, "Battery Park City is
a Triumph of Urban Design," *The
New York Times*, 31 August 1986, Arts
Section.

86 For the application of Chaos theory
and Ilya Prigogne's ideas to Japanese

urban development see Kazuo Shinohara, quoted in my *The New Moderns*, op. cit., chapter one.

87 For these characteristic reactions see Brendan Gill, "In the Classic Vein," *The New Yorker*, 14 August 1989; Robert Maxwell, "Compact at Ithaca," *The Architectural Review*, November 1989, p. 38.

88 K. Andersen, "An Architect for the New Age," *Time Magazine*, 11, 1988, p. 40.

89 For the global migrations to America see for instance the special issue of *Time Magazine*, Fall 1993 devoted to The New Face of America, pp. 14–15; for Los Angeles see my *Heteropolis, Los Angeles – The Riots and the Strange Beauty of Hetero-Architecture*, Academy Editions, Ernst & Sohn, London and New York, 1993, pp. 23–32.

90 See the writing of Edward Soja, Allen Scott, Michael Storper, Michael Dear and Mike Davis, as well as the 1990 census data, analysed by Eugene Turner and James P. Allen, Department of Geography, California State University, Northridge, *An Atlas of Population Patterns in Metropolitan Los Angeles and Orange County*, CSUN, Northridge, CA, 1991. Some references and maps are in my *Heteropolis*, ibid., pp. 26–29.

91 Ibid., p. 99 for these metaphors published in the *Los Angeles Times*.

92 Ibid., p. 97. The interview was with Leon Whiteson, *Los Angeles Times*, 15 Sept., 1991. K1, 14, 15.

93 For the notion of a positive "ex-centricity" see Linda Hutcheon, *A Poetics of Postmodernism, History, Theory, Fiction*, Routledge, New York, London, 1988. For the new urban dweller as a self-assured hunter and nomad see the architect Adriaan Geuze, *West 8*, Skira, Milan, 2000, pp. 11–13, and his work discussed below.

94 Just before Stirling died I gave a talk at the old Weimer Bauhaus at a symposium on Architecture and Power. The title was "The Nazis, the Modernists and Prince Charles" and my theme was that all three used one-sided arguments and caricature to gain power and that a democracy does not really function unless there is conflict at the top of an establishment, an idea that was not readily understood in East Germany. Stirling's attack on Prince Charles followed by his knighthood illustrated this point, an insight of Isaiah Berlin, Hannah Arendt and others. See the introduction to the Sixth Edition of *The Language of Post-Modern Architecture*, 1991, pp. 15–18 for a discussion "The Failure of Prince Charles' Crusade."

95 See "National Gallery – Sainsbury Wing, Robert Venturi, David Vaughan & Charles Jencks, An Interview" in "Post-Modern Triumphs in London," *Architectural Design*, 1991, pp. 49–57.

96 Rem Koolhaas, *S,M,L,XL*, The Monacelli Press, 1995, pp. 494–517, 1238–69.

97 Bart Lootsma, *Superdutch, New Architecture in the Netherlands*, Thames & Hudson, 2000, pp. 15–19.

98 Lootsma, ibid., p. 16. Quote from Bart Lootsma, "Rem Koolhaas, In search of the New Modernity," *Domus*, no. 800, January 1998. For Dirty Realism and the New Sobriety see *S,M,L,XL*, op. cit., pp. 570–77, 940–57.

99 *S,M,L,XL*, p. 692.

100 Ibid., pp. 495–516.

101 Ibid., p. xiii.

102 Richard Rogers, now Lord Rogers, designer of the Pompidou Center and Lloyd's, has from the beginning of his work in the 1960s, been a strong Modernist both in practice and in word. Yet from the middle 1980s his work has become contextually sensitive and responsive to urban history, and his Urban Task Force, set up under Tony Blair's government, has promoted an agenda that includes many Post-Modern values. Among these are a commitment to building on brownfield sites, the support of local communities and their further empowerment, an emphasis on mixed use, and the major goal of an urban renaissance. All these points, underlined by the example of Barcelona, resist those economic and political forces that Koolhaas shows are eroding the city. Significantly, Rogers is the first major architect since Le Corbusier to effectively change public urban policy, and unlike his forbear Rogers actually loves the city as he finds it. Rogers is, in effect, Jane Jacobs in high-tech garb, proof that even if there is not progress in architecture there is learning.

103 For this list and others see Bart Lootsma, *Superdutch*, op. cit., pp. 16, 19.

104 Ibid.

105 In addition to *Superdutch*, see Bart Lootsma, "Synthetic Regionalization: The Dutch Landscape Toward a Second Modernity," in *Recovering Landscape, Essays in Contemporary Landscape Architecture*, edited by James Corner, Princeton Architectural Press, 1999, pp. 251–74, particularly p. 254.

106 For the requirements see Paul Groenendijk, *Piet Vollaard, Guide to Modern Architecture in the Netherlands*, Uitgeverij 010 Publishers, Rotterdam, p. 171, and Kathy Battista and Florian Migsch, *The Netherlands Guide to Recent Architecture*, Ellipsis, London, 1998, pp. 34–37.

107 Bart Lootsma, *Superdutch*, op. cit., p. 19, and quoting MVRDV on this point see his *Synthetic Regionalization*, op. cit., pp. 261–63

108 See Sigrún Davídsdóttir, "Farm of the Future," *The Guardian*, August 21, 2001, pp. 23–24.

109 Adriaan Geuze, *West 8*, Skira, Milan, 2000, pp. 10–13.

110 Ibid., pp. 10, 11 and 13.

111 Notes from RIBA talk, April 2001.

112 *West 8*, op. cit., p. 24.

113 This point was made by Sanford Kwinter at the 1997 *Anyhow Conference* in Rotterdam in a critique of the previous generation, and reported by Andreas Ruby in "The Spectre of Research," *Archilab, Radical Experiments in Global Architecture*, Thames & Hudson, London, 2001, p. 528.

114 The historical specificity of every city was recognised as a matter of theory and policy at the Habitat Conference on Cities, in 1995.

115 For the notion of the "ex-centric" see Linda Hutcheon, op. cit., "Decentering the Postmodern: The Ex-centric", pp. 57–73.

116 Howard Raggatt, *Fringe de Cringe* and

A Fringe Dweller's Diatribe, written in 1992. See *Tangled Destinies, National Museum of Australia*, edited by Dimiti Reed, Images Publishing Group, Victoria, Australia, 2002.

117 See Melvin Webber, "Order in Diversity: Community without Propinquity," 1963, p. 23, or "The Urban Place and Non-Place Urban Realm," in *Explorations into Urban Structure*, Pennsylvania, 1964.

118 Ibid.

119 William Mitchell, *e-topia*: "Urban life, Jim – but not as we know it," MIT Press, Cambridge, 1999.

120 See Michael Batty and Paul Longley, *Fractal Cities*, Academic Press, San Diego, CA., 1994.

121 I have written on this theme as a basic metaphor in *The Architecture of the Jumping Universe, A Polemic: How Complexity Science is Changing Architecture and Culture*, Academy/Wiley, London and New York, 1995, Second Edition, 1997.

122 Peter Eisenman, "Visions unfolding: architecture in the age of electronic media," *Domus* no. 734, 1992, pp. 17-21.

123 Gilles Deleuze, *The Fold Leibniz and the Baroque*, Foreword and translation by Tom Conley, University of Minnesota Press, Minneapolis, 1993.

124 However, it was true he was looking at philosophy too. I remember when, on one occasion that I happened to be visiting him, he appeared with a copy of *Le Pli* in his hands, quickly to be slipped out of sight. I mention this trivial incident because it makes the general point that motives are mixed, and influences are common in international architecture.

125 Christian Pongratz, Maria Rita Perbellini, *Natural Born CAD Designers*, Birkhäuser, Basel Switzerland, 2000. Other important titles in this series edited by Antonino Saggi include *Digital Eisenman, HyperArchitecture, Information Architecture* and *New Wombs*.

126 See for instance *Architectural Design*, "Architects in Cyberspace," guest edited by Martin Pearce and Neil Spiller, November 1995, and its follow up in November 1998; or *Hypersurface Architecture*, September–October 1998 and its follow up a year later, also edited by Stephen Perella.

127 *Folds blobs & boxes, Architecture in the Digital Era*, at the Heinz Architectural Center, Carnegie Museum of Pittsburgh, curated by Joseph Rosa, 3 February – 27 May, 2001. This included twenty-five architects, mostly Americans. Lynn's book of 1998 is called *folds, bodies & blobs*, all lower case – the influence is clear.

128 Peter Zellner, *Hybrid Space, New Forms in Digital Architecture*, Thames & Hudson, London, 1999.

129 The dislocation of the subject has been Eisenman's theme since his involvement with Deconstruction in the late 1970s, but for an early 1990s statement and the quote see the essay in *Domus*, note 122 above, also republished in Luca Galofaro, *Digital Eisenman, An Office of the Electronic Era*, Birkhäuser, Basel, 1999, pp. 84–89.

130 The most sophisticated account in the Birkhäuser series is Maria Luisa Palumbo, *New Wombs, Electronic Bodies and Architectural Disorders*, Birkhäuser, Basel, 2000. There are many important insights in this short treatment. See also Anthony Vidler, *Warped Space, Art, Architecture, and Anxiety in Modern Culture*, MIT Press, Cambridge, 2000.

131 For a recent book on emergence – the concept was current in the 1920s – see Steven Johnson, *Emergence*, Allen Lane, London, 2001.

132 Scientists are just as disputatious as architects, and some would question the priority of complexity, both as a direction of the universe and as a substitute for other terms, such as nonlinear dynamics and chaos. Perhaps the universe is a chaosmos, has no meaning and shows no pattern? This, the reigning Late-Modern view, is upheld by those such as Stephen Jay Gould and Steven Weinberg. The latter Nobel physicist opines that the more we study the universe, the less meaning we find. He ends a book on the origin of the universe with the summary: "The more the universe seems comprehensible, the more it also seems to be pointless." (Steven Weinberg, *The First Three Minutes*, Basic Books Inc., New York, 1977, updated edition 1988, p. 154.) But this nihilist conclusion stems from the view that there has to be one predetermined story to history, one outcome, whereas what we find, as the universe becomes more comprehensible, is that it reveals ever greater varieties of growth and meaning – is that pointless, or to the point? Increasing complexity of organization, sentience and thought, punctuated by regressions, is itself a meaningful story. The debate of whether the universe has a direction, shows a pattern or is a continuously random emergent is a long one. A recent, rather pop summary favouring increasing complexity, is Robert Wright, *Nonzero, the Logic of Human Destiny*, Little, Brown and Co., London, 2000. Other essays in the same recent genre include Mark Buchanan, *Ubiquity, The Science of History…Or Why the World is Simpler Than We Think*, Weidenfeld & Nicolson, London, 2000. It is fair to say we will not know the outcome of this debate for a long time, so opposite metaphysics are possible and therefore also opposite architectures based on them.

133 There are now countless books on Complexity Theory, but two early overviews stressed the way it emerges at the border between order and chaos: M.Mitchell Waldrop, *Complexity, The Emerging Science at the Edge of Order and Chaos*, Simon and Schuster, New York, 1992, and Roger Lewin, *Complexity, Life on the Edge of Chaos*, J. M. Dent, London, 1993. For my definition and architectural examples see "New Science =New Architecture?," *Architectural Design*, Nov.–Dec., 1997, p. 8.

134 See Peter Eisenman, *Diagram Diaries*, with an Introduction by R. E. Somol, Thames & Hudson, London, 1999, p. 31, pp. 48 ff.

135 Henry N. Cobb, "A Note on the criminology of Ornament: from Sullivan to Eisenman," *Eleven Authors in Search of a Building*, edited by Cynthia C. Davidson, The Monacelli Press, 1996, pp. 95–97. The new ornament is con-

structed as "figure/figure" not as the more usual "figure/ground," and made from the cheap gypsum wallboard in different colours – at human scale.

136 Peter Eisenman quoted in Joseph Giovannini, "Campus Complexity," *Architecture*, AIA Journal (Washington), August, 1996, pp. 14–25.

137 Sanford Kwinter, "The Genius of Matter: Eisenman's Cincinnati Project," *Re:working Eisenman*, Academy Editions (London), 1993, pp. 90–97.

138 Per Bak developed the notion of "self-organized criticality" using sand piles in 1986; see Per Bak and Kan Chen, "Self-Organized Criticality," *Scientific American*, January 1991, pp. 46–53.

139 Some of this work is summarized in M. Mitchell Waldrop, *Complexity, The Emerging Science at the Edge of Order and Chaos*, Simon and Schuster, New York, 1992.

140 Alfred North Whitehead, *Science and the Modern World*, A Mentor Book, New York, 1946, first published in 1925, p. 87, 101; see also David Ray Griffin, editor, *The Reenchantment of Science*, SUNY Press, New York, 1988, especially the introduction and pp. 151–57. This is part of a SUNY Series on Postmodern Proposals edited by Griffin.

141 Peter Eisenman, unpublished manuscript of complete works, pp. 9.1–9.3 to be published by Thames & Hudson, London, 2002.

142 "Visions Unfolding…," op. cit. See also Galafaro, op. cit., p. 87.

143 Unpublished manuscript, op. cit., p. 14.2.

144 The two major books are Greg Lynn, *folds, bodies & blobs*, Collected Essays, La Lettre Volèe, Brussels, 1998 and Greg Lynn, *Animate Form*, Princeton Architectural Press, New York, 1999.

145 Lynn, "the folded, the pliant and the supple," reprinted in *folds, bodies & blobs*, op. cit., pp. 121, 110.

146 Richard Weinstein interview with Greg Lynn, published in the Yale University School of Architecture journal, *Constructs*, Spring 2000, p. 5.

147 *Animate Form*, op. cit., pp. 30, 31.

148 Murray Gell-Mann, *The Quark and the Jaguar, Adventures in the Simple and Complex*, Little, Brown & Co., London 1994, pp. 58–60.

149 Charles Jencks, *The Architecture of the Jumping Universe*, op. cit., new edition 1997, pp. 34–38.

150 Jane Jacobs, *The Death and Life of Great American Cities*, New York: Vintage Books, 1961, last chapter.

151 Eco-Tech is a label often used by the British journal *Architecture Today*. For a picture survey see Catherine Slessor, *Eco-Tech, Sustainable Architecture and High Technology*, Thames & Hudson, London, 1997.

152 Ken Yeang publishes tirelessly his work and theories and his intentions are sprinkled throughout many sources and lectures. His intentions to measure and formalize green architecture is constantly reiterated, see for instance, Robert Powell, *Rethinking the Skyscraper, The Complete Architecture of Ken Yeang*, Thames & Hudson, 1999, Chapter 3, and Ken Yeang, *The Skyscraper Bioclimatically Considered*, Academy Editions, 1996.

153 Several writers and scientists have discussed these new insights, among them Brian Goodwin and Ian Stewart. See for instance Ian Stewart, *Nature's Numbers, Discovering Order and Pattern in the Universe*, Phoenix, London, 1995, pp. 157–66.

154 Alexander Tzonis, *Santiago Calatrava, The Poetics of Movement*, Universe, New York, 1999, p. 9.

155 See Maria Luisa Palumbo, op. cit., pp. 78–83 where the blinking eye is seen as exemplifying the post-organic part of the paradigm.

156 Zvi Hecker, quoted in pamphlet *Heinz-Galinski-Schule, Berlin, Aedes Galerie und Arckitekturforum*, January 1993, p. 14.

157 See *Ecstatic Architecture, The Surprising Link*, edited and with essays by Charles Jencks, Academy/Wiley, London and New York, 1999, pp. 11–13, 98–107.

158 Benoit Mandelbrot, *The Fractal Geometry of Nature*, W. H. Freeman & Co., New York, 1977, 1982, 1983.

159 This and other quotes are from the BBC2 film, *Close-Up – Daniel Libeicsd, The Spiral*, 25 March 1999.

160 Comparative figures have not been investigated but the 10–15 % estimate was given to me by one of the chief architects in charge, Carlos Iturriaga, who I met on the site several times in 1996 and 1997.

161 For the ideology behind this approach see Brian O'Doherty's *Inside the White Cube, The Ideology of the Gallery Space*, The Lapis Press, Santa Monica, San Francicso, 1986, first published in *Artforum*, 1976. London's most recent fashionable gallery is called *The White Cube²*, as if squaring a nullity would multiply the presence of the absence.

162 I have had several conversations with Gehry on this point over the years. The issue is explored in "The Surface of Complexity," *Architectural Design*, Nov.–Dec., 1997 entitled *New Science= New Architecture?* that I edited. His agreement on the point is contained in a film *The Garden of Cosmic Speculation*, Border TV, November 1997.

163 Hal Foster, "Slouching Toward Bilbao," Book Review section of the *Los Angeles Times*, 14 October 2001, pp. 6–8. Throughout the review Foster uses the qualifiers "often," "at least in part" where I would say "occasionally" or "a bit" – that is I agree there is a point, but not with his emphasis. His reliance on Carl Andre's tripartite history of modern sculpture is not only historicist, in the negative sense, but reductive and, in the end, daft.

164 Bettina von Hase, "After the Guggenheim," the Business section of the *Financial Times*, 18 March 2000, pp. 27–30, quote p. 28.

165 "Gehry and the Guggenheim," *BBC World Service*, 5 June 2001.

166 I have discussed the recent museum boom, and museum as cathedral, in "Spectacular Contradictions," a paper given as the inaugural address at the AICA 2000 Congress, National Gallery, London and published in several places including *d'Letzebuerger Land*, 18 May 2001, pp. 21–24, *The Art Newspaper*, no. 109, December 2000, *pinakotheke*, Moscow, 2001 and elsewhere.

167 "Measures of success," figures displayed at the launch of the New Guggenheim New York, April 2001.

168 For a sceptical assessment of the financial risks of the new museums see Adrian Ellis, "Bust to follow museum boom," *The Art Newspaper*, no. 116, July–August, p. 14. Anna Somers-Cox informs me that, after all the millions in lottery and building grants, the British Museum is now running at a deficit of £3 million per year. On top of this is the £4 million it must find to keep the new court, designed by Norman Foster, open until eleven at night. The Tate Modern has to raise £12 million a year to stay solvent. Such figures, by British standards, are extraordinarily high, perhaps unsustainable.

169 J. Fiona Ragheb, Associate Curator for Collections and Exhibitions at the Guggenheim, kindly supplied me with these figures and very helpfully led me through the Gehry Exhibition. See the catalogue she edited, *Frank Gehry, Architect*, Guggenheim Museum, New York, 2001, and, for the figures the museum paper, "Project for a New Guggenheim Museum in New York City", 2001, p. 3.

170 Frank Gehry talking to Elizabeth Nash in Madrid, "Buildings may never be the same, says Guggenheim architect," *The Independent*, London, 1 November 2001.

171 Celestine Bohlen, "The Guggenheim's Scaled-Back Ambition," *The New York Times*, 20 November 2001.

172 *Archilab, Radical Experiments in Global Architecture*, edited by Frédéric Migayrou and Marie-Ange Brayer, Thames & Hudson, London, 2001. There are interesting critical articles, hard to read because of the fashionable over-printing, and a feast of projects illustrated by 2300 images.

173 Paul Goldberger quoted from Rowan Moore's discussion of the tower's symbolism, "Minoru Yamasaki," *Prospect*, November 2001, pp. 48–50.

174 Two major explanations of the Risk Society are Ulrich Beck, Anthony Giddens, Scott Lash, *Reflexive Modernization, Politics, Tradition and Aesthetics in the Modern Social Order*, Polity Press, Cambridge, 1994, and *The Politics of Risk*, edited by Jane Franklin, Polity Press, Cambridge, 1998.

Index

A

Aalto, Alvar 257
　Imatra church, Finland 74
　Town Hall 66
Abromovitz, Harrison and 49
Abstract Expressionism 53
　geometry 238
　Representation 134–41
　see also Representation
ACE 127
ACT 140
Adam, Robert 10
Adams, Robert 63
Adhocism 2, 10, 71–5, 80
advocacy planners 75, 76
AEG
　see Behrens
Aida, Takefumi 123–4
AJM 164, 165, 166
Alberts, Anton 163
Alsop, Will 43, 51, 211, 222
Ambasz, Emilio 229
Amery, Colin 68
Amon Carter Museum 54
Amsterdam 69, 70
　face houses 83
　Nieumarket district 74
analogies 17
　see also code; metaphor; meaning;
　　language; semantics; syntax
"Anthropic Principle" 264
anthropology 81
anthropomorphism 3, 50, 83–4
　see also Biomorphic design;
　　metaphor
anthroposophical design 163
ARAU 73, 74
Archigram 67
Arets, Will 190
ARM 199–203, 211, 240
　Storey Hall, Melbourne (1993–6)
　　240–1
Armani 21
Art Deco 61, 90, 98, 104, 143
Arte Povera 94

Art Nouveau 197, 210
Ashton
　see ARM
AT&T building 163
auditoria 28
Aulenti, Gae 139–41
Australia 199–203
　National Museum Canberra (1998–2001)
　　198–99
　see also Utzon, Sydney Opera House

B

Babka 146
Banham, Reyner 53, 65
Barcelona 82
architects 61, 133
　see also Gaudi
　Cerda 160
　Park 160
　Pavilion 87, 110
　School 70
Barnes, Edward Larrabee 128
Baroque 53, 55, 91, 106, 119, 129, 133, 146,
　157, 207, 210
Bath 76
Battersea Power Station 7, 34–5
Battery Park City
　see Moore, Charles
Batty 211, 241
Baudrillard, Jean 97
Bauhaus 87
Bauman, Zygmunt 248
Beck, Ulrich 263
Beeby, Thomas 97, 143, 146
Behaviourism 9
Behrens, Peter
　AEG factory, Berlin (1909) 20
Benamo and Portzamparc 100
Benjamin, Walter 243
Berlin, Isaiah 79
Bernini, Gian Lorenzo 82
Bickerseiland Housing 69, 70
"Bilbao Effect" 258, 259
　see also Gehry, Bilbao, New
　Guggenheim

Biomorphic design 51, 207, 220
　see also "blob" architecture
"blob" architecture 51, 210–27
　The Blobmeisters 218–27
　blob grammar applied 228
　see also biomorphic design
Bloomer, Kent 81
BLR 164, 165, 166
"Blue Whale"
　see Pelli, Cesar
boat houses
　see Sausalito
Bofill, Ricardo 126, 132–4
Bohigas, Oriol 70, 71, 160
　see also MacKay, Martorell
Borromini 53
Bos 190
Bosch, Theo 69
Botta, Mario 119, 120, 121–3, 126, 146, 149,
　229
Boullée, Etienne 16
Bouman, Ole 190
Boyarsky, Alvin 78
brand/"Form follows Brand" 49
bricolage 79, 80
Brighton Pavilion
　see Nash
Broadgate 158
Brown, Denise Scott
　see Scott
Brunelleschi, Filippo 66, 129
Brussels 74
　Philips Pavilion, Brussels World's Fair
　　206–7
Brutalism 12, 53, 55, 119
bungalows/"bungaloids" 37, 65–6
Bunschaft, Gordon 39, 61
　Hirshhorn Museum 16
　Lever Tower 21
Buñuel 133
Burgee, John 129
Burton, Ahrends 68

C

Calatrava, Santiago 211, 231–4, 258

Canary Wharf 158
Capitalism 12
caricature 66
Carsons, Rachel 2
Celan, Paul 243
Celebration New Town, USA 63
Chicago Seven 97, 98
    Townhouse Project 97, 98
Christiaanse, Kees 190
Chrysler Building 163
churches
    see "consumer temples"
CIAM 9, 76
"cinematic sectioning" 235
Classicism 76, 110, 121, 122-3
    Post Modern C. 51
    Technological C. 134
    see also Prince Charles
classical architecture
    language/orders 17, 25, 28, 35, 43, 44,
        45, 106, 107, 147
    19th century villa 38
Clendinning, Max 68
Clotet and Tusquets 61-2
Coates, Nigel 149
Cobb, Harry 147
Coca-Cola 41
code visual 26
    see also analogies; metaphor; meaning;
        language; semantics; syntax
    architectural 69
    double/dual 19, 30, 55, 101
"Collage City" 76-80
Collins, George 78
column 34
    see also classical architecture, lan-
        guage/orders 17, 25
commercialization/commercialism 57
    see also brand; consumer temples
Communism 19, 84, 264
competitions 159, 178, 185, 259
Yokohama Port Terminal 235
Complexity
    architecture 207-34, 237, 243
    theory 1, 6, 189, 210
        "Complexity Two" 6
        "Complexity One" 80
computer (aided) design 1, 6, 51, 126,
    207-34
concrete
    see materials
Congress of International Modern
    Architects
    see CIMA
"consumer temples" 3, 22-24
    see also commercialization

contextualism 2, 3, 51, 76-80, 143, 179
Corbusier
    see Le Corbusier
Corinthian 44, 46, 133
    see also classical architecture
corporate
    architecture 20
    brand 49
cosmic metaphor 3
cosmogenisis 264
Covent Garden 158
crime
    see Newman, O
Critical Modernism 7
Csete, Gyorgy 130
Cubism 42, 55, 88
    photo Cubism 235
Cullinan, Edward 68
Culot, Maurice 74, 76
curtain wall construction 13, 21
Cusanus, Nicholas 119

D
Dalí, Salvador 133
Darbourne and Darke 67-8
Davidson, Cynthia 210
"decorated shed" 29, 58, 59, 148
De Kovel/De Vroom
    see DKV
De Ley 70
Denari, Neil 211
Derbyshire, Andrew 68-9
De Stijl 42, 123
digital media & design 207-34
Disney(land) 3, 12, 31, 39, 63, 66, 79, 152
    consumerism 22
Disney Development Corp 152-7
    Entertainment Architecture, mid-1980s
        23
    Concert Hall
        see Gehry, Frank
Dixon, Jeremy 98
DKV 190
Dobblelaar 190
Dolphin Hotel 152-7
Doric 43, 44, 45, 119, 123, 125
    see also classical architecture; New
        Tuscanism
double/dual coding
    see code
Doughnut ("Big Donut Drive-in") 30
Droog Design 190
Dulansky, Jeno 130
Düsseldorf Museum Project 80

E
Eclecticism 37, 70, 80, 198
    High-Tech 146
    Radical 51, 97-114, 131-32
Eco Tech 229
Eco, Umberto 24, 101, 110
Egyptian motifs 139
    see also Neo-
Ehrenkrantz, Exra 41
Eisenman, Peter 6, 41, 51, 88-9, 90, 96,
        125, 199, 207, 208-9, 210, 211-15
    Aronoff Center 211-15, 237
    City of Culture, Santiago de Compostela
        (1999) 217, 258
    House III 42-3
    Staten Island Institute for Arts &
        Sciences 216
electronic
    revolution 2
    see also digital
Ellul, Jacques 9
energy
    see renewable
engineering projects 22
Entertainment Architecture 157
    see also Disney
Environmental Education Center 134-5
Erith, Raymond and Quinlan Terry 62, 63
Ersatz 10-11, 37, 63, 67, 151, 152
Erskine, Ralph 10, 59, 71, 75, 197
    Clare College, Cambridge 71
    Byker
        Architects' Office 72
        Wall, Newcastle (1974) 72
Esher 89
Esherick, Joseph 70, 71
Evans, Arthur 65
"evolutionary tree" 50-1
EXPO
    2000 193
    1997-98 223-5
Expressionism 210
    see also Abstract Expressionism

F
face houses 83-5
factories 22
Farrell, Terry 3, 85, 130
Feilden and Mawson 69
Findlay, Urshida 211
Finland
    Imatra church 74
Five Architects The 41
flatness 126, 134
flat roofs 36, 71
FOA 211, 235

Yokohama International Port Terminal
(1995) 236
Foreign Office Architects
see FOA
formalism 16
Foster, Norman Sir 2–3, 166, 202, 222,
229, 230
Swiss Re HQ, London (1996–2002) 230
Fox, Kohn Petersen
see KPF
Fractal
architecture 235–64
Metropolis, The 203–5, 211, 234
Frampton, Kenneth 123, 128
Franzen, Ulrich 16, 128
Fuller, Buckminster 21, 231, 249
Futurists 40
see also Sant' Elia

G
Gaia Theory 215
Gaudi, Antonio 58, 231, 234, 235, 240
Gebhardt, David 63
Gehry, Frank 2, 6, 10, 40, 41, 44, 49, 51, 59,
61, 73, 75, 93–4, 95, 110, 149, 163, 207,
211, 249, 250–63
Chiat/Day/Mojo, LA 176
Condé Nast Cafeteria, New York
(1996–2000) 257–8
Der Neue Zollhof, Dusseldorf 174
Experience Music Project, Seattle
(1995–2000) 222, 257–8
Horse's Head 222
Loyola Law School, LA 75
New Guggenheim Museum, Bilbao
(1992–97) 31, 32, 211, 217,
250–57, 258
New Guggenheim Museum, New York
(1998–) 262
Santa Monica House 93
Walt Disney Concert Hall, LA (1987ff)
31, 177, 261
Gell-Mann, Murray 222
Georgian 61
see also Neo-
Geuze, Adriaan
see West 8
Giddens, Anthony 263
Giedon, Sigfried 87
gigantism 12
Gigliotti, Vittorio 53
glass
see materials
GLC 68, 69
Goldberger, Paul 19
Gombrich, E.H. 128

Gothic 10
Revival 62, 207
see also Neo-
Graves, Michael 3, 23, 40, 41, 59, 84, 86,
88, 97, 131, 134, 139, 149, 152
Benacerraf House addition, Princeton
(1969) 42
Environmental Education Center ("Frog
Museum") 134–5
Humana HQ Building (1982–86) 135–6
Portland Building 157
San Juan Capristrano Public Library
(1981–3) 135
Swan and Dolphin Hotels, Florida
(1987–90) 152–7
Walt Disney HQ, Burbank, Florida
(1988–90) 155
grids 88
see also materials, concrete
Grimshaw, Nicolas 211, 231
Waterloo Channel Tunnel Terminal,
London (1990–3) 231
Gris, Juan 42
Gropius, Walter 2, 26, 36, 49, 61, 128, 129
Fagus Factory (1911) 22
with TAC, Pan Am Building New York
(1958) 21
Group Pécs 84, 130
Gruen, Victor 66
Grumbach, Antoine 152
Guggenheim Museum 21, 237
see also Gehry, New Guggenheim
Gund, Graham 158
Gwathmy, Charles 38

H
Hadid 51, 211, 235
Hadrian's Villa, Tivoli 79–80
Hagmann, John 90
Hammond 146
"Handmade Houses" 10
Hara, Hiroshi 100, 164–5
Yamato International, Tokyo (1984–87)
164
Harrison, and Abromovitz 49
Harrison, Wallace 54
Hecker, Zvi 211, 237–8
Heinz-Galinski School, Berlin (1993–95)
238
Hertzberger, Herman 16–17
heterogeneity 6
Heteropolis, The 175–80
High-Tech 110, 123, 130, 146, 164, 229
Himmelblau, Coop 41, 51, 98, 211, 239
Cinema Center, Dresden (1993–98) 239
Musée des Confluences, Lyon 258–9

Hiroshima 7
Museum of Contemporary Art 169–71
historicism 53–5
see also Classicism; Neo-; revivalism
Hitchcock, Henry Russell 62
Hitler, Adolf 3, 110, 130
Hodgkinson, P
Foundling Estate (1973) 22
Holl, Steven 197
Hollein, Hans 40, 49, 97, 103–5, 114, 127,
131, 134, 163
Austrian Travel Agency 104–5
Generali-Media Tower (1998–2001)
48–9
Haas House, Vienna 179–80
Jewelry shop, Vienna 22–3
Museum, Mönchengladbach (1976–82)
138
Perchtoldsdorf Town Hall renovation
104
Holocaust 7, 248
see also Museums
Hong Kong and Shanghai Bank 163
Hot Dog
House 82–3
Stand 30
hotels 10
Florida, Swan and Dolphin 152–7
house, the popular 37
housing
mass/terraces 63
see also schemes
style 71
housing schemes
Amsterdam, Bickerseiland 69, 70
Communist and authoritarian countries,
1970s 19
England
London 22
Milton Keynes 22
Newcastle 72
Norwich 69
Germany 22
Tegel housing, Berlin 158
Weissenhof, Stuttgart 72
Russian 19, 22
"social condensers" 22
Switzerland 22
Zwolle 69, 70
see also Berlin; Bickerseiland; Le
Corbusier, Pessac; Odense; Yamasaki,
Pruitt-Igoe; Russia
Howard, Ebenezer 68
Hutcheon, Linda 24, 66
"ex-centricity" 66

I
IBE, Berlin 159, 160
Ideal Home Exhibition 36, 77
Illich, Ivar 9, 11
Industrial style 70
Ingemann, Paul 160
Instrumentalism 7
International style 10,12, 55, 61–2, 90, 126, 129
Internet, The 203–4
Ionic
  see classical architecture
irony 115
  see also parody
Ishii, Kazuhiro 100, 128–9
Isozaki, Arata 44, 49, 66, 101, 131–2, 139
  Museum of Contemporary Art, LA 139
Israel, Frank 176

J
Jacobs, Jane 1, 2, 6, 9, 67, 158, 159, 163, 189, 210
Jahn, Helmut 97
Jameson, Conrad 63, 68
Japan 67
  "new Japan style" 55
Jencks, Charles 85, 148, 203, 215
Jerde, Jon 66–7, 160, 161
  Canal City, Hakata, Japan (1966) 67
Johnson, Philip 16, 54–5, 97, 129, 143
  Amon Carter Museum (1961) 54
  Folie (1962) 54
  Synagogue, Port Chester (1956) 54
Jones, Edward 149–50, 151

K
Kahn, Louis 40, 57, 79, 121, 122
Kainz, Hans 127
Kapfinger, Otto 99
Kiesler, Frederick 222, 223
Kikutake, Kiyonori 55
  Tokoen Hotel, Yonago (1963–5) 55
Kipnis, Jeff 207, 210, 211, 218, 237
Kirkland, Michael 149–50
kitsch 3, 16, 54, 123, 143, 151ff
  see also PoMo
Kleinheus, Josef Paul 114, 159
Koetter, Fred 79
Kohn Pedersen, Fox
  see KPF
Koolhaas, Rem 180–9, 190, 195, 197, 207, 211, 235, 237, 258, 263
  Bibliothèques Jussieu, Paris (1993) 185, 188
  Grand Palais, Lille (1993–4) 187–8
  Parc de la Villette Paris (1982–3) 181

Seattle Public Library (2000–2003) 188
Zentrum für Kunst und Medientechnologie, Karlsruhe (1989–92) 184–5
Koons, Jeff 127
Koralek 68
KPF 97, 143
  Proctor and Gamble HQ, Cincinnati (1982–6) 143
Kresge College, University of California
Krier brothers 76, 80, 119, 197
  Leon 63, 99, 114, 159, 163, 189
    Echternach (1970) Luxembourg 76–7
    La Villette Competition (1976) 76–8
  Robert 125, 159
Krischanitz, Adolf 99
Kroll, Lucien 59, 72–3, 74, 75, 76, 197
Kuala Lumpur Airport (1991–3) 229
Kurokawa, Kisho 26–7, 55, 144–5, 146, 167, 211
  Museum of Contemporary Art, Hiroshima (1988) 169–71
  Nakagin Capsule Building, Tokyo (1972) 26
  Wacoal Building, Tokyo 82–5
Kwinter, Sanford 218

L
language 18–19
linguistic analogy in architecture 24, 25, 69
  see also code; metaphor; meaning; semantics; syntax
Las Vegas 20, 24, 29, 40, 57, 58, 59, 126
Le Corbusier 2, 9, 24, 40, 53, 54, 55, 76, 78, 81, 87, 88, 90, 134, 137, 178, 217, 218, 220, 243, 251, 257
  "house as a machine for living" (1922) 22
  La Roche house 87–8
  Le Style Corbu 38, 42–3
  Pessac housing 36
  Philips Pavilion, Brussels World's Fair (1958) 206–7
  Ronchamp chapel 4, 30, 31, 32, 51, 81, 134, 172, 173, 252
  Villa Savoye 66, 87, 110, 200–202
Ledoux, C.N. 16, 54, 78
Léger 24
Letchworth Garden Suburb 68
Levittown, USA 37, 58
Libeskind, Daniel 6, 51, 95–6, 200, 211, 241, 243–50, 258, 263
  Imperial War Museum, Trafford, Manchester (1998–2002) 248–9
Jewish Museum, Berlin 243–8

V&A, London 258
"Liminal, The" 87–96
Lissitsky, El 249
Lloyd Wright, Frank
  see Wright
London
  Clore Gallery 137–8
  Covent Garden 74
  "High Point II", Highgate 53
  "Thematic House" 84–5
  Victoria & Albert Museum 258
  see also South Bank
Longley 211, 241
Loos, Adolf 101, 119, 123, 125
  Chicago Tribune Column 35
Lorenz 213
Los Angeles 30, 74–5, 175–8
Loudon J. C. 43, 44
Louvain 73
Lubetkin, Berthold 80
  and TECTON, "High Point II", Highgate (1938) 53
Lutyens, Sir Edwin 58, 61, 91, 127, 178
Lynn, Greg 207, 211, 215, 218–22, 235, 237
Lyotard, Jean-François 97, 107, 110, 115, 248

M
McDougal
  see ARM
McLuhan, Marshall 203–4
MacEwan, M. 10
Machine Aesthetic 13, 17, 81
MacKay, Martorell 70
Maas, Winy
  see MVRDV
Maekawa, Kunio 67
Magritte, René 29, 62
Main Street 58, 66
Makovecz, Imre 84, 86, 87, 130
Mandelbrot, Benoit 235, 241
Mannerism 55, 58, 80, 81, 100, 120, 126, 149, 157
Martorell, Bohigas and Mackay 70
Marx 130
mass production 2, 3, 17
materials 13, 15, 46
  brick 46, 67, 68, 71
  concrete 126
    pre-cast grilles 26
  ETFE 231
  glass 46, 231, 255
  marble, imitation 65
  neon 106
  nylon 46
  sensuous 115

steel 46
  synthetic 65
  titanium 255, 257
  wood 46
Matthew, Johnson, Marshall & Ptrs 68–9
Mau, Bruce 189
Mawson 69
Maybeck, Bernard 84
Mayne, Thom 241, 243
MBM 160
meaning
  see also analogies; code; metaphor;
    language; semantics; syntax
Meier, Richard
  Douglas House, Michigan (1971–3) 38
Melnikov, Konstantin
  Russakov Club, Moscow (1928) 28
Mendini, Alessandro 198
Merrill 166
metabolism 2
metaphor 3, 51, 115
  animal 86
  anthropomorphic 36, 37, 81
  body 81–7
  cheesegrater 35
  confusing 14
  cosmic 3
  face 83–6
  factory 14, 22
    Weissenhof Siedlungen (1927) 22
  hospital 9
  linguistic 6, 17
  machine 6, 22, 26, 81, 134
  Mies van der Rohe 6
  nature 81, 228–34, 243
  negative m.s for Modern Architecture
    26–34, 35
  office 35
  organic 28
  parking 35
  PDC 33
  pitched roof/home 35
  sensuous 145
  "slips-of-the metaphor" 17
  suggested 30
  wedge-auditorium 35
metaphysics 81–7
Michaelangelo 66, 131
Micky Mouse 157
  see also Disney
"Mid-Cult" 15
Mies van der Rohe, Ludwig 2, 3, 6, 12–13,
    30, 87, 121, 194, 237, 243
  Crown Hall 6
  Lake Shore Drive, Chicago 13
  Seagram Building, New York 13, 21

Illinois Institute of Technology Campus,
    Chicago 13–14, 94
  Siegel Building, IIT, Chicago 14
Milton Keynes, housing 22
Minimalism 6, 13, 173
Miralles, Enric 51, 160, 197, 211 235
  Eurythmics Center, Alicante (1993–4)
    235
Missing Link 99
Modern Architecture (Modernism) 3
  see also Critical; Disneyworld; Late-;
    Neo-; New; Post-; Ultra-
    pejorative criticism
  death of 9
Monta, Mozuna 66
  Okawa House 66
Moore
  Charles 10, 41, 55, 59, 74, 81, 91, 97, 100,
    104, 127, 131, 159, 197
    Battery Park City, New York (1985–7)
      158, 161–2
    Episcopal Church of St. Matthew, LA
      74–5
    Piazza d'Italia, New Orleans 105–7
  Ruble and Yudell 158, 159
  and Turnbull
Mora-Pinon-Viaplana 61
Moretti, Luigi 80
Morimura, Yasamasa 66
Morphosis 41, 51, 176, 211, 243
Moss, Eric Owen 40, 41, 87, 176
Moussavi, Farshid
  see FAO
Mozuna, Monta 100
Muller, AJ 164–6
"multivalence" 12
Murphy, CF
  Chicago Civic Center 13, 16
musée imaginaire
museums 137
  Amon Carter Museum 54
  Australia, National Museum, Canberra
    (1998–2001) 198–99
  "cathedral of our time" 137
  Dusseldorf 80
  "Frog" Museum 134
  German Architectural Museum 120–1
  Getty Museum Malibu California 63–5
  Hiroshima 169
  Holocaust Museum 96, 248
  Hirshhorn Museum 16
  Imperial War Museum, Trafford,
    Manchester (1998–2002) 248–9
  Jewish Museum, Berlin 243–8
  LA, Museum of Contemporary Art 139
  Lyon, Musée des Confluences 258–9

Maastricht 119
  Manchester, Imperial War Museum
    248
  Neue Staatsgalerie, Stuttgart 108–13
  Portland, Maine 127
  Mönchengladbach 138
  Musée d'Orsay 141
  Soane 54
  Tate Modern, London 251, 258
  see also Gehry, Bilbao; Guggenheim,
    Victoria & Albert
MVDRV 71, 190–7, 204

N
Nash, John 45, 46, 47
  Royal Pavilion, Brighton (1815–18) 45,
    134
National Gallery, London, Sainsbury Wing
  179
NATO 149
Nazis 22, 151, 243
Nelson's Column 34, 35
Neo
  -Art Nouveau 53
  -Classical 45, 51–2
  -De Stijl 53
  -Egyptian 43–4, 139
  -Gothic 43
  -Hindu/Indian Gothic 45
  -humanism 81
  -Mies 97
  -Modernism 173
  -Neo 66
  -Palladianism 97
  -Rationalists 76, 80, 119, 120, 122
  -Vernacular 51, 67–71, 98
  Neoisms gone mad 53, 66
neon 106
Nervi, Pier Luigi 234
Neue Staatsgalerie, Stuttgart 108–13
Neutelings, Willem Jan 190
New
  Abstraction 119, 120
  Paradigm 7–8
  Representation 119
  Tuscanism 115, 119, 122–5, 17
  Urbanists 163
Newman, O. 8, 18, 19
Newton, Sir Isaac ("Newtronian"?) 7
Niemeyer 178
Nieumarket, Amsterdam 74
Nolli, Giambattista 78–9, 99
Norwich, housing 68, 69
Nouvel, Jean 82, 229
NOX 190, 223–5

O
Oakshott, Michael 9
office
  as village 163
  buildings 12, 13
Oosterhuis, Kas 211, 223
Orders
  see classical architectural language
"organitech" 231
ornament 3, 51, 97, 115, 126, 127, 128, 149
  reused 72
  see also "decorated shed"
Ornamentalism (1982) 127
Otto, Frei 21
Owings 16

P
Pacific Design Center
  see Pelli, Cesar
Palladio, Andrea 132
Palladianism 10, 100, 101, 134
  see also Neo-
Pantheon 3, 151
Paris 76, 78, 181, 185, 188
parody 66
participatory design 72–5
Passarelli Brothers 46–7, 49
pastiche 74, 89
Pécs
  see Group Pécs
Pei, I. M. 16, 128
Pelli, Cesar 143, 144, 146, 166
  Carnegie Hall ext., New York (1986) 144
  Pacific Design Center, LA ("the Blue
    Whale") 5, 32, 33, 81, 144
  Rice Jones School, Houston, Texas
    (1983–4) 144
  World Financial Center Towers (1982–7)
    161–2
Penrose, Roger 240, 241, 243
Pepper, Beverly 160
PER 62
Perrault, Dominique 229
Perret, Auguste 101
Pessac
  see Le Corbusier
Pevsner, Sir Nikolaus 31, 45, 53, 115
Pioneers of the Modern Movement (1936)
    49, 151–2
Piano, Renzo 211, 229, 234
Piazza d'Italia 7
Picasso, Pablo 24
Piranesi 100, 239, 249
planning 67, 158
  advocacy planning, USA 74
  failures 9, 264

see also Jacobs, Jane; participatory
    design; Post Modern urbanism; village
pluralism 6, 39, 72, 74, 115, 138, 158, 175,
    198
Poincaré, Henri 241
polychromy 115
PoMo 3, 6, 66, 97, 115, 127, 143
  death of 157
  see also kitsch
Pompeiian style 64–5
Pompidou Centre 110
Pop 30, 58, 59, 65, 70
Porphyrios, Demetri 122–3
Port Grimaud 38, 71, 73
Portman, John
  Bonaventure Hotel, LA (1976) 23
Portmeirion 38, 39, 63
Portoghesi
  Paolo 53, 115
  and Gigliotti 53
Portzamparc 100, 222–3
Post-Modernism 2
  takes off 97ff
  dying 129
Post Modern
  Classicism 7, 115, 127–9
    synthesis 119
  dance 7
  Urbanism 158–75
    see also Culot; Hollein; Krier; Kroll;
    Rogers; Rossi; Stirling
Pragmatism 9
Predock, Antoine 152, 167, 171–3
Prigogine, Ilya 215
Prince Charles 63, 76, 163, 175, 178, 179
Prix, Wolf 239
Pruitt-Igoe
  see Yamasaki
Pugin, A. W. N. 46, 68
Purism 9, 49, 90

Q
Queen Anne 99

R
Radical
  Eclecticism
    see Eclecticism
  Traditionalism 63
Raggatt, Howard 202, 240
  see also ARM
Rang, Berhof Landes 164
Rationalism 9, 76
Rauch 40
Reichstag conversion 2–3
Reiser 211, 235

renewable energy
  vegetable oil 3
Renaissance, The 66, 81–2, 83, 100, 122
Representation 126
Revisionism 67
revivalism 62–6
  see also historicism; Neo-
RIBA 10, 123
Rice Jones School, Texas 144
"Risk Society" 263–4
Roche, Kevin 128
Rococo 10, 104, 139, 210
Rogers, Richard 76, 189, 195, 229
Rohe
  see Mies
Romanesque 143
Rome 78–9, 99, 119
Ronchamp
  see Le Corbusier
Rossi, Aldo 76, 80, 97, 115, 116–19, 122,
    123, 126, 159, 197
  Bonnefanten Museum, Maastricht
    (1995) 119
  Il Teatro del Mondo (1979–80) 118
  Modena Cemetery (1971–) 118
  Social Housing, Berlin (1981–8) 159
Rouse Corporation 158
Rowe, Colin 79, 100, 107, 110, 119, 197, 218
Royal Incorporation of British Architects
  see RIBA
Ruble
  see Moore

S
Saarinen, Eero 55, 57
  CBS parallelepiped (1961) 21, 263
  Kresge Auditorium and chapel (1955)
    53–4
  Stiles and Morse College, Yale (1958–62)
    54
  TWA terminal, New York 3, 30–1, 32,
    81, 200
Sainsbury Wing, National Gallery, London
    179
San Francisco 74
Sant' Elia 4, 23–4
Sausalito boat houses San Francisco 10–11
scale 11
Schinkel, Karl Friedrich 110
Schoenberg 243
Schumacher, E. F. 9
Schwitter, Kurt 88
Scott Brown, Denise 39, 57, 58, 61, 69,
    126, 127, 148, 179–80
Scully, Vincent 79
Seaside new town, Florida 63–4

Second Empire 10
self-build 73
semantics 17, 25, 43–4, 120
    see also analogies; code; metaphor;
        meaning; language; syntax
semiotics 34
September 11 263
Serlio 125
Serra, Richard 251
Shane, Graham 78, 211
sheds
    see "decorated shed"
Sherman, Cindy 66
Shinto 123, 130
Shirai, Seiichi 66
shopping
    see consumer temples
"signolic" architecture 148
signs 29, 35
    see also code; language; meaning;
        metaphor; semantics
    architectural
        see also "decorated shed"
symbolic 35
    Venturi/Brown 29, 30
SITE 100–101, 228
Sitta, Vladimir 199
Sitte, Camillo 76, 78
Skidmore, Owings and Merrill 6
Smith
    Adam
    Adrian 158
    Thomas Gordon 127
Smithson, A & P 7,18
    Robin Hood Gardens, London 18–19
    see also Team Ten
Soane
    Sir John 132
    Musem 54
social
    class
        see semiotics
    criticism 39
    goals 2
    housing
        see main entry, housing
SOM 97, 143
South Bank, London 17, 25, 49
space 87–96
Speer, Albert 110
Spuybroek, Lars 211, 222
Freshwater Pavilion, EXPO 1997–8 223–5
    see also NOX
Staatsgalerie, Stuttgart 108–13
Steiner, Rudolf 87, 163
Stern, Robert 23, 40, 55, 61, 115, 127, 152

Casting Centre, Disney, Orlando
    (1987–9) 156–7
    and Hagmann John 90
Stewart, Jimmy
    house, Beverly Hills 37
Stirling, James 31, 76, 79, 80, 97, 100,
    104, 107, 108–13, 122, 134, 137–8, 152,
    157, 166, 171
    Clore Gallery, London (1982–6) 137–8
    and Gowan, James 167
    and Wilford, Michael 167–70, 178–80
Stone, Edward 54
Street, G. E. 67
Student movement 2
Stuttgart 72, 80, 107, 108–13, 122
Summerson, John 3
"SuperDutch" 190, 198, 237
Surrealism 62
Swan Hotel 152–7
Sydney Opera House
    see Utzon
symbolism 3
    new significance of everyday objects 24
    see also contextualism; Venturi
Synagogue, Port Chester 54
syntax 25, 41–3
    see also analogies; code; metaphor;
        meaning; language; semantics

T
TAC
    Pan Am Building New York (1958) 21
Taller de Arquitectura 132–4
Takeyama, Minoru 7, 66, 82, 83, 123
Tange, Kenzo 55
Theme Pavilion, EXPO 70, Osaka 21
    Olympic Gymnasium, Tokyo (1964) 23
TEAM 39
Team Ten 16, 18, 69
    see also Smithsons; Van Eyck
technology
    see computer aided design; digital;
        renewable energy
Technological Classicism 134
TECTON 53
Tegel Housing, Berlin 158
terraced housing 63
Terry, Quinlan 62, 63
Thatcher, M. 3
Thompson, Ben 158
Tigerman, Stanley 82–3
tourism 4
    see also commercialization
town planning
    see planning
tromp l'oeil 39, 65

Trump Tower 163
Turnbull, William 91
Tuscanism
    see New Tuscanism
Tusquets, Oscar 61–2, 160
TWA
    see Saarinen

U
Umemoto 211, 235
Ungers, O. M. 6, 76, 79, 80, 119–21, 122,
    126, 197
"univalence" 13
universalism 115
U. N. Studio 190
urbane
    mega-build 158–62
urban design
    see also housing; planning
urbanism
    see Post-Modern 76
Utzon, Jörn
    Sydney Opera House 27–8, 29, 30, 33,
        81, 134, 200, 203, 251

V
Van Berkel 190, 197, 211, 223, 225
Van den Bout
Vandenhove, Charles 146–7
Van Egeraat, Eric 190
Van Eyck, Aldo 69, 81
Van Rijs
    see MVRDV
Venice Biennale 115–18, 120, 127
Venturi, Rauch 126, 127
Venturi, Robert 1, 2, 6, 23, 29, 30, 35, 39,
    51, 55–62, 69, 74, 79, 80, 88, 90, 96,
    100, 107, 110, 126, 127, 128, 129, 134,
    148, 210
    Allen Art Museum 61
    Brant House, Greenwich (1971) 61
    Franklin Court, Philadelphia (1972–6)
        61
    HQ Building for Nurses and Dentists
        (1966) 55, 58
    Oberlin College Addition (1973–7)
        59–60
    Sainsbury Wing, National Gallery,
        London 179
    Tucker House, New York (1975) 40
        see also "decorated sheds"
vernacular 51
    see also Neo-
Victoria & Albert Museum, London 258
Victoriana 70
Villa

19th century 38
  Hadrian's 79–80
  Savoye 66, 87, 110
    "not Villa Savoye" 200–202
village planning 162–7
Vitruvius 45, 46, 127, 220

W
Wacoal building 82–5
Wagner, Otto 105
Walter, Thomas Ustick 44
Warsaw 24
Watanabe, Toyokaze 66, 123–5
Weller, Richard 199
West 8 190, 194–7, 204
"white architecture" 38
  see also Le Corbusier
Wigley, Mark 218
Wilford, Michael 107–13, 167–70, 178–80
William-Ellis, Sir Clough 39

Williams 213
Wines, James 228
Winter Garden, Battery Park City 158,
  161–2
Wittkower, Rudolf 79
Wolfe, Tom 19, 40, 122
Wood, John (II) 18
  Royal Crescent, Bath 18
Woolworth Tower 163
World Fairs 21
World
  Financial Center 161
  Trade Center 161
Wright, Frank Lloyd 49, 68, 230, 37
  Marin County Civic Center 16
  Johnson Wax Building 20–1
Wright, Lance 68

Y
Yamasaki, Minoru 8, 54, 263

Pruitt-Igoe housing scheme, St. Louis
  Missouri (1981) 8–9,18, 72, 129, 157,
  263, 264
Yamashita, Kazumasu 83–4
Yeang, Ken 211, 229
  Kuala Lumpur Airport (1991–3)
  229
Yoh, Shoei 211
Yudell, Buzz
  see Moore, Charles
Yokohama Port Terminal 235, 236

Z
Zaero Polo, Alejandro
  see FAO
Zevi, Bruno 115
zoomorphism 86
  see also metaphor
Zuccaro Federico 84
Zwolle Housing 69, 70